TEACH

D0761731

CANTONESE

CANTONESE

A COMPLETE COURSE FOR BEGINNERS

Hugh Baker
and
P.K. Ho

TEACH YOURSELF BOOKS

Long-renowned as the authoritative source for self-guided learning – with more than 30 million copies sold worldwide – the *Teach Yourself* series includes over 200 titles in the fields of languages, crafts, hobbies, sports, and other leisure activities.

British Library Cataloguing in Publication Data

A catalogue for this title is available from the British Library

Library of Congress Catalog Card Number: 95-68140

First published in UK 1995 by Hodder Headline Plc, 338 Euston Road, London NW1 3BH

First published in US 1996 by NTC Publishing Group, 4255 West Touhy Avenue, Lincolnwood (Chicago), Illinois 60646 – 1975 U.S.A.

Typeset by Graphicraft Typesetters Ltd, Hong Kong.
Printed in Great Britain by Cox & Wyman Ltd, Reading, Berkshire.

Impression number	10	9	8	7	6	5	4	3	2
Year	1999	1998	1997	1996					

CONTENTS

—— INTRODUCTION ——

Welcome to a new experience. If you have never tried to learn a Chinese language before you are in for a rare treat.

There are some real eye-openers. Have you ever met a language where verbs do not have more than one form and so cannot change according to tense or number or mood? Have you ever met a language where there are no cases (you can forget about vocatives, genitives, ablatives and their confusing brethren), where no gender differences are acknowledged (have you noticed how Chinese people speaking English frequently get *he* and *she* mixed up?), where there are no agreements of anything with anything else ('singular third person feminine', what's that?!) and where there are no subjunctives (would 'twere so for English!)?

On the other hand, have you ever tried to learn a language which has to be sung in order to be understood? Or where word orders are so crucial that if you get them wrong you will be totally unintelligible? Or where you can't count objects without specifying what kind of objects they are first? Or where almost every single syllable has a meaning (unlike English where the individual syllables of a word like 'trousers' mean nothing at all)?

Cantonese is a vital living language spoken by upwards of a hundred million people in South-east China (including Hong Kong and Macau), Malaysia, Europe, Australia, Fiji, North America and many other parts of the world where the adventurous Cantonese people have settled. It is one of a large family of Chinese languages and retains many more traces of its ancient roots than do most of the other Chinese languages. On the other hand, it is a language which seems unafraid to adopt or adapt, notably from English in the past century or so, and it invents, evolves and discards slang at a frenetic rate. As a result it is a very rich language.

The people who speak Cantonese are lively, quick-thinking, direct and fun-loving. They are tuned into their language so much that they cannot resist having fun with it – they pun all the time and often with great ingenuity. They love it when foreigners stammer out their first words of Cantonese, because it is bound to include a howler or two which can be punned into something funny. Don't be put off, you are brightening their lives, and they will not despise you for it.

And if you have the chance to get help from a Cantonese speaker you should of course seize the opportunity. The odds are that he or she will not want to be bothered with the romanised text which you are learning, and it is for this reason that we have supplied Chinese characters for the dialogues and new vocabulary. We are not attempting to teach you characters beyond the briefest of introductions in the Appendices, the reason being that it takes a great investment of time to learn to read and write Chinese characters, and you will learn to speak and to understand speech much sooner if you ignore the script. You can always learn it later on.

Most of the units of this book follow the same pattern: two dialogues (often humorous, if you think silly jokes are humorous), each with a list of the new vocabulary used and explanations of new grammar points, followed by some exercises. Units 7, 14, 21 and 26 are revision units, giving more material based on what has been learned and not introducing anything new. The Appendices summarise the most important grammar points and provide a brief introduction the Chinese writing. At the back of the book you will find the answers to all the exercises and complete translations of the revision units.

A few words of warning:

- Do not look for consistent characterisation of the people who appear in the dialogues. There is none, the Mr Wong of one unit being a totally different person from the Mr Wong who figures in another;
- Do not be put off by the fact that in our system of writing Cantonese Mr Wong is spelled **Wròng**, Mr Cheung is spelled **Jhèung**, etc. Our system is meant to work for *you the learner*,

but the person in the street does not need to be as precise about pronunciation as you do, so we also show you the spellings which he or she would probably normally use;

- You may be puzzled by the numbers of words which are pronounced the same but which have quite different meanings (**daai**, for instance, means both *to bring* and *to wear*). Cantonese, like all the Chinese languages, is full of homophones (words pronounced the same). It is a fact of life which you will have to accept – and it is one of the reasons why punning is so common;
- Please do not start on the text before reading the Pronunciation guide and listening to it on the tape. You don't want to get into bad pronunciation habits which may be hard to break.
- When you first hear Cantonese it sounds rather ugly, and even a normal chat can seem like a violent argument because of the vigour and velocity with which ideas are delivered. Fear not, you will quickly learn to detect beneath the coarse exterior melodic and beautiful cadences which can be as romantic, heart-warming or soft as anyone could desire.

We have had fun writing this book. We hope you will enjoy studying it. We *know* you will get a great kick out of speaking with Cantonese people.

——— **Symbols and abbreviations** ———

▣ = This indicates material included on the cassette.

▣ = This indicates dialogue.

▣ = This indicates exercises – places where you can practise using the language.

▣ = This indicates key words or phrases.

▣ = This indicates grammar explanations – the nuts and bolts of the language.

A NOTE ON ROMANISATION

This note is about the sounds used in Cantonese and how to write them down. You should read this section with your tape readily available so that you can hear a clear demonstration of what the sounds are.

Cantonese, like all the Chinese languages, is written in characters. As you will discover when you read the Appendices of this book, characters are ideographs – symbols representing ideas – whereas the letters of our alphabet are symbols representing sounds. Written English reproduces the sounds of speech using an economical 26 symbols, which are quite sufficient to do the job, but the Chinese writing system pays little attention to the sounds of the spoken language and tackles the massive problem of providing instead a separate symbol for most of the ideas which need to be written.

When you learn to write an English word you learn how to say it (even if the spelling is sometimes a little erratic). If you were to try to learn the basic Cantonese used in this book through Chinese characters, not only would you have the daunting task of learning nearly 1,500 different symbols, but even when you had learned them you would be none the wiser about how to speak the language.

So generations of foreign learners have struggled to find ways to 'romanise' Cantonese, that is, to represent Cantonese sounds using the Roman alphabet. Since there are very few sounds in Cantonese which are difficult for English speakers, this would be an easy task but for one thing: Cantonese is a *tonal language*, that is, each one of the sounds of Cantonese can be pronounced (or perhaps 'sung' would be a better word) in seven different ways (the *tones*). The Roman alphabet does not have any devices for representing tones, and musical notations added to letters of the alphabet would be much too awkward to handle.

Romanisation is only a tool to enable you to learn how to speak the language, it is useless outside the classroom, a private communication system just between us the teachers and you the learner. There is no official romanisation of Cantonese, and many different systems are in existence. We have chosen not to use any of them but to devise our own system, which we believe to be helpful for the following reasons:

- It distinguishes clearly each one of the sounds and each of the seven tones;
- Only two additional symbols (the grave (`) and acute (´) accent marks) are required to indicate the tones;
- The three pitches among which the tones are distributed are visually represented in the spelling and so are easily remembered;
- The entire system is regular, with no exceptions or special spellings.

If you intend to study Cantonese in depth you will certainly have to learn Chinese characters, and then you can discard this tool. But in the meantime we hope you find our system a useful aid.

 ## *The Cantonese tones*

Cantonese has seven tones which it is essential to master for fluent and comprehensible speech. The tones occur on all syllables and are located in three pitches (high, mid and low), the voice remaining level, rising or falling within those pitches. The seven tones are:

High level
High falling
  Mid rising
  Mid level
    Low falling
    Low rising
    Low level

- We show high pitch by the insertion of **h** after the initial consonant, and low pitch by the insertion of **r** after the initial consonant, leaving mid pitch unmarked;
- Rising tones are shown by the acute accent (′), and falling tones by the grave accent (`), leaving level tones unmarked;
- The accents are marked on the vowel or (where there is a vowel chain) on the first vowel of the syllable.

The seven tones of the sound **Maa** would be written:

High level	**Mhaa**
High falling	**Mhàa**
Mid rising	**Máa**
Mid level	**Maa**
Low falling	**Mràa**
Low rising	**Mráa**
Low level	**Mraa**

Listen to how these are spoken on the tape and do your best to copy them exactly.

Every now and then a word changes its tone in a particular context. We have pointed it out when it occurs in this book, and suggest that you try to accept these occurrences as the oddities they are rather than try to figure out why they change.

———— Pronunciation guide ————

🔲 *The sounds of Cantonese*

1 The consonant sounds which begin Cantonese syllables are simple for English speakers. The only exception is the initial consonant **ng-**, and that is only difficult because English does not have syllables which start with this sound. You can imagine how it is done if you think of the word *singalong* and try to pronounce it without the letters *si* at the front. If you have the cassette you should be able to pick up how **ng-** syllables are pronounced without much difficulty. For example:

ngan   ngaa   ngok   ngai   ngaam

A **q-** at the beginning of a syllable is not pronounced at all. It indicates that the syllable begins with a vowel. If we did not do this, there might be confusion between high pitch syllables without an initial consonant and other syllables which begin with *h*. For example:

qau   quk   qon   qou

2   There are very few consonants which can appear at the end of Cantonese syllables; in fact there only six (**-n, -ng, -m, -p, -t, -k**). Of these, the first three are completely straightforward, just as you would expect them to be if you were reading the sounds off in English. For example:

haan   seun   leng   mong   taam   gam

But the other three (**-p, -t, -k**) are hardly pronounced at all, the tongue and the lips getting into position to pronounce them and then not following through. So your lips should snap together to get ready to make the **-p** at the end of the syllable **sap**, but you should not open them again to release the puff of air which has built up to make the full *p* sound. Similarly with the sound **bat**, the tip of your tongue should make contact with the hard ridge behind your upper teeth, but the air should not puff out to make a full *t*. And with **baak** the flat top of your tongue should go up into your palate but not allow the air to escape to make the full *k* sound. Listen carefully to the cassette examples:

sap   jaap   kat   faat   sik   jek

3   The vowel sounds of Cantonese are a little more complicated. We have set out below a guide to the sounds based wherever possible on 'BBC English' pronunciations, but please note that this is only a rough guide. The best way to grasp the sounds is to listen carefully several times to the pronunciation section of the cassette. While your ear is getting used to hearing the sounds, your eye will be taking in the system which we use for spelling those sounds. To begin with, concentrate on the sound itself without being too much concerned with tone. You will get more pronunciation practice later, because each unit's dialogues and the early vocabulary lists are also on the tape. And of course, if you have the luxury of having a Cantonese friend, ask him or her to make the sounds for you as well.

-aa   is a long vowel sound, rather like the sound of the word *are* in English. It combines with **-i** to make a long vowel, as in a drawled version of *eye*, and it combines with **-u** to make a long version of cow. For example:

baa   baai   baau   baan   saam   laang   daap

-a   is a shorter version of the **aa** sound, pronounced somewhere between the English b*a*t and b*u*t. For example:

jam   pan   hang   tai   tau   sat

-e   is rather like the English f*ai*ry. For example:

be   che   leng   jek

-ei   is like the English d*ay*. For example:

bei   sei

-eu   is something like English f*ur*ther. For example:

jeun   leung   cheut   jeuk

-eui   is rather like h*er* *e*vening (but don't pronounce the *r*). For example:

deui   neui   heui

-i   is not too different from English s*ee*, except when it is followed by **-k** when it is more like English s*i*ck. For example:

ni   tiu   tim   min   ting   lip   mit   sik

-o   is somewhere between English th*aw* and g*o*ne. For example:

fo   qon   bong   hok   ngoi   mou

-u   is somewhere between English t*oo* and c*oo*k. For example:

fu   fun   hung   juk   mui

-ue   is like the German ü*ber* or the French t*u*. In English you can get close to the sound by saying *see you* very quickly. For example:

jue   suen   huet   yuet

m and **ng** can occur as full syllables without vowels: **mȓ   ngȓ**

4 You may be put off at first to see spellings such as **chhe**, where the basic **che** sound is to be prununced in high pitch and therefore has another **h**. This 'double h' problem affects only high pitch words with **ch** and **h** initials, and we think you will quickly get used to them. There are one or two other 'unhappy' spellings (such as **Wròng** for the surname *Wong*), but that kind of thing happens between many different languages, and we think it is better to put up with the odd spellings rather than devise exception rules in order to avoid them.

5 Cantonese syllables all carry virtually equal stress, and each therefore sounds more or less discrete. And Chinese characters each represent one syllable and are all written discretely. Our romanisation, therefore, could spell each syllable separately, but we have chosen to use hyphens where two or more syllables are so closely associated that they may be thought of as one word or one concept, as with **pràng-yráu** (*friend*), **jhùng-yi** (*to like*) and **Jhùng-gwok-wáa** (*Chinese language*).

6 Language never stands still, and Cantonese changes very rapidly. There are some important sound changes which seem to be going on in the late 20th century:

- Many people now do not use an initial **n-** sound at all, and all the words which appear in this book with an initial **n-** would be pronounced by them with an **l-** instead. You may if you wish, therefore, pronounce **nréi** as **lréi** and **nràam-yán** as **lràam-yán**. You will certainly meet some native speakers who do this constantly or who perhaps even alternate between the two.

- Some people now do not distinguish between initial **g-** and initial **gw-**, pronouncing **Jhùng-gwok** as **Jhùng-gok**. This change is not so common, but you should be prepared to understand it if you hear it.

- The initial **ng-** sound seems to have been gradually falling out of favour over many years, and some people have now dropped it altogether. So you may hear, for example, **qró** for **ngró** or **qràu-yruk** for **ngràu-yruk**.

- The distinction between the High Level and High Falling tones is becoming blurred and some people use only one or the other.

1

第一課　會面
WRUI-MRIN

Encounters

In this unit you will learn how to greet and address people, ask questions and use descriptive words.

 ──────── **Dialogue 1** ────────

Mr Wong and his boss Miss Cheung meet in the lift on the way up to the office.

早晨，王先生。
早晨，張小姐。你好嗎?
我好好。你呢?
好好。
你太太呢?
佢都好，有心。

Cheung	Jóu-sràn, Wròng Shìn-shàang.
Wong	Jóu-sràn, Jhèung Síu-jé. Nréi hóu maa?
Cheung	Ngró hóu hóu. Nréi nhe?
Wong	Hóu hóu.
Cheung	Nréi taai-táai nhe?
Wong	Kréui dhou hóu, yráu-shàm.

── 1 ──

早晨	**Jóu-sràn**	*good morning*
王	**Wròng**	*Wong (a surname)*
先生	**shìn-shàang**	*Mr, Sir, gentleman, husband*
張	**Jhèung**	*Cheung (a surname)*
小姐	**síu-jé**	*Miss, young lady*
你	**nréi**	*you*
好	**hóu**	*very; well, fine, OK, nice, good*
嗎?	**maa?**	*(a word that makes a sentence into a question)*
我	**ngró**	*I, me*
呢?	**nhe?**	*(a word for asking follow-up questions)*
太太	**taai-táai**	*Mrs, wife, married woman*
佢	**kréui**	*she, her, he, him, it*
都	**dhou**	*also*
有心	**yráu-shàm**	*kind of you to ask*

Just to test you. Now that you have read the dialogue, can you say whether **Jhèung Síu-jé** has a husband or not? Has **Wròng Shìn-shàang**? Are any of the three people unwell? How would you address the person that Miss Cheung enquires about?

(The answers, as if you didn't know, are no, no, no and **Wròng Taai-táai**.)

Grammar

1 Identifying people and things

ngró	*I, me*
nréi	*you* (singular)
kréui	*he, she, him, her, it*

Each of these personal pronouns can be made plural by the addition of **-drei**:

ngró-drei	*we, us*
nréi-drei	*you* (plural)
kréui-drei	*they, them*

2 Addressing people

Unlike English, Chinese surnames are always given before titles:

Wròng Shìn-shàang	*Mr Wong*
Wròng Taai-táai	*Mrs Wong*
Wròng Síu-jé	*Miss Wong*

Why does the surname come first?

As well as Mr, Mrs and Miss, other titles, such as President, Doctor, Professor, Ambassador, Sister, are also given after the surname. Personal names follow the surname too, so someone called Mr John Smith becomes *Smith John Mr* in the Cantonese order. It all fits in with the great stress which the Chinese people have traditionally placed on the family. The surname shows your family line and so it is the surname which comes first in the Cantonese order, as with **Wròng Gwok Mréi Shin-shàang**.

---

3 Adjectives or verbs? Both!

Hóu means *good, nice, well, fine, OK,* and so on. Just as in English, such words (adjectives) go in front of nouns, so a *good husband* is a **hóu shìn-shàang**. But in Cantonese all adjectives can also act as verbs to describe things (descriptive verbs), and so **hóu** means not only *good* but also *to be good*:

Kréui-drei hóu.	*They are well.*
Wròng Shìn-shàang hóu.	*Mr Wong is fine.*

Remember, it is not only the adjective **hóu** which is also a descriptive verb – all adjectives behave the same. So the word for *ugly* also means *to be ugly, difficult* can also mean *to be difficult,* and so on.

4 Simple questions

You can ask a question simply by adding the little word **maa?** onto the end of a statement:

Kréui hóu.	*She is well.*
Kréui hóu maa?	*Is she well?*

So **maa?** is a kind of spoken question mark.

5 Two for the price of one

When you learned **hóu** you got double value, because it not only means *good, well*, etc, but *very* as well. So **hóu hóu** means *very good*.

6 Follow-up questions

A special kind of short cut question is formed using the little word **nhe? Nhe?** asks a follow-up question without the tedium of repeating in full what went before:

Jhèung Taai-táai hóu maa?   *Is Mrs Cheung OK?*
Kréui hóu hóu. Wròng   *She's very well. And how's*
  Síu-jé nhe?   *Miss Wong?*

7 Dhou (also)

Dhou means *also, too*. It always comes just before a verb:

Ngró hóu.   *I'm well.*
Kréui dhou hóu   *She's well too.*

8 And now for the good news

It may have escaped your notice but verbs only have one form! The same word **hóu** was translated as *am well, is well* and *are well* above, and it was no accident. **Hóu** only ever appears in that form, whereas the English verb *to be well* takes many guises (*am well, is well, are well, will be well, have been well, was well, were well*, etc). Regardless of the tense, the mood, the subject or anything else, the form of the verb will always be simply **hóu**. And, better still, this applies to all verbs, there are no irregularities to make life difficult!

 —————— Dialogue 2 ——————

 When she gets to the office, Miss Cheung is surprised to find a visitor waiting for her.

噢，對唔住，貴姓呀？
我姓何，你係李小姐嗎？

唔係，我姓張。何先生，你係唔係美國人呀？
唔係，我係英國人，我賣美國車：美國車好靚，你要唔要呀？
唔要，唔要。美國車好貴：我要日本車。再見，何先生。
你唔要，李小姐要唔要呀？
李小姐都唔要。再見，再見。

Cheung	Qhòu, deui-mr̀-jrue, gwai-sing qaa?
Ho	Ngró sing Hrò. Nréi hrai Lréi Síu-jé maa?
Cheung	Mr̀ hrai, ngró sing Jhèung. Hrò Shìn-shàang, nréi hrai mr̀ hrai Mréi-gwok-yràn qaa?
Ho	Mr̀ hrai, ngró hrai Yhìng-gwok-yràn. Ngró mraai Mréi-gwok chhe: Mréi-gwok chhe hóu leng, nréi yiu mr̀ yiu qaa?
Cheung	Mr̀ yiu, mr̀ yiu. Mréi-gwok chhe hóu gwai: ngró yiu Yrat-bún chhe. Joi-gin, Hrò Shìn-shàang.
Ho	Nréi mr̀ yiu, Lréi Síu-jé yiu mr̀ yiu qaa?
Cheung	Lréi Síu-jé dhou mr̀ yiu. Joi-gin, joi-gin.

噢	**qhòu!**	*oh! (surprise)*
對唔住	**deui-mr̀-jrue**	*I'm sorry; excuse me; pardon me*
貴姓呀？	**gwai-sing qaa?**	*what is your name? (lit. distinguished surname?)*
姓	**sing**	*surname; to be surnamed*
何	**Hrò**	*Ho (a surname)*
係	**hrai**	*to be*
李	**Lréi**	*Li (a surname)*
唔	**mr̀**	*not*
美國人	**Mréi-gwok-yràn**	*American person*
美國	**Mréi-gwok**	*America, USA*
人？	**yràn**	*person*
呀？	**qaa?**	*(word used at the end of a question)*
英國人	**Yhìng-gwok-yràn**	*British person*
英國	**Yhìng-gwok**	*Britain, UK, England*
賣	**mraai**	*to sell*
車	**chhe**	*car, cars*
靚	**leng**	*pretty, good-looking, handsome; of good quality*
要	**yiu**	*to want*
貴	**gwai**	*expensive; distinguished*
日本人	**Yrat-bún-yràn**	*Japanese person*
日本	**Yrat-bún**	*Japan*
再見	**joi-gin**	*goodbye*

Questions

1 **Let's test again!** You should be able to answer these questions if you have under-stood the second dialogue. Why did Miss Cheung not want an American car? What kind of car did she want? Could Mr Ho supply it? Was he going to have better luck with Miss Li?

(Answers: too expensive; Japanese; no; no.)

2 **True or false?** Having read dialogue 2 again, can you say which of these statements is/are true and which false?

(*a*) Jhèung Síu-jé hrai Mréi-gwok-yràn.
(*b*) Hrò Shìn-shàang mr̀ mraai Mréi-gwok chhe.
(*c*) Wròng Shìn-shàang mraai chhe.
(*d*) Jhèung Síu-jé hrai taai-táai.

(Answers: all false.)

 ———————————— **Grammar** ————————————

9 People

Yràn means *person*, but it also means *people*. In fact, all nouns in Cantonese are the same whether singular or plural, and you can only tell which is meant from the sense of the conversation. There is usually no problem: by looking at the personal pronouns you can easily tell which is which in the following examples:

Ngró hrai Yhìng-gwok-yràn.
Kréui-drei hrai Yrat-bún-yràn.

More on surnames

You have already met a number of surnames (**Wròng, Jhèung, Hrò, Lréi**) and you will of course meet others. It is interesting that although there are several thousand different surnames in existence, the vast majority of the Chinese share just a few dozen of them. You will certainly meet many people with the four surnames you've just learned, but the most common surname of all among Cantonese people is **Chràn**.

---

10 Negatives

The word for *not* is **mÌ€**. It always comes in front of the word it refers to:

WrÒ²ng ShÌ€in-shÀaang mÌ€ leng.	*Mr Wong isn't handsome.*
NgrÓ mÌ€ yiu chhe.	*I don't want a car.*

11 Another way to ask questions

The most common way to ask a question in Cantonese is by using the positive and negative of a verb together and adding the little word **qaa?** at the end of the sentence:

KrÃ©ui leng mÌ€ leng qaa?   *Is she pretty?*

What you are really doing is offering your listener a choice of answers (*She pretty? Not pretty? Eh?*) and the answer is going to be either:

KrÃ©ui leng.	*She is pretty.* or:
KrÃ©ui mÌ€ leng.	*She's not pretty.*

In the same way you can ask:

NrÃ©i mraai mÌ€ mraai	*Are you selling American cars?*
MrÃ©i-gwok chhe qaa?	

Cantonese people like to have a comfortable noise to round off their sentences with, and they have a whole string of little words (usually called particles) which they use. **Qaa?** has no meaning on its own, it is just used to punch home the question which has been asked in the sentence. **Maa?** and **nhe?**, which you have already met, are other examples of particles.

12 The unspoken if

There are various words for *if* in Cantonese, but quite often none of them is used, the meaning seeming to flow naturally from the context.

In the dialogue, the sentence **NrÃ©i mÌ€ yiu, LrÃ©i SÃu-jÃ© yiu mÌ€ yiu qaa?** (literally, *You not want, Miss Li want not want, eh?*) should be understood to mean *If you don't want one, does Miss Li?*

—————— **Exercises** ——————

(The answers to all the exercises and tests from now on are at the back of the book.)

1 Here's a fine mess! The following words have got all jumbled up. Sort them out and make meaningful sentences of them. For example, **Taai-táai Wròng leng hóu** does not make sense, but rearranged into **Wròng Taai-táai hóu leng** it is a correct sentence meaning *Mrs Wong is very beautiful.*

   (*a*) **hóu kréui-drei hóu**
   (*b*) **Shìn-shàang Wròng hóu**
   (*c*) **dhou Jhèung hóu Síu-jé**

2 What would you reply to these expressions?

   (*a*) **Jóu-sràn.**
   (*b*) **Nréi hóu maa?**
   (*c*) **Joi-gin.**

3 Fill in the blanks with words which will make sense. You will have to think a bit to work out what the sentence must mean!

   (*a*) **Wròng Shìn-shàang ＿＿＿ yiu Mréi-gwok chhe.**
   (*b*) **Chràn Síu-jé leng ＿＿＿ leng qaa?**
   (*c*) **Kréui-drei hrai mr̀ ＿＿＿ Yrat-bún-yràn qaa?**
   (*d*) **Ngró mr̀ mraai Yrat-bún chhe, ngró mraai ＿＿＿.**

4 Translate these simple sentences into Cantonese. If you can do so, you can really congratulate yourself on having mastered this unit.

   (*a*) *Japanese cars aren't expensive.*
   (*b*) *He isn't nice.*
   (*c*) *You are very pretty.*
   (*d*) *Do they want cars?*
   (*e*) *He is good-looking too.*
   (*f*) *They are Americans.*
   (*g*) *Mr Wong sells cars.*
   (*h*) *British people don't sell American cars.*

2

第二課　個人財物
–GO-YRÀN CHRÒI-MRAT–
Personal property

This unit introduces numbers (which are quite easy) and the unfamiliar notion of 'classifiers', words which introduce different types of nouns. Don't be put off by classifiers. They soon become second nature, and you will find later on that they give you some nice opportunities for making your speech more flexible and clear.

 ——————— **Dialogue 1** ———————

Mr Ho is working in his office when a woman comes in.

太太，你搵邊個呀？
我搵王國美先生，佢係中國人，係我嘅朋友。
你搵王先生有乜嘢事呀？
我要賣我嘅美國車，王先生想買。
好，我帶你去王先生嘅寫字樓。
唔該你。

Ho	Taai-táai, nréi wán bhin-go qaa?
Woman	Ngró wán Wròng Gwok Mréi Shìn-shàang, kréui hrai Jhùng-gwok-yràn, hrai ngró ge pràng-yráu.
Ho	Nréi wán Wròng Shìn-shàang yráu-mhat-yré-sri-qaa?
Woman	Ngró yiu mraai ngró ge Mréi-gwok chhe, Wròng Shìn-shàang séung mráai.

— 9 —

Ho   Hóu, ngró daai nréi heui Wròng Shìn-shàang ge sé-jri-lràu.

Woman   Mr̀-ghòi nréi.

搵	**wán**	*to look for*
邊個	**bhin-go?**	*who? which person? which one?*
中國	**Jhùng-gwok**	*China*
嘅	**ge**	*-'s (shows possession)*
我嘅	**ngró ge**	*my*
朋友	**pràng-yráu**	*friend*
有	**yráu**	*to have*
乜嘢	**mhat-yré?**	*what? what kind of?*
事	**sri**	*matter, business, affair*
有乜嘢事呀?	**yráu-mhat-yré-sri-qaa?**	*for what purpose? why?*
想	**séung**	*to want to, intend to, would like to*
買	**mráai**	*to buy*
帶	**daai**	*to lead, to bring, to go with*
去	**heui**	*to go to, to go*
寫字樓	**sé-jri-lràu**	*office*
唔該（你）	**mr̀-ghòi (nréi)**	*thank you*

True or false? If you have understood the dialogue, you should be able to pass judgement on the following statements about it.

(*a*)   Wròng Gwok Mréi Shìn-shàang séung mraai chhe.

(*b*)   Wròng Shìn-shàang séung mraai Yrat-bún chhe.

(*c*)   Hrò Shìn-shàang, Wròng Shìn-shàang kréui-drei hrai pràng-yráu.

(*d*)   Wròng Taai-táai wán Wròng Shìn-shàang.

The Chinese characters for **sé-jri-lràu** (*office*) read from left to right.

Grammar

1 Question words

Question words like **bhin-go?** (*who?*) and **mhat-yré?** (*what?*) come in the same position in the sentence as the answer to them does. In English, question and answer have different word orders, but in Chinese they have the same word order. In the two following examples note how the English word order changes, whereas the Chinese does not:

Kréui sing mhat-yré qaa?	*What is he surnamed?*
Kréui sing Hrò.	*He is surnamed Ho.*
Kréui wán bhin-go qaa?	*Who is she looking for?*
Kréui wán Hrò Síu-jé.	*She is looking for Miss Ho.*

Some people say **mhi-yré?** instead of **mhat-yré?** There is no difference in meaning; you can please yourself which you say. Note how **qaa?** is used at the end of sentences which are questions.

2 Possession

The little word **ge** shows possession, like the apostrophe *s* (*'s*) in English. So **ngró ge** is *my* or *mine*, **nréi ge** is *your* or *yours*, **kréui ge** is *his*, *her*, *hers* or *its*, and **Lréi Taai-táai ge** is *Mrs Li's*:

kréui ge chhe	*her car*
ngró-drei ge sé-jri-lràu	*our office*
Chhe hrai Wròng Síu-jé ge.	*The car is Miss Wong's.*
Jhùng-gwok chhe hrai kréui ge.	*The Chinese car is his.*

When there is a close personal relationship with a person, **ge** is often left out, but the relationship term must have at least two syllables, as with **taai-táai** and **pràng-yráu** here:

ngró taai-táai	*my wife*
kréui pràng-yráu	*her friend*

3 M̀-ghòi (thank you)

M̀-ghòi literally means *ought not*, but it is the most common word for *thank you*. If someone holds the door open for you, or passes you the soy sauce, or tells you your shoelace is undone, you should politely say **m̀-ghòi** to them.

Dialogue 2

Miss Cheung has found a watch and a pen on her desk. She asks Mr Ho if they are his.

噢！一個手錶，一枝筆……何先生，呢個手錶同埋嗰枝筆係唔係你㗎？
呢個手錶唔係我嘅：嗰枝筆係我嘅。
呢個手錶好靚，係美國手錶。你估係邊個㗎？
我估係王先生嘅。
我都估係佢嘅。我哋去問佢，好唔好呀？
王先生而家唔喺佢嘅寫字樓。
唔緊要，我遲啲問佢。

Cheung	Qhòu! Yhat go sáu-bhiu, yhat jhì bhat . . . Hrò Shìn-shàang, nhi go sáu-bhiu trùng-mràai gó jhì bhat hrai m̀ hrai nréi gaa?
Ho	Nhi go sáu-bhiu m̀ hrai ngró ge: gó jhì bhat hrai ngró ge.
Cheung	Nhi go sáu-bhiu hóu leng, hrai Mréi-gwok sáu-bhiu. Nréi gwú hrai bhin-go gaa?
Ho	Ngró gwú hrai Wròng Shìn-shàang ge.
Cheung	Ngró dhou gwú hrai kréui ge. Ngró-drei heui mran kréui, hóu m̀ hóu qaa?
Ho	Wròng Shìn-shàang yrì-ghaa m̀ hái kréui ge sé-jri-lràu.
Cheung	M̀ gán-yiu. Ngró chrì-dhi mran kréui.

一	**yhat**	*one*
個	**go**	(classifier word for *people* and many *objects*)
手錶	**sáu-bhiu**	*wrist-watch*
枝	**jhì**	(classifier word for stick-like things)
筆	**bhat**	*pen, any writing tool*
呢	**nhi**	*this*

同埋	**trùng-mràai**	*and, with*
嗰	**gó**	*that*
㗎?	**gaa?**	*= ge + qaa?*
估	**gwú**	*to guess, reckon*
問	**mran**	*to ask a question*
而家	**yrì-ghaa**	*now*
喺	**hái**	*at/in/on, to be at/in/on*
唔緊要	**mŕ gán-yiu**	*never mind, it doesn't matter*
遲啲	**chrì-dhi**	*later on*

 ——————— **Grammar** ———————

4 This, that *and* which?

nhi go yràn	*this person*
gó go yràn	*that person*
Bhin go yràn?	*Which person?*

In English when you specify a word with *this, that* or *which?* you just put it in front of the relevant word (*this man, that ship, which pen?*), but in Cantonese you need to use a classifier word as well (*this* classifier *man, that* classifier *ship, which* classifier *pen?*). It is not necessarily easy to guess which classifier goes with which noun, although you can expect, for instance, that almost any object which is thin, straight and stick-like will be classified with **jhì**. You will be given the correct classifier for each noun you meet from now on. The classifier for people is **go**, so:

| **nhi go yràn** | *this person* |
| **Bhin go Mréi-gwok-yràn qaa?** | *Which American?* |

The classifier for wrist-watch is also **go**:

| **gó go sáu-bhiu** | *that watch* |

The classifier for pen is **jhì**:

| **gó jhì bhat** | *that pen* |

If it is clear what is meant, it is possible to leave out the noun, but the classifier must still be used. Note the following question and answer:

Nréi yiu bhin jhì bhat qaa?　　*Which pen do you want?*
Ngró yiu nhi jhì.　　　　　*I want this one.*

5　How about it?

Hóu m̀ hóu qaa? literally means *is it good?*, but it is also used at the ends of sentences and means *what do you say?*, *how about it?*, *OK?* (And there is **qaa** at the end of a question sentence again!)

6　Counting things

The Cantonese numbering system is very straightforward. The numbers one to ten are all single syllable words; eleven is 10 + 1, twelve is 10 + 2, thirteen is 10 + 3, and so on up to twenty which is 2×10; twenty-one is $2 \times 10 + 1$, twenty-nine is $2 \times 10 + 9$; thirty is 3×10, thirty-one is $3 \times 10 + 1 \ldots$. Memorise the numbers 1–10 given below and then try counting up to ninety-nine (and back again if you are really confident).

1 yhat	11 srap-yhat	21 yri-srap-yhat
2 yri	12 srap-yri	22 yri-srap-yri
3 shàam	13 srap-shàam	23 yri-srap-shàam
4 sei	14 srap-sei	24 yri-srap-sei
5 ngf́	15 srap-ngf́	25 yri-srap-ngf́
6 lruk	16 srap-lruk	26 yri-srap-lruk
7 chhat	17 srap-chhat	27 yri-srap-chhat
8 baat	18 srap-baat	28 yri-srap-baat
9 gáu	19 srap-gáu	29 yri-srap-gáu
10 srap	20 yri-srap	30 shàam-srap

40 sei-srap	41 sei-srap-yhat	47 sei-srap-chhat
50 ngf́-srap	52 ngf́-srap-yri	58 ngf́-srap-baat
60 lruk-srap	63 lruk-srap-shàam	69 lruk-srap-gáu
70 chhat-srap	74 chhat-srap-sei	75 chhat-srap-ngf́
80 baat-srap	85 baat-srap-ngf́	87 baat-srap-chhat
90 gáu-srap	96 gau-srap-lruk	99 gáu-srap-gáu

When things are counted (*one person, three pens*, etc.) the classifier must be used in the same way as with specifying words. So:

yhat go yràn	*one person*
sei jhì bhat	*four pens*
srap-yri go sáu-bhiu	*twelve watches*

The whole numbering system is nice and regular with one exception: the number *two* is not **yri** but **lréung** when it is followed by a classifier, so:

yhat, yri, shàam, sei, . . .	*one, two, three, four, . . .*, but:
yhat jhì bhat, lréung jhì	*one pen, two pens, three pens,*
bhat, shàam jhì bhat,	*four pens, . . .*
sei jhì bhat, . . .	

It is only the number *two* itself which plays this trick, complex numbers which end in a two are not affected, as you can see from the example of *twelve watches* above. (And don't feel too hard done by: English is even crazier about the number two: think of *brace of, pair of, couple of, twin, duo-* and *bi-*!)

The magic of numbers

Cantonese people are very interested in numbers and many people believe that numbers can influence fate. Everybody loves the number eight because **baat** sounds rather like **faat** which means *get rich*. On the other hand, four is considered an unlucky number because **sei** sounds like **séi**, which means *to die*. Two and eight are good because **yri baat** sounds like **yri faat**, *easy to get rich*, but five and eight are bad because **ngŕ baat** resembles **mŕ faat**, *not get rich*. A Chinese purchaser recently insisted on paying £80,000 for a house in the south of England rather than the asking price of £79,500, believing that the larger sum was much luckier sounding! For many years, the Hong Kong Government auctioned 'lucky' car registration numbers for charity: an astronomical price was paid for 8888, which adorned one of the Territory's many Rolls-Royces.

 ———————— **Exercises** ————————

1 Try to give answers to the following questions. You cannot be sure of the answer to the second one, but common sense should help you.

    (*a*) **Gwai-sing qaa?**

    (*b*) **Wròng Shìn-shàang hrai mŕ hrai Jhùng-gwok-yràn qaa?**

(c) **Nréi mráai mř mráai chhe qaa?** *(answer: no)*

(d) **Nréi yráu Yrat-bún pràng-yráu maa?** *(answer: yes)*

2 See if you can understand what these sentences mean. Practise saying them out loud until they sound fluent.

(a) **Sáu-bhiu trùng-mràai bhat dhou hrai Hrò Shìn-shàang ge.**

(b) **Gó go sáu-bhiu hóu leng.**

(c) **Hrò Shìn-shàang chrì-dhi heui mran Wròng Taai-táai.**

(d) **Bhin jhì bhat hrai Jhèung Síu-jé gaa?**

3 Fill in the blanks to make correct and meaningful sentences.

(a) **Nhi ____ sáu-bhiu hrai Hrò Taai-táai ge.**

(b) **Nréi hrai mř hrai Yhìng-gwok ____ qaa?**

(c) **Ngró gwú Yrat-____ chhe hóu gwai.**

(d) **Wròng Síu-jé leng ____ leng qaa?**

(e) **Nréi séung mráai ____-yré qaa?**

(f) **____-go hrai Jhèung Síu-jé qaa?**

(g) **Kréui mř hrai Yhìng-gwok-yràn, ____ mř hrai Mréi-gwok-yràn; kréui hrai Yrat-bún-yràn.**

(h) **Ngró ____ Wròng Shìn-shàang, 'Nréi yráu Yhìng-gwok chhe maa?'**

4 Make up your own conversation. Tell Mr Wong that you want to go to England to buy a British car. He tells you that British cars are expensive. Ask him what kind of car he's got. He says that he has a British car too.

5 In the picture opposite all the women are American, all the men are Chinese, and all the children are Japanese. Try saying in Cantonese how many of each there are, say how many watches Mr Wong is selling, and describe what the woman is doing with her money at the stationery stall.

3

第三課　家人同朋友

GHÀA-YRÀN TRÙNG PRÀNG-YRÁU

Family and friends

In Unit 3 you will meet one of the only two irregular verbs that there are in Cantonese – the verb *to have*. You will also learn some important words for family members. And there is a neat summary of the useful little words known as final particles which round off sentences.

────── Dialogue 1 ──────

Mr Ho meets Mr Wong on the street.

王先生，你去邊處呀？
早晨，何先生，我返屋企。
你返屋企做乜嘢呀？
我帶我媽媽去睇醫生。
你同媽媽一齊住吖？
係，我同爸爸，媽媽，兄弟，姊妹，七個人一齊住。
七個人一齊住……噉樣，你哋間屋一定好大嘞。
係，都幾大。對唔住，何先生，我要走嘞，再見。
再見，王先生。

Ho　Wròng Shìn-shàang, nréi heui bhin-sue qaa?
Wong　Jóu-sràn, Hrò Shìn-shàang, ngró fhàan qhuk-kéi.

── 18 ──

Ho Nréi fhàan qhuk-kéi jrou-mhat-yré qaa?

Wong Ngró daai ngró mraà-mhaa heui tái-yhi-shang.

Ho Nréi trùng mràa-mhaa yhat-chrài jrue qràa?

Wong Hrai, ngró trùng bràa-bhaa, mràa-mhaa, hhìng-drai, jí-mrui, chhat go yràn yhat-chrài jrue.

Ho Chhat go yràn yhat-chrài jrue ... gám-yéung, nréi-drei ghàan qhuk yhat-dring hóu draai laak.

Wong Hrai, dhou-géi draai. Deui-mȑ-jrue, Hrò Shìn-shàang, ngró yiu jáu laak, joi-gin.

Ho Joi-gin, Wròng Shìn-shàang.

邊處、邊度	**bhin-sue?** or **bhin-drou?**	*where? which place?*
返	**fhàan**	*to return, to return to*
屋企	**qhuk-kéi**	*family; home*
做乜嘢	**jrou-mhat-yré?**	*why? for what reason?*
做 ·	**jrou**	*to do*
媽媽	**mràa-mhaa**	*mother*
睇醫生	**tái-yhi-shang**	*to see the doctor*
醫生	**yhi-shang**	*doctor*
同	**trùng**	*with, and* (a shorter form of **trùng-mràai**)
一齊	**yhat-chrài**	*together*
住	**jrue**	*to dwell, to live*
吖?	**qràa?**	(a question word: *that's right, isn't it?*)
爸爸	**bràa-bhaa**	*father*
兄弟	**hhìng-drai**	*brothers*
姊妹	**jí-mrui**	*sisters*
噉，噉樣	**gám** or **gám-yéung**	*in that case, so*
間	**ghàan**	(classifier for *houses* and *rooms*)
屋	**qhuk**	*house*
一定	**yhat-dring**	*certainly*
大	**draai**	*big*
嘞、嗱	**laak** or **laa**	(a statement word: *that's how the case stands now*)
都幾、幾	**dhou-géi** or **géi**	*quite, rather, fairly*
要	**yiu**	*must, need to*
走	**jáu**	*to run; to run away; to leave*

Here is the Wong family. How would C address A? How would D address B? How would D address A? How would you address D? How would you address B? Which one do you think is the Mr Wong who figures in the dialogue?

(a) (b) (c) (d) (e) (f) (g)

Grammar

1 Where?

Bhin-sue? (*where?*) works according to the same rules as **bhin-go?** (*who?*) and **mhat-yré?** (*what?*) (see Unit 2, grammar point 1):

    Nréi heui bhin-sue qaa?   *Where are you going?*
    Ngró heui sé-jri-lràu.   *I'm going to the office.*

Bhin-sue? and **bhin-drou?** both mean *where?* and you can use whichever of them you prefer.

2 Fhàan (to return)

Fhàan means *to return*. It combines easily with **heui** (*to go*) as **fhàan-heui**, meaning *to go back*, that is, *to return in a direction away from me the speaker*.

    Nréi fhàan-heui m̀r fhàan-heui   *Are you going back?*
    qaa?

or in its more commonly shortened form:

    Nréi fhàan m̀r fhàan-heui qaa?   *Are you going back?*

Fhàan also means *to go where one usually goes*:

Wròng Síu-jé fhàan qhuk-kéi.	*Miss Wong is going home.*
Ngró fhàan sé-jri-lràu.	*I'm going to the office.*

3 Why?

Jrou-mhat-yré? literally means *to do what?*, but it has come to mean *why?* It can be positioned quite freely in the sentence without any change of meaning. All the following examples mean *Why must you sell your car?*

Nréi jrou-mhat-yré yiu mraai chhe qaa?
Jrou-mhat-yré nréi yiu mraai chhe qaa?
Nréi yiu mraai chhe jrou-mhat-yré qaa?

Yes and No

There are no words for *yes* and *no* in Cantonese. You should use the positive or negative form of the appropriate verb, so in answer to **Nréi heui mř heui Jhùng-gwok qaa?** (*Are you going to China?*) you can reply **heui** (*yes*) or **mř heui** (*no*). If it is not the verb itself which is the focus of the question, it is useful to use **hrai** (*it is the case*), or **mř hrai** (*it is not the case*), as in the dialogue. **Hrai** and **mř hrai** come as close to *yes* and *no* as Cantonese gets.

---

4 The adverb yhat-chrài (together)

Yhat-chrài (*together, all together*) is an adverb and like almost all adverbs it comes in front of the verb in the sentence. So **yhat-chrài jrue** is *to live together* and **yhat-chrài fhàan Yhìng-gwok** means *to return to Britain together*.

5 That's right, isn't it?

The word **qràa?** comes at the end of a sentence to ask for confirmation that what you have said is correct:

Nréi hrai Jhèung Shìn-shàang qràa?	You're Mr Cheung, aren't you?
Nréi heui Yhìng-gwok qràa?	I take it you're going to England, right?

6 That's how the case stands now

Laak (sometimes pronounced **laa**) comes at the end of the sentence to state what the current position is. Naturally enough, that means that often there has been some change before that position has been arrived at:

Ngró yiu jáu laak.	I must be going now.
Kréui mr̀ séung mráai chhe laak.	He doesn't want to buy a car any more.

Dialogue 2

Mr Ho hasn't seen Mr Cheung for a long while. They meet by chance.

張先生，好耐冇見。你好嗎？你而家喺邊處住呀？
我而家住喺香港花園道二十八號三樓。
花園道好唔好住呀？
好住。花園道有好多巴士同的士搭。何先生，你住喺邊處呀？
我重住喺𠻹啡街七十三號地下。你有時間請嚟坐喇。
你有心。你間屋有車房嗎？
我唔係住一間屋，我住一層樓啫。呢層樓唔係幾大，冇車房嘅。
好，有時間我嚟探你，再見。
再見。

Ho	Jhèung Shìn-shàang, hóu-nroi-mróu-gin. Nréi hóu maa? Nréi yrì-ghaa hái bhin-sue jrue qaa?
Cheung	Ngró yrì-ghaa jrue hái Hhèung-góng Fhàa-yrùen Drou yri-srap-baat hrou shàam láu.
Ho	Fhàa-yrùen Drou hóu mr̀ hóu jrue qaa?
Cheung	Hóu jrue. Fhàa-yrùen Drou yráu hóu dhò bhaa-sí trùng dhik-sí daap. Hrò Shìn-shàang, nréi jrue hái bhin-sue qaa?
Ho	Ngró jrung jrue hái Gaa-fhe Ghaai chhat-srap-shàam hrou drei-háa. Nréi yráu srì-gaan chéng lrài chró lhaa.

Cheung Nréi yráu-shàm. Nréi ghàan qhuk yráu chhe-fròng maa?

Ho Ngró mř hrai jrue yhat ghàan qhuk, ngró jrue yhat chràng láu jhe. Nhi chràng láu mř-hrai-géi-draai, mróu chhe-fròng ge.

Cheung Hóu, yráu srì-gaan ngró lrài taam nréi. Joi-gin.

Ho Joi-gin.

耐	**nroi**	*a long time*
好耐冇見	**hóu-nroi-mróu-gin**	*long time no see*
冇	**mróu**	*have not* (negative of **yráu** to have)
香港	**Hhèung-góng**	*Hong Kong*
花園道	**Fhàa-yrùen Drou**	*Garden Road*
花園	**fhàa-yúen**	*garden* (note the tone change from **yrùen** to **yúen**)
道	**drou**	*street, road*
......號	**... hrou**	*number . . .*
樓	**láu**	*flat; high building; storey*
多	**dho**	*many, much*
巴士	**bhaa-sí**	*bus*
的士	**dhik-sí**	*taxi*
搭	**daap**	*to travel by/catch/take* (public transport)
重	**jrung**	*still, yet*
㗎啡	**gaa-fhe**	*coffee*
街	**ghaai**	*street*
地下	**drei-háa**	*ground floor; ground; floor*
時間	**srì-gaan**	*time*
請	**chéng**	*please*
嚟	**lrài**	*to come, to come to*
坐	**chró**	*to sit*
喇	**lhaa**	(a word urging someone to agree with you or to do something for you)
車房	**chhe-fròng**	*garage*
層	**chràng**	(classifier for a *flat, storey, deck*)
啫	**jhe** or **jhek**	*only; and that's all*
唔係幾／好	**mř-hrai-géi/hóu**	*not very*
嘅	**ge**	(makes a statement more emphatic: *that's how it is and that's how it's going to stay*)
探	**taam**	*to see, to visit*

The Chinese characters for **Yhì-yúen Drou** (*Hospital Road*) read from left to right.

The Chinese characters for **dhik-sí** (*taxi*) read from left to right.

Questions

1 **Hrai m̀r hrai qaa?** Test your understanding of Dialogue 2 by answering **hrai** (*it is so*) or **m̀r hrai** (*it is not so*) to the following statements.

(*a*) **Fhàa-yrùen Drou mr̀ hóu jrue.**
(*b*) **Hrò Shìn-shàang jrue hái yhat ghàan qhuk.**
(*c*) **Hrò Shìn-shàang jrue hái drei-háa.**
(*d*) **Hrò Shìn-shàang ge chhe-fròng hóu draai.**
(*e*) **Jhèung Shìn-shàang heui Hrò Shìn-shàang qhuk-kéi.**

2   Now answer the following questions in Cantonese.

(*a*) **Hrò Shìn-shàang jrue hái bhin-sue qaa?**
(*b*) **Jhèung Shìn-shàang jrue hái bhin-sue qaa?**
(*c*) **Hrò Shìn-shàang ge láu yráu mróu chhe-fròng qaa?**
(*d*) **Jhèung Shìn-shàang séung mr̀ séung taam Hrò Shìn-shàang qaa?**
(*e*) **Yráu mróu bhaa-sí heui Fhàa-yrùen Drou qaa?**

Grammar

7 *The verb* yráu

The verb **yráu** (*to have*) is an oddity. It is not made negative with **mr̀**. Instead, the negative of **yráu** is another verb **mróu** (*not to have*). So *Are you English?* is:

Nréi *hrai mr hrai* Yhìng-gwok-yràn qaa?

But *Have you got an English car?* is:

Nréi *yráu mróu* Yhìng-gwok chhe qaa?

And *I haven't got a car* is:

Ngró *mróu* chhe.

From the general to the particular

When Mr Cheung gives his address in the dialogue, you will see that he gives it in the order Hong Kong, Garden Road, No. 28, 3rd floor, that is, in the opposite way to English. Chinese always prefers to work from the general to the particular, from the large to the small. We shall see later that it is the same with dates and times, so that the Chinese would translate *3.18 p.m. on 17th May 1995* in the order *1995, May, 17th, p.m., 3.18.*

---

8 Jhe or jhek

Jhe (pronounced by some people as **jhek**) is a very useful little word which is tacked onto the end of sentences to give the meaning *only, that's all*:

Ngró yráu lréung jhì bhat.	*I've got two pens.*
Kréui yráu yhat jhì bhat jhe.	*He's only got one pen.*

9 Not very

The negative of **draai** (*big*) is **mr̀ draai** (*not big*), just as you would expect. The negative of **hóu draai** (*very big*), however, is **mr̀-hrai-géi-draai** or **mr̀-hrai-hóu-draai**, both of which mean *not very big*. So you will need to remember that the verb **hrai** is included in this *not very* construction:

Nhi chràng láu mr̀-hrai-géi-gwai.	*This flat is not very dear.*
Wròng Síu-jé mr̀-hrai-hóu-leng.	*Miss Wong is not very pretty.*

10 A recap: final particles

You have now met quite a few words like **jhe**, that is, words which are added to the end of a sentence to round it off or to give an extra meaning. They are usually called final particles and they are used a great deal in everyday speech. Before you meet any more of them, here is a reminder of those you already know. So that you can check back, we have given in brackets the reference to where you first met them.

maa?	A spoken question mark. It makes a statement into a question. (Unit 1, grammar point 4)
nhe?	The short cut question word which asks follow-up questions. (Unit 1, grammar point 6)
qaa?	The final particle which is added to sentences which already contain positive–negative type

questions or question words like **mhat-yré?**
(Unit 1, grammar point 11; Unit 2, grammar
point 1)

gaa?   The particle made when **ge** is followed by **qaa?**
(Unit 2, Dialogue 2 vocabulary)

qràa?   The question word which expects the listener to
be in agreement: *that's right, isn't it?* (Unit 3,
grammar point 5)

laak/laa The word which shows that things were different
before but this is how the situation stands now.
(Unit 3, grammar point 6)

jhe/jhek *Only.* (Unit 3, grammar point 8)

lhaa   The word you use when you are trying to urge
someone to do something for you or to persuade
someone to agree with you. (Unit 3, Dialogue 2
vocabulary)

ge   Makes a statement more emphatic: *that's the way
it is!* (Unit 3, Dialogue 2 vocabulary)

 ———————— **Exercises** ————————

1 Sort out these jumbled words into meaningful sentences.

   (*a*) **bràa-bhaa yhi-shang Hrò Shìn-shàang hrai.**
   (*b*) **jrou-mhat-yré hái qhuk-kéi Wròng Taai-táai qaa?**
   (*c*) **tái yhi-shang ngró heui mr̀ séung.**
   (*d*) **ngró-drei sé-jri-lràu yhat-chrài fhàan.**

2 Fill in the blanks with words which will make sense of the
following sentences.

   (*a*) **Wròng Taai-táai heui tái ___-___.**
   (*b*) **Ngró-drei ___ heui Wròng Shìn-shàang ___-___.**
   (*c*) **Ngró bràa-bhaa hrai ___-___.**
   (*d*) **Ngró-drei jrue hái ___-___.**

3 You have just bumped into your old friend Mr Wong in the street in Hong Kong. You haven't seen him for several months. How do you greet him? Ask after his wife and where he lives now. Apologise to him and say that you have to catch a bus to Garden Road now to visit your father whom you have to take to see the doctor.

4

第四課　食嘢
SRIK-YRÉ
Eating in and eating out

The Chinese have made cuisine one of the most important features of their culture, and the Cantonese have refined the art to its highest form. If you are ever stuck for a topic of conversation, food is the one subject which is guaranteed to liven everyone up. In this unit you will learn about 'lonely verbs', some more about classifiers, some useful endings to attach to verbs and some other basic grammar points, but (very properly) the whole unit is dominated by food.

—————————— Dialogue 1 ——————————

Mr Ho invites Mr Wong to his home for a meal.

何先生，你太客氣啦，煮咁多餸請我食飯。
便飯啫，隨便食喇。要唔要茶呀？
唔要，唔該。何太太呢？佢喺邊處呀？
佢喺廚房煮緊飯，唔駛等佢啦。
何太太煮嘅餸真好食嘞。好似酒樓嘅一樣。何先生你有冇幫佢手呀？
冇呀！
何太太一定用咗好多時間預備呢餐飯嘞。
佢用咗半個鐘頭啫。
只係半個鐘頭吖？我唔信。
係真㗎。啲餸都係佢去附近嘅酒樓買嘅。
哦！

Wong Hrò Shìn-shàang, nréi taai haak-hei laa, júe gam dhò sung chéng ngró srik-fraan.

Ho Brin-fraan jhe, chrèui-bín srik lhaa. Yiu mǐ yiu chràa qaa?

Wong Mǐ yiu, mǐ-ghòi. Hrò Taai-táai nhe? Kréui hái bhin-sue qaa?

Ho Kréui hái chrùe-fóng júe-gán fraan, mǐ-sái dáng kréui laa.

Wong Hrò Taai-táai júe ge sung jhàn hóu-srik laak. Hóu-chrí jáu-lràu ge yhat-yreung. Hrò Shìn-shàang nréi yráu mróu bhòng kréui sáu qaa?

Ho Mróu qaa!

Wong Hrò Taai-táai yhat-dring yrung-jó hóu dhò srì-gaan yrue-brei nhi chhàan fraan laak.

Ho Kréui yrung-jó bun go jhung-tràu jhe.

Wong Jí-hrai bun go jhung-tràu qràa? Ngró mǐ seun.

Ho Hrai jhàn gaa. Dhi sung dhou hrai kréui heui fru-gran ge jáu-lràu mráai ge.

Wong Qró!

太......(啦)	taai . . . (laa)	too . . . , exceedingly . . .
客氣	haak-hei	polite
煮	júe	to cook
咁	gam	so
餸	sung	food; a course or dish other than rice or soup
請	chéng	to invite
食飯	srik-fraan	to eat, to eat a meal
食	srik	to eat
飯	fraan	rice; food
便飯	brin-fraan	pot-luck, a meal of whatever comes to hand
隨便	chrèui-bín	as you please, feel free
茶	chràa	tea
廚房	chrùe-fóng	kitchen
......緊	-gán	(a verb ending for continuing action: -ing)
唔駛	mǐ-sái	no need to, not necessary to
等	dáng	to wait, to wait for
真(係)	jhàn(-hrai)	truly, really; true, real
好食	hóu-srik	delicious
好似......一樣	hóu-chrí . . . yhat-yreung	just like . . .
酒樓	jáu-lràu	Chinese restaurant
幫......手	bhòng . . . sáu	to help . . . , to give . . . a hand
用	yrung	to use, to spend
......咗	-jó	(a verb ending for completed action: -ed)
預備	yrue-brei	to prepare, to get ready

餐	chhàan	(classifier for *food, a meal*)
半	bun	*half*
鐘頭	jhung-tràu	*an hour* (classifier = **go**)
只(係)	jí(-hrai)	*only*
信	seun	*to believe, to trust*
啲	dhi	(plural classifier, classifier for uncountable things)
都	dhou	*all, both*
附近	fru-gran	*nearby*
哦	qró!	*oh, really! oh, now I understand!*

 True or false?

(*a*) Hrò Shìn-shàang chéng Wròng Shìn-shàang heui jáu-lràu srik-fraan.

(*b*) Hrò Shìn-shàang júe-jó lréung go sung chéng Wròng Shìn-shàang srik.

(*c*) Hrò Shìn-shàang bhòng Hrò Taai-táai sáu júe-fraan.

(*d*) Hrò Shìn-shàang, Hrò Taai-táai yrung-jó lréung go bun jhung-tràu júe-fraan.

(*e*) Hrò Taai-táai mŕ júe sung, kréui jí-hrai heui jáu-lràu mráai-sung.

 —————————— **Grammar** ——————————

1 Chéng (to invite)

In Unit 3 you saw that **chéng** means *please*. It also has another meaning, *to invite*:

Kréui chéng ngró heui kréui qhuk-kéi.　　*He invites me to go to his home.*

2 'Lonely verbs'

Some verbs feel incomplete if they have no object, so Cantonese supplies an all-purpose object to comfort their loneliness! In English we have no problem with saying *he is eating*, but the Cantonese verb **srik** is unhappy on its own and if what is being eaten is not specified, the all-purpose object **fraan** (*rice*) will be added. The normal translation of *he is eating* is thus **Kréui srik-fraan**. **Júe** (*to cook*) is another verb which takes **fraan** for want of anything more definite, and you will meet other such verbs and other all-purpose objects as we go on.

3 Adverbs of place

The adverb which tells you where an action is happening comes either before or after the subject depending on the sense, but in any case it always comes before the verb:

Kréui hái qhuk-kéi chró.	*She is sitting indoors.*
Hái sé-jri-lràu nréi yráu mróu bhat qaa?	*Have you got a pen in the office?*

4 Tags on verbs

No verb ever changes its form in any way, but it is possible to modify the effect of a verb by tagging on to it one of a number of verb endings:

-gán is tagged onto a verb to emphasise that the action is actually going on at the time:

Wròng Shìn-shàang tái-gán yhi-shang.	*Mr Wong is in with the doctor.*

-jó is tagged onto a verb in the same way to show that the action has been completed. Usually the particle **laak** is added at the end of the sentence to back it up:

Kréui tái-jó yhi-shang laak.	*He saw the doctor.*
Ngró mráai-jó Mréi-gwok chhe laak.	*I bought an American car.*

5 An irregular verb: yiu/sái!

Here's a rare treat, another oddity in the way a verb is used. *To need to* is **yiu**, but *not to need to* is **mr̀ sái**:

Ngró-drei yiu dáng kréui.	*We need to wait for her.*
Ngró-drei mr̀ sái dáng kréui laa.	*We don't need to wait for her.*
Ngró yiu mráai chhe.	*I need to buy a car.*
Ngró mr̀ sái mráai chhe.	*I don't need to buy a car.*

However, when **yiu** means *to want* its negative is **mr̀ yiu**:

Ngró mr̀ yiu fraan.   *I don't want any rice.*

The question form for *to need to* is **sái mr̀ sái**:

Ngró-drei sái mr̀ sái dáng kréui qaa?   *Do we need to wait for her?*

The question form for *to want* is **yiu mr̀ yiu**:

Nréi yiu mr̀ yiu fraan qaa?   *Do you want some rice?*

6 Another use of ge

You saw in Unit 2, grammar point 2 that **ge** shows possession: **ngró ge chhe** (*my car*). It also is used to link a descriptive phrase to a noun:

hóu gwai ge gaa-fhe	*very expensive coffee, coffee which is very expensive*
mráai-gán bhat ge yràn	*the person who is buying a pen*
kréui jrue ge qhuk	*the house that he lives in*

7 Have you done it?

To ask if an action has been completed, Cantonese (like English) can use the verb *to have* (**yráu**):

Nréi taai-táai yráu mróu fhàan-heui qaa?	*Has your wife gone back?*
Kréui yráu mróu srik-fraan qaa?	*Has he eaten?*

The answer is a simple **yráu** (*yes*) or **mróu** (*no*).

8 More on classifiers

In Unit 2, grammar points 4 and 6 you met classifiers used with numbers and with specifying words like *this* and *that*. Some nouns are 'uncountable' – think of *water* and *air*, for instance – and the classifier to use then is **dhi**:

Nhi dhi sung hóu hóu-srik.   *This food is delicious.*

Dhi is also used as the classifier for all nouns when they are 'plural but not counted'. Compare the classifiers in the following examples:

nhi go yràn	*this person*
gó jhì bhat	*that pen*
gó ngŕ jhì bhat	*those five pens*
shàam go Yhìng-gwok-yràn	*three British people*
Gó dhi yràn	*those people* (plural but not counted)
Bhin dhi bhat qaa?	*Which pens?* (plural but not counted)

When a sentence starts with a definite noun (*The pen...*, *The food...*, *The Americans...*) Cantonese uses the appropriate classifier where English uses *The*:

Jhì bhat hóu leng.	*The pen is very nice.*
Dhi sung mŕ gwai.	*The food is not expensive.*
Dhi Mréi-gwok-yràn lrài mŕ lrài qaa?	*Are the Americans coming?*

9 The adverb dhou *again*

In Unit 1, grammar point 7 you met the adverb **dhou**, meaning *also*. Other meanings are *all* and *both*. **Dhou** must come immediately before a verb, and it obeys a further rule that it must come after the noun it refers to. Note carefully the placing of **dhou** in the following examples:

Nréi yráu bhat, kréui dhou yráu bhat.	*You have a pen, and he has too.*
Ngró-drei dhou yráu chhe.	*All of us have cars.*
Wròng Shìn-shàang Wròng Síu-jé dhou fhàan-jó sé-jri-lràu laak.	*Both Mr and Miss Wong have gone to the office.*
Gó lréung go Yhìng-gwok-yràn dhou mŕ séung srik-fraan.	*Neither of those two British people wants to eat.*

Rice

Rice is the staple food in the south of China and it is much appreciated as the superior grain in the north too. Not surprisingly, rice figures large in Chinese culture. It is offered in religious sacrifices to the ancestors, it is thrown over newly-weds to bring fertility to them, bags of it are laid on babies' stomachs to comfort them and stop them crying, the language is full of sayings about it. English has only the one word *rice*, but Cantonese has many words for it. **Fraan** means *rice* only when it is *cooked rice*. There are different words for *rice when growing*, *rice when harvested but not husked*, *rice husked but not cooked* and *rice cooked into a gruel*, as well as yet more terms for different kinds of rice such as *red rice*, *glutinous rice* and *non-glutinous rice*.

———— Dialogue 2 ————

Mr Ho tries to order a meal from a waiter.

伙記，我想要一個湯。你哋嘅湯新唔新鮮呀？
先生，你要個牛肉湯喇。好新鮮㗎。
好，我就要個牛肉湯。主菜有乜嘢好介紹呀？
龍蝦飯喇，好好味㗎。如果你要呢個飯，我哋送生果沙律俾你。
點解送生果沙律呀？
因為我哋嘅廚房昨日整咗太多，今日重有唔少，所以就送俾你食喇。
你哋昨日整嘅生果沙律今日俾我食，你識唔識做生意㗎？
先生，你唔好嬲。我再送今朝早整嘅甜品俾你，好嗎？重係好好味㗎。
乜嘢話？昨日嘅生果沙律；今朝早嘅甜品！你當我係垃圾桶吖！

Ho	Fó-gei, ngró séung yiu yhat go thòng. Nréi-drei ge thòng shàn mr̀ shàn-shìn qaa?
Waiter	Shìn-shàang, nréi yiu go ngràu-yruk thòng lhaa. Hóu shàn-shìn gaa.
Ho	Hóu, ngró jrau yiu go ngràu-yruk thòng. Júe-choi yráu mhat-yré hóu gaai-sriu qaa?
Waiter	Lrùng-hhaa-fraan lhaa, hóu hóu-mrei gaa. Yrùe-gwó nréi yiu nhi go fraan, ngró-drei sung shàang-gwó shàa-léut béi nréi.
Ho	Dím-gáai sung shàang-gwó shàa-léut qaa?

Waiter Yhàn-wrai ngró-drei ge chrùe-fóng jrok-yrat jíng-jó taai dhò, ghàm-yrat jrung yráu mȑ síu, só-yrí jrau sung béi nréi srik lhaa.

Ho Nréi-drei jrok-yrat jíng ge shàang-gwó shàa-léut ghàm-yrat béi ngró srik, nréi shik mȑ shik jrou-shàang-yi gaa?

Waiter Shìn-shàang, nréi mȑ-hóu nhàu. Ngró joi sung ghàm-jhìu-jóu jíng ge trìm-bán béi nréi, hóu maa? Jrung hrai hóu hóu-mrei gaa.

Ho Mhat-yré wáa? Jrok-yrat ge shàang-gwó shàa-léut; ghàm-jhìu-jóu ge trìm-bán! Nréi dong ngró hrai lraap-saap-túng qràa!

伙記	**fó-gei**	*waiter*
湯	**thòng**	*soup*
新鮮	**shàn-shìn**	*fresh*
牛肉	**ngràu-yruk**	*beef*
牛	**ngràu**	*cow, ox, cattle*
肉	**yruk**	*meat, flesh*
就	**jrau**	*then*
主菜	**júe-choi**	*main course*
介紹	**gaai-sriu**	*to recommend; to introduce*
龍蝦	**lrùng-hhaa**	*lobster*
好味	**hóu-mrei**	*delicious*
如果	**yrùe-gwó**	*if*
送……俾……	**sung X béi Y**	*to give X as a present to Y*
生果	**shàang-gwó**	*fruit*
沙律	**shàa-léut**	*salad*

點解?	**dím-gáai?**	*why?*
因為	**yhàn-wrai**	*because*
昨日	**jrok-yrat**	*yesterday*
整	**jíng**	*to make; to prepare*
今日	**ghàm-yrat**	*today*
少	**síu**	*few; little*
所以	**só-yrí**	*therefore, so*
識	**shik**	*to know how to, to be able to*
做生意	**jrou-shàang-yi**	*to do business, to run a business*
唔好	**mr̀-hóu**	*don't*
嬲	**nhàu**	*angry*
再	**joi**	*in addition; again*
朝早	**jhìu-jóu**	*morning; in the morning*
早	**jóu**	*early*
甜品	**trìm-bán**	*dessert*
話	**wáa**	*words, language, speech, saying*
當	**dong**	*to regard as*
垃圾桶	**lraap-saap-túng**	*rubbish bin*
垃圾	**lraap-saap**	*rubbish*

 ———————— **Grammar** ————————

10 To give

Sung means *to present, to make a gift*. It usually appears with **béi** which itself means *to give, to give to*. The word order for giving a present to someone is a comfortable one for an English speaker:

  Kréui sung yhat jhì bhat   *He gives a pen to me (as a*
    béi ngró.   *gift)*.

Béi is sometimes used on its own to mean *to present*, but it is more commonly found meaning just *to give to, to hand over to*:

  Kréui béi yhat jhì bhat   *He hands a pen to me/hands me*
    ngró.   *a pen.*

11 Don't!

To tell someone not to do something, Cantonese uses **mr̀-hóu** (*it's not good to . . .*) or **Nréi mr̀-hóu** (*it's not good that you should . . .*):

  Mr̀-hóu heui!   *Don't go!*
  Nréi mr̀-hóu mráai chhe!   *Don't buy a car!*

12 Short cuts

Cantonese is a lively quick-fire language, and speakers often find ways of shortening phrases which seem to them to be tediously long. Here is a list of shortened forms of phrases which you have met so far:

ghàm-yrat jhìu-jóu   → ghàm-jhìu-jóu or even shorter →
                         ghàm-jhìu

jrok-yrat jhìu-jóu   → jrok-yrat-jhìu or → jrok-jhìu

Wròng Shìn-shàang → Wròng Shàang

Wròng Taai-táai   → Wròng Táai

mr̀-hóu   → mrái (both mean *don't*, but mrái
                          is a bit ruder because it
                          is so abrupt sounding)

 ———————— **Exercises** ————————

1 Make meaningful sentences from the jumbled words below. You have done exercises like this before, but it gets more difficult now that you know more complicated patterns.

    (*a*) Hrò Taai-táai séung Wròng Shìn-shàang srik-fraan dáng yhat-chrài.

    (*b*) chrùe-fóng hái júe-gán fraan Hrò Taai-táai.

    (*c*) maa? mran Wròng Shìn-shàang Hrò Taai-táai hóu-mrei júe ge sung kréui.

    (*d*) sáu Hrò Taai-táai Hrò Shìn-shàang yráu qaa? mróu bhòng.

    (*e*) júe ge sung jáu-lràu yhat-yreung ge hóu-chrí Hrò Taai-táai.

2 Try to answer these questions in Cantonese.

    (*a*) Nréi shik mr̀ shik júe ngràu-yruk thòng qaa? (*answer: yes*)

    (*b*) Nréi qhuk-kéi fru-gran yráu mróu jáu-lràu qaa? (*answer: no*)

    (*c*) Jrok-yrat nréi yráu mróu bhòng nréi mràa-mhaa sáu júe-fraan qaa? (*answer: no*)

    (*d*) Dím-gáai nréi ghàm-jhìu-jóu gam nhàu qaa? (*answer: I'm not*)

(e) **Nréi jí-hrai shik jrou shàang-yi mŕ shik júe-fraan, hrai mŕ hrai qaa?** (*answer: it's not so*)

3

(a) **Hái chrùe-fóng yráu mhat-yré qaa?** See how many answers you can make up on the lines **Hái chrùe-fóng yráu lrùng-hhaa, dhou yráu ...**

(b) **Hái chrùe-fóng yráu mróu lraap-saap-túng qaa?** If your answer is *yes*, try to explain it. If your answer is *no*, think again but less seriously!

5

第五課　購物
KAU-MRAT
Shops and markets

Here you will find yet more on classifiers and verb endings, and two different ways of saying *thank you* are explained. One of the two shopping trips on which you are taken is of course for food.

Dialogue 1

Miss Wong and Miss Cheung are shopping in a fashion store.

今日係禮拜一，唔係禮拜日，點解呢間舖頭咁多人呢？
呢間舖頭大減價吖嗎。我哋入去睇吓好嗎？
好呀，嘩！你睇，嗰件衫裙真係好平嘛！
係嘛。質地又好；款式又新；顏色又靚；真係好嘞。
噉，我就買呢件喇。
我都想買嗰件紅色嘅。
咦，呢處有少少爛咗嘛。
係咩？哦！係嘛！我呢件都有少少爛咗。等我睇吓其他嘅有冇爛呢。
唔駛睇啦，件件都有少少爛嘅，因為佢哋都係次貨，所以咁平。

Wong　Ghàm-yrat hrai Lrái-baai-yhat, mr̀ hrai Lrái-baai-yrat, dím-gáai nhi ghàan pou-táu gam dhò yràn nhe?

Cheung　Nhi ghàan pou-táu draai-gáam-gaa qhaa-maa. Ngró-drei yrap-heui tái-hráa hóu maa?

— 40 —

Wong	Hóu qaa. Whàa! Nréi tái, gó grin shaam-kwràn jhàn-hrai hóu prèng bo!
Cheung	Hrai bo. Jhat-déi yrau hóu; fún-shik yrau shàn; ngràan-shik yrau leng: jhàn-hrai hóu laak.
Wong	Gám, ngró jrau mráai nhi grin lhaa.
Cheung	Ngró dhou séung mráai gó grin hrùng-shik ge.
Wong	Yí, nhi-sue yráu síu-síu lraan-jó bo!
Cheung	Hrai mhe? Qhòu! Hrai bo! Ngró nhi grin dhou yráu síu-síu lraan-jó. Dáng ngró tái-hráa krèi-thàa ge yráu mróu lraan nhe.
Wong	Mr̀-sái tái laa, grin-grin dhou yráu síu-síu lraan ge, yhàn-wrai kréui-drei dhou hrai chi-fo, só-yrí gam prèng.

禮拜、星期	**lrái-baai** or **shìng-krèi**	*week*
禮拜一	**Lrái-baai-yhat**	*Monday*
禮拜日	**Lrái-baai-yrat**	*Sunday*
舖頭	**pou-táu**	*shop*
大減價	**draai-gáam-gaa**	*a sale*
丫嗎	**qhaa-maa**	(final particle: *you should realise, don't you know*)
入	**yrap**	*to enter*
睇	**tái**	*to look at*
......吓	**-hráa**	(verb ending: *have a little . . .*)
嘩！	**whàa!**	*wow!*
件	**grin**	(classifier for most items of *clothing*)
衫裙	**shaam-kwràn**	*a dress*

平	prèng	cheap
嚩	bo!	(final particle: *let me remind you, let me tell you*)
質地	jhat-déi	quality
又......又......	yrau . . . yrau . . .	both . . . and . . .
款色	fún-shik	style
新	shàn	new; up-to-date
顏色	ngràan-shik	colour
紅色嘅	hrùng-shik ge	red
咦	yí	(exclamation of surprise: *hullo, what's this?*)
呢處	nhi-sue	here
少少	síu-síu	a little bit, somewhat
爛	lraan	broken, damaged
咩?	mhe?	(final particle: *do you mean to say that . . . ?*)
等	dáng	let, allow
其他	krèi-thàa	other
次貨	chi-fo	seconds

The six Chinese characters above the shops read **Draai-gáam-gaa: Draai-chhàu-jéung** (*Great sale: Great lucky draw*) from left to right.

Picture quiz

(a) Wròng Síu-jé gó grin shaam-kwràn prèng mř prèng qaa? Leng mř leng qaa?

(b) Wròng Síu-jé gó grin shaam-kwràn yráu mróu lraan gaa? Jhèung Síu-jé gó grin nhe?

Grammar

1 The week

Lrái-baai means *week*. It is classified with **go**, so *one week* is **yhat go lrái-baai**, *two weeks* is **lréung go lrái-baai**, and so on.

The days of the week are simply numbered 1–6 from Monday to Saturday:

Lrái-baai-yhat	*Monday*	**Lrái-baai-sei**	*Thursday*
Lrái-baai-yri	*Tuesday*	**Lrái-baai-ngŕ**	*Friday*
Lrái-baai-shàam	*Wednesday*	**Lrái-baai-lruk**	*Saturday*

However, Sunday is not numbered. Instead, the word for *sun* (**yrat**) is used, so **Lrái-baai-yrat** is Sunday. Go very carefully with your tones or you will mix up Sunday (**Lrái-baai-yrat**) and Monday (**Lrái-baai-yhat**)!

Some people say **shìng-krèi** instead of **lrái-baai**, and you may do so too if you wish. Simply substitute **shìng-krèi** for **lrái-baai** in any of the above.

2 Nhe? *again*

You have met **nhe?** as a final particle which asks a follow-up question (see Unit 1, grammar point 6). It is also used after rhetorical questions, that is, questions where you do not expect an answer, or perhaps when you are wondering to yourself:

Gó go yràn hrai bhin-go nhe?	*I wonder who that can be?*

There are two examples in the dialogue. Can you find them?

3 Coming *and* going

Lrài (*to come*) and **heui** (*to go*) are often used with other verbs of movement to show which direction the movement is in. For instance:

fhàan	*to return*	**yrap**	*to enter*
fhàan-heui	*to go back*	**yrap-heui**	*to go in*
fhàan-lrài	*to come back*	**yrap-lrài**	*to come in*

4 Another verb ending: -hráa

In Unit 4, grammar point 4 you met the verb endings -jó and -gán.
Another one is -hráa, which gives the idea of *doing something for a bit*:

tái-hráa	have a glance at (lit. *look a bit*)
dáng-hráa	wait for a moment (lit. *wait a bit*)
chró-hráa	sit for a while (lit. *sit a bit*)

5 Yrau ... yrau ... (both ... and ...)

Yrau basically means *furthermore* and it is an adverb. It has to obey
the rule for such adverbs and come in front of a verb (see **dhou** in
Unit 1, grammar point 7 and Unit 4, grammar point 9), even when
it is being repeated to give the meaning *both... and....* In the
dialogue you can see that it does obey (the three verbs are **hóu** (*to
be good*), **shàn** (*to be new*) and **leng** (*to be pretty*)). If you bear that
rule in mind you will easily understand why the translation of *both
Mr and Mrs Wong are going* might be **Wròng Shìn-shàang yrau
heui, Wròng Taai-táai yrau heui.**

6 Colours

Hrùng means *red*, but it is most easily used in combination with
shik (*colour*) as **hrùng-shik** (*red-coloured*). **Ge** is added to link
hrùng-shik with a noun (see Unit 4, grammar point 6):

| Kréui ge chhe hrai mhat-yré ngràan-shik gaa? | *What colour's his car?* |
| Hrai hrùng-shik ge chhe. | *It's a red car.* |

7 Here *and* there

In Unit 3 you met **bhin-sue?** and **bhin-drou?** (*where?*). **Bhin** means
which?, and **sue** and **drou** both mean *place*, so **bhin-sue?** and
bhin-drou? mean *which place?, where?*

Logically enough, *here* and *there* are made from *this place* and *that
place*:

| nhi-sue or nhi-drou | here |
| gó-sue or gó-drou | there |

8 *Final particle* mhe?

If you want to express great incredulity in a question in English (for example, *You can speak 57 languages fluently??!!*) you raise your voice almost to a squeak at the end of the question, but of course it is less easy to do that in Cantonese because of the need to observe tones. **Mhe?** does the job for you. It indicates great surprise, astonishment, near disbelief: *surely that's not the case, is it?*; *do you mean to say that . . . ?* The answer given is almost always **hrai** or **mr̀ hrai** (*it is the case* or *it is not the case*).

9 Dáng *again*

Dáng means *to wait*, as you saw in Unit 4. **Dáng ngró** means *wait for me* or *wait for me to*, and so **dáng ngró srik-fraan** means *wait for me to eat*. From *wait for me to eat* to *let me eat* is not a big jump, and you will find that Cantonese often uses **dáng ngró** where English would say *let me . . . .* Generally, if **dáng ngró** comes at the beginning of a sentence it is likely to be used in the sense of *let me . . .* , and if it is embedded within a sentence it is likely to mean *wait for*:

Dáng ngró bhòng nréi sáu.	*Let me help you.*
Mr̀-hóu dáng ngró srik-fraan.	*Don't wait for me to eat.*

10 *Double classifiers*

Doubling up classifiers and adding **dhou** (*all*) before the verb is a useful way of conveying the idea *every one of, each one of*:

Ghàan-ghàan qhuk dhou hóu leng.	*All the houses are very nice.*
Jhì-jhì Mréi-gwok bhat dhou gwai.	*All American pens are expensive.*
Grin-grin shaam-kwràn dhou mr̀ prèng.	*None of the dresses is cheap.*

Let me pay!

In restaurants you will often hear Chinese customers vying with each other to pay the bill, the winner gaining in 'face' what he/she loses in pocket. The standard wording used is **Dáng ngró béi!** (*Let me pay!*) (Literally: *Let me give!*) You, too, can play that game, but be sure you have the money about you in case you should be (un)lucky enough to win!

 ——————— **Dialogue 2** ———————

 Miss Cheung gets a bargain (perhaps) from the fish seller in the market.

呢啲蝦幾多錢一斤呀?
八十五蚊一斤
呢啲蝦咁細,八十五蚊一斤太貴勒。七十蚊一斤得唔得呀?
唔得!小姐,你睇,隻隻蝦都好新鮮會游水。八十五蚊一斤唔貴嘅啦。
嗰處嘅檔口只係要七十二蚊一斤啫。點解你哋要八十五蚊一斤呀?
因為我哋係"買一送一"丫嗎。
點樣買一送一呀?
即係買一斤蝦,免費送一斤蝦喇。
好!我要一斤喇。嗱,呢處八十五蚊。
多謝。嗱,呢處兩斤蝦。
點解咁多死蝦㗎?
買一斤游水蝦,送一斤死蝦丫嗎。

Cheung	Nhi dhi hhaa géi-dho chín yhat ghàn qaa?
Seller	Baat-srap-ngŕ mhan yhat ghàn.
Cheung	Nhi dhi hhaa gam sai, baat-srap-ngŕ mhan yhat ghàn taai gwai laak. Chhat-srap mhan yhat ghàn dhak mr̀ dhak qaa?
Seller	Mr̀ dhak! Síu-jé, nréi tái, jek-jek hhaa dhou hóu shàn-shìn wrúi yràu-séui. Baat-srap-ngŕ mhan yhat ghàn mr̀ gwai ge-laa.
Cheung	Gó-sue ge dong-háu jí-hrai yiu chhat-srap-yri mhan yhat ghàn jhe. Dím-gáai nréi-drei yiu baat-srap-ngŕ mhan yhat ghàn qaa?
Seller	Yhàn-wrai ngró-drei hrai 'mráai-yhat-sung-yhat' qhaa-maa.

Cheung	Dím-yéung mráai-yhat-sung-yhat qaa?
Seller	Jhik-hrai mráai yhat ghàn hhaa, mrín-fai sung yhat ghàn hhaa lhaa.
Cheung	Hóu! Ngró yiu yhat ghàn lhaa. Nràa, nhi-sue baat-srap-ngŕ mhan.
Seller	Dhò-jre. Nràa, nhi-sue lréung ghàn hhaa.
Cheung	Dím-gáai gam dhò séi hhaa gaa?
Seller	Mráai yhat ghàn yràu-séui hhaa, sung yhat ghàn séi hhaa qhaa-maa.

蝦	hhaa	*prawn*
幾多?	géi-dho?	*how much? how many?*
錢	chín	*money*
斤	ghàn	*a catty (= 20 ounces)*
蚊	mhan	*dollar*
細	sai	*small*
得	dhak	*OK, 'can do', acceptable*
隻	jek	*(classifier for animals)*
會	wrúi	*to be able to, to know how to*
游水	yràu-séui	*to swim*
水	séui	*water*
嘅啦	ge-laa	*(final particle giving strong emphasis)*
檔口	dong-háu	*street stall*
點樣?	dím-yéung?	*how? in what way?*
即係	jhik-hrai	*that is, that is to say*
免費	mrín-fai	*free of charge*
嗱	Nràa	*'there', 'here you are', 'here it is, look'*
多謝 (你)	dhò-jre (nréi)	*thank you*
死	séi	*dead; to die*

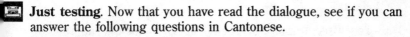

Just testing. Now that you have read the dialogue, see if you can answer the following questions in Cantonese.

(a) Jhèung Síu-jé hái dong-háu séung mráai mhat-yré qaa?

(b) Dhi hhaa géi-dho chín yhat ghàn qaa?

(c) Krèi-thàa dong-háu ge hhaa, géi-dho chín yhat ghàn qaa?

(d) Jhèung Síu-jé mráai-jó hhaa dím-gáai hóu nhàu qaa?

———————— **Grammar** ————————

11 So much each

Note the simple formula for giving prices:

Géi-dho chín yhat ghàn qaa?	*How much per catty?*
Lréung mhan yhat ghàn.	*Two dollars a catty.*

The same kind of formula can be used with other terms:

Shaam-kwràn lruk-srap mhan yhat grin.	*Dresses cost $60 each.*
Yhat go yràn shàam jhì bhat.	*Three pens per person.*

12 *More on* How about it?

In Unit 2, grammar point 5 you met **hóu mr̀ hóu qaa?** as a way of asking someone's opinion after making a statement. **Dhak mr̀ dhak qaa?** is perhaps even more commonly used for the same purpose, meaning *will that do?, is that OK by you?, are you happy with that?*

13 Thank you

You have now met two words for *thank you*: **mr̀-ghòi** and **dhò-jre**. They are used in different ways, and it is important to try to sort them out.

Mr̀-ghòi is used for everyday minor politenesses, such as thanking someone for holding a door open, or for passing the soy sauce, or for doing the washing-up.

Dhò-jre is used for more heartfelt thanks, for example, in gratitude to someone for a present received, or for saving your life, or for finding you a job. It is always used when receiving money.

So when you take goods from a shopkeeper, you may or may not say **mr̀-ghòi** (depending on how polite you feel like being), but he will certainly say **dhò-jre** when he takes your money.

The polite response to someone who thanks you is **mr̀-sái** (*there's no need to*). The longer forms **mr̀-sái mr̀-ghòi** and **mr̀-sái dhò-jre** can be used too.

Pidgin English

Pidgin English was developed in the early eighteenth century in Canton. It was a strange language which was a kind of halfway house between English and Cantonese, and therefore was presumed to be equally easy/difficult for both sides to learn and to speak as they transacted 'pidgin' (*business*) together. It used English vocabulary but often with Cantonese grammar patterns. Like Cantonese, it did not really have any plural forms, tenses or agreements, and it invented the word *piecee* to take the place of the Cantonese classifiers (*four piecee man, that piecee pen*). Some of its expressions have passed into regular English, such as *to have a look-see, long time no see, chop-chop* and *no can do*. This last phrase comes from the Cantonese **m̀r dhak** which you met in this lesson.

 ——————— **Exercises** ———————

1 Insert the bracketed element to make a sentence which is still meaningful. For example, the answer to the first question would be **Hrùng-shik ge Mréi-gwok chhe hóu gwai.**

   (*a*)   Mr̀ei-gwok chhe hóu gwai. (hrùng-shik ge)
   (*b*)   Ngró shik yràu-séui. (bràa-bhaa)
   (*c*)   Wròng Taai-táai heui mráai-yré. (pou-táu)
   (*d*)   Kréui ghàm-yrat m̀r srik-fraan. (séung)
   (*e*)   Hrò Shàang m̀r srik Hrò Táai júe ge sung. (Taai-)

2 Here is a test of your understanding of classifiers. See if you can put the correct classifier into the blank space. Beware: *there are two trick sentences*, so you will need to keep your wits about you!

   (*a*)   Gó ____ qhuk hrai Hrò Shìn-shàang ge.
   (*b*)   Kréui ge ____ shaam-kwràn yráu síu-síu lraan-jó.
   (*c*)   Wròng Síu-jé ge bràa-bhaa m̀r hrai ____ Jhùng-gwok-yràn.
   (*d*)   Nhi ____ Mréi-gwok bhat hóu gwai.

(e) Gó ____ lrùng-hhaa dhou hóu draai.

(f) ____-____ hhaa dhou séi-jó.

3

Now test your mathematical skills!

(a) Lrùng-hhaa srap-sei mhan yhat jek. Wròng Táai
     mráai-jó lréung jek. Kréui yiu béi géi-dho chín qaa?

(b) Nhi go dong-háu ge hhaa mr̀ gwai: shàam-srap-yri
     mhan yhat ghàn, mráai yhat ghàn sung bun ghàn.
     Wròng Táai yiu shàam ghàn – kréui yiu béi géi-dho
     chín qaa?

6

第六課　交通
GHÀAU-THÙNG

Getting around

Chinese cities are not models of grid-like planning, although ideally they were meant to be. However, people still tend to point the way to places by giving compass directions rather than left and right. In this unit you will be concentrating on means of transport and how to get to places.

Dialogue 1

Mr Wong is a stranger in town and asks a local person the way.

我要搭飛機返英國，請問去飛機場要搭幾多號巴士呀？

呢處有巴士去飛機場嘛。你要先由呢處搭小巴一直去，過三個街口到
　　大馬路，喺巴士站你要落小巴，再轉搭十五號巴士去飛機場喇。

噉，有冇小輪去飛機場呢？

冇小輪去機場嘛。

我好想搭地下鐵路。有冇地下鐵路去機場呢？

都冇嘛！地鐵只去市區啫。

噉，我去大會堂喇！有冇地鐵去呀？地鐵站喺邊處呀？

有，地鐵站喺嗰度，但係你話要搭飛機返英國。喺大會堂冇飛機場嘛。

Wong　Ngró yiu daap fhèi-ghèi fhàan Yhìng-gwok, chéng-mran
　　　　heui fhèi-ghèi-chrèung yiu daap géi-dho hrou bhaa-sí qaa?

Local　Nhi-sue mróu bhaa-sí heui fhèi-ghèi-chrèung bo. Nréi yiu
　　　　shìn yràu nhi-sue daap síu-bhaa yhat-jrik heui, gwo

The Chinese characters for **sréung** (*board*) can be seen on the front left door of the bus in white. The other door reads **lrok** (*alight*).

shàam go ghàai-háu dou draai mráa-lrou, hái bhaa-sí-jraam nréi yiu lrok síu-bhaa, joi júen daap srap-ngѓ hrou bhaa-sí heui fhèi-ghèi-chrèung lhaa.

Wong	Gám, yráu mróu síu-lrèun heui fhèi-ghèi-chrèung nhe?
Local	Mróu síu-lrèun heui ghèi-chrèung bo.
Wong	Ngró hóu séung daap drei-hraa-tit-lrou. Yráu mróu drei-hraa-tit-lrou heui ghèi-chrèung nhe?
Local	Dhou mróu bo! Drei-tit jí heui srí-khèui jhe.
Wong	Gám, ngró heui Draai-wrui-tròng lhaa! Yráu mróu drei-tit heui qaa? Drei-tit-jraam hái bhin-sue qaa?
Local	Yráu, drei-tit-jraam hái gó-drou, draan-hrai nréi wraa yiu daap fhèi-ghèi fhàan Yhìng-gwok. Hái Draai-wrui-tròng mróu fhèi-ghèi-chrèung bo.

飛機	**fhèi-ghèi**	*aircraft*
飛機場	**fhèi-ghèi-chrèung**	*airport*
請問	**chéng-mran . . . ?**	*please, may I ask . . . ?*
先	**shìn**	*first*
由	**yràu**	*from*
小巴	**síu-bhaa**	*mini-bus*
一直	**yhat-jrik**	*straight, directly*
過	**gwo**	*go past, go across, go by*
街口	**ghàai-háu**	*road junction*

到	**dou**	*to arrive, arrive at, reach*
馬路	**mráa-lrou**	*road*
巴士站	**bhaa-sí-jraam**	*bus stop*
落	**lrok**	*to alight from*
轉	**júen**	*to turn, to change to*
小輪	**síu-lrèun**	*ferry*
地下鐵路	**drei-hraa-tit-lrou**	*underground railway*
市區	**srí-khèui**	*urban area*
大會堂	**Draai-wrui-tròng**	*City Hall*
地鐵站	**drei-tit-jraam**	*underground station*
但係	**draan-hrai**	*but*
話	**wraa**	*to say*

Testing again. Re-read the dialogue. Then decide whether the following are true or false?

(*a*) Wròng Shìn-shàang yiu daap fhèi-ghèi fhàan Yhìng-gwok.

(*b*) Wròng Shìn-shàang yiu daap srap-ngŕ hrou bhaa-sí heui fhèi-ghèi-chrèung.

(*c*) Yráu síu-lrèun heui fhèi-ghèi-chrèung.

(*d*) Dhou yráu drei-hraa-tit-lrou heui fhèi-ghèi-chrèung.

(*e*) Draan-hrai mróu drei-tit heui Draai-wrui-tròng.

Grammar

1 Chéng-mran . . . ? (please may I ask . . . ?)

Chéng-mran, a combination of *please* and *ask*, is the polite way to begin a question to a stranger and is therefore very useful when asking for directions. It is also the respectful way to begin a question to someone of higher status than yourself.

2 To travel by

In Unit 3 you were introduced to **daap** (*to travel by*), and in the same unit you met **chró** (*to sit*). **Chró** can actually be used like **daap** to mean *to travel by* as well, probably because when you use a form of transport you sit on it (if you're lucky!). So **daap bhaa-sí** and **chró bhaa-sí** both mean *to travel by bus*. Beware, though, you cannot do the opposite and get away with making **daap** mean *to sit*!

3 First this, then that

The adverbs *first* and *then* are **shìn** and **joi**. Being adverbs they come before verbs (see Unit 1, grammar point 7, Unit 4, grammar point 9 and Unit 5, grammar point 5):

Kréui shìn heui	*He's going first to the airport*
ghèi-chrèung joi chró	*and then he's taking the bus*
bhaa-sí fhàan qhuk-kéi.	*home.*

4 More short cuts

The airport in Hong Kong, the **fhèi-ghèi-chrèung**, is such a common feature of everybody's life that the shortening of this term was almost inevitable. People mostly reduce it just to **ghèi-chrèung**. Similarly, the full formal word for an underground railway **drei-hraa-tit-lrou** is far too much of a mouthful for most people, who reduce it to **drei-tit**.

The Mass Transit Railway

The underground railway in Hong Kong, the **drei-hraa-tit-lrou** or **drei-tit** for short, is known in English as the MTR, short for Mass Transit Railway. The first section of it was opened in 1979 and the total length of 43 kilometres was in service by 1989. It is air-conditioned throughout (including the tunnels), clean, fast and efficient, and fares are low. Hong Kong people are noticeably proud of the system. The trains have no barriers between the coaches, so that you can stand at one end and look down the full length of the inside of the train as it snakes its way through the tunnels. For speed of travel through crowded Hong Kong it cannot be bettered.

Dialogue 2

Mr Wong visits Britain and is met by his friend Mr Chan.

老陳，我第一次嚟倫敦，請你話我聽去邊處玩好呢？
等我帶你去玩喇。我哋搭火車先向北行，去參觀劍橋大學。
好呀。劍橋大學係世界最有名嘅大學之一。
參觀完之後，我哋搭巴士去英國東部睇吓嗰處嘅鄉下。
好主意。我好中意去鄉下地方玩。
喺嗰處我有一個好朋友，我哋可以喺佢屋企住一晚。第二日請佢揸車
　送我哋去英國南部嘅漁港睇吓。
香港都有漁港，我去過好多次嘅。
我哋由漁港再搭小輪去離島。
我唔想去離島嘞。兩日之內去咁多地方，又搭咁耐車，我話好似走難
　唔似去玩噉。

Wong	Lróu Chán, ngró drai-yhat chi lrài Lrèun-dheun, chéng nréi wraa ngró thèng heui bhin-sue wáan hóu nhe?
Chan	Dáng ngró daai nréi heui wáan lhaa. Ngró-drei daap fó-chhè shìn heung bhak hràng, heui chhàam-gwhùn Gim-krìu Draai-hrok.
Wong	Hóu qaa. Gim-krìu Draai-hrok hrai sai-gaai jeui yráu-méng ge draai-hrok jhì yhat.
Chan	Chhàam-gwhùn-yrùen jhì-hrau, ngró-drei daap bhaa-sí heui Yhìng-gwok dhùng brou tái-hráa gó-sue ge hhèung-háa.
Wong	Hóu júe-yi. Ngró hóu jhùng-yi heui hhèung-háa drei-fhòng wáan.
Chan	Hái gó-sue ngró yráu yhat go hóu pràng-yráu, ngró-drei hó-yrí hái kréui qhuk-kéi jrue yhat mráan. Drai-yri yrat chéng kréui jhàa-chhe sung ngró-drei heui Yhìng-gwok nràam brou ge yrùe-góng tái-hráa.
Wong	Hhèung-góng dhou yráu yrùe-góng, ngró heui-gwo hóu dhò chi laak.
Chan	Ngró-drei yráu yrùe-góng joi daap síu-lrèun heui lrèi-dóu.
Wong	Ngró mr̀ séung heui lrèi-dóu laak. Lréung yrat jhì-nroi heui gam dhò drei-fhòng, yrau daap gam nroi chhe ngró wraa hóu-chrí jáu-nraan mr̀-chrí heui wáan gám.

老	lróu	elderly, aged, old
第	drai-	(makes ordinal numbers: *the first, the second*, etc.)
倫敦	Lrèun-dheun	London
聽	thèng	to listen
玩	wáan	to play, to enjoy, to amuse oneself
火車	fó-chhè	train
向	heung	towards
北	bhak	north
行	hràng	to journey, to go towards
參觀	chhàam-gwhùn	to visit
劍橋	Gìm-krìu	Cambridge
大學	draai-hrok	university
世界	sai-gaai	the world
最	jeui	most
有名	yráu-méng	famous
……之一	. . . jhì-yhat	one of the . . .
……完	-yrùen	finished
之後	jhì-hrau	after
東	dhùng	east
部	brou	area, part, portion
鄉下	hhèung-háa	countryside
主意	júe-yi	idea
中意	jhùng-yi	to like, to be fond of
地方	drei-fhòng	place
可以	hó-yrí	can, may
晚	mráan	evening, night
日	yrat	day
揸車	jhàa-chhe	to drive (a vehicle)
送	sung	to deliver, escort, send
南	nràam	south
漁港	yrùe-góng	fishing port
……過	-gwo	(verb ending: *to have experienced*)
次	chi	a time, an occasion
離島	lrèi-dóu	outlying island
之內	jhì-nroi	within
好似……唔似	hóu-chrí . . . mr̀-chrí	to be more like . . . than like . . .
走難	jáu-nraan	to flee from disaster, to be a refugee

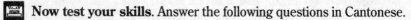 **Now test your skills.** Answer the following questions in Cantonese.

(*a*) Chràn Shìn-shàang hrai mr̀ hrai drai-yhat chi lrài Lrèun-dheun qaa?

(*b*) Gìm-krìu Draai-hrok hrai mr̀ hrai hái Lrèun-dheun fru-gran qaa?

(c) **Yhìng-gwok dhùng brou yráu hóu dhò yráu-méng ge yrùe-góng, hrai mr̀ hrai qaa?**

(d) **Chràn Shìn-shàang hóu jhùng-yi heui lrèi-dóu wáan, hrai mr̀ hrai qaa?**

Grammar

5 Lróu

Lróu means *elderly, aged*, and is used only of people and animals (that is, you would not describe a building or a book as **lróu**). It is often used with the surname as a familiar or affectionate term of address to a man (rarely to a woman):

    Lróu Wóng, . . .   *Wong, old chap, . . .*

However, you should note that when this is done the tone of the surname is changed to a mid rising tone from the original low falling tone. So the surname **Wròng** becomes **Lróu Wóng** and **Chràn** becomes **Lróu Chán**.

6 Ordinal numbers

You met the cardinal numbers (1, 2, 3, 4, etc.) in Unit 2. The ordinal numbers (the first, the second, the third, the fourth, etc.) are formed by putting **drai-** in front of the cardinal number:

    yhat go yràn   *one person*
    drai-yhat go yràn   *the first person*

You will remember from Unit 2, grammar point 6 that the number *two* obeys different rules, so that **yri** becomes **lréung** in front of classifiers. You should note that with ordinal numbers there is no such exception:

    lréung go yràn   *two people*
    drai-yri go yràn   *the second person*

While we are on the subject, we might as well look at a couple of other peculiarities of the number *two*. **Drai-yri**, as well as meaning *the second*, can quite logically extend to mean *the next*:

    Drai-yri yrat kréui jáu-jó laak.   *He left the next day.*

It can also logically extend to mean *the other*:

Ngró jrung yráu drai-yri jhì   *I've still got another pen.*
bhat.

But you need to stretch your mind a little further to take in the notion that **drai-yri** can mean *the others*:

Drai-yri dhi bhat dhou hrai   *The other pens are all hers.*
kréui ge.

7 To tell

Tell has various meanings in English, and they are not all translated by the same word in Cantonese. When *tell* means *tell someone about something* you can use **wraa . . . thèng . . .** :

Kréui wraa ngró thèng   *He told me he doesn't know*
kréui mr̀ shik jhàa-chhe.   *how to drive.*

8 Directions

dhùng	*east*
nràam	*south*
shài	*west*
bhak	*north*

Cantonese lists the four directions in the above order, whereas English speakers normally start with *north*. The intermediate directions are straightforward provided you remember that they are always the opposite way round from English, that is, Cantonese says *east-north* where English says *north-east*:

dhùng-bhak	*north-east*
dhùng-nràam	*south-east*
shài-nràam	*south-west*
shài-bhak	*north-west*

9 Another verb ending: -yrùen (finished)

Yrùen means *the end* or *to finish*. It is used as a verb ending to show that the action of the verb is all over:

| srik-yrùen | *finished eating* |
| chàam-gwhùn-yrùen | *finished visiting* |

10 'Time when'

Time expressions which begin with *after* are translated with jhì-hrau in Cantonese. However, jhì-hrau is placed at the end of the time expression, not at the beginning:

Nréi jáu-jó jhì-hrau, kréui wraa ngró thèng nréi mr̀ jhùng-yi srik hhaa.

After you'd gone she told me you don't like prawns.

In English, *after you'd gone* could come at the end of the sentence (*She told me you don't like prawns after you'd gone*), but with expressions which pinpoint the *time when* something happens Cantonese likes to have the information before the verb of the main statement is given, so you do not have the option of putting nréi jáu-jó jhì-hrau at the end. Other 'time when' expressions you have met so far, such as ghàm-yrat (*today*) and Lrái-baai-nǵr (*Friday*), as well as the many you haven't yet met (*at 6 o'clock*; *on May 12th last year*; *when I got there*; *before he had breakfast*; *in 1492 AD*), all obey the same rule:

Lrái-baai-lruk nréi heui mr̀ heui qaa?

Are you going on Saturday?

Ngró ghàm-yrat séung heui yràu-séui.

I'd like to go swimming today.

11 Can, able to

You met **shik** in Unit 4, and this unit introduces you to **hó-yrí**. Both mean *can, able to*. They are not usually interchangeable. **Shik** really means *to have learned how to* and implies that you are able to do something because you have acquired the skill to do it (speak a foreign language, ride a bicycle, eat with chopsticks, etc.). **Hó-yrí** operates in the realm of permission (*may*) and the absence of obstacles to doing something:

Nréi shik mr̀ shik jhàa-chhe qaa?	*Can you drive? (Do you know how to drive?)*
Nréi hó-yrí mr̀ hó-yrí jhàa-chhe qaa?	*Can you drive? (Have you a licence? Is the car available?)*

Another way to say *can, be able* is by using the verb ending **-dhak**. This is actually the same word that you met in Unit 5, grammar point 12, but in this use it must be added to the end of a verb, for example, **Ngró mr̀ heui-dhak** (*I can't go*):

Kréui jhàa-dhak chhe.	*He can drive.*

With **-dhak** there is no guidance as to whether he can drive because he knows how to, or because his father says he may, or because he is in possession of his full physical powers, or because there is a car available, so it is a good all-purpose way of saying *can*. Do remember, though, that **-dhak** can only be added to the end of a verb, not to any other part of speech.

12 'Time how long'

Time expressions which show *how long* something goes on for (as opposed to the *time when* something happens) come *after* the main verb in Cantonese:

daap gam nroi chhe	*travelling in a car for so long*
Ngró-drei hái Hhèung-góng jrue lréung go lrái-baai.	*We're staying in Hong Kong for two weeks.*
Kréui chró-jó ngf go jhung-tràu fhèi-ghèi.	*He was on the plane for five hours.*

13 Yet another verb ending: -gwo (to have had the experience)

Gwo literally means *to go past*, as you saw in the first part of this unit. As a verb ending, **-gwo** shows that the verb has been experienced at some time in the past:

Ngró srik-gwo hhaa.	*I have had prawns* (lit. *I have experienced eating prawns*).

The following pairs of sentences illustrate the difference between the two verb endings **-jó** and **-gwo**. The ending **-jó**, as we saw in Unit 4, grammar point 4, shows that an action has been completed at a particular point in time. The ending **-gwo** shows that an action has occurred at some time or other:

Kréui heui-jó Hhèung-góng.	*He went to Hong Kong.*
Kréui heui-gwo Hhèung góng.	*He has been to Hong Kong.*
Wròng Taai-táai ghàm-yrat tái-jó yhi-shang.	*Mrs Wong went to the doctor's today.*
Nréi tái-gwo yhi-shang maa?	*Have you ever been to the doctor's?*

 ——————— **Exercises** ———————

1 All of the following sentences (*a*)–(*e*) are already complete, but each of them will allow one of the phrases numbered (i)–(v) to be inserted and still make sense. For example, if you insert phrase (iii) into sentence (*a*) you create a new sentence which reads: **Gim-krìu Draai-hrok hrai sai-gaai jeui yráu-méng ge draai-hrok jhì-yhat.** (*Cambridge is one of the most famous universities in the world.*)

Now try the rest.

(*a*) **Gim-krìu Draai-hrok hrai draai-hrok jhì-yhat.**

(*b*) **Yràu Lrèun-dheun heui Gim-krìu Draai-hrok chhàam-gwhùn**

(i) **daap chhe**
(ii) **srap-ngŕ hrou**
(iii) **sai-gaai jeui yráu-méng ge**
(iv) **mŕ heui fhèi-ghèi-chrèung**

yiu heung bhak hràng.

(c) Yràu nhi-sue daap bhaa-sí heui fhèi-ghèi-chrèung yiu géi-dho chín qaa?

(d) Nhi-sue ge drei-hraa-tit-lrou jí heui srí-khèui.

(e) Nréi yiu daap bhaa-sí heui fhèi-ghèi-chrèung.

(v) gwo shàam go ghàai-háu dou draai mráa-lrou

2

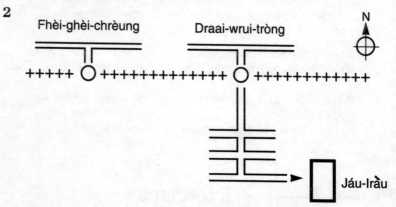

Fhèi-ghèi-chrèung   Draai-wrui-tròng   N

Jáu-lràu

Jhèung Shìn-shàang Jhèung Taai-táai chéng ngró srik-fraan. Mr̀-ghòi nréi wraa ngró thèng yràu fhèi-ghèi-chrèung dím-yéung heui jáu-lràu qaa?

(You should note that **mr̀-ghòi nréi** is used here to mean not *thank you* but *please*. It is very commonly used in this way, and is quite often used to attract someone's attention as well, rather as we might say *excuse me*, so it is a kind of all-purpose expression of politeness.)

7

第七課　溫習（一）

– WHÀN-JRAAP (YHAT) –

Revision (1)

This unit gives you no new vocabulary or grammar rules. Instead it goes back over a lot of the material from the first six units, presenting it in a new way so that you can become more fluent through extra practice. If you are stuck for any of the words, remember that there is a glossary at the end of the book to help you. Units 14, 21 and 26 will also be revision units, and just to make sure that you can check on your progress properly you will find a complete set of translations and answers at the end of the book.

───── Passage 1 ─────

Read this passage aloud.

 Jrok-yrat mràa-mhaa mran ngró-drei séung mr̀ séung srik shàa-léut? Ngró-drei go-go dhou wraa hóu séung srik. Mràa-mhaa wraa, 'Hóu hóu, ngró jrau jíng lrùng-hhaa shàa-léut béi nréi-drei srik lhaa. Nràa, yrì-ghaa ngró heui mráai lrùng-hhaa, nréi-drei heui mráai dhi shàn-shìn shàang-gwó fhàan-lrài lhaa.' Ngró-drei mráai-jó hóu dhò shàn-shìn shàang-gwó fhàan qhuk-kéi, yrau* yhat-chrài hái chrùe-fóng yrue-brei gó dhi shàang-gwó. Bun go jhung-tràu jhì-hrau mràa-mhaa fhàan-lrài laak. Kréui wraa, 'Ghàm-yrat dhi lrùng-hhaa yrau sai yrau mr̀ shàn-shìn, só-yrí ngró mróu mráai, jí-hrai mráai-jó

dhi draai hhaa jhe. Nréi-drei jrau srik draai hhaa shàa-léut
dong lrùng-hhaa shàa-léut lhaa!'

*See Unit 5: **yrau** (*furthermore*).

 ─────────── **Exercises** ───────────

1 Are the following statements true or false?

(a) Jrok-yrat mràa-mhaa wraa kréui hóu séung srik shàa-
léut.
(b) Mràa-mhaa jeui shik jíng lrùng-hhaa shàa-léut.
(c) Ngró-drei mráai-jó hóu dhò shàn-shìn shàang-gwó
fhàan qhuk-kéi.
(d) Mràa-mhaa mráai-jó yhat jek hóu draai ge lrùng-hhaa.
(e) Mràa-mhaa jíng ge lrùng-hhaa shàa-léut hóu hóu-mrei.

 2 Answer the following questions in Cantonese.

(a) Mràa-mhaa mráai-jó mhat-yré fhàan qhuk-kéi qaa?
(b) Ngró-drei mráai-jó mhat-yré fhàan qhuk-kéi qaa?
(c) Jrok-yrat dhi lrùng-hhaa shàn mr̀ shàn-shìn qaa?
(d) Nréi shik mr̀ shik jíng shàa-léut qaa?
(e) Hái nréi qhuk-kéi fru-gran ge jáu-lràu yráu mróu
shàa-léut mraai qaa?

3 Translate the following into Cantonese.

(a) *Have you ever tasted beef salad?*
(b) *This American pen is one of the pens I most want to buy.*
(c) *This is the first time I've been to your office.*

4 Eavesdropping – you can hear one end of a phone conversation:
see if you can guess what the other end might be.
X: ___
Y: Mr̀ gán-yiu. Nréi yrì-ghaa hái bhin-drou qaa?
X: ___
Y: Qhòu, hái qhuk-kéi. Mhat-yré sri qaa?
X: ___
Y: Hóu, hóu. Dhò-jre, dhò-jre. Hái bhin-sue srik qaa?

Easy isn't it? Now try this one.

X: ___
Y: Hóu, hóu. Nréi nhe?

X: ___
Y: Kréui dhou géi hóu. Yráu-shàm. Nréi taai-táai nhe?

X: ___
Y: Deui-mỉ-jrue, ngró ghàm-yrat mỉ fhàan sé-jri-lràu, mỉ hó-yrí trùng nréi fhàan. Shìng-krèi-sei, hóu mỉ hóu qaa?

X: ___
Y: Ngró mỉ séung jhàa-chhe heui, séung chró bhaa-sí heui.

X: ___
Y: Chró lruk hrou lhaa.

X: ___
Y: Hóu, Lrái-baai-sei joi-gin.

5 Fill in the blanks in the following sentences.

(a) Wròng Shàang hrai kréui bràa-bhaa, Wròng Táai hrai ____ ____-____.

(b) Ngró mróu bràa-bhaa, mràa-mhaa, hhìng-drai, jí-mrui, qhuk-kéi jí yráu ngró ____ go yràn jhe.

(c) Chró fhèi-ghèi gwai, draan-hrai chró bhaa-sí ____.

(d) Ngró-drei Lrái-baai-yrat ____ sái fhàan sé-jri-lràu.

(e) Hrò Shìn-shàang mróu chín, mỉ ____-____ daap dhik-sí.

6 Insert the appropriate phrases (i)–(v) in sentences (a)–(e) to create meaningful new sentences.

(a) Ngró-drei nhi go Shìng-krèi-lruk daap fhèi-ghèi heui Yhìng-gwok wáan.

(b) Wròng Taai-táai trùng Wròng Shìn-shàang lrài ngró ge sé-jri-lràu.

(c) Nréi ge júe-yi hrai jeui hóu ge.

(d) Nhi ghàan draai-hrok hrai yráu-méng ge draai-hrok.

(e) Lrèun-dheun hrai Yhìng-gwok jeui dhò yràn ge drei-fhòng.

(i) sai-gaai
(ii) shàam go yràn
(iii) jhì-yhat
(iv) yhat-dring
(v) yhat-chrài

———— **Passage 2** ————

Finally, here is another passage for you to read and understand. When you have understood it, read it aloud several times until it feels natural and easy on the tongue.

Ghàm-yrat ngró fhàan sé-jri-lràu. Hrò Shìn-shàang wraa ngró thèng Lrái-baai-lruk kréui yiu daap fhèi-ghèi fhàan-heui Yhìng-gwok, só-yrí hái Lrái-baai-shàam jhì-hrau jrau mr̀ fhàan sé-jri-lràu laak. Hrò Shìn-shàang hrai ngró jeui hóu ge pràng-yráu jhì-yhat, kréui nhi chi fhàan-heui Yhìng-gwok jhì-hrau, ngró gwú jrau mr̀ fhàan-lrài ge laak. Gám, ngró yiu sung mhat-yré béi kréui hóu nhe? Ngró séung-jó hóu nroi dhou mróu júe-yi, jrau heui mran Wròng Síu-jé trùng Jhèung Taai-táai. Wròng Síu-jé wraa, 'Ngró-drei shàam go yràn yhat-chrài chéng Hrò Shìn-shàang srik-fraan lhaa! Hóu maa?' Jhèung Taai-táai wraa, 'Yrùe-gwó Hrò Taai-táai hó yrí trùng Hrò Shìn-shàang yhat-chrài lrài, gám jrau jeui hóu laak.'

Ngró wraa síu-jé trùng taai-táai ge júe-yi yhat-dring hrai jeui hóu ge. Nréi wraa hrai mr̀ hrai qaa?

8

第八課　天氣
THÌN-HEI

Blowing hot and cold

The Cantonese-speaking world is almost everywhere subject to seasonal climatic change, in some places more so than in others. It doesn't ever snow in Hong Kong or Guangzhou, but it does in Canada and northern Europe, and it is surprising how cold it can feel in winter even in frost-free Hong Kong. This unit introduces some of the vocabulary you will need to cope with heat and cold.

━━━━━━━ Dialogue 1 ━━━━━━━

A husband and wife agree about the temperature, but not about much else.

而家天氣漸漸冷嘞。我好怕冷，我最中意晒太陽嘅。天文臺話今日會
　　落雨，呢個星期六重會落雪添。
我已經預備咗啲冷天衫啦。
我想聽日買個電暖爐返嚟，你話好唔好呀？
唔好。
噉，我要幾時買呀？
唔好買電暖爐啦！你買嘅嘢時時都唔實用嘅。
我唔同意，我買嘅嘢最實用嘅嘞。
你要知道買唔實用嘅嘢即係嘥錢。
你話我聽，我買咗乜嘢唔實用呀？
擠喺走廊牆角嗰個手提滅火筒，你舊年買嘅，一年之內都冇用過，你
　　話係唔係唔實用吖！

Mr Wong	Yrì-ghaa thìn-hei jrim-jím lráang laak. Ngró hóu paa lráang: ngró jeui jhùng-yi saai-taai-yrèung ge. Thìn-mràn-tròi wraa ghàm-yrat wrúi lrok-yrúe, nhi go Shìng-krèi-lruk jrung wrúi lrok-suet thìm.
Mrs Wong	Ngró yrí-ghìng yrue-brei-jó dhi lráang-thin shaam laa.
Mr Wong	Ngró séung thìng-yrat mráai go drin-nrúen-lròu fhàan-lrài, nréi wraa hóu mr̀ hóu qaa?
Mrs Wong	Mr̀ hóu.
Mr Wong	Gám, ngró yiu géi-sí mráai qaa?
Mrs Wong	Mr̀-hóu mráai drin-nrúen-lròu laa! Nréi mráai ge yré srì-srì dhou mr̀ srat-yrung ge.
Mr Wong	Ngró mr̀ trùng-yi. Ngró mráai ge yré jeui srat-yrung ge laak.
Mrs Wong	Nréi yiu jhì-dou mráai mr̀ srat-yrung ge yré jhik-hrai shàai-chín.
Mr Wong	Nréi wraa ngró thèng, ngró mráai-jó mhat-yré mr̀ srat-yrung qaa?
Mrs Wong	Jhài hái jáu-lóng chrèung-gok gó go sáu-trài mrit-fó-túng, nréi grau-nín mráai ge, yhat nrìn jhì-nroi dhou mróu yrung-gwo. Nréi wraa hrai mr̀ hrai mr̀ srat-yrung qhaa!

天氣	**thìn-hei**	*weather*
漸漸	**jrim-jím**	*gradually*
冷	**lráang**	*cold*
晒太陽	**saai-taai-yrèung**	*to sunbathe*
怕	**paa**	*to fear; to dislike*
天文臺	**thìn-mràn-tròi**	*observatory*
落雨	**lrok-yrúe**	*to rain* (lit. *to fall down rain*)
重	**jrung**	*in addition, furthermore*
會	**wrúi**	*it is likely that* (future possibility)
落雪	**lrok-suet**	*to snow*
添	**thìm**	*as well, also, what's more* (final particle)
已經	**yrí-ghìng**	*already*
冷天	**lráang-thin**	*cold weather, winter*
衫	**shaam**	*clothing*
聽日	**thìng-yrat**	*tomorrow*
電暖爐	**drin-nrúen-lròu**	*electric heater*
幾時?	**géi-sí?** or **géi-srì?**	*when?*
嘢	**yré**	*thing, object*
時時（都）	**srì-srì (dhou)**	*always, frequently*
實用	**srat-yrung**	*practical*
同意	**trùng-yi**	*to agree*

知道、知	**jhì-dou** or **jhì**	*to know a fact, to understand*
嘥	**shàai**	*to waste*
擠	**jhài**	*to put, to place*
走廊	**jáu-lóng**	*passage, corridor*
牆角	**chrèung-gok**	*corner (of house, room, etc.)*
手提	**sáu-trài**	*hand-held, portable*
滅火筒	**mrit-fó-túng**	*fire extinguisher*
舊年	**grau-nín**	*last year*
年	**nrìn**	*year*
丫?	**qhaa?**	*(particle) (triumphantly scoring a point: didn't I tell you so!)*

Have you understood? Read the dialogue again and then select the correct phrases from those in brackets in the following sentences. You will no doubt feel insulted if we tell you that the answer to the first one is **drin-nrúen-lròu** . . . so we won't!

(*a*) **Wròng Shìn-shàang dáa-suen mráai (drin-nrúen-lròu/ mrit-fó-túng).**

(*b*) **Wròng Taai-táai wraa Wròng Shìn-shàang mráai ge yré srì-srì dhou (yráu-yrung/mróu-yrung/mr̀ srat-yrung).**

(*c*) **Gó go sáu-trài mrit-fó-túng jhài hái (jáu lràu/sé-jri-lràu/chrèung-gok).**

(*d*) **Gó go sáu-trài mrit-fó-túng (yrung-gwo yhat chi/mróu yrung-gwo/srì-srì yrung).**

 —————— **Grammar** ——————

1 What's more

Jrung means *furthermore, in addition* (you met the same word in Unit 3 where it meant *still, yet*). It is an adverb and therefore, as you now know, it comes before the verb in the sentence. The final particle **thìm** is usually added at the end of the sentence to give additional force to **jrung**:

Ngró jrung yráu lréung go thìm.   *I've got two more as well.*

> Kréui jrung séung heui
> Mréi-gwok yhat chi thìm.

What's more she wants to go to the States once as well.

2 When?

Géi-sí? (*when?*) is the question word which asks for a 'time when' answer. Not surprisingly then, you will find géi-sí? in the same place in the sentence where the 'time when' answer comes. If you have forgotten the rule, refresh your memory by re-reading Unit 6, grammar point 10.

> Nréi géi-sí heui qaa?
> Ngró Lrái-baai-yrat heui.

When are you going?
I'm going on Sunday.

3 *More on* dhou

You by now are well aware that **dhou** is an adverb which means *all, both, also*, and that it is placed like other adverbs immediately in front of the verb. Sometimes it is used where there seems no need for it in English: for instance, in the dialogue Mrs Wong says **Nréi mráai ge yré srì-srì dhou mr̀ srat-yrung ge** (*The things you buy are always impractical*). What **dhou** is doing is backing up the word **srì-srì** (*always*), and it does so because **srì-srì** feels like a plural idea in Cantonese – it literally means *time-time*. You first met this in Unit 5, grammar point 10, where **dhou** was used to back up doubled classifiers. So whenever there are plural ideas (*the cows all . . . ; Mr and Mrs Wong . . . ; electric heaters . . .*) or ideas of wholeness (*the entire population . . . ; the whole busload . . .*), you can expect **dhou** to be thrown in for good measure.

4 *More about* most

In Unit 6 you met **jeui** (*most*), and you will have had no difficulty in using it to make superlatives (*biggest, coldest, best*, etc.) Quite often you will find that the final particle **laak** is tacked on at the end of the sentence to back up **jeui**, just as **thìm** backs up **jrung**:

> jeui draai laak
> jeui hóu-srik laak

biggest
most delicious

jeui hóu laak	*best*
Rolls-Royce hrai Yhìng-	*The Rolls-Royce is Britain's most*
gwok jeui gwai ge	*expensive car.*
chhe laak.	

5 Tone changes

Up to now you have met no exceptions to the rule that a word is always pronounced in the same tone. Alas, Cantonese is not in fact quite so straightforward, and from time to time you will come across the odd word which does not obey this rule. In the last speech of the dialogue you will notice that the word for *year* appears in two different tones. The usual tone is **nrìn** (low falling), but in *last year* (**grau-nín**) it becomes mid rising. There is no obvious reason why this tone change should occur, but take heart, it only happens in the following common words:

grau-nín	*last year*
ghàm-nín	*this year*
chheut-nín	*next year*

In all other cases, *year* is pronounced in the low falling tone **nrìn**.

6 Years and days

While we are talking about **nrìn** you might note that it is one of a very small number of nouns which do not need a classifier. You have learned that nouns must have a classifier when they are counted or specified with words like *this, that* and *which?* (see Unit 2, grammar points 4 and 6), so you know that *two pens* must be **lréung jhì bhat** and *three Americans* must be **shàam go Mréi-gwok-yràn**. **Nrìn** (*year*) and **yrat** (*day*), however, along with one or two other nouns that you have not met, do not have a classifier; they seem to combine the role of classifier and noun at the same time. So *one day* is **yhat yrat** and *two years* is **lréung nrìn**. This is a convenient place to set out in a clear form the words for years and days that you have met so far:

ghàm-yrat	*today*	**ghàm-nín**	*this year*
jrok-yrat	*yesterday*	**grau-nín**	*last year*
thìng-yrat	*tomorrow*	**chheut-nín**	*next year*

Dialogue 2

Mr Chan and Mr Cheung demonstrate how buying an air conditioner can lead to a conflict of stinginess.

張先生，你好。去邊處呀？

我去買冷氣機。

係呀！天氣漸漸熱，買冷氣機係時候啦。

陳先生，你有乜嘢打算呢？

我冇錢買冷氣機。天氣太熱嘅時候，我會去海灘游水，飲啤酒，食雪
糕，咁就唔熱喇。

但係如果打風就唔可以去海灘，落雨就唔可以去買雪糕……咁，就點
呀？冷氣機唔算好貴，但係好有用：你都唔買，真係慳嘞！

我唔算慳啦！我話你太太重慳喇！

佢點樣慳法呀？

呢個禮拜二我喺百貨公司買游水褲嘅時候，見到你太太，佢好開心咁話
我知，佢只係用咗一條你嘅舊領呔就可以改成一套"比堅尼"嘞。
你話佢慳唔慳呢？

Chan	Jhèung Shìn-shàang, nréi hóu. Heui bhin-sue qaa?
Cheung	Ngró heui mráai lráang-hei-ghèi.
Chan	Hrai qaa! Thìn-hei jrim-jím yrit, mráai lráang-hei-ghèi hrai srì-hrau laa.
Cheung	Chràn Shìn-shàang, nréi yráu mhat-yré dáa-suen nhe?
Chan	Ngró mróu chín mráai lráang-hei-ghèi. Thìn-hei taai yrit ge srì-hrau, ngró wrúi heui hói-thaan yràu-séui, yám bhe-jáu, srik suet-ghou, gám jrau mr̀ yrit lhaa.
Cheung	Draan-hrai yrùe-gwó dáa-fhùng jrau mr̀ hó-yrí heui hói-thaan, lrok-yrúe jrau mr̀ hó-yrí heui mráai suet-ghou … gám, jrau dím qaa? Lráang-hei-ghèi mr̀ suen hóu gwai, draan-hrai hóu yráu-yrung: nréi dhou mr̀ mráai, jhàn-hrai hhàan laak!
Chan	Ngró mr̀ suen hhàan laa! Ngró wraa nréi taai-táai jrung hhàan lhaa!
Cheung	Kréui dím-yéung hhàan-faat qaa?
Chan	Nhi go Lrái-baai-yri ngró hái baak-fo-ghung-shi mráai yràu-séui-fu ge srì-hrau, gin-dóu nréi taai-táai, kréui hóu hhòi-sham gám wraa ngró jhì kréui jí-hrai yrung-jó yhat trìu nréi ge grau lréng-thàai jrau hó-yrí gói-srèng yhat tou béi-ghìn-nrèi laak. Nréi wraa kréui hhàan mr̀ hhàan nhe?

冷氣機	**lráang-hei-ghèi**	air conditioner (lit. *cold air machine*)
熱	**yrit**	hot
時候	**srì-hrau**	time
打算	**dáa-suen**	to intend; intention
海灘	**hói-thaan**	beach
飲	**yám**	to drink
啤酒	**bhe-jáu**	beer
酒	**jáu**	any alcoholic drink
雪糕	**suet-ghou**	ice-cream
打風	**dáa-fhùng**	to have a typhoon
風	**fhùng**	wind
算	**suen**	to be regarded as, to be reckoned
有用	**yráu-yrung**	useful
慳	**hhàan**	to save; to be parsimonious, stingy
重	**jrung**	even more
點樣……法?	**dím-yéung . . . -faat?**	in what way . . . ?
百貨公司	**baak-fo-ghung-shi**	department store
公司	**ghung-shi**	a company
游水褲	**yràu-séui-fu**	swimming trunks
見	**gin**	to see, to meet
到	**-dóu**	to succeed in (verb ending)
開心	**hhòi-sham**	happy
話……知 = 話……聽	**wraa . . . jhì** or **wraa . . . thèng**	to tell
條	**trìu**	(classifier for long, thin flexible things)
舊	**grau**	old, used
領呔	**lréng-thàai**	neck-tie
改	**gói**	to alter, to change (usually for the better)
成	**-srèng**	. . . to become, . . . into (verb ending)
套	**tou**	(classifier: *a set of, a suit of*)
比堅尼	**béi-ghìn-nrèi**	bikini

Look at the picture. Answer these questions if you can!

(*a*) **Nréi wraa Jhèung Táai yrung nhi trìu lréng-thàai gói-srèng béi-ghìn-nrèi dhak m̀ dhak qaa?**

(*b*) **Yhat tou béi-ghìn-nrèi hrai géi-dho grin qaa?**

 ———————— **Grammar** ————————

7 In what way?

You first met **dím-yéung** (*in what way? how?*) in Unit 5. In the above dialogue it appears with the verb ending **-faat** (*way of...*). You do not have to use this new form, but it makes for quite good, racy-sounding Cantonese to do so. Here are two example sentences, each using both forms:

(*a*) **Kréui dím-yéung heui fhèi-ghèi-chrèung qaa?**
    Fhèi-ghèi-chrèung kréui dím-yéung heui-faat qaa?

(*b*) **Kréui dím-yéung hhàan chín qaa?**
    Chín kréui dím-yéung hhàan-faat qaa?

Sentence (*a*) means *how is he going to the airport?* and sentence (*b*) means *how does she save money?* When the **-faat** form is used, note how in each case the object of the verb moves to the front of the sentence, and **-faat** is tacked onto the end of the verb. There is a useful principle to be learned: Cantonese verbs are sensitive creatures (remember how some of them feel lonely?) and they don't feel happy with too many ideas attached to them. Verb endings *must* be added directly onto the verb, and so if there is an object as well and it makes the verb feel overburdened, it often feels more comfortable to shift that object to the front of the sentence.

8 Srì-hrau (time)

Hrai srì-hrau is a colloquial way to say *it is the right time to . . . .*
Here are two ways of using it, both of which mean *it's time to go to
the office now*:

> Yrì-ghaa hrai srì-hrau fhàan sé-jri-lràu laa.
> Yrì-ghaa fhàan sé-jri-lràu hrai srì-hrau laa.

Perhaps more common is the expression **. . . ge srì-hrau**, which
means *when . . .* or *while. . . .* Study these two sentences carefully:

Ngró júe-sung ge srì-hrau mȑ séung mràa-mhaa bhòng ngró sáu.	*I don't want mummy to help me while I'm cooking.*
Kréui hái Yhìng-gwok ge srì-hrau srì-srì dhou lrài taam ngró.	*She often comes to see me when she's in Britain.*

Now look back to Unit 4, grammar point 6 and see how **. . . ge srì-
hrau** is really just like other **ge** phrases:

hóu gwai ge gaa-fhe	*coffee which is very expensive*
mráai-gán bhat ge yràn	*the person who is buying a pen*
kréui hái Yhìng-gwok ge srì-hrau	*the time when she is in Britain*

9 Making adverbs from adjectives

If you bracket an adjective with **hóu . . . gám** you turn it into an
adverb:

hhòi-sham	*happy*	→	hóu hhòi-sham gám	*happily*
haak-hei	*polite*	→	hóu haak-hei gám	*politely*
Kréui hóu nhàu.			*He's very angry.*	
Kréui hóu nhàu gám wraa ngró jhì.			*He told me angrily.*	

10 -dóu (to succeed in)

It is not easy to put a specific meaning on the verb ending **-dóu**.
Sometimes you might want to translate it as *to succeed in*, sometimes as *successfully*, sometimes as *actually* and quite often it seems

to add nothing much at all to the meaning of the verb to which it is attached. Here are four examples of it with different verbs:

Ngró tái-dóu Wròng Síu-jé hái gó-sue.	*I caught sight of Miss Wong there.*
Ngró gwú-dóu nréi hái chrùe-fóng.	*I guessed right that you were in the kitchen.*
Kréui daap-dóu bhaa-sí.	*He actually caught the bus.*
Ngró gin-dóu nréi taai-táai.	*I met your wife.*

11 -srèng (to become)

As a verb ending -srèng means *to become* or *to make into*. You will find an example in the dialogue where Mrs Cheung claims to make a tie into a bikini. Here is another one:

Ngró yrung ngràu-yruk júe-srèng yhat go thòng.	*I'm making the beef into a soup.*

 ──────── **Exercises** ────────

1 Match the correct part (b) with its part (a) to make meaningful sentences.

(a) Thìn-hei jrim-jím yrit...
Lráang-hei-ghèi mr̀ suen hóu gwai...
Yrùe-gwó mráai mr̀ srat-yrung ge yré...
Ngró yrí-ghìng yrue-brei-jó...

(a) ...jhik-hrai shàai chín.
...mráai lráang-hei-ghèi hrai srì-hrau laa.
...ngró-drei dhi lráang-thin shaam laa.
...draan-hrai hóu yráu-yrung.

2 How can you turn these two sentences into one?
(i) Gó-sue yráu chhe.   (ii) Chhe hóu gwai.
Answer: **Gó-sue yráu hóu gwai ge chhe.** Easy, isn't it? Now try to do the same with the following sentences.

(a) (i) Jhèung Síu-jé hrai Yrat-bún-yràn.
    (ii) Kréui hóu leng.

(b) (i) **Ngró mř séung mráai bhat.**
    (ii) **Chràn Shìn-shàang ge pou-táu mraai Mréi-gwok bhat.**
(c) (i) **Ngró hóu séung srik lrùng-hhaa.**
    (ii) **Hrò Táai jíng lrùng-hhaa.**

3   Select the correct words and phrases (i)–(ix) to complete sentences (a)–(d). (You will have to reject five of them as unsuitable or less suitable.)

(a)   ____ **mrit-fó-túng hóu yráu-yrung.**
(b)   **Hái nhi-sue yám séui hrai ____ ge: nréi mř sái béi chín.**
(c)   ____ **béi-ghìn-nrèi mř prèng.**
(d)   **Yruè gwó dhi ngràu-yruk mř ____, ngró jrau mř séung srik.**

(i) **shàn-shìn**	(ii) **Mréi-gwok ge**	(iii) **Yhìng-gwok ge**
(iv) **sáu-trài**	(v) **mrín-fai**	(vi) **yhat tou leng ge**
(vii) **gaai-sriu**	(viii) **hrùng-shik**	(ix) **yrùe-góng**

4   **A creative test.**

Can you supply the cartoon caption in Cantonese? Mr Wong is saying: *Don't be angry. I told you the fire extinguisher was a practical object!*

9

第九課 娛樂同運動
YRUE-LROK TRÙNG WRAN-DRUNG
Fun and games

This unit lives up to its title: there is little in the way of heavy new grammar, and the new vocabulary lists are not too intimidating. You deserve it. Enjoy!

──────────── Dialogue 1 ────────────

Mr Chan finds out how his colleague Miss Cheung spends her time off.

張小姐，昨日同前日都放假。你有冇去打波呀？
我唔中意打波嘅。
有冇去其他地方玩呢？
我都唔中意離開香港嘅，我只係中意睇電影啫。
我知道昨日喺大會堂有一齣好有名嘅電影。你有冇去睇呀？
有呀！真係好好睇呀。而且重好刺激添。
刺激！我唔覺得噃。你記唔記得嗰齣電影嘅內容呀？
對唔住，我一啲都唔記得嘞，因為我同男朋友一齊去睇嘅。

Mr Chan	Jhèung Síu-jé jrok-yrat trùng chrìn-yrat dhou fong-gaa. Nréi yráu mróu heui dáa-bho qaa?
Miss Cheung	Ngró mr̀ jhùng-yi dáa-bho ge.
Mr Chan	Yráu mróu heui krèi-thàa drei-fhòng wáan nhe?

─── 78 ───

Miss Cheung	Ngró dhou m̀ jhùng-yi lrèi-hhòi Hhèung-góng ge, ngró jí-hrai jhùng-yi tái-drin-yíng jhe.
Mr Chan	Ngró jhì-dou jrok-yrat hái Draai-wrui-tròng yráu yhat chheut hóu yráu-méng ge drin-yíng. Nréi yráu mróu heui tái qaa?
Miss Cheung	Yráu qaa! Jhàn-hrai hóu hóu-tái qaa. Yrì-ché jrung hóu chi-ghik thim.
Mr Chan	Chi-ghik! Ngró m̀ gok-dhak bo. Nréi gei m̀ gei-dhak gó chheut drin-yíng ge nroi-yrùng qaa?
Miss Cheung	Deui-m̀-jrue, ngró yhat-dhi dhou m̀ gei-dhak laak, yhàn-wrai ngró trùng nràam-pràng-yráu yhat-chrài heui tái ge.

前日	**chrìn-yrat**	the day before yesterday
放假	**fong-gaa**	to be on holiday, take days off
打波	**dáa-bho**	to play a ball game
離開	**lrèi-hhòi**	to leave, depart from
電影	**drin-yíng**	cinema film, movie
齣	**chheut**	(classifier for *films* and *stage plays*)
而且	**yrì-ché**	moreover
刺激	**chi-ghik**	exciting
覺得	**gok-dhak**	to feel
記得	**gei-dhak**	to remember
內容	**nroi-yrùng**	contents
一啲	**yhat-dhi**	a little bit
男	**nràam**	male

Give the cartoon a caption. Supply the caption for the market researcher's question. He is asking: *Did you feel that this was an exciting film?*

───── **Grammar** ─────

1 Plurality with dhou again

In Unit 8, grammar point 3 you learned about the use of **dhou** to back up plurals. Did you spot the new example in the first speech of the dialogue?

2 Fong-gaa (to have a holiday)

Fong-gaa literally means *to release a day off*. It is one of quite a large group of expressions which are made up of a verb and an object, and these expressions can all be split up if the sense of the sentence allows it. Here are a couple of examples:

Ngró nhi go shìng-krèi   *I have three days holiday this*
fong **shàam yrat** *gaa.*   *week.*
Kréui *jrou* **jáu-lràu ge**   *He is in the restaurant business*
shàang-yi.

3 Playing ball

The word **bho** originally came from the English word *ball*. **Dáa** means *to hit*, and **dáa-bho** is the regular way to say *to play a ball game*.

The problem is: which ball game? For a majority of people it means *soccer*, but if you happen to be a snooker fan then it means *snooker*, or for a basketball fan it means *basketball*. And then of course there is table-tennis, rugby, etc. For the moment **dáa-bho** is all you need, but you might note the very logical difference between the following:

Ngró heui dáa-bho.   *I'm going off to play ball.*
Ngró heui tái dáa-bho.   *I'm going off to watch the game.*

4 Going to the movies

Tái-drin-yíng means *to see a film* and **heui tái-drin-yíng** is *to go to the movies*. You will notice that **tái-drin-yíng** is also a verb plus object expression, so another example for grammar point 2 might be:

Wròng Táai séung heui   *Mrs Wong wants to go to see*
tái **Mréi-gwok** *drin-yíng.*   *an American film.*

There is another expression, **tái-hei**, which means *to see a play*, but
far more people go to the cinema than go to the live theatre, and it
is now very common to hear someone say **ngró heui tái-hei** when
they mean *I'm going to the pictures.*

5 Overkill

You may or may not have realised that in Miss Cheung's third
speech in the dialogue, she uses three different ways of saying
moreover (**yrì-ché/jrung/thìm**). This may feel like overkill in English, but it is perfectly acceptable, indeed common, in Cantonese.

6 Taking short cuts again

In Unit 3, grammar point 2 you met the sentence **Nréi fhàan mr̀**
fhàan-heui qaa? and it was explained that this was a common
shortened form of **Nréi fhàan-heui mr̀ fhàan-heui qaa?** You can
do the same thing with any two-syllable verb. In the dialogue you
will have noticed **nréi gei mr̀ gei-dhak** where Mr Chan might
equally well have said **nréi gei-dhak mr̀ gei-dhak.** Here is another example:

Nréi jhùng mr̀ jhùng-yi Lrèun-   *Do you like London?*
dheun qaa?

7 Not even a little bit!

Yhat-dhi means *a little bit*, and combined with **dhou** and the nega-
tives **mr̀** or **mróu** it means *not even a little bit.* In a later unit you
will find that this fits in with a regular grammatical pattern, but for
the time being you should just accept it as an idiomatic expression.
Along the same lines you can also say **Ngró-drei yhat-dhi chín**
dhou mróu. If you are like us you probably need to say it quite
often!

It's electric!

In this unit you have met the word **drin-yíng** for *movie film*. It literally means *electric shadows* and was an ingenious way of coping with a new concept when it first burst upon the Chinese world. The word **drin** (*electric*) was itself originally borrowed from the word meaning *lightning*, and it has been put to very good use ever since. You met *electric heater* (**drin-nrúen-lròu**) in Unit 8. Nowadays everyone is familiar with **drin-chhè** (*electric vehicle*) for *tram*, **drin-wáa** (*electric speech*) for *telephone*, **drin-sri** (*electric vision*) for *television*, **drin-nróu** (*electric brain*) for *computer*, and many more.

 ———————— **Dialogue 2** ————————

 Mr Wong and Mr Cheung discuss keeping fit, but Mr Wong is not sure that the theories apply to his wife!

張先生，你話時時運動可以減少身體裡便多餘嘅脂肪，對健康好好，
　係唔係呀？
係呀！我時時都行路，爬山，同打波。你睇我已經五十幾歲嘞，重係
　好健康，好似四十歲咁上下。
但係我覺得運動對我太太一啲用都冇。
一定有用嘅。只要你太太時時運動，身體裡便一定冇多餘脂肪嘅。
我太太成日講嘢，口部嘅肌肉有好多運動喇。點解佢重有一個好多脂
　肪嘅雙下巴呢？

Mr Wong	Jhèung Shìn-shàang, nréi wraa srì-srì wran-drung hó-yrí gáam-síu shàn-tái lréui-brin dhò-yrùe ge jhì-fhong, deui grin-hhòng hóu hóu, hrai mr̀ hrai qaa?
Mr Cheung	Hrai qaa! Ngró srì-srì dhou hràang-lrou, pràa-shàan, trùng dáa-bho. Nréi tái ngró yrí-ghìng ngr̀-srap-géi seui laak, jrung hrai hóu grin-hhòng, hóu-chrí sei-srap seui gam-sreung-háa.
Mr Wong	Draan-hrai ngró gok-dhak wran-drung deui ngró taai-táai yhat-dhi yrung dhou mróu.
Mr Cheung	Yhat-dring yráu yrung ge. Jí-yiu nréi taai-táai srì-srì wran-drung, shàn-tái lréui-brin yhat-dring mróu dhò-yrùe jhì-fhong ge.

Mr Wong   Ngró taai-táai srèng-yrat góng-yré, háu-brou ge
                ghèi-yruk yráu hóu dhò wran-drung lhaa. Dím-gáai
                kréui jrung yráu yhat go hóu dhò jhì-fhong ge
                sheung hraa-pràa nhe?

運動	**wran-drung**	*physical exercise; to exercise*
減少	**gáam-síu**	*to reduce, cut down*
身體	**shàn-tái**	*the body*
裡便	**lréui-brin**	*inside*
多餘	**dhò-yrùe**	*surplus*
脂肪	**jhì-fhong**	*(body) fat*
對	**deui**	*with regard to, towards*
健康	**grin-hhòng**	*health*
行路	**hràang-lrou**	*to walk*
爬山	**pràa-shàan**	*to climb mountains, walk the hills*
山	**shàan**	*mountain, hill*
幾	**géi**	*several*
歲	**seui**	*year of age*
咁上下	**gam-sreung-háa**	*approximately, thereabouts*
只要	**jí-yiu**	*so long as, provided that*
成日	**srèng-yrat**	*the whole day*
講	**góng**	*to speak, talk, say*
口部	**háu-brou**	*mouth*
肌肉	**ghèi-yruk**	*muscle*
雙	**sheung**	*double*
下巴	**hraa-pràa**	*chin*

────── Grammar ──────

8 Géi (several)

You met **géi** in the expression **géi-dho?** (*how many?*) in Unit 5 and
géi-sí? (*when?*) in Unit 8. On its own **géi** can also mean *how many?*
However, it also has the meaning *several*, and that is potentially
quite confusing. Supposing someone were to say to you **géi go
yràn,** you couldn't be sure whether they were saying *how many
people?* or *several people*. Obviously the context in which they said
it would help a lot, but in practice if it were a question most people
would add **qaa?** on the end, and that would of course make it clear.

In its *several* meaning, **géi** gets involved with numbers quite a lot;
you can see one example in Mr Cheung's first speech in the dialogue. Here are a few other examples:

yrì-srap-géi go yràn	*more than twenty people* (i.e. *more than twenty but fewer than thirty*)
srap-géi seui ge Jhùng-gwok-yràn	*a Chinese in his teens*
géi-srap go yràn	*dozens of people* (lit. *several tens of people*)
géi-srap nrìn	*several decades*

9 Seui (years of age)

There are two points to be noted about **seui**. First, it is one of those few words which (like **yrat** and **nrìn**) do not need a classifier. Second, it is often used without a verb. Look again at the dialogue where Mr Cheung says **ngró yrí-ghìng ngí-srap-géi seui laak**. There is no verb in this expression, yet it is perfectly acceptable Cantonese. If you want to or feel the need to put in a verb, the most commonly used one is **hrai** (*to be*). Mr Cheung could have said **ngró yrí-ghìng hrai ngí-srap-géi seui laak**, and it would have meant the same thing.

10 Approximately

Gam-sreung-háa literally means *thus up and down* and from that comes to mean *approximately*. It usually follows whatever it refers to, as it does in the dialogue: **sei-srap seui gam-sreung-háa** (*about forty years old*).

11 Srèng (the whole)

Srèng- combines with classifiers to make *the whole* . . . . So **srèng-go lrái-baai** is *the whole week*, **srèng-yrat** is *the whole day* or *all day long*, and **srèng-nrìn** is *the whole year long*. (Remember that **yrat** and **nrìn** are nouns which act like classifiers – see Unit 8, grammar point 6).

12 Another 'lonely verb'

In Mr Wong's last speech, he says **Ngró taai-táai srèng-yrat góng-yré**. **Yré** means *things*, as you learned in Unit 8, but here it is merely providing the object for the verb **góng** which is one of those which gets lonely on its own. **Yré** is quite handy for this purpose. Here are a few more examples of its use with 'lonely verbs':

Nréi séung mǐ séung srik-yré?	*Do you want to eat?*
Ngró taai-táai heui-jó mráai-yré.	*My wife's gone shopping.*
Kréui srèng-yrat dhou yám-yré.	*He drinks all day long.*

A problem of age

When someone gives his or her age he or she will give it in **seui**, not in **nrìn** – it would be wrong to use **nrìn** in this way. That in itself is easy enough. What is sometimes a problem is sorting out what **seui** means, because traditionally Chinese people were born one **seui** old and then added another **seui** to their age at each lunar new year. So a Chinese born on the last day of the lunar year would already be **Iréung seui** old the next day, while a Western baby born on the same day would not even have reached 'one'! Worse still, if the Chinese baby were born just before the beginning of a short lunar year (the lunar years vary in length and can be much longer or much shorter than the Western solar year), he or she has time to become **shàam seui** before the poor little Western baby has even opened his score! If it is important to be certain of someone's correct age, you can always ask whether the Chinese or the Westerner (**Shài-yràn**) **seui** is meant (see also Unit 22, page 211.)

 ——————— **Exercises** ———————

1 Here are some jumbled phrases for you to rearrange to make meaningful sentences.

    (a) **gam-sreung-háa/Hrò Shìn-shàang/ngǐ-srap seui/hóu-chrí**

    (b) **hóu hóu/srì-srì/deui/wran-drung/grin-hhòng**

(c)   ngró/dáa-bho/jhùng-yi/jhe/pràa-shàan/jí-hrai/trùng
      yràu-séui

2   There is a relationship between each of the words in list (a) and
    one of the words in list (b). Make the connections.

(a)	sung	(b)	yràu-séui
	fó-gei		shàn-shìn
	draai-gáam-gaa		jáu-lràu
	lraan		lraap-saap-túng
	hói-thaan		drin-nrúen-lròu
	lrok-suet		baak-fo-ghung-shi

3   You've made it to the big time: you are a professional inter-
    preter. The fate of nations hangs in the balance, so make sure
    you translate the following remarks by the British Foreign Sec-
    retary accurately or there may be a diplomatic incident with the
    state of Cantonia!

FS   *Good morning, Mr Wong.*
You   ____
Wong   Jóu-sràn.
FS   *Would you like to have a beer?*
You   ____
Wong   Ngró mr̀ jhùng-yi yám bhe-jáu.
FS   *Oh, well how about coffee? Or tea?*
You   ____
Wong   Gaa-fhe trùng chràa dhou deui shàn-tái mr̀ hóu.
        Ngró jí-hrai yám séui jhe.
FS   *I'm sorry, we have no water. The waiter told me that the
        water here is not good to drink. Why don't you have some
        beer?*
You   ____
Wong   Nréi srèng-yrat wraa ngró yiu yám bhe-jáu. Ngró
        yrí-ghìng wraa nréi jhì ngró mr̀ jhùng-yi yám. Nréi
        jhàn-hrai hóu mr̀ haak-hei.
FS   *The beer is very good, it's British beer. Please drink a little.*
You   ____
Wong   Nhi go yràn jeui mr̀ haak-hei laak! Ngró jáu laak!
FS   *Oh, he's gone!*
You   ____

Oh dear, it doesn't look as though that went too well, and you
wasted your breath translating the last remark, didn't you? Still
it wasn't your fault, was it? Or was it?

4 Pair off the most likely objects in list (*b*) with their verbs in list (*a*). Some of those in (*b*) won't be suitable, but sometimes there may be more than one possible pairing.

(*a*)	(*b*)
tái	yré
júe	drin-yíng
góng	trìm-bán
chhàam-gwhùn	chrùe-fóng
srik	yhi-shang
	chi-fo
	chrèung-gok
	Gim-krìu Draai-hrok

5

Answer these questions in Cantonese so that all the answers have one word in common.

(*a*) Wròng Shàang jrou mhat-yré qaa?
(*b*) Wròng Táai jrou mhi-yré qaa?
(*c*) Wròng Síu-jé jrou mhi-yré qaa?
(*d*) Jhèung Shìn-shàang jrou mhi-yré qaa?
(*e*) Nhi shàam go yràn jrou mhat-yré qaa?

10

第十課 健康
──── GRIN-HHÒNG ────
Health care for beginners

Don't be fooled by the lighthearted approach of this unit: the vocabulary is serious enough and you may need to consult a doctor at some point. We hope it will be a better one than Mr Wong's!

──────── Dialogue 1 ────────

Mr Wong phones his family doctor to make an appointment. The nurse answers the phone.

喂！呢處係唔係張醫生嘅診所呀？
係呀！
我想睇醫生，唔該你幫我掛號喇。
你貴姓呀？有乜嘢唔舒服呀？
我係王一港先生，我覺得有啲頭痛，間中有啲頭暈，重有啲作嘔添。
你嘅病唔算好嚴重。我話你知，張醫生好忙……
噉，我幾時可以睇醫生呀？
我估你要等三四日先至可以見到張醫生嘫！
乜嘢話？三四日之後！我估嗰陣時我已經死咗啦！
唔緊要，嗰陣時請你太太打電話嚟話我知取消掛號就得喇！
唔得，唔得！我唔想等嘞，我而家就要去醫院嘞！

Mr Wong	Wái! Nhi-sue hrai m̀r hrai Jhèung Yhi-shang ge chán-só qaa?
Nurse	Hrai qaa!

── 88 ──

Mr Wong Ngró séung tái-yhi-shang, mr̀-ghòi nréi bhòng ngró gwaa-hrou lhaa.

Nurse Nréi gwai-sing qaa? Yráu mhat-yré mr̀ shùe-fruk qaa?

Mr Wong Ngró hrai Wròng Yhat Góng Shìn-shàang, ngró gok-dhak yráu-dhi tràu-tung, gaan-jhung yráu-dhi tràu-wràn, jrung yráu-dhi jok-qáu thìm.

Nurse Nréi ge breng mr̀ suen hóu yrìm-jrung. Ngró wraa nréi jhì, Jhèung Yhi-shang hóu mròng . . .

Mr Wong Gám, ngró géi-sí hó-yrí tái-yhi-shang qaa?

Nurse Ngró gwú nréi yiu dáng shàam-sei yrat shìn-ji hó-yrí gin-dóu Jhèung Yhi-shang bo!

Mr Wong Mhat-yré wáa? Shàam-sei yrat jhì-hrau? Ngró gwú gó-jran-srì ngró yrí-ghìng séi-jó laa!

Nurse Mr̀ gán-yiu. Gó-jran-srì chéng nréi taai-táai dáa-drin-wáa lrài, wraa ngró jhì chéui-shìu gwaa-hrou jrau dhak lhaa!

Mr Wong Mr̀ dhak, mr̀ dhak! Ngró mr̀ séung dáng laak, ngró yrì-ghaa jrau yiu heui yhì-yúen laak!

喂！	**wái!**	hello! (especially on the phone)
診所	**chán-só**	clinic
幫	**bhòng**	on behalf of, for the benefit of
掛號	**gwaa-hrou**	to register
舒服	**shùe-fruk**	comfortable
唔舒服	**mr̀ shùe-fruk**	unwell, uncomfortable
有啲、有一啲	**yráu-dhi** or **yráu-yhat-dhi**	some, a little bit
頭痛	**tràu-tung**	headache
頭	**tràu**	head
痛	**tung**	pain, ache
間中	**gaan-jhung**	occasionally, periodically
頭暈	**tràu-wràn**	dizzy
作嘔	**jok-qáu**	to retch, be about to vomit
嘔	**qáu**	to vomit
病	**breng**	illness
嚴重	**yrìm-jrung**	serious, desperate
忙	**mròng**	busy
先至	**shìn-ji**	only then
嗰陣時	**gó-jran-srì**	at that time
打電話	**dáa-drin-wáa**	to make a phone call
取消	**chéui-shìu**	to cancel
醫院	**yhì-yúen**	hospital

Chinese and Western medicine

Chinese medicine (**Jhùng-yhì**) and Western medicine (**Shài-yhì**) have very different traditions and practices. Each has begun to acknowledge and learn from the other in recent years, and some practitioners now combine elements of both schools in their treatments. The contrast between Chinese (**Jhùng**) and Western (**Shài**) is echoed in a number of expressions, perhaps most basically in **Jhùng-gwok-yràn** (*a Chinese*) and **Shài-yràn** (*a Westerner*). Another pair of terms which are more earthy and less formal are **Tròng-yràn** (*a Chinese*) and **Gwái-lóu** (*a ghost fellow*). This last term for a Westerner is in very common use and is not really to be considered offensive, although the strictly 'politically correct' would probably avoid it.

 ———————— **Grammar** ————————

1 Bhòng (on behalf of)

You met the verb **bhòng** (*to help*) in Unit 4. It can be used with other verbs to mean *on behalf of, for the benefit of* and *for*, but you should note that it always comes *in front of* the other verbs:

Ngró bhòng nréi jíng shàa-léut.	*I'll make the salad for you.*
Kréui bhòng ngró heui mráai-yré.	*She does the shopping for me*

2 Shùe-fruk (comfortable)

Shùe-fruk nicely translates the English word *comfortable*, and it follows naturally enough that **mȑ shùe-fruk** should mean *uncomfortable*. Indeed it does, but it is also very commonly used to mean *unwell, poorly, off-colour* and, rather as in English, someone may tell you that they are *a bit off-colour* even if they are quite seriously ill.

3 Yráu-dhi (a certain amount of)

Yráu-dhi can be put in front of many other words to indicate *a certain quantity of, some*. Here are some useful examples:

yráu-dhi yràn	*some people*
yráu-dhi mǐ shùe-fruk	*a bit off-colour*
yráu-dhi mǐ séung heui	*a bit reluctant to go*

4 Approximate numbers

In the dialogue the nurse tells Mr Wong he will have to wait *three or four days* (**shàam-sei yrat**). You can make approximate numbers up like that whenever you want to. Here are a few chosen at random:

chhat-baat go yràn	*seven or eight people*
Kréui srap-yri-shàam seui.	*She's twelve or thirteen.*
sei-ngǐ-srap jek ngràu	*forty or fifty head of cattle*

But beware! There is one combination you cannot use in this way. If you think about it, **gáu-srap** cannot mean *nine or ten* because it already means *ninety*. So some other way of saying *nine or ten* had to be found, and Cantonese has come up with a real humdinger – **srap-go-baat-go** (*ten or eight classifiers*). So *nine or ten days* is **srap-yrat-baat-yrat,** and *nine or ten pens* is **srap-jhì-baat-jhì bhat**.

5 Shìn-ji (only then)

Shìn-ji is an adverb and obeys the usual rule for adverbs: it must come directly in front of a verb. (In case you have forgotten the rule, go back to Unit 1, grammar point 7, Unit 4, grammar point 9 and Unit 5, grammar point 5.) It is best remembered as meaning *only then*, but you will find it very useful in coping with the English expression *not until*:

Kréui thìng-yrat shìn-ji heui Yrat-bún.	*She's not going to Japan until tomorrow.* (lit. *She tomorrow only then is going to Japan.*)

6 Dáa (to hit)

Although **dáa** does literally mean *to hit* (**kréui dáa ngró** – *he hits me*), you will meet it used in many idiomatic ways as a general purpose verb. Here are a few:

dáa-bho	*to play ball*
dáa-lréng-thàai	*to tie a neck-tie*
dáa-drin-wáa	*to make a phone-call*
dáa-suen	*to reckon on, to intend to*

A word of warning: don't try to invent idiomatic usages for yourself
(by definition you cannot *invent* idioms).

—————— Dialogue 2 ——————

Mr Wong talks to his sick son, William.

威廉，你做乜嘢左搖右擺，跳高踎低呀？你唔舒服吖？

係呀！爸爸，我起身嗰陣時覺得個肚唔舒服。去完廁所之後，都重有
啲痛，所以我就飲咗上個禮拜媽媽買返嚟嗰樽藥水嘞。

而家點呀？個肚重痛唔痛呀？

我啱啱飲咗藥水十分鐘啫，重未知。

噢，做乜嘢你要左搖右擺呢？

次次飲藥水之前，媽媽都要我搖勻啲藥水先然後至飲，但係頭先飲藥
水嗰陣時，我唔記得搖勻，所以而家左搖右擺，希望可以補返數
啦。

Mr Wong	Whài-lrìm, nréi jrou-mhat-yré jó-yrìu-yrau-báai, tiu-ghòu-mhàu-dhài qaa? Nréi mř shùe-fruk qràa?
William	Hrai qaa! Bràa-bhaa, ngró héi-shàn gó-jran-srì gok-dhak go tróu mř shùe-fruk. Heui-yrùen chi-só jhì-hrau, dhou jrung yráu-dhi tung, só-yrí ngró jrau yám-jó sreung-go-lrái-baai mràa-mhaa mráai-fhàan-lrài gó jhèun yreuk-séui laak.
Mr Wong	Yrì-ghaa dím qaa? Go tróu jrung tung mř tung qaa?
William	Ngró nghaam-nghaam yám-jó yreuk-séui srap fhàn jhung jhe, jrung mrei jhì.
Mr Wong	Gám, jrou-mhat-yré nréi yiu jó-yrìu-yrau-báai nhe?
William	Chi-chi yám yreuk-séui jhì-chrìn, mràa-mhaa dhou yiu ngró yrìu-wràn dhi yreuk-séui shìn yrìn-hrau ji yám. Draan-hrai tràu-shin yám yreuk-séui gó-jran-srì, ngró mř gei-dhak yrìu-wràn, só-yrí yrì-ghaa jó-yrìu-yrau-báai, hhèi-mrong hó-yrí bóu-fhàan-sou lhaa.

威廉	**Whài-lrìm**	(a Cantonese version of *William*)
左搖右擺	**jó-yrìu-yrau-báai**	*shaking from side to side*
跳高踎低	**tiu-ghòu-mhàu-dhài**	*jumping up and down*
起身	**héi-shàn**	*to get up in the morning*
肚	**tróu**	*stomach, abdomen*
廁所	**chi-só**	*toilet, lavatory*
上個禮拜	**sreung-go-lrái-baai**	*last week*
樽	**jhèun**	*bottle, bottle of*
藥	**yreuk**	*medicine*
藥水	**yreuk-séui**	*(liquid) medicine*
點呀 = 點樣呀?	**dím qaa?** or **dím-yéung qaa?**	*how is it? how are things?*
啱啱	**nghaam-nghaam**	*a moment ago, a moment before*
一分鐘	**yhat fhàn jhung**	*minute*
未	**mrei**	*not yet*
之前	**jhì-chrìn**	*before*
搖勻	**yrìu-wràn**	*to shake up*
然後	**yrìn-hrau**	*afterwards, after that*
頭先	**tràu-shìn**	*just now*
希望	**hhèi-mrong**	*hope*
補返數	**bóu-fhàan-sou**	*to make up for*

True or false? Answer **hrai** or **mr̀ hrai** to the following questions, and then write out a complete answer in Cantonese. So for the first question, you could reply **Mr̀ hrai. Dhi yreuk-séui hrai mràa-mhaa sreung-go-lrái-baai mráai-fhàan-lrài ge.**

(*a*)   **Gó jhèun yreuk-séui hrai mràa-mhaa jrok-yrat mráai-fhàan-lrài ge.**

(*b*)   **Chi-chi yám yreuk-séui jhì-chrìn, mràa-mhaa dhou yiu Whài-lrìm yrìu-wràn dhi yreuk-séui shìn.**

(*c*)   **Whài-lrìm gok-dhak go tràu mr̀ shùe-fruk.**

(*d*)   **Whài-lrìm yám-jó yreuk lréung go jhung-tràu laak.**

 ———————— **Grammar** ————————

7 Four-character phrases

All the Chinese languages seem to thrive on using combinations of four characters as set phrases. Mr Wong uses two of them in his first speech in the dialogue. It can often be misleading to translate these phrases literally, so we generally will not do so, but in this case the second four-character phrase is made up of two common useful words which it will help you to learn now:

tiu-ghòu means *to jump high* (**ghòu** = *high, tall*), and in athletics is *high jump*.

mhàu-dhài means *to squat down, to crouch down*.

8 Last week, this week *and* next week

Sreung-go-lrái-baai means *last week*. **Sreung** means *above*, so **sreung-go-lrái-baai** really means *the week above*. Logically enough, the word for *next week* is *the week below* (**hraa-go-lrái-baai**). You now have the full set:

sreung-go-lrái-baai/shìng-krèi	*last week*
nhi-go-lrái-baai/shìng-krèi	*this week*
hraa-go-lrái-baai/shìng-krèi	*next week*

And you can go further:

sreung-go-Lrái-baai-sei	*Thursday of last week*
nhi-go-Shìng-krèi-lruk	*Saturday of this week*
hraa-go-Shìng-krèi-shàam	*Wednesday of next week*

As a matter of fact you have met **sreung** and **hraa** as a pair meaning *up and down, above and below* before (see Unit 9, grammar point 10 – the word **hraa** in that case had changed its tone), and you will meet them again later.

9 'Time how long' again

In Unit 6, grammar point 12 you met the idea of 'time how long', and you will remember that such time expressions are placed *after* the verb. *An hour* was **yhat go jhung-tràu**, and now you can deal in minutes too: *a minute* is **yhat fhàn jhung**. In the dialogue, William says **Ngró nghaam-nghaam yám-jó yreuk-séui srap fhàn jhung jhe.** (*I've only had the medicine down me for ten minutes.*).

10 Before *and* after

In Unit 6 you met **jhì-hrau** meaning *after*. Its opposite is **jhì-chrìn** (*before*). Both of these words follow the phrases they refer to, whereas in English they come in front of them:

Ngró srik-fraan jhì-chrìn, hóu séung heui mráai bhe-jáu.	*Before I eat, I would very much like to go and buy some beer.*
Kréui fhàan qhuk-kéi jhì-hrau, nréi yiu wraa kréui jhì!	*After he returns home, you must tell him!*

Like **sreung** and **hraa** (see grammar point 8), **chrìn** and **hrau** are a regular pair. You learned **chrìn-yrat** (*the day before yesterday*) in Unit 9, so you can now make a good guess at what *the day after tomorrow* must be .... Of course, it is **hrau-yrat!**

chrìn-yrat	*the day before yesterday*
hrau-yrat	*the day after tomorrow*
chrìn-nín	*the year before last*
hrau-nín	*the year after next*

11 Shìn-ji *again*

You met **shìn-ji** in grammar point 5. It is actually made up of two separate words **shìn** (*first*) and **ji** (*only then*), and sometimes they can be separated, although the meaning remains the same. In William's last speech in the dialogue you will see a good example:

Mràa-mhaa dhou yiu ngró yrìu-wràn dhi yreuk-séui shìn yrìn-hrau ji yám.

Translated literally this means *Mummy requires me to shake the medicine first (and) afterwards only then to drink it.* It is a little more long-winded than **mràa-mhaa dhou yiu ngró yrìu-wràn dhi yreuk-séui shìn-ji yám,** and for that reason sounds slightly more emphatic, as though William is relaying the lesson which his mother has carefully taught him.

 ——————— **Exercises** ———————

1   Read these questions aloud in Cantonese, then give the answer clearly and as quickly as you can. Remember that most of the answer will be the same as the question, but there will of course be no **qaa**?!

(a) **Yhi-shang hái bhin-drou tái breng-yràn qaa?**
(b) **Wròng Shìn-shàang hrai bhin-gwok-yràn qaa?**
(c) **Mràa-mhaa hái bhin-sue mráai-yré qaa?**
(d) **Hhèung-góng-yràn hái bhin-drou jrue qaa?**
(e) **Wròng Whài-lrìm ge bràa-bhaa sing mhat-yré qaa?**

 2   Read the passage below and then make up some lines for a very severe Dr Li, who tells two people that they are both ruining their health and then tells each of them separately not to indulge their favourite vice any more.

Wròng Shàang, Wròng Táai dhou yráu-breng. Dím-gáai yráu-breng nhe? Yhàn-wrai Wròng Taai-táai yám gaa-fhe yám-jó taai dhò laak, Wròng Shìn-shàang yám bhe-jáu yám-jó taai dhò laak. Lréung go yràn dhou heui tái Lréi Yhi-shang. Nréi gwú yhi-shang deui kréui-drei dím-yéung góng nhe?

3   You are advanced enough now to translate a suitably modified nursery rhyme into Cantonese. A pig is **jhue** and the word for *a son* (**jái**) can be tacked onto the end of any noun to show that it is a little one, so **jhue-jái** is a *piglet*, a *piggy*, or just a *small pig*; and **jhùe-yruk** is *pork*. OK, off you go . . . and forgive us for the last line!

This little piggy went to market (went shopping).
This little piggy stayed at home.
This little piggy had roast beef. (Well, you can forget the roast bit.)
And this little piggy had none.
And this little piggy went 'Oh! Oh! Oh!' to see the doctor.

4   Describe in Cantonese what Mr Chan is doing in each of the pictures on page 97. Begin the first sentence with **Chràn Shàang . . .** , and the others with **Kréui . . . .**

11

第十一課 時裝
SRÌ-JHONG

The world of fashion

It is not easy keeping up with fashion, and Hong Kong in particular feels it has to do so. In this unit you will learn some ways of passing judgements and expressing likes and dislikes.

 ───── **Dialogue 1** ─────

Miss Wong shops for a new hat and finally thinks she has found the very thing. However . . .

呢頂帽嘅設計唔錯，顏色又好可惜太貴嘞！

小姐，試吓呢頂喇：係最新運到㗎。

我唔中意佢嘅質地，我覺得太硬嘞，戴起嚟好唔舒服。

小姐，再試吓呢兩頂啦。佢哋都唔錯㗎。

係，佢哋都唔錯，但係呢兩頂帽都係舊年嘅款式，你哋重有冇啲新款嘅呀？......咦！呢頂唔錯嘛，又新款又大方。等我試吓！

真係好靚！

你都話靚吖！唔知要幾多錢呢?

九百五十蚊。

佢都冇價錢牌，你點知呀?

小姐，你戴住嘅帽正係我嘅！

Miss Wong	Nhi déng móu ge chit-gai mr̀-cho, ngràan-shik yrau hóu – hó-shik taai gwai laak!
Assistant	Síu-jé, si-hráa nhi déng lhaa: hrai jeui shàn wran-dou gaa.

─── **98** ───

Miss Wong	Ngró mr̀ jhùng-yi kréui ge jhat-déi, ngró gok-dhak taai ngraang laak, daai-héi-lrài hóu mr̀ shùe-fruk.
Assistant	Síu-jé, joi si-hráa nhi lréung déng lhaa. Kréui-drei dhou mr̀-cho gaa.
Miss Wong	Hrai, kréui-drei dhou mr̀-cho, draan-hrai nhi lréung déng móu dhou hrai grau-nín ge fún-shik. Nréi-drei jrung yráu mróu dhi shàn-fún ge qaa? . . . Yí! Nhi déng mr̀-cho bo, yrau shàn-fún yrau draai-fhong. Dáng ngró si-hráa!
Customer	Jhàn-hrai hóu leng!
Miss Wong	Nréi dhou wraa leng qràa! Mr̀-jhì yiu géi-dho chín nhe?
Customer	Gáu-baak-ngf́-srap mhan.
Miss Wong	Kréui dhou mróu gaa-chrìn-páai, nréi dím jhì qaa?
Customer	Síu-jé, nréi daai-jrue ge móu jing-hrai ngró ge!

頂	**déng**	(classifier for *hats*)
帽	**móu**	*hat, cap*
設計	**chit-gai**	*design, to design*
唔錯	**mr̀-cho**	*not bad, pretty good*
可惜	**hó-shik**	*it is a pity that, unfortunately*
試	**si**	*to try, to test*
運到、運輸到	**wran-dou** or **wran-shùe-dou**	*to arrive by transport*
運、運輸	**wran** or **wran-shùe**	*to transport*
硬	**ngraang**	*hard, unyielding*
帶	**daai**	*to wear, put on (accessories)*
......起嚟	**-héi-lrài**	(verb ending: *when it comes to, once you start*)
新款	**shàn-fún**	*new-style*
大方	**draai-fhong**	*tasteful, sophisticated*
唔知	**mr̀-jhì**	*I wonder*
百	**baak**	*hundred*
價錢牌	**gaa-chrìn-páai**	*price tag*
價錢	**gaa-chrìn**	*price*
住	**-jrue**	(verb ending: *ongoing state of*)
正係	**jing-hrai**	*just happens to be*

——————— **Grammar** ———————

1 -héi-lrài (when it comes to it)

-héi-lrài is a verb ending which means *once you start . . .* or *when it comes to . . .* , depending on the context. Here are two examples which should give you a feeling for its use:

Góng-héi-lrài, ngró dhou
shik Hrò Shìn-shàang.
Yrung-héi-lrài, nréi jrau
gok-dhak hóu shùe-fruk.

*Now you come to mention
it, I know Mr Ho as well.
When you start using it,
you will find it very
comfortable.*

2 Higher numbers

Up to now you have only been able to count as far as 99. One hundred is **yhat-baak**, 200 is **yri-baak**, 999 is **gáu-baak-gáu-srap-gáu**, and 1,000 is **yhat-chhìn**. Two thousand is **yri-chhìn**, 9,999 is **gáu-chhìn-gáu-baak-gáu-srap-gáu**. After that Cantonese differs from English. The Chinese have a special word for 10,000 (**mraan**), so 10,000 is **yhat-mraan**, 20,000 is **yri-mraan**, 90,000 is **gáu-mraan**, 100,000 is **srap-mraan** and 1,000,000 is **yhat-baak-mraan**. In short, Cantonese goes up to 10,000 and then starts counting in units of ten thousand, whereas English goes up to 1,000 and starts counting in units of a thousand until it gets to units of a million. Here it is in table form:

1	yhat
10	(yhat-)srap
100	(yhat-)baak
1,000	(yhat-)chhìn
10,000	(yhat-)mraan
100,000	(yhat-)srap-mraan
1,000,000	(yhat-)baak-mraan

Be warned that some overseas Chinese (notably those in Singapore and Britain) seem to be slipping into Western ways, so you might hear them saying **srap-chhìn** instead of **yhat-mraan** for 10,000.

The natural progression in Cantonese, then, is from **srap** to **baak** to **chhìn** to **mraan**. If one or more of these categories is missed out, as for instance with the number 103 where there is a zero in the **srap** column, Cantonese indicates this by throwing in the word **lrìng** (*zero*). So 103 is **yhat-baak-lrìng-shàam**. If more than one category is represented by zero it is still only necessary to put in one **lrìng**, so 10,003 is **yhat-mraan-lrìng-shàam**.

Round numbers

The Chinese love round numbers. *May you have a hundred sons and a thousand grandsons* was a very common good wish to someone at New Year or on other happy occasions. *The Old Hundred Surnames* is a regular way of talking of *The Chinese People*. *Thousand Mile Eyes* was the name of a protective God who acted as lookout for trouble. *The Ten Thousand Mile Long Wall* is what is known in English as *The Great Wall*. None of these numbers is meant to be taken literally: they all mean something like *lots of*.

---

3 The verb endings -jrue *and* -gán *compared*

In Unit 4 **-gán** was introduced as a verb ending which indicated a continuing action. At first sight **-jrue** does not seem so different, but the two endings are not interchangeable. **-gán** tells us that an activity is still going on, but **-jrue** says that the activity has come to a halt and that we are left with a steady ongoing state. The following examples should make it clear:

Wròng Táai daai-gán yhat déng hóu leng ge móu.	*Mrs Wong is putting on a beautiful hat.*
Wròng Táai daai-jrue yhat déng hóu leng ge móu.	*Mrs Wong is wearing a beautiful hat.*
Ngró tái-gán kréui.	*I'm taking a glance at her.*
Ngró tái-jrue kréui.	*I'm keeping an eye on her.*

Dialogue 2

Mrs Wong explains to her husband why she talked so much at a party.

太太，今晚我哋參加嘅時裝展覽酒會你一定覺得好開心嘞。

唔係嘛！啱啱相反，我覺得好唔開心。

唔係丫：我睇見你坐喺梳化椅處，唔停咁同張太太，何太太，王小姐
佢哋傾偈。你重大聲讚王小姐件衫裙好靚，又讚張太太件外套嘅款
式好新。

我係被迫要唔停嗽大聲傾偈啫，實在我唔想㗎。

點解呢？

因為我著嗰套衫裙嘅顏色同花樣，同啲梳化椅嘅布料一樣。我坐喺梳
化椅處，如果唔講嘢，有人經過以為有一張空椅，想坐落嚟添。

Mr Wong	Taai-táai, ghàm-mráan ngró-drei chhàam-ghàa ge sṙi-jhong jín-lráam jáu-wúi nréi yhat-dring gok-dhak hóu hhòi-sham laak.
Mrs Wong	Mṙ hrai bo! Nghaam-nghaam shèung-fáan. Ngró gok-dhak hóu mṙ hhòi-sham.
Mr Wong	Mṙ hrai qhaa: ngró tái-gin nréi chró hái sho-fáa-yí sue, mṙ trìng gám trùng Jhèung Taai-táai, Hrò Taai-táai, Wròng Síu-jé kréui-drei khìng-gái. Nréi jrung draai-shèng jaan Wròng Síu-jé grin shaam-kwràn hóu leng, yrau jaan Jhèung Taai-táai grin ngroi-tou ge fún-shik hóu shàn.
Mrs Wong	Ngró hrai brei-bhik yiu mṙ trìng gám draai-shèng khìng-gái jhe, srat-jroi ngró mṙ séung gaa.
Mr Wong	Dím-gáai nhe?
Mrs Wong	Yhàn-wrai ngró jeuk gó tou shaam-kwràn ge ngràan-shik trùng fhaa-yéung, trùng dhi sho-fáa-yí ge bou-líu yhat-yreung. Ngró chró hái sho-fáa-yí sue, yrùe-gwó mṙ góng-yré, yráu-yràn ghìng-gwo yrí-wrài yráu yhat jhèung hhùng yí, séung chró-lrok-lrài thìm.

今晚	**ghàm-mráan**	*tonight, this evening*
參加	**chhàam-ghàa**	*to take part in*
時裝	**srì-jhong**	*fashion*
展覽	**jín-lráam**	*show, exhibition*
酒會	**jáu-wúi**	*reception, cocktail party*
相反	**shèung-fáan**	*on the contrary*
梳化椅	**sho-fáa-yí**	*sofa, easy chair*
椅	**yí**	*chair*
停	**trìng**	*to stop*
傾偈	**khìng-gái**	*to chat*
大聲	**draai-shèng**	*loud, in a loud voice*
讚	**jaan**	*to praise*
外套	**ngroi-tou**	*jacket*
被迫	**brei-bhik**	*to be forced to, compelled to*
實在	**srat-jrol**	*in fact, really*
著	**jeuk**	*to wear (clothes)*
花樣	**fhaa-yéung**	*pattern*
布料	**bou-líu**	*material, fabric*
一樣	**yhat-yreung**	*the same*
有人	**yráu-yràn**	*somebody*
經過	**ghìng-gwo**	*to pass by*
以為	**yrí-wrài**	*to think, to assume, to regard as*
張	**jhèung**	*(classifier for flat things: paper, chairs, tables, sheets, etc.)*
空	**hhùng**	*empty*
......落嚟	**-lrok-lrài**	*(verb ending: downwards)*

The Chinese character for **trìng** (*to stop*).

Questions

1 **Have you understood?** What does the cartoon caption mean?

`Jrok-yrat
ngró yrí-wrài
nhi jhèung yí hóu
shùe fruk,draan-hrai
yrì-ghaa...!´

2 Quickly decide which of the alternatives in brackets to strike out, so that you leave a correct statement.

(a) Wròng Shìn-shàang trùng Wròng Taai-táai chhàam-ghàa ge hrai (jrou-shàang-yi/drin-yíng/srì-jhong) jáu-wúi.

(b) Wròng Táai wraa, kréui (mr̀ hhòi-sham/hóu hhòi-sham).

(c) Wròng Táai jaan Jhèung Táai (shàn-tái hóu hóu/hóu shik júe-sung/hóu shik yràu-séui/grin ngroi-tou hóu leng).

(d) Wròng Taai-táai tou shaam-kwràn ge ngràan-shik, fhaa-yéung trùng (sho-fáa-yí/lraap-saap-túng/drin-nrúen-lròu) yhat-yreung.

⊡ ——————— Grammar ———————

4 Late in the day

Mr̀aan means *evening, late in the day* (not *late for an appointment*). *This evening* or *tonight* is **ghàm-mráan**. More terms using **mráan** include:

jrok-mráan	*yesterday evening, last night*
thìng-mráan	*tomorrow evening, tomorrow night*
chrìn-mráan	*the evening of the day before yesterday*
hrau-mráan	*the evening of the day after tomorrow*

5 Nghaam-nghaam *again*

In Unit 10 we met **nghaam-nghaam** meaning *a moment ago*. It has a second meaning – *exactly, precisely*. In the dialogue Mrs Wong says **nghaam-nghaam shèung-fáan** (*it's exactly to the contrary*), and you should also note these other examples:

nghaam-nghaam yhat go jhung-tràu	*exactly one hour*
nghaam-nghaam hóu	*exactly right*

6 Hái-sue/hái-drou (at the indicated place)

You met **nhi-sue/nhi-drou** (*here*), **gó-sue/gó-drou** (*there*) and **bhin-sue?/bhin-drou?** (*where?*) way back in Units 3 and 5. **Hái-sue** and **hái-drou** (lit. *at the place*) are used rather loosely to mean either *here* or *there*, and they really seem to mean *at the place we both know about*. So you might say **Nréi hái-sue jrou mhat-yré qaa?** to someone on the phone and it would mean *What are you doing there?*, or you might say it to someone who is in the same room as you and it would mean *What are you doing here?*

Hái-sue or **hái-drou** can be split to surround a noun. They then indicate a rather vague relationship with the noun, meaning *in/on/ at/in the general vicinity of*. In the dialogue Mr Wong says **ngró tái- gin nréi chró hái sho-fáa-yí sue** (*I saw you sitting there on the sofa*); *on* seems the most likely place for Mrs Wong to be. However, if you were to ask someone where they had thoughtlessly left their keys, they might reply **hái chhe sue** and you would not be sure whether the keys were in, on top of, under, or just somewhere on the ground near the car. It can be quite useful to be able to be so vague, so **hái-sue** and **hái-drou** are worth remembering.

7 *Three verbs for* to wear

You have now met three verbs which can all be translated as *to wear* in English:

Jeuk	*to wear clothing*, that is, shirts, jackets, trousers, underclothes, shoes and socks.
Daai	*to wear accessories*, that is, hats, spectacles, watches, rings, jewellery, gloves, etc.
Dáa	the least common, meaning *to wear something which has to be tied on*, like a neck-tie or head-scarf.

8 Yrí-wrài (to think wrongly)

Yrí-wrài means *to assume* or *to think, to consider*, but it is probably most often used when the speaker already knows that what he/she thought was actually wrong. In the dialogue Mrs Wong says that she was talking so much so that no-one would fail to know she was there and *think (wrongly) that there was a vacant chair*. Here are some more examples:

Ngró yrí-wrài kréui hrai Yrat-bún-yràn.	*I thought she was Japanese (but now I know that she is actually Korean).*
Kréui yrí-wrài ghàm-yrat hrai Lrái-baai-yrat.	*He thought that today was Sunday (but of course it's actually Saturday).*

And you might like to learn a very slangy expression: **Nréi yrí-wrài lhaa!**, which corresponds to the English *You reckon!, That's what you think!, Think again, pal!*

9 Verb ending: -Irok-Irài

You met **lrok** in **lrok síu-bhaa** (*to alight from the mini-bus*) and in **lrok-suet** (*to snow*). The basic meaning of **lrok** is *to come down, to fall down, to go down*. As a verb ending **-lrok-lrài** shows that the action of the verb is happening in a downward direction:

chró-lrok-lrài	*sitting down*
yràu fhèi-ghèi gó-sue tái-lrok-lrài	*looking down from the aircraft*

 —————— **Exercises** ——————

1 Test your skill with numbers by translating the phrases below into Cantonese. You probably know that one of the hardest

things to do is to count naturally in a second language, so the more you practise the better.

16 young women	*200 sheets of paper*
$5,600	*1,000,000 Chinese people*
12,750	*8,034*
11 hours	*2 lobsters*

2   Warning: only do this when you are not driving! When you are in a car or a bus, watch the vehicles that come towards you and try to read off their number plates before they have gone by. Until you get better at it, you can do it by saying **shàam-baat-chhat** rather than the full version **shàam-baak-baat-srap-chhat**. It's quite an addictive little game, you'll find, but *very* good for making you proficient with numbers.

3   Give the opposites of the words on the left by filling in the blanks on the right.

(*a*)	**shàn-fún**	____-fún
(*b*)	**taai gwai**	taai ____
(*c*)	**mráai qhuk**	____ qhuk
(*d*)	**jhì-hrau**	jhì-____
(*e*)	**lráang**	____
(*f*)	**dhùng-bhak**	____-____

4   Here's a brain-teaser for you. Miss Ho's cryptic answer does contain enough information to reveal all the facts, but you will have to work hard to find them out!

Hraa-go-shìng-krèi Hrò Shìn-shàang, Hrò Taai-taái, Hrò Síu-jé dhou wrúi fong yhat yrat gaa. Hó-shik kréui-drei mȑ hrai yhat-chrài fong: yhat go fong Lrái-baai-yhat, yhat go fong Lrái-baai-yri, yhat go fong Lrái-baai-shàam. Kréui-drei fong-gaa séung jrou mhat-yré nhe? Yhat go séung heui tái-hei, yhat go séung heui pràa-shàan, yhat go séung heui jáu-lràu srik lrùng-hhaa. Ngró mran Hrò Síu-jé bhin-go séung hái bhin yhat yrat heui bhin-drou qaa? Kréui wraa:

'Bràa-bhaa séung heui pràa-shàan. Ngró Lrái-baai-yri fong-gaa. Yráu yràn séung Lrái-baai-yhat heui srik lrùng-hhaa.'

Nràa! Nréi hó mȑ hó-yrí wraa ngró jhì nhi shàam go yràn lréui-brin bhin-go séung heui tái-hei? bhin-go séung heui srik lrùng-hhaa? Shìng-krèi-shàam fong-gaa hrai bhin-go qaa?

12

第十二課 教育

GAAU-YRUK

Education for life

Education looms large in Chinese culture, and all over the world the Chinese have a reputation for application and dedication to learning. This unit provides you with some of the terms you will need to carry on a conversation on the subject, and it also introduces colours, tells you how to make comparisons, and how to describe the relative position of one thing to another.

Dialogue 1

Parents chat about the hardships of education.

我覺得香港學生讀書真係辛苦嘞。

係呀！我都同意。佢哋每日都要讀中文、英文、數學、地理、歷史同科學。而且平均每個禮拜都有兩三科要測驗。

重有呀！佢哋嘅課本又重又多，每日要帶返學校嘅課本同練習簿就唔會少過十磅重。

我個仔今年只係十歲之嘛，喺小學讀書，但係佢晚晚都要溫習差唔多四個鐘頭先至可以做完啲功課。我唔明白啲先生上堂嘅時候點樣教書嘅。

我話喺中學教書重麻煩呀！又要教佢哋又要管佢哋，尤其是管佢哋，因為而家啲後生仔個個都唔中意被人管嘅喇。

好彩我哋個個都唔係教書先生啫。如果唔係，我哋都冇時間一齊喺呢處傾偈啦。

Mr Wong	Ngró gok-dhak Hhèung-góng hrok-shaang druk-shùe jhàn-hrai shàn-fú laak.
Mr Cheung	Hrai qaa! Ngró dhou trùng-yi. Kréui-drei mrúi yrat dhou yiu druk Jhùng-mràn, Yhìng-mràn, Sou-hrok, Drei-lréi, Lrik-sí trùng Fho-hrok. Yrì-ché prìng-gwhàn mrúi go lrái-baai dhou yráu lréung-shàam fho yiu chhaak-yrim.
Mr Wong	Jrung yráu qaa! Kréui-drei ge fo-bún yrau chrúng yrau dhò, mrúi yrat yiu daai-fhàan hrok-hraau ge fo-bún trùng lrin-jraap-bóu jrau mr̀ wrúi síu-gwo srap brong chrúng.
Mrs Lee	Ngró go jái ghàm-nín jí-hrai srap seui jhi-mráa, hái síu-hrok druk-shùe, draan-hrai kréui mráan-mráan dhou yiu whàa-jraap chhàa-mr̀-dho sei go jhung-tràu shìn-ji hó-yrí jrou-yrùen dhi ghùng-fo. Ngró mr̀ mrìng-braak dhi shìn-shàang sréung-tròng ge srì-hrau dím-yéung gaau-shùe ge.
Mr Wong	Ngró wraa hái jhùng-hrok gaau-shùe jrung mràa-fràan qaa! Yrau yiu gaau kréui-drei yrau yiu gwún kréui-drei, yràu-krèi-sri gwún kréui-drei, yhàn-wrai yrì-ghaa dhi hrau-shaang-jái go-go dhou mr̀ jhùng-yi brei yràn gwún ge lhaa.
Mr Cheung	Hóu-chói ngró-drei go-go dhou mr̀ hrai gaau-shùe shìn-shàang jhe. Yrùe-gwó-mr̀-hrai, ngró-drei dhou mróu srì-gaan yhat-chrài hái nhi-sue khìng-gái laa.

學生	**hrok-shaang**	*student, pupil*
讀書	**druk-shùe**	*to study*
讀	**druk**	*to read*
書	**shùe**	*book*
辛苦	**shàn-fú**	*hard, distressing*
每	**mrúi**	*each, every*
中文	**Jhùng-mràn**	*Chinese language*
英文	**Yhìng-mràn**	*English language*
數學	**Sou-hrok**	*Mathematics*
地理	**Drei-lréi**	*Geography*
歷史	**Lrik-sí**	*History*
科學	**Fho-hrok**	*Science*
平均	**prìng-gwhàn**	*average, on average*
科	**fho**	*subject, discipline*
測驗	**chhaak-yrim**	*to test; evaluation*
課本	**fo-bún**	*textbook*
重	**chrúng**	*heavy*

學校	**hrok-hraau**	*school*
練習薄	**lrin-jraap-bóu**	*exercise book*
過	**gwo**	*than*
磅	**brong**	*pound* (weight)
之嘛	**jhi-mráa**	(particle: *only*)
小學	**síu-hrok**	*primary school*
溫習	**whàn-jraap**	*to revise lessons*
差唔多	**chhàa-mr̀-dho**	*almost*
功課	**ghùng-fo**	*homework*
明白	**mrìng-braak**	*to understand, be clear about*
先生	**shìn-shàang**	*teacher*
上堂	**sréung-tròng**	*to attend class*
中學	**jhùng-hrok**	*secondary school*
教書	**gaau-shùe**	*to teach*
麻煩	**mràa-fràan**	*trouble, troublesome*
管	**gwún**	*to control, be in charge of*
尤其是	**yràu-krèi-sri**	*especially*
後生仔	**hrau-shaang-jái**	*youngsters*
後生	**hrau-shaang**	*young*
被	**brei**	*by; to endure, suffer*
好彩	**hóu-chói**	*lucky, fortunately*
如果唔係（呢）	**yrùe-gwó-mr̀-hrai(-nhe)**	*otherwise*

Whoops! Something is wrong! Each of the following sentences contains an error either in the sense or in the grammar. Can you spot the deliberate mistakes?

(*a*) Gó dhi hrok-shaang jek-jek dhou shik góng Yhìng-mràn.

(*b*) Ngró mr̀ shik góng Jhùng-mràn.

(*c*) Wròng Táai go jái mr̀ yráu lrik-sí fo-bún.

(*d*) Gó lréung Mréi-gwok síu-jé mr̀ jhùng-yi jeuk hrùng-shik ge shaam-kwràn.

(*e*) Wròng Shìn-shàang ge bràa-bhaa ghàm-nín jí-hrai baat seui jhi-mráa.

 —————— **Grammar** ——————

1 Mrúi (each, every)

There are two things to remember about using **mrúi**. First, it requires the use of a classifier:

mrúi go yràn	*each person, everybody*
mrúi jhì bhat	*each pen*
mrúi yrat	*every day* (refer back to Unit 8, grammar point 6 if this one puzzles you)

Second, because **mrúi** involves *wholeness* and *inclusiveness* it is almost always backed up by **dhou** placed before the verb. (You met this in Unit 5, grammar point 10, Unit 8, grammar point 3 and Unit 9, grammar point 1.)

| **Mrúi grin shaam-kwràn** | *Each one of the dresses is* |
| **dhou yráu síu-síu lraan-jó.** | *slightly damaged.* |

2 Simple comparisons with gwo

The same word **gwo** which you met in Unit 6 (meaning *to go past, to go by*) is used to make simple comparisons (*X is —er than Y*):

Ngró ge chhe draai-gwo	*My car is bigger than yours.*
nréi ge chhe.	
Yhìng-gwok chhe gwai	*Are British cars more expensive*
mr̀ gwai-gwo Yrat-bún	*than Japanese cars?*
chhe qaa?	

The pattern, then, is **X adjective *gwo* Y**, and you can probably see how logically it works – *X is* adjective *surpassing Y*:

| **Ngró ghòu-gwo kréui.** | (lit. *I am tall surpassing him.*) |
| | *I am taller than he is.* |

In the dialogue Mr Wong talks about the heavy load of books and exercise books carried by students, and he says **mr̀ wrúi *síu-gwo* srap brong chrúng** (*they cannot be less than ten pounds in weight*).

3 Classifiers as possessives

You learned in Unit 2, grammar point 2 that **ge** shows possession, so that *my pen* is **ngró ge bhat**. There is a minor snag with this. As you know, nouns can be either singular or plural without changing their form, and so **ngró ge bhat** actually can mean either *my pen* or *my pens*. In many cases it doesn't matter that this is unclear, or else the context makes it obvious whether you mean *pen* or *pens*. If you wish to be more precise, however, you can use the classifier:

ngró ge bhat	*my pen* or *my pens*
ngró jhì bhat	*my pen* (singular only)
ngró dhi bhat	*my pens* (plural only)

In the dialogue Mrs Lee talks about **ngró go jái**, and that tells you that she only has one son, or at least that she is only talking about one son in this instance.

4 Brei: *the passive construction*

Brei literally means *to suffer, to endure*. You will usually only meet it when it is used like the English word *by* in the passive construction. The following two examples should suffice to show how it works:

> **Hrò Shìn-shàang chéng Wròng Shìn-shàang heui srik-fraan.**
> **Wròng Shìn-shàang brei Hrò Shìn-shàang chéng heui srik-fraan.**

The first sentence is active (*Mr Ho invites Mr Wong out for a meal.*) and the second is passive (*Mr Wong is invited out for a meal by Mr Ho.*) Cantonese does not use the passive construction very often, but you need to be aware that it exists so that you will not be taken by surprise when you do meet it.

5 Recap on classifiers

You have now met all the major uses of classifiers, so the following checklist summarising their uses should be helpful to you:

(*a*)   When you specify a noun with **nhi, gó, bhin, mrúi, géi, srèng-** (*this, that, which?, each, how many?/several, the whole*) you should use the correct classifier between the specifier and the noun:

nhi go yràn	gó chràng láu
bhin jek lrùng-hhaa?	mrúi grin shaam-kwràn
géi trìu mráa-lrou	srèng-go lrái-baai

(*b*)   When you count nouns you should use the correct classifier between the specifier and the noun:

| yhat go Yrat-bún-yràn | lréung chhàan fraan |
| shàam ghàan qhuk | yri-srap-sei jhì bhat |

(*c*)   The classifier for uncountable things (like *water*) is **dhi**.
Dhi is also the plural classifier, that is, the classifier used when
a noun is plural but uncounted:

gó dhi séui	nhi dhi sung
nhi dhi Yhìng-gwok- yràn	bhin dhi Jhùng-mràn shùe?

(*d*)   The classifier can be used at the beginning of a sentence
where English uses the definite article *The*:

Dhi sung hóu hòu- srik.	Grin shaam leng mȓ leng qaa?

(*e*)   Doubling the classifier and adding **dhou** before the verb
gives the meaning *every one of, each one of*:

Grin-grin shaam-kwràn dhou hóu leng.
Ghàan-ghàan qhuk lréui-brin dhou mróu yràn.

(*f*)   The correct classifier or the plural classifier **dhi** can be
used to indicate possession:

kréui ghàan qhuk
Wròng Shìn-shàang dhi chhe

(*g*)   A small number of words seem to act as noun and
classifier combined. Of these you have already met the most
common – **nrìn, yrat** and **seui**:

shàam nrìn   lréung yrat   srap seui

(*h*)   Finally, here are three new classifiers which you will find
useful:

brou	classifier for *books* (interchangeable with **bún**)
bún	classifier for *books* (interchangeable with **brou**)
gaa	classifier for *vehicles, aircraft* and *machinery*

Large, medium and small

Have you noticed how neatly Cantonese copes with the different levels of the school education system? Primary or junior
school is **síu-hrok** (*small learning*); middle or secondary
school is **jhùng-hrok** (*middle learning*); and university is
draai-hrok (*large learning*).

You will find the same words (**draai**, **jhùng**, **síu**) used on Chinese restaurant menus, showing that you can have different sized dishes of any one order, and of course the menu will also show different prices for the three sizes. Quite often, off-the-peg clothes are marked in the same way.

—————— Dialogue 2 ——————

An encounter with a traffic policeman shows that education does not always succeed in getting the main point across.

香港政府教育香港市民真係失敗嘞。
你講邊方面嘅教育呢?
好多方面喇,尤其是一般嘅公共秩序方面。
咦!前便有個警察好似要檢控個汽車司機噃!我哋去睇吓喇。
先生,你睇唔睇到嗰盞交通燈呀?
睇到丫!
你睇唔睇到係紅燈呀?
睇到丫!
噉,點解你重要衝紅燈呢?
因為我睇唔到你!
張先生,你睇吓,呢啲就係香港人對一般公共秩序嘅教育嘞!
每個社會都有一啲壞份子,唔好話個個人都一樣,香港嘅教育都有好
　嘅方面嘅。

Mr Wong	Hhèung-góng jing-fú gaau-yruk Hhèung-góng srí-mràn jhàn-hrai shat-braai laak.
Mr Cheung	Nréi góng bhin fhòng-mrin ge gaau-yruk nhe?
Mr Wong	Hóu dhò fhòng-mrin lhaa, yràu-krèi-sri yhat-bhùn ge ghùng-grung drit-jreui fhòng-mrin.
Mr Cheung	Yí! Chrìn-brin yráu go gíng-chaat hóu-chrí yiu gím-hung go hei-chhe shi-ghei bo! Ngró-drei heui tái-hráa lhaa.
Policeman	Shìn-shàang, nréi tái mr̀ tái-dóu gó jáan ghàau-thùng-dhang qaa?
Driver	Tái-dóu qhaa!
Policeman	Nréi tái mr̀ tái-dóu hrai hrùng-dhang qaa?
Driver	Tái-dóu qhaa!

Policeman	Gám, dím-gáai nréi jrung yiu chhùng hrùng-dhang nhe?
Driver	Yhàn-wrai ngró tái-mr̀-dóu nréi!
Mr Wong	Jhèung Shìn-shàang, nréi tái-hráa, nhi dhi jrau hrai Hhèung-góng-yràn deui yhat-bhùn ghùng-grung drit-jreui ge gaau-yruk laak!
Mr Cheung	Mrúi go sré-wúi dhou yraú-yhat-dhi wraai-fran-jí, mr̀-hóu wraa go-go yràn dhou yhat-yreung. Hhèung-góng ge gaau-yruk dhou yráu hóu ge fhòng-mrin ge.

政府	**jing-fú**	*government*
教育	**gaau-yruk**	*education; to educate*
市民	**srí-mràn**	*citizen*
失敗	**shat-braai**	*a loss, a failure*
方面	**fhòng-mrin**	*aspect*
一般	**yhat-bhùn**	*general, common, the general run of*
公共	**ghùng-grung**	*public*
秩序	**drit-jreui**	*order*
前便	**chrìn-brin**	*in front; the front side*
警察	**gíng-chaat**	*policeman*
檢控	**gím-hung**	*accuse*
汽車	**hei-chhe**	*vehicle, car*
司機	**shi-ghei**	*driver*
盞	**jáan**	*(classifier for lamps and lights)*
交通燈	**ghàau-thùng-dhang**	*traffic light*
交通	**ghàau-thùng**	*traffic, communications*
燈	**dhang**	*a light*
衝	**chhùng**	*to rush, dash against*
社會	**sré-wúi**	*society*
壞	**wraai**	*bad*
份子	**fran-jí**	*element, member*

 ———————— **Grammar** ————————

6 Colours

Hrùng-dhang is *a red light*. The other important traffic light colour is **lruk** (*green*), and **lruk-dhang** is *a green light*. It will help you to introduce all the major colours now. You should note that they work with **-shik ge** in the same way as does **hrùng** (see Unit 5, grammar point 6).

braak-shik	*white*	**hrùng-shik**	*red*
cháng-shik	*orange*	**jí-shik**	*purple*
fhui-shik	*grey*	**lràam-shik**	*blue*
gaa-fhe-shik	*brown*	**lruk-shik**	*green*
gham-shik	*gold*	**ngràn-shik**	*silver*
hhaak-shik or		**wròng-shik**	*yellow*
hhak-shik	*black*		

Colour symbolism in Chinese culture

The dominant colour in Chinese culture is red. It stands for happiness and good luck. Brides traditionally dress in red and weep into red handkerchiefs, their grooms wear red sashes, and the house where they set up home is decorated with auspicious sayings written on red paper. White is the colour for funerals (although most people wear a flash of something red about them in order to offset the bad luck which surrounds death and burial). Yellow was the Imperial colour, and the roofs of the Forbidden City in Beijing are still covered with yellow tiles. Yellow also stands for China, prob ably because it is the colour of the loess soil which covers the northern homeland of the Chinese, the same soil which is carried along by the Yellow River and deposited in the Yellow Sea. You will have noticed that the word for brown is *coffee colour*, clearly a comparatively recent import. In traditional colour schemes, red ran into yellow uninterrupted by brown, and browns were classified either as **hrùng** or **wròng**. What English calls a brown cow, Cantonese calls a **wròng-ngràu**, and dark tan shoes are deemed to be **hrùng-shik**.

---

7 Telling your whereabouts

In the dialogue you met the word **chrìn-brin** (*in front, in front of, the front side*). Other associated expressions include:

hrau-brin	*the back, behind, the rear side*
sreung-brin	*the top, on top of, above, the top side*

hraa-brin	*the underneath, under, beneath, the underside*
jó-(sáu-)brin	*on the left, the left(-hand) side*
yrau-(sáu-)brin	*on the right, the right(-hand) side*
lréui-brin or **yrap-brin**	*inside, in, the inside*
ngroi-brin or **chheut-brin**	*outside, out, the outside*
dhùng-brin	*the east side*
nràam-brin	*the south side*
shài-brin	*the west side*
bhak-brin	*the north side*
deui-mrin	*opposite, the opposite side*

Note that **deui-mrin** is exceptional in that **-brin** is replaced by **-mrin**. All these whereabouts words combine happily with **hái** (*at, in, on; to be at, to be in, to be on*):

Kréui *hái* **lréui-brin.**	*She is inside.*
Ghàan qhuk *hái* **fhèi-ghèi-chrèung** *nràam-brin.*	*The house is on the south side of the airport.*
Brou shùe *hái* **sho-fáa-yrí** *sreung-brin.*	*The book is on the sofa.*
Wròng Síu-jé *hái* **nréi** *hrau-brin.*	*Miss Wong is behind you.*
Hái **qhuk jó-brin yráu chhe-fròng.**	*There is a garage on the left of the house.*
Chró *hái* **gó ghàan jáu-lràu** *chheut-brin* **yráu lréung go wraai-fran-jí.**	*There are two bad lots sitting outside that restaurant.*

Notice that in the last two examples the verb **yráu** (*to have*) is used to mean *there is* or *there are*. If you have learned French, you will find a similarity with the expression *il-y-a* (*there is, there are*) which also uses the verb *to have*.

Another whereabouts word is **jhùng-ghaan** (*in the middle of, in between*). When it means *in the middle of* it acts just like the other words:

Kréui chró *hái* **fhàa-yúen** *jhùng-ghaan.*	*She is sitting in the middle of the garden.*

However, when it means *in between* it has a pattern all its own (**hái X Y jhùng-ghaan** or **hái X trùng Y jhùng-ghaan**):

Kréui chró *hái* Wròng Shàang (trùng) Chràn Táai *jhùng-ghaan*.

She is sitting between Mr Wong and Mrs Chan.

 —————————— **Exercises** ——————————

1 Go back and read the first dialogue of this unit just once more. Then without looking at it again try to choose from the brackets the words which will complete the following sentences correctly.

   (*a*) **Wròng Shìn-shàang wraa dhi hrok-shaang ge fo-bún (yrau gwai yrau leng/yrau prèng yrau shàn/yrau chrúng yrau dhò).**

   (*b*) **Lréi Taai-táai go jái mráan-mráan dhou yiu whàn-jraap (sei go jhung-tràu/shàam go jhung-tràu/yhat go jhung-tràu).**

   (*c*) **Wròng Shìn-shàang wraa gaau (síu-hrok/jhùng-hrok/draai-hrok) jrung mràa-fràan.**

   (*d*) **Jhèung Shàang wraa hóu-chói kréui-drei mř hrai (gíng-chaat/shi-ghei/gaau-shùe shìn-shàang/jáu-lràu fó-gei).**

2 Imagine you are a worried parent trying to place your son in a Hong Kong school. You have an interview with the Headmaster tomorrow and are preparing some questions to ask him, but you are afraid that your newly acquired language skills will let you down, so you are writing out the following questions in Cantonese on a piece of paper.

   (*a*) *Does my son need to study Chinese?*

   (*b*) *How many hours of homework must he do each evening?*

   (*c*) *My son has studied at junior school in London for five years. British pupils do not go to secondary school until they are eleven years old. Is it the same in Hong Kong?*

   (*d*) *How much a year does it cost to study in your school?*

   (*e*) *Does the pupil need to buy textbooks and exercise books?*

3 Here are the answers which we happen to know the Headmaster will give to your questions, but he is so bored with hearing the same thing from every parent who sees him that he deliberately gives the answers in the wrong order. You will have to

match the answers numbered (i)–(v) below with the questions above before you know what is what, but our advice is to try another school for your son!

(i) **Yiu. Hóu gwai thìm!**

(ii) **Yiu. Kréui yhat go shìng-krèi yiu hrok shàam-srap go jhung-tràu.**

(iii) **Hhèung-góng ge gaau-yruk trùng Yhìng-gwok ge chhàa-mr̀-dho laak.**

(iv) **Mr̀-sái hóu dhò jhe. Ngŕ-lruk go jhung-tràu jhe.**

(v) **Mr̀-sái hóu dhò jhe. Yhat nrìn sei-baak-mraan mhan jhe.**

4 Describe the scene you see here by answering the questions in Cantonese.

(*a*) **Hái qhuk ngroi-brin yráu mhat-yré qaa?**

(*b*) **Wròng Shàang hái Wròng Táai bhin-brin qaa?**

(*c*) **Brou shùe hái bhin-drou qaa?**

(*d*) **Nréi gwú Wròng Shàang Wròng Táai jrou-yrùen mhat-yré fhàan-lrài qaa?**

(*e*) **Hái Wròng Táai chrìn-brin yráu mhat-yré qaa?**

(*f*) **Nréi gei mr̀ gei-dhak gó go mrit-fó-túng hrai bhin-go mráai gaa?**

(*g*) **Wròng Shàang Wròng Táai go jái hái bhin-drou qaa?**

(*h*) **Nréi wraa Wròng Táai hhòi mr̀ hhòi-sham qaa?**

13

第十三課 投機
TRÀU-GHÈI
Speculation

This unit contains a lot of new vocabulary, but by way of compensation the new grammar is uncomplicated and should give you no problems. Speculation is a big part of Cantonese life, so do not be afraid that the vocabulary will be of no use to you!

——————— Dialogue 1 ———————

Mr Cheung lets slip that he is not entirely immune to Hong Kong's passion for gambling.

昨日電台嘅新聞廣播話，舊年香港市民投注喺賽馬嘅錢有一百三十二
　　億元，入馬場嘅人數係三百二十萬人！

嘩！香港人真係有錢嘞。張先生，你中唔中意賭馬㗎。

唔中意。賭馬、賭狗、賭啤牌、賭股票......樣樣我都唔中意。

你真係乖嘞！喺香港好似你一樣嘅人而家真係好少嘞。

有人話，香港咁繁榮係同香港人中意賭錢有關係嘅噃！你話啱唔啱呀？

我話冇關係，但係賭錢同罪案嘅增加就有關係嘞。

對唔住，王先生，我而家夠鐘要去參加一個慈善籌款抽獎會。

抽獎會吖！獎品豐唔豐富㗎？

頭獎係一間屋，二獎係一架車。

咦！嗽算唔算係賭錢呢？

Mr Cheung　　Jrok-yrat drin-tròi ge shàn-mràn gwóng-bo wraa,
　　　　　　　　grau-nín Hhèung-góng srí-mràn tràu-jue hái choi-

—— 120 ——

mráa ge chín yráu yhat-baak-shàam-srap-yri-yhik yrùen, yrap mráa-chrèung ge yràn-sou hrai shàam-baak-yri-srap-mraan yràn!

Mr Wong Wràa! Hhèung-góng-yràn jhàn-hrai yráu-chín laak. Jhèung Shìn-shàang, nréi jhùng mř jhùng-yi dóu-mráa gaa?

Mr Cheung Mř jhùng-yi. Dóu-mráa, dóu-gáu, dóu-phe-páai, dóu-gwú-piu . . . yreung-yreung ngró dhou mř jhùng-yi.

Mr Wong Nréi jhàn-hrai gwhàai laak! Hái Hhèung-góng hóu-chrí nréi yhat-yreung ge yràn yrì-ghaa jhàn-hrai hóu síu laak.

Mr Cheung Yráu-yràn wraa, Hhèung-góng gam fràan-wrìng hrai trùng Hhèung-góng-yràn jhùng-yi dóu-chín yráu gwhàan-hrai ge bo! Nréi wraa nghaam mř nghaam qaa?

Mr Wong Ngró wraa mróu gwhàan-hrai, draan-hrai dóu-chín trùng jreui-qon ge jhàng-ghàa jrau yráu gwhàan-hrai laak.

Mr Cheung Deui-mř-jrue, Wròng Shìn-shàang, ngró yrì-ghaa gau-jhung yiu heui chhàam-ghàa yhat go chrì-srin chràu-fún chhàu-jeúng-wúi.

Mr Wong Chhàu-jéung-wúi qràa! Jéung-bán fhùng mř fhùng-fu gaa?

Mr Cheung Tràu-jéung hrai yhat ghàan qhuk, yrì-jéung hrai yhat gaa chhe.

Mr Wong Yí! Gám, suen mř suen hrai dóu-chín nhe?

電台	**drin-tròi**	*radio station*
新聞	**shàn-mràn**	*news*
廣播	**gwóng-bo**	*broadcast*
投注	**tràu-jue**	*to stake, to bet*
賽馬	**choi-mráa**	*to race horses, horse-racing*
馬	**mráa**	*horse*
億	**yhik**	*a hundred million, a billion*
元	**yrùen**	*dollar*
馬場	**mráa-chrèung**	*race-track*
人數	**yràn-sou**	*number of people*
有錢	**yráu-chín**	*rich*
賭馬	**dóu-mráa**	*to bet on horses*
賭	**dóu**	*to gamble on, to bet on*
賭狗	**dóu-gáu**	*to bet on dogs*
狗	**gáu**	*dog*

賭啤牌	dóu-phe-páai	to gamble at cards
啤牌	phe-páai	playing cards
賭股票	dóu-gwú-piu	to gamble on shares
股票	gwú-piu	stocks and shares
樣樣	yreung-yreung	all kinds of, all sorts of
乖	gwhàai	well-behaved, obedient, a 'good boy'/'good girl'
繁榮	fràan-wrìng	prosperous
賭錢	dóu-chín	to gamble with money
關係	gwhàan-hrai	relationship, connection, relevance
啱	nghaam	correct
罪案	jreui-qon	criminal case
增加	jhàng-ghàa	increase, to increase
夠鐘	gau-jhung	time's up, it's time to
慈善	chrì-srin	charity
籌款	chràu-fún	to raise money, fund-raising
抽獎	chhàu-jéung	lucky draw
會	wúi	meeting; club, association
獎品	jéung-bán	prize
豐富	fhùng-fu	rich, abundant
頭獎	tràu-jéung	first prize

The Cantonese as gamblers

The Cantonese have been renowned for their love of gambling for a long time, and they pursue their love with dedication and not infrequently with recklessness. A 19th century missionary reported that in the city of Canton (**Gwóng-jhàu**) the orange sellers would take bets with their customers on the number of pips which the oranges they bought might contain, offering different odds on various numbers. It would hardly be an exaggeration to say that next to eating the favourite pastimes of Hong Kong have for many years been mah-jong and horse-racing, and since the 1960s the stock exchange has become a fourth passion. At weekends high-speed ferries, jet-driven hydrofoils and helicopters carry thousands of Hong Kong people the forty miles to Macau where other forms of gambling are legally available; and many Cantonese high rollers are to be found in casinos all over the world.

Grammar

1 Different dollars

In Unit 5 you learned the word **mhan** for *dollar*. Now you have learned a different word **yrùen** which has the same meaning. There are in fact two different systems for talking about money, a colloquial system (**mhan**) and a more formal written system (**yrùen**). When people write they always use the formal system, and when they speak they usually but not always use the colloquial system. The closest comparison is perhaps the American *dollars* and *bucks* system, where no banknote carries the word *bucks* but where in speech either *bucks* or *dollars* is acceptable. In the dialogue Mr Cheung uses **yrùen** because a figure as large and important as *130 billion* seems to command more formality, and the radio newscaster he is quoting would certainly not descend into the colloquial **mhan** for such an important item. The money system will be explained further in Unit 20.

2 Dropping classifiers

In Mr Cheung's first speech you will notice that he talks of **shàam-baak-yri-srap-mraan yràn** (*3,200,000 people*), but he does not use the classifier **go** which you would expect between the number and the noun. The larger numbers get, the less likely it is that a classifier will be used: as a rule of thumb you can assume that the classifier will be used up to 100 and will seldom be used for numbers greater than 100. However, if you are in doubt put it in; it is never wrong to do so.

3 Striking it rich

The reason why **yráu-chín** means *rich* is clear enough – it comes from *having money*. But notice that although **yráu-chín** is made up of a verb plus a noun (**yráu** + **chín**) it behaves like any other adjective:

Hrò Shìn-shàang hóu yráu-chín.	*Mr Ho is very rich.*
Yráu-chín yràn chró hái chhe hrau-brin.	*The rich ride in the back.*

4 The same, almost the same *and* related to

In the dialogue Mr Cheung says *trùng* **Hhéung-góng-yràn jhùng-yi dóu-chín** *yráu gwhàan-hrai* (*is related to Hong Kong people's loving to gamble*). Notice how **trùng** introduces the construction. You have met similar constructions before, and you might like to consolidate your understanding of them here:

hóu-chrí **jáu-lràu ge** **yhat-yreung**	*seems like restaurant food* (Unit 4)
trùng **dhi sho-fáa-yí ge** **bou-líu** *yhat-yreung*	*the same as the material of the sofa* (Unit 11)
hóu-chrí **sei-srap seui** **gam-sreung-háa**	*seem like about forty* (Unit 9)
trùng **Yhìng-gwok ge** **chhàa-mr̀-dho**	*almost like the British* (Unit 12)

 ───────── **Dialogue 2** ─────────

 Why Mr Chan is welcomed at the mah-jong table.

老陳,你咁中意去澳門賭錢,老實話俾我聽,你贏錢嘅時候多定係輸錢嘅時候多呢?

當然係贏錢嘅時候多喇。但係每次都係贏少少啫。

你中意賭輪盤定係廿一點呀?

兩樣都唔中意;我中意賭番攤。

你去賭場定係喺屋企賭錢呀?

我有時去賭場,有時喺屋企,但係我一定唔去大檔賭錢,因為係非法嘅。

噉,賭波同賭外匯呢?

我估你話"賭波"就係賭英國足球嘞。呢樣嘢我冇興趣。賭外匯就一定要有好多本錢。所以兩樣都唔適合我。

香港人最中意打麻雀嘅嘞;噉你呢?

我覺得打麻雀最好玩,最吸引我,但係我好少贏錢嘅。

真好嘞!下個禮拜如果你得閒請嚟我屋企,我哋一齊打場麻雀喇!

Mr Lee	Lróu Chán, nréi gam jhùng-yi heui Qou-mún dóu-chín, lróu-srat wraa béi ngró thèng, nréi yrèng chín ge srì-hrau dhò dring-hrai shùe chín ge srì-hrau dhò nhe?
Mr Chan	Dhòng-yín hrai yrèng chín ge srì-hrau dhò lhaa. Draan-hrai mrúi chi dhou hrai yrèng síu-síu jhe.

Mr Lee	Nréi jhùng-yi dóu lrèun-pún dring-hrai yraa-yhat-dím qaa?
Mr Chan	Lréung yreung dhou mr̀ jhùng-yi; ngró jhùng-yi dóu fhaan-thaan.
Mr Lee	Nréi heui dóu-chrèung dring-hrai hái qhuk-kéi dóu-chín qaa?
Mr Chan	Ngró yráu-srì heui dóu-chrèung, yráu-srì hái qhuk-kéi, draan-hrai ngró yhat-dring mr̀ heui draai-dong dóu-chín, yhàn-wrai hrai fhèi-faat ge.
Mr Lee	Gám, dóu-bho trùng dóu ngroi-wrui nhe?
Mr Chan	Ngró gwú nréi wraa 'dóu-bho' jrau hrai dóu Yhìng-gwok jhuk-kràu laak. Nhi yreung yré ngró mróu hing-cheui. Dóu-ngroi-wrui jrau yhat-dring yiu yráu hóu dhò bún-chrìn. Só-yrí lréung yreung dhou mr̀ shik-hrap ngró.
Mr Lee	Hhèung-góng-yràn jeui jhùng-yi dáa-mràa-jeuk ge laak: gám nréi nhe?
Mr Chan	Ngró gok-dhak dáa-mràa-jeuk jeui hóu-wáan, jeui khap-yrán ngró, draan-hrai ngró hóu síu yrèng chín ge.
Mr Lee	Jhàn hóu laak! Hraa-go-lrái-baai yrùe-gwó nréi dhak-hràan chéng lrài ngró qhuk-kéi, ngró-drei yhat-chrài dáa chrèung mràa-jeuk lhaa!

澳門	**Qou-mún**	*Macau*
老實	**lróu-srat**	*honest, honestly*
贏	**yrèng**	*to win*
定係	**dring-hrai**	*or, or rather*
輸	**shùe**	*to lose*
當然	**dhòng-yín**	*of course*
輪盤	**lrèun-pún**	*roulette*
廿一點	**yraa-yhat-dím**	*blackjack, pontoon*
樣	**yreung**	*kind, sort, type*
番攤	**fhaan-thaan**	*fantan*
賭場	**dóu-chrèung**	*casino*
有時	**yráu-srì**	*sometimes*
大檔	**draai-dong**	*gambling den*
非法	**fhèi-faat**	*illegal*
賭波	**dóu-bho**	*to bet on football*
賭外匯	**dóu-ngroi-wrui**	*to gamble on foreign exchange*
外匯	**ngroi-wrui**	*foreign exchange*
足球	**jhuk-kràu**	*soccer*
興趣	**hing-cheui**	*interest*
本錢	**bún-chrìn**	*capital*
適合	**shik-hrap**	*suitable to, fitting*

打麻雀	**dáa mràa-jeuk**	to play mah-jong
好玩	**hóu-wáan**	good fun, amusing, enjoyable
吸引	**khap-yrán**	to attract
得閒	**dhak-hràan**	to be free, at leisure
場	**chrèung**	(classifier for performances, bouts, games)

 ———— **Grammar** ————

5 Telling options

In Unit 6 you met **wraa . . . thèng** meaning *to inform someone, to tell someone about something*, and in Unit 8 you were told that **wraa . . . jhì** meant the same. Now you can add some more variants, because **gong** (*to speak*), which you met in Unit 9, can be substituted for **wraa** in either of the above two phrases, and you can include **béi** (*to*) in any of them. So all of the following forms mean the same – *she tells me* . . . :

Kréui wraa ngró thèng . . .   Kréui wraa béi ngró thèng . . .
Kréui wraa ngró jhì . . .   Kréui wraa béi ngró jhì . . .
Kréui góng ngró thèng . . .   Kréui góng béi ngró thèng . . .
Kréui góng ngró jhì . . .   Kréui góng béi ngró jhì . . .

6 Dring-hrai (or rather)

Dring-hrai nicely translates *or* when a question is being asked, and the final particle **nhe?** is usually included to back it up:

Kréui hrai Jhùng-gwok-yràn
dring-hrai Yrat-bún-yràn
nhe?

Is she Chinese or Japanese?

Nréi Lrái-baai-yhat
dring-hrai Lrái-baai-yri
heui Qou-mún nhe?

*Is it Monday or Tuesday
that you are going to
Macau?*

Nréi séung srik ngràu-yruk
dring-hrai jhùe-yruk nhe?

*Which do you want to have,
beef or pork?*

But remember that it is only in questions that **dring-hrai** will translate as *or*. If you think back to Unit 10, grammar point 4 you will remember that *seven or eight people* was translated by **chhat-baat**

go yràn. The difference can be shown by comparing the following two examples:

Gó-drou yráu chhat-baat go yràn.	*There are (approximately) seven or eight people over there.*
Gó-drou yráu chhat dring-hrai baat go yràn nhe?	*Are there seven or eight people over there, which is it?*

7 Blackjack teaches you numbers!

The card game blackjack, sometimes known as pontoon or *vingt-et-un*, is popular amongst the Cantonese, who call it **yraa-yhat-dím** (*21 spots*). **Dím** means *a dot, a spot*, and **yraa-yhat** is an alternative way of saying **yri-srap-yhat** (*twenty-one*). Here is a list of the alternative forms of numbers, all of which really consist of nothing more than slurring over the word **srap** in numbers above twenty:

yri-srap-yhat	=	**yri-qraa-yhat**	=	**yraa-yhat**	= **yre-yhat**
shàam-srap-yhat	=	**shàam-qraa-yhat**	=	**shàa-qraa-yhat**	
sei-srap-yhat	=	**sei-qraa-yhat**			
ngŕ-srap-yhat	=	**ngŕ-qraa-yhat**			
lruk-srap-yhat	=	**lruk-qraa-yhat**			
chhat-srap-yhat	=	**chhat-qraa-yhat**			
baat-srap-yhat	=	**baat-qraa-yhat**			
gáu-srap-yhat	=	**gáu-qraa-yhat**			

We have only shown 21, 31, 41, etc., but the same short cuts work for 22, 32, 42, . . . and any other such number up to 99. You can use these alternatives quite freely provided you observe one rule – you should not use the short cuts for the round numbers 20, 30, 40, . . . 90, which are almost always given in their full **yri-srap, shàam-srap, sei-srap, . . . gáu-srap** form.

8 Making adjectives with **hóu**

In the dialogue you met the word **hóu-wáan** (*good fun, enjoyable*). You may have realised that this is a new word made up of two that you already know: **hóu** (*good*) and **wáan** (*to play, enjoy, amuse oneself*), and hence *good to enjoy, good to play*. If you are brave enough, you can make up such words for yourself. Here are a few common ones:

hóu-srik	lit. *good to eat*	= *delicious*
hóu-yám	lit. *good to drink*	= *delicious*
hóu-tái	lit. *good to look at*	= *good-looking, attractive*
hóu-thèng	lit. *good to listen to*	= *harmonious, melodic*

9 At leisure

Dhak-hràan literally means *attaining leisure*, and so *not busy*. In Unit 10 you learned the word **mròng** (*busy*). The Cantonese usually seem to like to take short cuts with their language, but many people prefer to say **mr̀ dhak-hràan** and **hóu mr̀ dhak-hràan** rather than **mròng** and **hóu mròng** despite the extra syllables involved.

10 Another short cut: dropping yhat

In the dialogue Mr Lee delightedly invites Mr Chan to **dáa chrèung mràa-jeuk lhaa!** (*have a round of mah-jong*). You might have expected the Cantonese to read **dáa yhat chrèung mràa-jeuk lhaa!**, and of course that would be grammatically correct, but quite often **yhat** is missed out when it comes between a verb and a classifier with its noun:

| srik chhàan fraan | *have a meal* |
| mráai gaa chhe | *buy a car* |

Mah-jong and fantan

Fantan is a Chinese gambling game which consists of guessing how many stones will be left when a random pile is diminished by taking away four stones at a time – that is, the gamblers bet on whether there will be one, two, three or four stones left at the end. There is no skill involved at all, it is just a pure gamble. Mah-jong is played by four players with heavy plastic or bone tiles which are crashed down onto a deliberately resonant table to enhance the noise and excitement. It can be equally well played with paper cards, but that would be quiet and far less fun! Luck plays its part, but skilled players have an advantage over unskilled players. While *to play fantan* is called **dóu-fhaan-thaan**, the far more active process of playing mah-jong is called **dáa-mràa-jeuk**.

Exercises

1 In the following sentences interchange **mròng** and **dhak-hràan** without altering the sense.

    (*a*)   Chràn Táai ghàm-mráan hóu mròng.
    (*b*)   Ngró bràa-bhaa srèng-nrìn dhou mròng.
    (*c*)   Mr̀-ghòi nréi wraa béi ngró thèng nréi go jái thìng-
         yrat dhak mr̀ dhak-hràan qaa?
    (*d*)   Kréui Lrái-baai-yri hóu mr̀ dhak-hràan.
    (*e*)   Ngró jeui mròng ge srì-hrau hrai jhìu-jóu.

2 Insert the correct classifiers in the gaps below.

    (*a*)   ____ Jhùng-mràn shùe dhou hrai Hrò Ṣhàang ge.
    (*b*)   Hái gó ____ qhuk chrìn-brin yráu ngŕ ____ jhùe-jái.
    (*c*)   Jrok-yrat gó ____ jhuk-kràu hóu hóu-tái qràa.
    (*d*)   Bhin lréung ____ chhe hrai Chràn Shàang mráai gaa?

3 From list (*a*) find the words which are the opposites of the words in list (*b*).

    (*a*)   gwhàai, síu-síu, tràu-jue, dhak-hràan, shùe, shàn-
         fú, shìn-shàang, jhàng-ghàa, srí-mràn, gwóng-bo, srì-
         srì, fhèi-ghèi, drin-wáa.
    (*b*)   mròng, shùe-fruk, gaan-jhung, yrèng, hrok-shaang,
         jing-fú, fhùng-fu, gáam-síu.

4

`Gáu hrou!
Gáu hrou!´

(a) Nréi gwú hrai Wròng Shàang yrèng chín dring-hrai Wròng Táai yrèng chín nhe?

(b) Wròng Shìn-shàang hóu hhòi-sham, hrai mr̀ hrai qaa?

(c) Drai-lruk jek mráa hrai géi-dho hrou qaa?

(d) Bhin jek mráa yrèng qaa?

(e) Nréi wraa hrai Wròng Taai-táai hóu shik dóu-mráa dring-hrai Wròng Shìn-shàang hóu shik dóu-mráa nhe?

(f) Sei hrou mráa hóu-gwo gáu hrou mráa, nghaam mr̀ nghaam qaa?

(g) Shàam hrou mráa nhe? Hóu mr̀ hóu-gwo gáu hrou qaa?

(h) Jeui hóu gó jek mráa hrai mr̀ hrai lruk hrou mráa qaa?

(i) Nhi yhat chrèung choi-mráa yráu géi-dho jek mráa qaa?

(j) Wròng Shìn-shàang dóu-mráa mrúi chrèung dhou jhùng-yi dóu hóu draai, yrùe-gwó yrèng jrau yrèng hóu dhò, shùe jrau shùe hóu dhò. Wròng Táai mr̀ hrai gám ge, kréui chrèung-chrèung dhou dóu hóu sai jhe. Gám, nréi gwú, nhi chrèung kréui-drei hrai shùe dhò-gwo yrèng dring-hrai yrèng dhò-gwo shuè nhe?

14

第十四課　溫習（二）
— WHÀN-JRAAP (YRI) —
Revision (2)

Another six units under your belt. It all gets more interesting now; you can say so many more things and begin to have some flexibility in your use of language. Remember that what you are learning is a living, colourful language spoken by a very dynamic people, not a bookish, sober exercise in style and complex grammar. Try to speak what you learn so that you can hear the cadences and become familiar with the zest of it. Cantonese people enjoy life, they talk loudly and laugh a lot – a Cantonese whisper is almost a contradiction in terms. Start by reading this first passage through, then read it aloud several times until it begins to feel part of you. Even better, learn it off by heart so that you can recite it.

——————————— Passage 1 ———————————

Wròng Shìn-shàang chhat seui ge jái jrok-yrat fhàan hrok-hraau gó-jran-srì hóu hhòi-sham gám wraa ngró jhì, kréui bràa-bhaa sreung-go-lrái-baai mráai-jó yhat ghàan shàn qhuk. Gó ghàan qhuk yrau draai yrau leng, yráu shàam ghàan fan-fóng*, ghàan qhuk chrìn-brin jrung yráu go fhàa-yúen trùng-mràai yhat ghàan chhe-fròng thìm. Kréui wraa: 'Yrì-ghaa ngró yhat-go-yràn yrung yhat ghàan fan-fóng, jhàn-hrai shùe-fruk laak. Draan-hrai mràa-mhaa jrau yiu trùng bràa-bhaa yhat-chrài yrung yhat ghàan. Ngró gwú mràa-mhaa yhat-dring

mŕ hhòi-sham laak. Ngró mŕ jhì dím-gáai bràa-bhaa mŕ béi
mràa-mhaa yrung drai-shàam ghàan fan-fóng nhe? Gó ghàan
fan-fóng yrì-ghaa mróu yràn yrung, jí-hrai bràa-bhaa jhài-jó
hóu dhò shùe hái gó-sue jhe.'

*fan-fóng = *bedroom*

 ———————— **Exercises** ————————

1 Try to answer these questions now without referring back to
the passage.

(a) **Wròng Shìn-shàang ge jái géi-dho seui qaa?**

(b) **Wròng Shàang sreung-go-shìng-krèi mráai-jó mhat-
yré qaa?**

(c) **Qhuk chrìn-brin yráu dhi mhat-yré qaa?**

(d) **Bhin-go yràn yiu trùng bràa-bhaa yhat-chrài yrung
yhat ghàan fan-fóng qaa?**

(e) **Drai-shàam ghàan fan-fóng lréui-brin yráu dhi mhat-
yré qaa?**

(f) **Yráu mróu yràn yrung drai-shàam ghàan fan-fóng qaa?**

2 It is time to remind you that you should be paying attention to
your tones: if you don't you will never sound like a Cantonese!
Put the correct tone marks on the following words. Those you
have forgotten you will have to look up, but that at least will
help to cement them in your mind.

(a)	**hhei-mrong**	(e)	**drin-ying**	(i)	**grin-hhong**
(b)	**thin-hei**	(f)	**wran-drung**	(j)	**nroi-yrung**
(c)	**lraang-thin**	(g)	**ghei-yruk**	(k)	**siu-lreun**
(d)	**daa-suen**	(h)	**dho-yrue**	(l)	**pring-gwhan**

3 Hunt the **yrat**. All the words here use **yrat** (*sun* or *day*). What
are they?

(a)	tomorrow	(d)	the whole day	(g)	today
(b)	Sunday	(e)	yesterday	(h)	every day
(c)	the day before yesterday	(f)	Japan	(i)	the day after tomorrow

4 The following sentence pairs differ by only one word, but the
sense changes a great deal. Try to translate them into English
in a way which will bring out the meanings clearly.

(a)   (i)   **Drai-yhat jek mráa jhik-hrai gáu hrou mráa.**

     (ii)   **Drai-yhat jek mráa mr̀ hrai gáu hrou mráa.**

(b)   (i)   **Jhùng-shàan Síu-jé jing-hrai Yrat-bún-yràn.**

     (ii)   **Jhùng-shàan Síu-jé jhàn-hrai Yrat-bún-yràn.**

(c)   (i)   **Kréui thìng-yrat jrau heui Gwóng-jhàu.**

     (ii)   **Kréui thìng-yrat shìn-ji heui Gwóng-jhàu.**

(d)   (i)   **Chràn Taai-táai heui-gwo Mréi-gwok srap-géi chi laak.**

     (ii)   **Chràn Taai-táai heui-gwo Mréi-gwok géi-srap chi laak.**

5   Choose the right item from the brackets to complete the sense of the following sentences.

(a)   **Yhat go yràn yrung yhat ghàan fan-fóng hóu (shàn-fú, yráu-méng, yráu-yrung, shùe-fruk).**

(b)   **Chhe-fròng yrung lrài (jhài shùe ge, júe-fraan ge, wran-drung ge, trìng-chhe ge).**

(c)   **Hái gó ghàan ghung-shi jrou-yré hóu hóu yhàn-wrai wrúi yráu (hóu dhò chín, mr̀ shik júe-sung, hóu síu chín, hóu mràa-fràan).**

6   Make one sentence out of each of the following sentence pairs using the words in brackets to make the link and by making whatever other slight adjustments are necessary. For instance, the first pair would give the sentence **Kréui sréung-tròng jhì-chrin, srì-srì dhou heui taam kréui nràam pràng-yráu.**

(a)   **Kréui sréung-tròng. Kréui srì-srì dhou heui taam kréui nràam-pràng-yráu. (jhì-chrin)**

(b)   **Wròng Táai séung mráai gó gaa chhe. Gaa chhe hóu leng. (yhàn-wrai)**

(c)   **Ngró mr̀ mrìng-braak. Gó go yràn lráang-thin séung mráai lráang-hei-ghèi. (jrou-mhat-yré?)**

(d)   **Gó dhi hhaa mr̀ shàn-shìn. Chràn Táai mr̀ séung mráai. (só-yrí)**

(e)   **Kréui srik-gán yré. Kréui mr̀ góng-wáa. (ge srì-hrau)**

7   Here are the answers to some questions. What were the questions?

(a)   **Mráai gó gaa chhe yiu *srap-ngŕ-mraan mhan jhe.***

(b)   **Wròng Shàang *Shìng-krèi-lruk* lrèi-hhòi Yrat-bún.**

(c) **Hái Lréi Táai jó-sáu-brin gó jek gáu-jái hrai *Lréi Shìn-shàang* sung béi kréui ge.**

(d) **Gó dhi yràn *ji-hrai Hrò Síu-jé* gaau-shùe jhe.**

8 Try to solve this simple crossword puzzle.

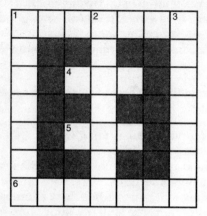

Across

1 **Trùng 'srì-hrau' yhat-yreung. (3–4)**
4 **____-ghòu-mhàu-dhài. (3)**
5 **Dóu jhuk-kràu jhik-hrai dóu ____. (3)**
6 **Yráu-méng ge draai-hrok. (3–4)**

Down

1 **Yruè-gwó nréi yrung sáu dáa hóu ngraang ge yré nréi jrau wrúi gok-dhak hóu ____. (3–4)**
2 **Yrùe-gwó nréi séung hrok Jhùng-mràn nréi yiu ____ hóu dhò yré. (3–4)**
3 **'Gó-sue' ge shèung-fáan. (3–4)**

Passage 2

This little anecdote finishes with a pun. You may as well get used to this – Cantonese people love punning. The particular pun involved is one that all gamblers know about, and it is safe to say that no one other than the naïve Mr Ho would have taken the bad advice which his wife gives him here!

Hrò Shìn-shàang Mráai-Mráa

Yrùe-gwó yhat go yráu-chín yràn séung mráai mráa, kréui jrau heui mráai mráa, draan-hrai gám-yéung mráai mráa hóu gwai bo! Hái Hhèung-góng nréi srì-srì dhou wrúi thèng-dóu mróu chín ge yràn dhou wraa 'Ghàm-yrat ngró séung mráai-mráa.' Dím-gáai nhe? Nréi gwú-hráa, mróu chín ge yràn wraa 'mráai-mráa' hrai mhat-yré nhe? Nghaam laak, 'mráai-mráa' jhik-hrai 'dóu-mráa', só-yrí mróu chín ge yràn wraa kréui séung heui mráai-mráa jhik-hrai wraa kréui séung heui dóu-mráa.

Hrò Shìn-shàang mr̀ hrai hóu yráu-chín. Yráu yhat yrat kréui ge hóu pràng-yráu Jhèung Shìn-shàang dáa-drin-wáa lrài mran kréui: 'Ghàm-mráan choi-mráa. Ngró séung chéng nréi trùng ngró yhat-chrài heui mráa-chrèung wáan-hráa, nréi wraa hóu m̀ hóu nhe?' Hrò Shàang hóu hhòi-sham gám wraa: 'Hóu! Hóu! Hóu júe-yi!'

Thèng-yrùen drin-wáa jhì-hrau kréui wraa béi Hrò Táai thèng. Hrò Táai wraa: 'Nréi mróu heui-gwo tái choi-mráa, nhi chi hrai nréi drai-yhat chi jhe. M̀ jhì-dou nréi wrúi m̀ wrúi jhùng-yi tái nhe?' Hrò Shàang wraa: 'Qhòu! Hrai bo! Hrai ngró drai-yhat chi heui tái choi-mráa bo! Yrùe-gwó m̀ jhùng-yi tái, gám ngró yiu chró hái-drou, mróu yré jrou bo! Dím-suen-hóu-nhe?*' Hrò Táai wraa: 'Nréi jeui hóu mráai bún shùe shìn-ji heui mráa-chrèung laak. Nréi yrùe-gwó gok-dhak tái choi-mráa hóu-wáan, jrau hó-yrí m̀-sái tái-shùe. Yrùe-gwó-m̀-hrai-nhe, gám nréi jrau hó-yrí chró hái-drou tái-shùe lhaa. Nréi wraa hóu m̀ hóu nhe?' Hrò Shàang hóu gwhàai: taai-táai wraa mhat-yré, kréui jrau jrou mhat-yré. Dhòng-yín kréui gó mráan heui mráa-chrèung jhì-chrìn mráai-jó bún shùe shìn.

Hóu-chói Hrò Shìn-shàang gok-dhak choi-mráa dhou-géi hóu-wáan, m̀-sái tái-shùe. Draan-hrai kréui yhat-dhi chín dhou mróu yrèng, shèung-fáan jrung shùe-jó hó dhò chín thìm! Kréui fhàan qhuk-kéi, hóu nhàu gám wraa béi taai-táai thèng: 'Ngró drai-yri chi heui dóu-mráa m̀ wrúi thèng nréi góng

laak! Mráai-mráa yiu mráai yrèng, mr̀-hóu mráai shùe qhaa-máa!'

* **Dím-suen-hóu-nhe?** = *What's to be done about it? What can I do?*

 ———————— **Exercise** ————————

9 That second passage was just to get you used to the idea of puns and wordplay. When you are sure that you understand how the pun worked, try this one. This time the only clue you have is a hyphen!

Jhèung Shìn-shàang yràu gáu-chrèung dóu-gáu fhàan qhuk-kéi. Kréui go jái mran kréui:
'Bràa-bhaa, nréi ghàm-yrat dóu-chín dím qaa? Yrèng mr̀ yrèng chín qaa?'
'Srap chrèung gáu chrèung yrèng!'
'Wràa! Bràa-bhaa, nréi jhàn-hrai hóu shik dóu-chín qaa. Dóu srap chrèung jí-hrai shùe yhat chrèung.'
'Lróu-srat góng, ngró yhat-dhi chín dhou mróu yrèng. Ngró dóu srap chrèung dhou hrai gáu-chrèung yrèng bo!'

15

第十五課　旅遊
LRÉUI-YRÀU

Travelling

Here you will find useful vocabulary for the traveller, and a very important grammar pattern which helps you to describe the way in which actions are performed.

──────── Dialogue 1 ────────

Mrs Lee talks of an inclusive hotel deal.

李太，你行得咁快，趕住去邊處呀？

我趕住去買旅遊飛啫。旅遊公司而家舉辦一個"澳門兩日遊"節目，
　喺澳門玩兩日一晚，費用只係一千蚊之嘛。

咁平，我唔信。呢個旅遊節目有啲乜嘢服務同享受呢？

日頭有啲乜嘢服務同享受我唔知，但係夜晚喺五星級酒店住一晚就已
　經好抵嘞。呢啲酒店房間當然唔少得有電視機喇、雪櫃喇、雙人床
　喇、洗身房喇，酒店重有暖水泳池等等。

李太，你對澳門嘅酒店服務同設備都好熟識嘛！

當然喇，我係澳門一間大酒店嘅公關經理嘛。

你係內行人都話呢個旅遊節目抵玩，嗽我都去買飛參加囉。

Mr Chan	Lréi Táai, nréi hràang-dhak gam faai, gón-jrue heui bhin-sue qaa?
Mrs Lee	Ngró gón-jrue heui mráai lréui-yràu fhei jhe. Lréui-yràu ghung-shi yrì-ghaa géui-braan yhat go 'Qou-mún lréung yrat yràu' jit-mruk, hái Qou-mún wáan lréung

yrat yhat mráan, fai-yrung jí-hrai yhat-chhìn mhan jhì-
mráa.

Mr Chan Gam prèng, ngró mɾ̀ seun. Nhi go lréui-yràu jit-mruk
yráu dhi mhat-yré fruk-mrou trùng héung-srau nhe?

Mrs Lee Yrat-táu yráu dhi mhat-yré fruk-mrou trùng héung-
srau ngró mɾ̀ jhì, draan-hrai yre-máan hái ngɾ̀-shing-
khap jáu-dim jrue yhat mráan jɾ̀au yrí-ghìng hóu dái
laak. Nhi dhi jáu-dim fròng-ghàan dhòng-yín mɾ̀-síu-
dhak yráu drin-sri-ghèi lhaa, suet-gwrai lhaa, shèung-
yràn-chròng lhaa, sái-shàn-fóng lhaa; jáu-dim jrung
yráu nrúen-séui wring-chrì, dáng-dáng.

Mr Chan Lréi Táai, nréi deui Qou-mún ge jáu-dim fruk-mrou
trùng chit-brei dhou hóu sruk-shik bo!

Mrs Lee Dhòng-yín lhaa, ngró hrai Qou-mún yhat ghàan draai
jáu-dim ge ghùng-gwhàan ghìng-lréi bo.

Mr Chan Nréi hrai nroi-hóng-yràn dhou wràa nhi go lréui-yràu
jit-mruk dái wáan, gám ngró dhou heui mráai fhei
chhàam-ghàa lo.

行(路)	hràang(-lrou)	to walk
......得	-dhak	(verb ending: *in such a way that*)
快	faai	*quick, quickly, fast*
趕住	gón-jrue	*hurrying to*
旅遊	lréui-yràu	*to travel; tourism*
飛	fhei	*ticket, fare*
舉辦	géui-braan	*to run, hold, conduct*
遊	yràu	*a tour, to tour*
節目	jit-mruk	*programme*
費用	fai-yrung	*cost, fee*
服務	fruk-mrou	*service, to give service*
享受	héung-srau	*to enjoy; enjoyment, entertainment, treat*
日頭	yrat-táu	*daytime, by day*
夜晚	yre-máan	*night-time, at night*
五星級	ngɾ̀-shing-khap	*five-star grade, top class*
酒店	jáu-dim	*hotel*
抵	dái	*to be worth it, a bargain, a good buy*
房間	fròng-ghàan	*a room*
唔少得	mɾ̀-síu-dhak	*not less than, must be at least*
電視機	drin-sri-ghèi	*television set*
雪櫃	suet-gwrai	*refrigerator*
雙人床	shèung-yràn-chròng	*double bed*

床	chròng	bed
洗身房	sái-shàn-fóng	bathroom
洗身	sái-shàn	to bath (lit. *to wash the body*)
洗	sái	to wash
暖	nrúen	warm
泳池	wring-chrì	swimming pool
等等	dáng-dáng	etc., and so on facilities, appointments, equipment
熟識	sruk-shik	familiar with, well acquainted with
公關	ghùng-gwhàan	public relations
經理	ghìng-lréi	manager
內行人、行內人	nroi-hóng-yràn or hròng-nroi-yràn	insider, expert
囉	lo	(final particle: agreement with previous speaker; strong emotion)

Check on yourself. See if you have understood the dialogue by trying to give answers in Cantonese to these questions.

(a) **Jáu-dim fròng-ghàan lréui-brin yráu mróu lráang-hei-ghèi qaa? Mrit-fó-túng nhe?**

(b) **Mhat-yré hrai 'ngŕ-shing-khap' jáu-dim qaa?**

(c) **Ngŕ-shing-khap jáu-dim lréui-brin yráu mróu chán-só qaa? Wran-drung-fóng nhe?**

 ──────── **Grammar** ────────

1 To walk

Hràang means *to walk*. It is a 'lonely verb', and the normal object supplied for it is **lrou** (*road*), so **hràang-lrou** also means *to walk*. You met **lrou** in **mráa-lrou** (Unit 6). **Mráa-lrou** literally means *horse road* and generally is used for a main road, while **lrou** is used for any grade of road or path. You might note two other common uses of **hràang**:

| **hràang-shàan** | (lit. *walk hills*) to go for a country walk |
| **hràang-ghaai** | (lit. *walk street*) to go out into the streets |

2 Making adverbs with the verb ending -dhak

Adding -**dhak** to a verb enables you to describe in what way that verb is performed, that is, it provides you with a way of forming adverbs. It might be helpful to think of -**dhak** as meaning something like *in such a way that, to the extent that*:

Kréui hràang-dhak faai.	*He walks quickly. (lit. He walks in such a way that it is quick.)*
Nréi góng-dhak nghaam.	*You spoke correctly.*
Wròng Síu-jé jeuk-dhak leng.	*Miss Wong is dressed beautifully.*

Each of these three examples converts a simple adjective into an adverb, but what comes after -**dhak** does not have to be so simple. In fact, this is a very flexible pattern, as the following examples show:

Kréui hràang-dhak hóu faai.	*He walks very quickly.*
Kréui hràang-dhak mr̀-hrai-géi-faai.	*He doesn't walk very quickly. (lit. He walks in such a way that it is not very quick.)*
Kréui hràang-dhak taai faai laa.	*He walks too quickly.*
Kréui hràang-dhak faai-gwo ngró.	*He walks faster than I do.*

But do remember that -**dhak** must be added directly onto a verb, nothing can come between the verb and -**dhak**. If the verb has an object which you want to put in you should give the verb and its object first and then repeat the verb so that -**dhak** can be added to it. Compare these two sentences:

Kréui *góng-dhak* hóu faai.	*He speaks very fast.*
Kréui *góng* Jhùng-mràn *góng-dhak* hóu faai.	*He speaks Chinese very fast.*

3 Questions expecting a plural answer

In the dialogue Mr Chan says **nhi go lréui-yràu jit-mruk yráu dhi mhat-yré fruk-mrou trùng héung-srau nhe?** (*what services* *and entertainments does this tour programme offer?*). Note how the use of the plural classifier **dhi** presupposes that the answer is going to list more than one item. You can do this whenever you ask a question and you are expecting a plural answer. Of course you can also show that you expect a singular answer by using the appropriate classifier for whatever you are talking about:

Nréi séung mráai mhat-yré shùe qaa?	*What kind of book/books do you want to buy?*
Nréi séung mráai *bún* mhat-yré shùe qaa?	*What kind of book do you want to buy?*
Nréi séung mráai *dhi* mhat-yré shùe qaa?	*What kind of books do you want to buy?*

4 Double *and* single

In **shèung-yràn-chròng** (*double (person) bed*), **shèung** means *double*, and it can also mean *a pair of*. The opposite word *single* is **dhaan**, and *a single bed* is **dhaan-yràn-chròng**.

A bargain may not be cheap

You now know two similar words, **prèng** (*cheap*) and **dái** (*a bargain*), but take care that you do not confuse the two. A Rolls Royce bought at a bargain price might still be several years' salary for most of us, so it would not really be appropriate to say that it was *cheap*, and Cantonese would be unlikely to use **prèng** to describe it either. If you are treated to a meal in a restaurant by a friend and you see the bill and think it small it would give offence to say it was **hóu prèng** – that would sound as though your friend should have spent more money on you. You could happily comment **hóu dái**, though, because that sounds as if it was a very good meal and your friend was clever to choose it and not get cheated into paying over the top. Interestingly, your friend *could* say **hóu prèng jhe**, because it is quite good manners to belittle one's own efforts as a host.

Dialogue 2

 A tourist checks in at the airport.

小姐，我要搭一五零號班機去倫敦。請問我喺呢處報到，啱唔啱呀？
一五零號班機喺下晝四點半鐘起飛去倫敦。你喺呢處報到就啱嘞。
　請你交你嘅護照，簽証同飛機票俾我嘞。
呢兩件係我嘅行李，請你幫我過磅喇。
先生，你嘅行李過重嘀！重有冇其他行李呀？
重有兩件手提行李都係好輕嘅。我嘅行李過重咗幾多磅呀？
唔算好多，只係兩磅啫。
對唔住，請你通融一吓喇，得嗎？
問題唔大，但係下次你就要多啲注意行李嘅重量啦。好嘞，你攞返你
　嘅護照同機票喇。
唔該你話我知旅遊保險嘅櫃枱喺邊處呀？免税洋酒又喺邊處買呢？
嗰兩個櫃枱都喺四號閘口附近，你唔會搵唔到嘅。
唔該晒。

Tourist	Síu-jé, ngró yiu daap yhat-ngɍ-lrìng hrou bhaan-ghèi heui Lrèun-dheun. Chéng-mran ngró hái nhi-sue bou-dou, nghaam mɍ nghaam qaa?
Clerk	Yhat-ngɍ-lrìng hrou bhaan-ghèi hái hraa-jau sei-dím-bun-jhung héi-fhèi heui Lrèun-dheun. Nréi hái nhi-sue bou-dou jrau nghaam laak. Chéng nréi ghàau nréi ge wru-jiu, chhìm-jing trùng fhèi-ghèi-piu béi ngró lhaa.
Tourist	Nhi lréung grin hrai ngró ge hràng-lréi, chéng nréi bhòng ngró gwo-bóng lhaa.
Clerk	Shìn-shàang, nréi ge hràng-lréi gwo-chrúng bo! Jrung yráu mróu krèi-thàa hràng-lréi qaa?
Tourist	Jrung yráu lréung grin sáu-trài hràng-lréi dhou hrai hóu hhèng ge. Ngró ge hràng-lréi gwo-chrúng-jó géi-dho brong qaa?
Clerk	Mɍ suen hóu dhò, jí-hrai lréung brong jhe.
Tourist	Deui-mɍ-jrue, chéng nréi thùng-yrùng yhat-hráa lhaa, dhak maa?
Clerk	Mran-trài mɍ draai, draan-hrai hraa chi nréi jrau yiu dhò-dhi jue-yi hràng-lréi ge chrúng-lreung laa. Hóu laak, nréi ló-fhàan nréi ge wru-jiu trùng ghèi-piu lhaa.
Tourist	Mɍ-ghòi nréi wraa ngró jhì lréui-yràu bóu-hím ge gwrai-tói hái bhin-sue qaa? Mrín-seui yrèung-jáu yrau hái bhin-sue mráai nhe?

Clerk   Gó lréung go gwrai-tói dhou hái sei hrou jraap-háu fru-gran, nréi mr̀ wrúi wán-mr̀-dóu ge.

Tourist   Mr̀-ghòi-saai.

班機	**bhaan-ghèi**	scheduled flight
報到	**bou-dou**	check in, register, report for duty
下晝	**hraa-jau**	afternoon, p.m.
四點半鐘	**sei-dím-bun-jhung**	half past four o'clock
起飛	**héi-fhèi**	to take off (of aircraft)
交	**ghàau**	to hand over
護照	**wru-jiu**	passport
簽証	**chhìm-jing**	visa
(飛)機票	**(fhèi-)ghèi-piu**	air ticket
行李	**hràng-lréi**	luggage
過磅	**gwo-bóng**	to weigh
過重	**gwo-chrúng**	overweight
輕	**hhèng**	light (in weight)
通融	**thùng-yrùng**	stretch a point, bend the rules, make an accommodation
一下	**yhat-hráa**	a little bit, one time
問題	**mran-trài**	problem, question
多啲	**dhò-dhi**	a little more
注意	**jue-yi**	pay attention to
重量	**chrúng-lreung**	weight
攞	**ló**	to collect, to take
保險	**bóu-hím**	insurance
櫃枱	**gwrai-tói**	counter
免稅	**mrín-seui**	tax-free, duty-free
洋酒	**yrèung-jáu**	liquor, (non-Chinese) alcoholic drinks
閘口	**jraap-háu**	gate, gateway
......晒	**-saai**	(verb ending; *completely*)

 ———————— **Grammar** ————————

5 Sreung *and* hraa *again*

In Unit 10, grammar point 8 you met **sreung-go-lrái-baai** (*last week*) and **hraa-go-lrái-baai** (*next week*). In the dialogue you have just read there are two more cases where **hraa** appears. **Hraa-jau** means *afternoon, p.m.,* and you will not be surprised to learn that *a.m.* is **sreung-jau**. **Hraa chi** or **hraa yhat chi** means *next time, on the next occasion,* and as expected **sreung chi** or **sreung yhat chi** means *last time, on the previous occasion.*

6 Clock time

Telling the hours by the clock is very simple; they are called **dím** (*dots* – you met that in Unit 13), and of course there are twelve of them on the clock (**jhung**). *One o'clock* is *one dot of the clock*, that is, **yhat-dím-jhung**, *two o'clock* is **lréung-dím-jhung**, and so on up to *twelve o'clock* (**srap-yri-dím-jhung**). *What time is it?* is *How many dots of the clock?* (**Géi-dho dím jhung qaa?**)

Half past uses the word **bun** (*half*), which you met in Unit 4. So *half past one* is **yhat-dím-bun(-jhung)**, *half past two* is **lréung-dím-bun(-jhung)**, and *half past twelve* is **srap-yri-dím-bun(-jhung)**. The brackets around **jhung** are to show that people do not usually bother to say it unless for some reason they want to speak particularly clearly.

You met the word for *minutes* (**fhan**) in Unit 10, and you can give precise times to the minute as follows:

1.01 **yhat-dím-lrìng-yhat-fhan-jhung** (for **lrìng** see Unit 11, grammar point 2)
1.09 **yhat-dím-lrìng-gáu-fhan-jhung**
1.10 **yhat-dím-srap-fhan-jhung**
1.59 **yhat-dím-ngŕ-srap-gáu-fhan-jhung**

Actually, it is quite uncommon for people to bother to give such precise times. They normally deal in five-minute periods only, just as you might say *Oh, it's twenty past two* even if your watch showed that it was 2.19 or 2.22. The five-minute periods are called *characters* (**jri**) after the figures which appear on clock faces:

1.05 is **yhat-dím-yhat-go-jri**
1.10 is **yhat-dím-lréung-go-jri**
1.25 is **yhat-dím-ngŕ-go-jri**
1.50 is **yhat-dím-srap-go-jri**

Some people like to use the word **gwhat** (from the English word *quarter*) in the following way:

yhat-dím-yhat-go-gwhat	*quarter past one*
yhat-dím-shàam-go-gwhat	*quarter to two*

But if you prefer, you can always say:

yhat-dím-shàam-go-jri	*quarter past one*
yhat-dím-gáu-go-jri	*quarter to two*

Finally, remember that Cantonese likes to put the large before the small, and that applies to time as well, so *4.35 p.m. on Tuesday* is **Shìng-krèi-yri hraa-jau sei-dím-chhat-go-jri**.

7 Fhei *and* piu (tickets)

The formal word for *ticket* is **piu**, but generally Cantonese people prefer to use the colloquial word **fhei**. (**Fhei** is probably a corruption of the English word *fare*.) In the case of the word for *air ticket* most people now simply say **ghèi-piu**, or if there could be any doubt what that means they use its fuller form **fhèi-ghèi-piu**. **Fhèi-ghèi-fhei** sounds rather odd and is not common.

8 Sáu-trài (portable)

In Unit 8 you met **sáu-trài mrit-fó-túng** (*portable fire extinguisher*), and in the dialogue you met **sáu-trài hràng-lréi** (*hand baggage*). **Sáu-trài** can be used freely with many other nouns, but probably the most common in the 1990s is the **sáu-trài drin-wáa** (*portable phone*).

9 Mran-trài (a problem)

Mran-trài mr̀ draai means *the problem is not a big one, no great problem.* You will frequently hear people respond to a request by saying **mróu mran-trài**, a phrase echoed almost precisely in the English *no problem!*

10 *Verb ending* -saai (completely)

The verb ending **-saai** is a very useful one. In the dialogue it was attached to **mr̀-ghòi** (*thank you*). **Mr̀-ghòi-saai** literally means *thank you totally*, but it has been devalued so that many people say it rather than just **mr̀-ghòi**, much as many English speakers say *thank you very much* rather than just *thank you* without meaning to show any great degree of gratitude. In the same way, **dhò-jre-saai** is very common. Otherwise, **-saai** means what it says, as the following examples illustrate:

Dhi yràn dhou jáu-saai.   *All the people left.*
Ngró mróu-saai chín.   *I've got no money at all.*
Kréui ge sáu hhak-saai.   *His hands were completely black.*

 ──────── **Exercises** ────────

1 Change the following pairs of sentences into single sentence
questions using **dring-hrai . . . nhe?** The first pair would thus
become **Nréi hrai Yhìng-gwok-yràn dring-hrai Mréi-gwok-
yràn nhe?**

    (*a*) Nréi hrai Yhìng-gwok-yràn. Nréi hrai Mréi-gwok-yràn.
    (*b*) Fó-chhe faai. Fhèi-ghèi faai.
    (*c*) Kréui Lrái-baai-shàam lrài. Kréui Lrái-baai-sei lrài.
    (*d*) Hrò Shìn-shàang séung heui Hhèung-góng. Hrò Shìn-
shàang séung heui Gwóng-jhàu.
    (*e*) Lréi Táai mróu chín. Chràn Táai mróu chín.

2 Give the opposites of these words.

    (*a*) yre-máan
    (*b*) mr̀-síu-dhak
    (*c*) nrúen-séui
    (*d*) chrúng
    (*e*) ghìng-lréi

3 Make adverbial sentences from the following using **-dhak** and
your translations of the phrases in brackets. The answer to the
first one is **Kréui góng-dhak faai**.

    (*a*) Kréui góng. (*quickly*)
    (*b*) Wròng Shàang mráai hhaa. (*very cheaply*)
    (*c*) Nréi hràang-lrou. (*faster than Miss Cheung*)
    (*d*) Nréi yám yrèung-jáu. (*more than I do*)
    (*e*) Lréi Shìn-shàang jhàa-chhe. (*not very well*)

4 What are the correct classifiers for the following? You have not
been specifically told some of them, but you should by now be
able to make a guess with a very good chance of being right.

    (*a*) dhaan-yràn-   (*d*) wran-drung-   (*g*) jáu-dim
        chròng   fóng   (*h*) fhèi-ghèi-
    (*b*) gáu-jái   (*e*) mráa-lrou   piu
    (*c*) drin-sri-ghèi (*f*) fhèi-ghèi   (*i*) hràng-lréi

5 These questions are quite difficult. Answer them in Cantonese.

   (*a*) **Yhat ghàn trùng yhat brong bhin yreung chrúng qaa?**

   (*b*) **Hái Yhìng-gwok mráai grin-hhòng bóu-hím gwai mr̀ gwai qaa?**

   (*c*) **Hái fhèi-ghèi-chrèung lréui-brin trùng-mràai hái bhin-sue yráu mrín-seui yrèung-jáu mraai qaa?**

   (*d*) **Daap fhèi-ghèi ge srì-hrau, sáu-trài hràng-lréi yiu mr̀ yiu gwo-bóng qaa?**

   (*e*) **Hái Lrèun-dheun yráu géi-dho go fhèi-ghèi-chrèung qaa?**

6 Here are some clock times. How do you say them in Cantonese? See if you can come up with *three* different ways of saying the last one!

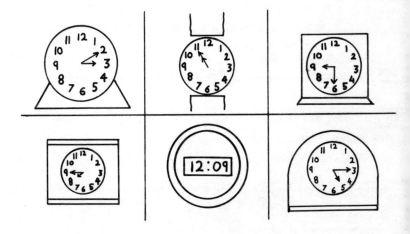

7 A question of time. Can you give the answer (in Cantonese) to this puzzle?

Ghàm-yrat hrai Shìng-krèi-yri.
Ngró shàam yrat jhì-chrìn heui-jó mráa-chrèung.
Ngró hái mráa-chrèung wáan-jó shàam go bun jhung-tràu.
Ngró lruk-dím-jhung lrèi-hhòi-jó mráa-chrèung.
Gám, ngró séung mran nréi: ngró Lrái-baai-géi géi-dho-dím-jhung dou-jó mráa-chrèung nhe?

16

第十六課　駕駛
GAA-SÁI
Driving

In this unit you will really get to grips with comparisons.

━━━━━ Dialogue 1 ━━━━━

Mr Lee has just come back from his driving test.

你咁開心，我估你今朝早參加嘅汽車駕駛考試成績一定好好嘞。
我都估我嘅成績幾好。
考試官考咗你啲乜嘢呀？
佢考咗我好多嘢，譬如泊位喇，斜路開車喇，慢駛喇，停車喇，窄路
　掉頭喇，手掣同腳掣用得好唔好喇，對路面嘅情況反應夠唔夠快喇
　等等.
結果係點樣，你知唔知呀？
佢冇講嘢嘛！我揸車返駕駛考試局嘅寫字樓嗰陣時，佢可能覺得好舒
　服，瞓咗喺車裡便重未醒，要我同佢嘅同事兩個人一齊抬佢落車.

Mrs Lee	Nréi gam hhòi-sham, ngró gwú nréi ghàm-jhìu-jóu
	chhàam-ghàa ge hei-chhè gaa-sái háau-srí srìng-jhik
	yhat-dring hóu hóu laak.
Mr Lee	Ngró dhou gwú ngró ge srìng-jhik géi hóu.
Mrs Lee	Háau-srí-gwhùn háau-jó nréi dhi mhat-yré qaa?
Mr Lee	Kréui háau-jó ngró hóu dhò yré, pei-yrùe paak-wái lhaa,
	che-lóu hhòi-chhe lhaa, mraan sái lhaa, trìng-chhe
	lhaa, jaak-lrou driu-tràu lhaa, sáu-jai trùng geuk-jai

yrung-dhak hóu mr̀ hóu lhaa, deui lrou-mín ge chrìng-fong fáan-ying gau mr̀ gau faai lhaa, dáng-dáng.

Mrs Lee   Git-gwó hrai dím-yéung, nréi jhì mr̀ jhì qaa?

Mr Lee   Kréui mróu góng-yré bo! Ngró jhàa-chhe fhàan Gaa-sái Háau-srí-gruk ge sé-jri-lràu gó-jran-srì, kréui hó-nràng gok-dhak hóu shùe-fruk, fan-jó hái chhe lréui-brin jrung-mrei séng, yiu ngró trùng kréui ge trùng-sri lréung go yràn yhat-chrài tròi kréui lrok chhe.

駕駛	**gaa-sái**	to drive, driving
考試	**háau-srí**	examination, test; to sit an examination
成績	**srìng-jhik**	result, score, report
官	**gwhùn**	an official, officer
考	**háau**	to examine, to test
譬如	**pei-yrùe**	for example, for instance
泊位	**paak-wái**	to park a car
斜路	**che-lóu**	steep road
斜	**che**	steep
開車	**hhòi-chhe**	to start a car; to drive a car
慢	**mraan**	slow, slowly
駛	**sái**	to drive
窄	**jaak**	narrow
掉頭	**driu-tràu**	to turn to face the other way
手掣	**sáu-jai**	handbrake
腳掣	**geuk-jai**	footbrake
腳	**geuk**	foot, leg
路面	**lrou-mín**	road surface
情況	**chrìng-fong**	situation, circumstances
反應	**fáan-ying**	reaction, response; to respond, react
夠	**gau**	enough
結果	**git-gwó**	the end result
局	**gruk**	bureau, department, office
可能	**hó-nràng**	it is possible that, possibly; possibility
瞓、瞓覺	**fan** or **fan-gaau**	to sleep; to lie down; to go to bed
重未	**jrung-mrei**	still not yet
醒	**séng**	to wake up, recover consciousness
同事	**trùng-sri**	colleague
抬	**tròi**	to carry, to lift

Háau-srí

Ngró-drei séung mran nréi: nréi gwú gó go háau-srí-gwhùn jhàn-hrai fan-jó gaau dring-hrai yhàṇ-wrai Lréi Shàang jhàa-chhe jhàa-dhak mr̀ hóu só-yrí kréui paa-dou tràu-wràn fan-jó hái chhe lréui-brin nhe?

Grammar

1 Reactions to ...

You first met **deui** (*with regard to, towards*) in Unit 9, and further examples of its use are to be found in Units 10, 12 and 15. In the dialogue above it teams up with **fáan-ying** to mean *reactions to road conditions*. When you know that, you will find it easier to make sense of the long section **deui lrou-mín ge chrìng-fong fáan-ying gau mr̀ gau faai lhaa** (*whether reactions to road conditions are fast enough*).

2 Gau (enough)

Gau means *enough*. It acts very consistently because it always goes in front of the word it refers to, regardless of whether that word is a noun or an adjective. However, as you will see from the translations of the examples, English is not so consistent:

Nréi *gau mr̀ gau chín* mráai fhei qaa?   *Do you have enough money to buy the tickets?*

Gó déng móu *gau mr̀ gau draai* qaa?   *Is that hat big enough?*

Carrying things

Cantonese uses a number of different verbs meaning *to carry*. To carry slung over the shoulder is one, to carry in the arms is another, to carry on the back is another, to carry on a pole over one shoulder is another, and so on. **Tròi** is used for *to carry* between two people either holding the load or with it suspended from a pole between them.

Dialogue 2

A lucky escape?

對唔住，先生，我一時唔小心用架單車撞到你，你有冇事呀？

大問題就冇，但係我隻腳而家好痛，有啲傷。你睇，重流緊血添.

你真好彩嘞，只係被架單車撞到啫。

豈有此理，你騎線喋，你唔小心撞到我，重話我好彩?！

係呀，先生！我係認真喋，唔係講笑喋，千祈唔好誤會呀！

我點樣誤會呀，你講喇！

我係的士司機，又係電單車賽車手，今日喺的士公司輪到我放假，所以唔駛揸的士，啱啱我架電單車又壞咗，撐咗去修理，所以我先至用我個仔嘅單車咋。如果係我嘅的士或者電單車撞到你，噉你就冇咁好彩啦。

Mr Chan	Deui-mȑ-jrue, shìn-shàang, ngró yhat-srì mȑ siú-shàm yrung gaa dhaan-chhe jrong-dóu nréi. Nréi yráu mróu sri qaa?
Victim	Draai mran-trài jrau mróu, draan-hrai ngró jek geuk yrì-ghaa hóu tung, yráu-dhi shèung. Nréi tái, jrung lràu-gán huet thìm.
Mr Chan	Nréi jhàn hóu-chói laak, jí-hrai brei gaa dhaan-chhe jrong-dóu jhe.
Victim	Héi-yráu-chí-lréi, nréi chhì-sin gràa. Nréi mȑ síu-shàm jrong-dóu ngró, jrung wraa ngró hóu-chói?!
Mr Chan	Hrai qaa, shìn-shàang! Ngró hrai yring-jhan gaa, mȑ hrai góng-siu gaa. Chhìn-krèi mȑ-hóu ngr-wrui qaa!
Victim	Ngró dím-yéung ngr-wrui qaa? Nréi góng lhaa!
Mr Chan	Ngró hrai dhik-sí shi-ghei, yrau hrai drin-dhaan-chhe choi-chhe-sáu. Ghàm-yrat hái dhik-sí ghung-shi lrèun-dou ngró fong-gaa, só-yrí mȑ-sái jhàa dhik-sí, nghaam-nghaam ngró gaa drin-dhaan-chhe yrau wraai-jó, nhìng-jó heui shàu-lréi, só-yrí ngró shìn-ji yrung ngró go jái ge dhaan-chhe jaa. Yrùe-gwo hrai ngró ge dhik-sí wraak-jé drin-dhaan-chhe jrong-dóu nréi, gám nréi jrau mróu gam hóu-chói laa.

一時	**yhat-srì**	momentarily, briefly
小心	**síu-shàm**	careful
單車	**dhaan-chhe**	bicycle
撞	**jrong**	run into, knock into
有事	**yráu sri**	to have something wrong with you
傷	**sheùng**	a wound; to wound
流	**lràu**	to flow
血	**huet**	blood
豈有此理	**héi-yráu-chí-lréi**	that's ridiculous; how could that be?
黐線	**chhì-sin**	crazy; mixed-up; off the rails
認真	**yring-jhan**	serious, sincere
講笑	**góng-siu**	to joke
笑	**siu**	to smile, to laugh, to laugh at
千祈	**chhìn-krèi**	whatever you do don't, don't ever
誤會	**ngr-wrui**	to misunderstand, to get it wrong
電單車	**drin-dhaan-chhe**	motor bike
賽車手	**choi-chhe-sáu**	racing driver
賽車	**choi-chhe**	motor racing
輪到	**lrèun-dou**	the turn of, it has come to the turn of
壞	**wraai**	to go wrong, break down
擰	**nhìng**	to bring, to take
修理	**shàu-lréi**	to repair, mend
或者	**wraak-jé**	or, perhaps

Grammar

3 Jek (one of a pair)

Things that come in pairs are classified with **shèung** or with **deui**:

> **yhat deui sáu** — *a pair of hands, pair of arms*
> **yhat shèung faai-jí** — *a pair of chopsticks* (**faai-jí** = *chopsticks*)

One of a pair is usually **jek**, regardless of the shape:

> **yhat jek sáu** — *a hand, an arm*
> **yhat jek faai-jí** — *a chopstick*

An exception is the case of human beings, such as *husband and wife*, where as a couple they are **shèung**, but where one of the pair on his or her own is still referred to as **go**. Other exceptions are *trousers, spectacles* and *scissors*, which the Cantonese do not consider to be *pairs* at all – logically enough, since they are each single objects – and so they do not use **deui** or **shèung** for them.

4 Accentuating the negative

Chhìn-krèi is a useful word when you want to make a negative command particularly strong:

> **Chhìn-krèi mȑ-hóu góng-**   *Whatever you do don't joke!*
> **siu laa!**
> **Chhìn-krèi mȑ-hóu mȑ**   *You really must not forget!*
> **gei-dhak laa!**

5 When electric is not electric

In Unit 9 you met a number of useful words which were made up using **drin** (*electricity, electric*). Cantonese seems to have got rather carried away with the idea, though, and has applied **drin** to things which have very little to do with electricity. So when motor bikes came along they dubbed them *electric bikes* (**drin-dhaan-chhe**). Here is another example:

> **drin-yràu**   *petrol, gasoline*
> **yrap drin-yràu**   *to refuel, put petrol in*

6 Broken and broken down

You met **wraai** meaning *bad* in Unit 12. **Wraai-jó** means *gone bad* or *broken down* and can be applied to fruit, meat, machinery, watches, radios, and so on. But if the object is clearly physically damaged, then the word to use is **lraan-jó** which you met in Unit 5:

> **Ngró ge drin-dhaan-chhe**   *Something's gone wrong with*
> **wraai-jó.**   *my motor bike.*
> **Nrgó ge drin-dhaan-chhe**   *My motor bike is smashed.*
> **lraan-jó.**

7 More on or

Remember **dring-hrai**? Now you have also met **wraak-jé**, and they both mean *or*. The difference is that **dring-hrai** means *or is it the case that?* and always appears in questions, while **wraak-jé** means *or maybe it is, or perhaps* and it always appears in statements:

Kréui géi-sí lrài qaa? Hrai ghàm-yrat dring-hrai thìng-yrat lrài nhe?	*When is she coming? Is it today or tomorrow that she is coming? (Which is it? It must be one or the other.)*
Kréui (wraak-jé) ghàm-yrat wraak-jé thìng-yrat lrài.	*She's coming today or maybe tomorrow. (It could be either.)*
Kréui yiu gaa-fhe dring-hrai chràa nhe?	*Does he want coffee or tea?*
Kréui wraak-jé yiu gaa-fhe wraak-jé yiu chràa.	*He may want coffee or he may want tea. (I'm not sure.)*

8 Negative comparisons

In the last line of the dialogue Mr Chan says **nréi jrau mróu gam hóu-chói laa** (*you wouldn't be as lucky then*), and this gives you a clue as to how to make negative comparisons. The pattern is:

X mróu Y gam ____.	*X isn't as ____ as Y.*
Kréui mróu ngró gam ghòu.	*He's not as tall as I am.*
Hei-chhe mróu fhèi-ghèi gam faai.	*Cars aren't as fast as planes.*
Ngró hràang-dhak mróu nréi gam mraan.	*I don't walk as slowly as you do.*

9 A recap on comparisons

Now we can set out the full range of comparisons so that you can bring real subtlety into your speech:

Ngró hóu ghòu.	*I am tall.*
Kréui ghòu dhi.	*He's taller.*
Kréui ghòu hóu-dhò.	*He's a lot taller.*
Nréi jrung ghòu.	*You are even taller.*
Kréui mróu gam ghòu.	*He's not so tall.*
Kréui ghòu gwo ngró.	*He is taller than I am.*
Kréui ghòu gwo ngró siú-siú. or:	
Kréui ghòu gwo ngró yhat-dhi.	*He is a bit taller than I am.*
Kréui ghòu gwo ngró hóu-dhò.	*He is a lot taller than I am.*
Kréui mróu ngró gam ghòu.	*He is not as tall as I am.*

And of course there is also the equivalent and the superlative:

Kréui trùng ngró yhat-yreung gam ghòu.	*He is just as tall as I am.*
Kréui mróu ngró yhat-yreung gam ghòu.	*He is not exactly the same height as I am.*
Kréui jeui ghòu laak.	*He is tallest.*

Laughing and smiling

The word **siu** is heavily used in Cantonese, and Chinese culture in general stresses the need to smile. You will notice that Chinese people smile a great deal, and sometimes in circumstances where Westerners would think it inappropriate, in the face of tragedy or horror, for example. Chinese novels are full of *I smiled, she smiled coldly, he smiled sadly*, and so on, where English novels use another set of words like *he said, she exclaimed, they expostulated, I sighed*. One of the reasons why Chinese faces are said to be 'inscrutable' may well be because Westerners do not know how to read the various subtleties of smiling. Chinese people often find Western faces disconcerting too – *Why doesn't he smile? Have I said something wrong?*

—————— **Exercises** ——————

1 Here are five English sentences. Which of the two possibilities given is the correct translation?

(a) *I think he is also a Japanese.*
    (i) **Ngró gwú kréui dhou hrai Yrat-bún-yràn.**
    (ii) **Ngró dhou gwú kréui hrai Yrat-bún-yràn.**

(b) *I give him ten dollars.*
    (i) **Ngró béi srap mhan gwo kréui.**
    (ii) **Ngró béi kréui srap mhan.**

(c) *Mrs Lee is going to Japan by air.*
    (i) **Lréi Taai-táai daap fhèi-ghèi heui Yrat-bún.**
    (ii) **Lréi Taai-táai heui Yrat-bún daap fhèi-ghèi.**

(d) *Mr Wong and I are going to dine at City Hall.*
    (i) **Ngró trùng Wròng Shìn-shàang heui Draai-wrui-tròng srik-fraan.**
    (ii) **Wròng Shìn-shàang trùng ngró heui Draai-wrui-tròng srik-fraan.**

(e) *Which lady is ill?*
    (i) **Bhin-go taai-táai yráu breng qaa?**
    (ii) **Bhin-go ge taai-táai yráu breng qaa?**

2 Fine, now write out the translations of the sentences which you think are incorrect.

3

Here's a really tough one. Can you say who is sitting in each of the six seats?

Ghàm-mráan Lrùng Shàang, Lrùng Táai chéng Lréi Shàang, Lréi Táai trùng-mràai Chràn Shàang, Chràn Táai srik-fraan. Lréi Shàang chró haí bhak-brin; Chràn Shàang hái Lrùng Táai yrau-brin; Chràn Táai hái Lrùng Shàang deui-mrin; Lréi Táai hái Lrùng Shàang jó-sáu-brin.

4   Can you match each of the six verbs (*a*)–(*f*) with a suitable noun from the list (i)–(xii)?

(*a*)   **dáa**   (*c*)   **chhàu**   (*e*)   **chhùng**
(*b*)   **dóu**   (*d*)   **thèng**   (*f*)   **tái**

(i)   **jéung-bán**   (v)   **drin-yíng**   (ix)   **hrùng-dhang**
(ii)   **thìn-hei**   (vi)   **mràa-jeuk**   (x)   **sou-hrok**
(iii) **gwóng-bo**   (vii) **hói-thaan**   (xi)   **yrèung-jáu**
(iv)   **phe-páai**   (viii) **nroi-yrùng**   (xii) **jit-mruk**

5

Mr Wong   Mr Chan   Mr Lee   Mrs Chan   Mrs Lee   Mrs Wong

Use Cantonese to describe Mr Wong's height in comparison with each of the other five people. How would you describe Mr Lee in comparison with Mrs Wong? How would you describe Mr Lee without reference to anyone else?

6   Here are definitions of four words which you have learned in this unit. Can you work out what they are?

(*a*)   **Jhik-hrai yhat go yràn góng ge yré, jrou ge yré, séung ge yré yhat-dhi dhou mr̀ nghaam.**

(b) Jhik-hrai nréi góng nhi yreung yré, kréui mr̀ mrìng-braak, yrí-wrài nréi góng gó yreung yré.

(c) Jhik-hrai dhi yré lraan-jó, wraai-jó jhì-hrau, joi yhat chi jíng-fhàan hóu.

(d) Jhik-hrai 'srì-srì' ge shèung-fáan.

17

第十七課　紀律部隊

GÉI-LREUT BROU-DÉUI

The uniformed services

In this unit you will tackle complicated descriptive phrases – and you'll find that they aren't so complicated after all.

 ──────── **Dialogue 1** ────────

Problems with a photograph on an immigration application.

小姐，你呢張用嚟申請移民嘅相片唔合規格嘛！

點樣唔合規格呀？

移民局規定申請人嘅相片唔准著軍服。

好彩我唔係軍人，我已經離開咗軍隊兩年嘞。

噉，你而家做緊乜嘢呀？

我而家係女警，不過下個月尾我會加入消防局做女消防員……嘩！警察同消防員都要著制服嘅嘛！我點算好呢？

小姐，移民局規定申請移民嘅人唔准著任何制服影相，你可以唔著㗎。

乜嘢話?！你叫我唔著衫裸體影相吖？

唔……唔……係……你……你唔好誤會。我嘅意思係叫你唔著制服著便服啫！

Official	Síu-jé, nréi nhi jhèung yrung lrài shàn-chíng yrì-mràn ge seung-pín mř hrap-kwhài-gaak bo!
Applicant	Dím-yéung mř hrap-kwhài-gaak qaa?

Official	Yrì-mràn-gruk kwhài-dring shàn-chíng yràn ge seung-pín mr̀ jéun jeuk gwhàn-fruk.	
Applicant	Hóu-chói ngró mr̀ hrai gwhàn-yràn, ngró yrí-ghìng lrèi-hhòi-jó gwhàn-déui lréung nrìn laak.	
Official	Gám, nréi yrì-ghaa jrou-gán mhat-yré qaa?	
Applicant	Ngró yrì-ghaa hrai nréui-gíng, bhat-gwo hraa-go-yruet-mréi ngró wrúi ghàa-yrap Shìu-fròng-gruk jrou nréui-shìu-fròng-yrùen . . . . Brai! Gíng-chaat trùng shìu-fròng-yrùen dhou yiu jeuk jai-fruk ge bo! Ngró dím-suen-hóu-nhe?	
Official	Síu-jé, Yrì-mràn-gruk kwhài-dring shàn-chíng yrì-mràn ge yràn mr̀ jéun jeuk yram-hrò jai-fruk yíng-séung. Nréi hó-yrí mr̀ jeuk gaa.	
Applicant	Mhat-yré wáa?! Nréi giu ngró mr̀ jeuk shaam ló-tái yíng-séung qràa?	
Official	Mr̀ . . . mr̀ . . . hrai. . . . Nréi . . . nréi mr̀-hóu ngr-wrui. Ngró ge yi-shì hrai giu nréi mr̀ jeuk jai-fruk, jeuk brin-fruk jhe!	

申請	**shàn-chíng**	to apply
移民	**yrì-mràn**	to migrate; immigration, emigration
相片	**seung-pín**	photograph
合規格	**hrap-kwhài-gaak**	to qualify, meet requirements
規定	**kwhài-dring**	to regulate, lay down a rule
准	**jéun**	to allow, permit
軍服	**gwhàn-fruk**	military uniform
軍人	**gwhàn-yràn**	soldier, military personnel
軍隊	**gwhàn-déui**	army
女警	**nréui-gíng**	policewoman
女	**nréui**	female
不過	**bhat-gwo**	but, however
月	**yruet**	moon, month
尾	**mréi**	tail, end
加入	**ghàa-yrap**	to join, recruit into
消防局	**Shìu-fròng-gruk**	fire brigade
消防員	**shìu-fròng-yrùen**	fireman
嘩！	**brai!**	oh dear! oh, heck! alas!
制服	**jai-fruk**	uniform
任何	**yram-hrò**	any
影相	**yíng-séung**	to take a photograph, have a photo taken
裸體	**ló-tái**	naked, nude
意思	**yi-shì**	meaning, intention
叫	**giu**	to tell someone to, to order someone to
便服	**brin-fruk**	plain clothes

Grammar

1 Adjectives

In Unit 4, grammar point 6 you first met **ge** used to link descriptive phrases or clauses to a noun, for example, **hóu gwai ge gaa-fhe** (*very expensive coffee*), **mráai-gán bhat ge yràn** (*the person who is buying a pen*). The first line of the above dialogue has a more complicated version of that **ge** pattern (**nhi jhèung yrung lrài shàn-chíng yrì-mràn ge seung-pín**). At first sight this phrase looks rather frightening, but keep cool, you can quite easily break it down to see how it works. The basic unit is **nhi jhèung seung-pín** – *this photograph* (remember **jhèung** is the classifier for sheet-like things). Splitting **nhi jhèung** and the noun **seung-pín** is the adjective **yrung lrài shàn-chíng yrì-mràn** (*used for applying for immigration*) and **ge** does the same job that it was doing when you met it in Unit 4, grammar point 6, that is, it is linking the complex adjective to the noun. So the whole thing means *this photograph which is being used for applying for immigration*. In fact, although the phrase looks complicated, when you break it down it is really only the same basic pattern as **nhi go Mréi-gwok-yràn** – specifier – classifier – adjective – noun. Here are some examples:

gó gaa Wròng Shàang séung mráai ge Yrat-bún chhe	*that Japanese car which Mr Wong wants to buy*
nhi chheut nràam-yán hóu jhùng-yi tái ge drin-yíng	*this movie that men love watching*

2 Possessives with adjectives

Look again at the same speech by the immigration official in the dialogue and you will see that **nréi** (*you*) is positioned in front of the complex adjectival phrase discussed above, and the entire meaning is *this photograph of yours which is being used for applying for immigration*. This is the regular position for the possessive in such cases, and the normal possessive indicator (**ge**) is not necessary:

nréi gó gaa Wròng Shàang séung mráai ge Yrat-bún chhe	*that Japanese car of yours which Mr Wong wants to buy*

— **161** —

3 Jéun: *a two-way verb*

Jéun can mean either *to allow* or *to be allowed*, so it can work two ways, both actively and passively:

Kréui mr̀ jéun yám-jáu.	*He's not allowed to drink alcohol.*
Kréui mr̀ jéun (ngró) yám-jáu.	*He doesn't let me drink alcohol.*

As you become more familiar with Cantonese you will find other two-way verbs like **jéun**. Already in this unit you will find **yíng-séung**, which can mean *to photograph* or *to be photographed*.

4 *Vive la différence!*

You met **nràam** (*male*) in Unit 9, and in this unit you have met **nréui** (*female*). As you can see from the dialogue, **nréui** can be attached fairly freely to nouns – **nréui-gíng** (*policewoman*), **nréui-shìu-fròng-yùen** (*firewoman*). In these cases the nouns are assumed to be males, so you would only meet the terms **nràam-gíng** and **nràam-shìu-fròng-yùen** if someone was specifically making a contrast between the two sexes. In other cases there is no assumption that a noun is male: **yràn** (*person*), for example, is completely non-commital, and so you will meet **nràam-yán** (*man*) just as often as you will meet **nréui-yán** (*woman*) (note how the tone changes from **yràn** to **yán**). Here are some more examples:

nràam-pràng-yráu/nréui-pràng-yráu	*boyfriend/girlfriend*
nràam-chi(-só)/nréui-chi(-só)	*gentlemen's/ladies' toilet*
nràam-hrok-shaang/nréui-hrok-shaang	*boy/girl pupils*

You should note that **nréui** changes its tone to become **néui** (*daughter*), the pair to **jái** (*son*).

5 Yruet (month)

Yruet means *the moon*, and by extension has also come to mean *a month*. The classifier for it is **go**, so *one month* is **yhat go yruet**, *two months* is **lréung go yruet**, and so on. As with **lrái-baai** and **shìng-krèi**, *last, this* and *next* are **sreung, nhi** and **hraa**, so *last month* is

sreung-go-yruet, *this month* is **nhi go yruet,** and *next month* is **hraa-go-yruet.**

The months of the year do not have fancy names as in English; they are just numbered without classifiers. The two sets below should make the system clear to you:

Yhat-yruet	*January*	**yhat go yruet**	*one month*
Yri-yruet	*February*	**lréung go yruet**	*two months*
Shàam-yruet	*March*	**shàam go yruet**	*three months*
Chhat-yruet	*July*	**chhat go yruet**	*seven months*
Srap-yri-yruet	*December*	**srap-yri go yruet**	*twelve months*

6 To tell

To tell has different meanings in English, and different words are also used for them in Cantonese. When *to tell* means *to inform, to tell a fact,* you have learned that it is translated by **wraa/góng . . . jhì/thèng** (see Unit 13, grammar point 5). When *to tell* means *to tell someone to do something, to order someone to do something,* then **giu** is used:

Shìn-shàang giu hrok-shaang tái Yhìng-mràn shùe.	*The teacher told the children to read their English books.*
Ngró giu kréui mr̀-hóu lrài.	*I told him not to come.*

Sometimes English uses *to tell* when it would be more fitting to use *ask* or *invite* (**chéng** in Cantonese). Note the following sentence carefully:

Ghìng-lréi giu fó-gei chéng Wròng Yhi-shang yrap-lrài.	*The manager told the waiter to tell Dr Wong to come in.*

A waiter is unlikely to feel able to *order* a doctor around, although the manager feels quite happy with *ordering* the waiter around, so in this example *told* and *tell* become **giu** and **chéng**, respectively.

Dialogue 2

A plain-clothes police officer has a tough time with some suspects.

喂！你哋幾個，唔好郁呀！快啲跍低，擸你哋嘅身份証出嚟。

你哋係乜嘢人呀？你哋有權睇我哋嘅身份證嘛！

我係王沙展，呢位係我上司陳幫辦。我哋懷疑你哋販毒，你哋企埋路邊，俾我搜身。

你哋都冇著制服，又唔係坐警察巡邏車。你哋話係警察，要拉人，要搜身，邊個信你呀？

我哋冇著警察制服，係因為方便我哋做嘢。我哋兩個都係便衣警察。你哋瞪大對眼睇吓我哋嘅警員証喇！

你哋連手槍都冇，警員証都可能係假嘅，我哋信你哋係警察就難啦。喂，手足！我哋散水囉！

咪走呀！你班死仔，等我拉晒你哋上警察局先！

Sergeant	Wai, nréi-drei géi go, mř-hóu yhuk qaa! Faai-dhi mhàu-dhài, nhìng nréi-drei ge shàn-fán-jing chheut-lrai.
Youth	Nréi-drei hrai mhat-yré yràn qaa? Nréi-drei mróu krùen tái ngró-drei ge shàn-fán-jing bo!
Sergeant	Ngró hrai Wròng Shàa-jín, nhi wái hrai ngró sreung-shi Chràn Bhòng-báan. Ngró-drei wràai-yrì nréi-drei fráan-druk. Nréi-drei kréi-mràai lrou-bhin, béi ngró sáu-shàn.
Youth	Nréi-drei dhou mróu jeuk jai-fruk, yrau mř hrai chró gíng-chaat chreun-lrò-chhe. Nréi-drei wraa hrai gíng-chaat, yiu lhàai-yràn, yiu sáu-shàn, bhin-go seun nréi qaa?
Sergeant	Ngró-drei mróu jeuk gíng-chaat jai-fruk, hrai yhàn-wrai fhòng-brin ngró-drei jrou-yré. Ngró-drei lréung go dhou hrai brin-yhì gíng-chaat. Nréi-drei dhàng-draai-deui-ngráan tái-hráa ngró-drei ge gíng-yrùen-jing lhaa!
Youth	Nréi-drei lrìn sáu-chheung dhou mróu, gíng-yrùen-jing dhou hó-nràng hrai gáa ge, ngró-drei seun nréi-drei hrai gíng-chaat jrau nràan laa. Wai, sáu-jhuk! Ngró-drei saan-séui lo!
Sergeant	Mrái jáu qaa! Nréi bhàan séi-jái, dáng ngró lhàai-saai nréi-drei sréung gíng-chaat-gruk shìn!

喂！	**wai!**	*hoy! héy!*
郁	**yhuk**	*to move, make a movement*
身份証	**shàn-fán-jing**	*identity card*
証	**jing**	*a certificate, a pass*
出	**chheut**	*out*
權	**krùen**	*right, authority, powers*
沙展	**shàa-jín**	*sergeant*
位	**wái**	*(polite classifier for people)*
上司	**sreung-shi**	*superior officer, direct boss*
幫辦	**bhòng-báan**	*inspector*
懷疑	**wràai-yrì**	*to suspect*
販毒	**fráan-druk**	*to peddle drugs*
企	**kréi**	*to stand*
……埋	**-mràai**	*(verb ending: close up to)*
路邊	**lrou-bhin**	*the roadside*
搜身	**sáu-shàn**	*to conduct a body search*
巡邏車	**chreun-lrò-chhe**	*patrol car*
拉	**lhàai**	*to arrest; to pull*
方便	**fhòng-brin**	*convenient*
便衣	**brin-yhì**	*plain-clothes, civilian clothes*
瞌大對眼	**dhàng-draai-deui-ngráan**	*to take a good look*
瞌	**dhàng**	*to stare, open the eyes*
眼	**ngráan**	*eye*
警員証	**gíng-yrùen-jing**	*warrant card*
連……都……	**lrìn . . . dhou . . .**	*even . . .*
手槍	**sáu-chheung**	*handgun, pistol*
假	**gáa**	*false*
難	**nràan**	*difficult, hard*
手足	**sáu-jhuk**	*brothers (secret society slang)*
散水	**saan-séui**	*to scatter away*
班	**bhàan**	*(classifier: group of, gang of)*
死仔	**séi-jái**	*'dead-beats', 'bastards', 'rats' (strong abuse)*

You are a Hong Kong immigration official. A foreign national in army uniform and wearing a handgun comes up to your desk. Ask him for his passport and visa, ask him when he will be leaving Hong Kong, and tell him that he is not allowed to bring a handgun into the territory and will he please hand it to the police sergeant at Counter No. 41.

——————— **Grammar** ———————

7 Hurry up!

Faai-dhi means *quicker, faster,* as you will remember from your work on comparatives in Unit 16, but it has become the most common way of saying *get a move on!, hurry up!* Harrassed mothers say it to their children constantly.

8 Wái: *the polite classifier*

The normal classifier for people is of course **go**, but if you wish to be polite to someone or about someone, you should use **wái** instead. So you might say **nhi go yràn** (*this person*), but you would almost certainly say **nhi wái shìn-shàang** (*this gentleman*) and **gó wái síu-jé** (*that young lady*). In the dialogue the sergeant uses **wái** when he refers to his superior officer, Inspector Chan. If you are introducing someone, you say **nhi wái hrai Wròng Taai-táai, gó wái hrai Lréi Síu-jé . . .**, etc.

9 -mràai (close up to)

The verb ending **-mràai** can be used to indicate movement towards something, or location close to something. Its opposite, showing movement away from something, or location away from something is **-hhòi**. You can use these two words quite freely where you feel them to be appropriate.

Kréui hràang-hhòi-jó.	*He's walked away.* (= *He is not here.* Often said by secretaries over the telephone when you want to talk to their boss.)
Chró-mràai-dhi.	*Sit a bit closer.* (*Cuddle up to me!*)
Chró-hhòi-dhi.	*Sit further away.* (*Stop crowding me!*)

10 Lhàai (to pull)

Lhàai is the normal verb meaning *to pull,* and it is the character which you see marked on doors: the opposite is **thèui** (*push*). **Lhàai** is also used to mean *to pull someone in, to arrest.*

11 Lrìn ... dhou ... (even ...)

Lrìn is a very useful word provided you remember how to position it. The golden rule is that **lrìn** is placed before the word which it refers to and that both *must* come before **dhou**. You will also remember from as far back as Unit 1, grammar point 7 that **dhou** must itself always come before a verb, so there is a certain rigidity about this pattern. A few examples will show you how to use it:

Lrìn Wròng Shìn-shàang dhou mŕ jhùng-yi Wròng Síu-jé.
Even Mr Wong doesn't like Miss Wong.

Ngró lrìn yhat mhan dhou mróu.
I haven't got even one dollar.

Kréui lrìn fraan dhou mŕ séung srik.
She doesn't fancy even rice.

12 sréung (to go up)

The real meaning of **sréung** is *to go up, to ascend*. **Sréung-shàan** means *to go up the hill*, and **sréung-chhe** is *to get (up) onto the vehicle*. In some cases, though, **sréung** is used to mean *to go to*. You met in Unit 12 **sréung-tròng** (*to go to class*), and in the dialogue there is another example, **sréung gíng-chaat-gruk** (*to go to the police station*). You are advised not to make up your own phrases using **sréung** in the sense of *to go to*, only use the ones you meet in this book.

Secret society slang

One of the biggest influences on contemporary Cantonese language has been the great popularity of gangster films and programmes on television and in the cinema. The racy slang which gives authenticity to the shows passes rapidly into ordinary people's speech, but it is discarded again equally quickly. At the end of the dialogue we included a couple of terms which seem likely to stay around, but there is little point in your learning any more – by the time you are able to use them they may well not be current any longer!

Exercises

1

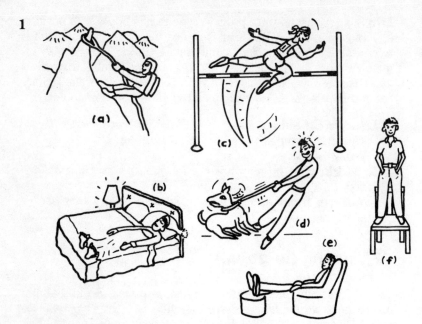

Try to describe in Cantonese what Mr Wong is doing in each of these pictures.

2 Fill in the blanks to show the occupations of each of the following people.

(a) Chràn Shìn-shàang lhàai fráan-druk ge yràn: kréui hrai ____.

(b) Wròng Síu-jé hái jhùng-hrok gaau-shùe: kréui hrai ____.

(c) Lréi Shàang srèng-yrat jhàa dhik-sí: kréui hrai ____.

(d) Jhèung Shàang hái jáu-lràu nhìng yré béi yràn srik: kréui hrai ____.

(e) Ngró bràa-bhaa hái chán-só jrou-yré: kréui hrai ____.

3 Into each of the following sentences put one of the randomly listed inserts (i)–(v), then translate the sentence into English.

(a) Kréui wraa kréui Shìng-krèi-yhat wrúi fhàan-lrài, draan-hrai kréui Shìng-krèi-shàam ____ fhàan.

(b) Nréi jáu-jó ____, ngró jrau dáa drin-wáa béi nréi taai-táai laak.

(c) Sreung-go-yruet Wròng Táai ____ yhat gaa chhe dhou mraai-mr̀-dóu: kréui ge ghìng-lréi hóu mr̀ hhòi-sham.

(d) Kréui yrat-yrat ____ dáa-mràa-jeuk, só-yrí mr̀ dhak-hràan trùng ngró heui mráai-sung.

(e) Yràu-séui ge srì-hrau ____ mr̀ hrai géi fhòng-brin.

(i) dhou
(ii) lrìn
(iii) jeuk shaam-kwràn
(iv) shìn-ji
(v) jhì-hrau

4 Answer the following questions briefly in Cantonese.

(a) Yhat nrìn yráu géi-dho yrat qaa?
(b) Chrìn-yrat hrai Lrái-baai-sei: thìng-yrat nhe?
(c) Sei-yruet yráu géi-dho yrat qaa?
(d) Shàam go shìng-krèi dhò mr̀ dhò yrat gwo yhat go yruet qaa?
(e) Yhat-chhìn yrat nroi dring-hrai shàam nrìn nroi nhe?

5 Here are three complicated sentences laden with adjectives for you to put into Cantonese. Remember, keep cool, they aren't so bad if you work out what the basic patterns are.

(a) *That young woman who is standing on the left of Mrs Chan is Mr Wong's seventeen-year-old daughter.*

(b) *Which is the Japanese car which you bought when you were touring in the States?*

(c) *This old fire extinguisher of yours is not big enough. How about buying a bigger one?*

18

第十八課 治安

JRI-QHÒN

Law and order

The subject may be a hard one, but there is no difficult grammar in this unit and you should not find the vocabulary too taxing either.

Dialogue 1

Three friends discuss the crime rate.

我每日睇報紙都一定睇到啲令我好唔開心嘅新聞嘅，譬如係謀殺喇，強姦喇，吸毒喇，打交喇，打劫喇，打荷包喇等等。

李太，呢啲噉嘅情況唔只喺香港好普遍，喺外國好多大城市都一樣普遍㗎。

前幾年我住喺紐約，喺我住嘅附近，幾乎每日都有罪案發生，而且都係我親眼睇見嘅，但係都唔見本地報紙有報導，你可以想像罪案多到幾咁嚴重嘞！

張太，聽你咁樣講，香港嘅治安雖然唔係十分好，但係都唔算太壞嗌！

係呀，真係唔算太壞，最少到而家為止，我哋普通人重敢一個人喺夜晚出街買嘢。

Mrs Lee	Ngró mrúi yrat tái bou-jí dhou yhat-dring tái-dóu dhi lring ngró hóu mr̀ hhòi-sham ge shàn-mán ge, pei-yrùe hrai mràu-saat lhaa, krèung-ghàan lhaa, khap-druk lhaa, dáa-ghaau lhaa, dáa-gip lhaa, dáa-hrò-bhaau lhaa, dáng-dáng.
Mrs Wong	Lréi Táai, nhi dhi gám ge chrìng-fong mr̀-jí hái Hhèung-góng hóu póu-pin, hái ngroi-gwok hóu dhò draai srìng-srí dhou yhat-yreung póu-pin gaa.

Mrs Cheung	Chrìn-géi-nrìn ngró jrue hái Náu-yeuk, hái ngró jrue ge fru-gran, ghèi-frù mrúi yrat dhou yráu jreui-qon faat-shàng, yrì-ché dhou hrai ngró chhàn-ngráan tái-gin ge, draan-hrai dhou mř gin bún-drei bou-jí yráu bou-drou. Nréi hó-yrí séung-jreung jreui-qon dhò dou géi-gam-yrìm-jrung laak!
Mrs Wong	Jhèung Táai, thèng nréi gám-yéung góng, Hhèung-góng ge jri-qhòn shèui-yrìn mř hrai srap-fhàn hóu draan-hrai dhou mř suen taai wraai bo!
Mrs Cheung	Hrai qaa, jhàn-hrai mř suen taai wraai. Jeui-síu dou-yrì-ghaa-wrài-jí ngró-drei póu-thùng-yràn jrung gám yhat-go-yràn hái yre-máan chheut-ghaai mráai-yré.

報紙	**bou-jí**	newspaper
令	**lring**	to cause, to make
謀殺	**mràu-saat**	murder, to murder
強姦	**krèung-ghàan**	rape, to rape
吸毒	**khap-druk**	to take drugs
打交	**dáa-ghaau**	brawling, to fight
打劫	**dáa-gip**	robbery, to rob
打荷包	**dáa-hrò-bhaau**	purse-snatching, to pick pockets
唔只	**mř-jí**	not only
普遍	**póu-pin**	common (widespread)
外國	**ngroi-gwok**	foreign, foreign country
城市	**srìng-srí**	city, town
前幾年	**chrìn-géi-nrìn**	a few years ago
紐約	**Náu-yeuk**	New York
幾乎	**ghèi-frù**	almost but not quite
發生	**faat-shàng**	to occur, happen, transpire
親眼	**chhàn-ngráan**	with one's own eyes
本地	**bún-drei**	local, indigenous
報導	**bou-drou**	report, to report
想像	**séung-jreung**	to imagine
幾咁……嘞！	**géi-gam-…laak!**	how very …!
治安	**jri-qhòn**	law and order, public order
雖然……但係	**shèui-yrìn … draan-hrai**	although … yet …
十分	**srap-fhàn**	totally, 100 per cent
最少	**jeui-síu**	at least
到而家為止	**dou-yrì-ghaa-wrài-jí**	up to now
普通	**póu-thùng**	common, ordinary
敢	**gám**	to dare, to dare to
一個人	**yhat-go yràn**	alone
出街	**chheut-ghaai**	to go out into the street

Things foreign

Ngroi means *outside*, as you will remember from **ngroi-brin**. **Ngroi-gwok** (*outside country*) is the standard word for *foreign country*, and as you might expect **ngroi-gwok-yràn** means *a foreigner* and **ngroi-gwok-wáa** means *a foreign language*. **Ngroi-gwok** is contrasted with **Jhùng-gwok** (*central country*), the country round which all others revolve, China. The Chinese have always considered themselves to be at the centre of the world, just as the Romans did with their tellingly named 'Medi-terranean' Sea, and this means that it is something of a contradiction in terms for Chinese in another country to describe themselves as **ngroi-gwok-yràn** – wherever they go they remain Chinese, and so the indigenous peoples tend to be called *foreigners* in their own lands.

 —————— **Grammar** ——————

1 Póu-thùng *and* póu-pin (common)

Both **póu-pin** and **póu-thùng** mean *common*, but there is a difference between them. Póu-pin means *common* in the sense of *widespread, universal, two-a-penny*: and **póu-thùng** means *common* in the sense of *ordinary, normal*. A **póu-thùng-yràn** is *an ordinary chap, the man on the Clapham/Shanghai omnibus*. **Póu-thùng-wáa** is *common language*, that is, the language which is used universally throughout China, what in English is usually called Mandarin and in China is known officially as Putonghua.

One use of **póu-thùng** is as a way of responding to a compliment: *How beautiful your handwriting is, Mr Wong*! – **Póu thùng jhe.** (*It's just run-of-the-mill.*) However, sometimes this very modest response is said with a cock of the head which belies its apparent humility, and Mr Wong can be understood in a boastful way to be saying something like *I'm just an ordinary genius, you know!*

2 Póu-thùng-wáa *and other languages*

Wraa means *to say*, as you learned in Unit 6, but when its tone is changed to **wáa** it means *speech, language* and often appears as the object of the 'lonely verb' **góng** (*to speak*). *To speak Mandarin* is **góng Póu-thùng-wáa**, and *to speak a foreign language* is **góng ngroi-gwok-wáa**. You can add **wáa** to the name of any country to give the language spoken in that country:

Yhìng-gwok-wáa	*English language*
Yrat-bún-wáa	*Japanese language*
Jhùng-gwok-wáa	*Chinese language*

You already know the words **Yhìng-mràn** and **Jhùng-mràn** for English and Chinese languages, and the addition of -**mràn** can be made to the roots of other country names too, but it is a risky thing to do – could you have predicted that the -**mràn** word for **Yrat-bún** is **Yrat-mràn**, for instance? You are safer sticking to the -**wáa** words.

The **mràn** and **wáa** forms are not quite the same in meaning. **Mràn** refers to the notion of both spoken and written language, while **wáa** really refers only to the spoken language. However, in practice they are mostly used interchangeably.

3 Up to now

Dou-yrì-ghaa-wrài-jí seems an awful mouthful to represent *up to now*. It may help you to remember it if you break it down into its component parts. **Dou** means *to arrive at*, **yrì-ghaa** means *now*, **wrài-jí** means *as a stop*, so *arriving at now as a stop* comes to mean *up to now*. You can adapt the expression to some extent, for example, **dou ghàm-nín wrài-jí** (*up until this year*) and **dou jrok-yrat wrài-jí** (*up until yesterday*).

 ———————————— **Dialogue 2** ————————————

 A thoughtful prisoner makes a special plea.

你犯咗偷嘢罪，而且罪名成立。我判你坐兩年監。你如果唔同意可以
　上訴。你明白未？

法官大人，我明白，不過如果我坐完兩年監之後出嚟，一定搵唔到嘢

做，因為我坐過監，冇人會請我做嘢。 所以我搵唔到錢，冇辦法生活，會再次偷嘢……噉，又會再次坐監嘅嘛！

噉，你想點樣呢? 係唔係唔想坐監，想罰錢呢?

唔係呀，大人，我實在冇錢俾你罰，啱啱相反，我希望你而家就判我坐二十五年監啫。

點解你自願要坐二十五年監咁耐呢?

因為坐完二十五年監之後，嗰陣時我會成為一個六十歲嘅老人，可以去攞老人救濟金，唔駛再做嘢嘞。

Judge   Nréi fraan-jó thàu-yré jreui, yrì-ché jreui-mrìng srìng-lraap. Ngró pun nréi chró lréung nrìn ghaam. Nréi yrùe-gwó mŕ trùng-yi hó-yrí sreung-sou. Nréi mrìng-braak mrei?

Prisoner   Faat-gwhùn Draai-yràn, ngró mrìng-braak, bhat-gwo yrùe-gwó ngró chró-yrùen lréung nrìn ghaam jhì-hrau chheut-lrài, yhat-dring wán-mŕ-dóu yré jrou, yhàn-wrai ngró chró-gwo ghaam, mróu yràn wrúi chéng ngró jrou-yré. Só-yrí ngró wán-mŕ-dóu chín, mróu braan-faat shàng-wrut, wrúi joi-chi thàu-yré . . . gám, yrau wrúi joi-chi chró-ghaam ge bo!

Judge   Gám, nréi séung dím-yéung nhe? Hrai mŕ hrai mŕ séung chró-ghaam, séung frat-chín nhe?

Prisoner   Mŕ hrai qaa, Draai-yràn. Ngró srat-jroi mróu chín béi nréi frat. Nghaam-nghaam shèung-fáan, ngró hhèi-mrong nréi yrì-ghaa jrau pun ngró chró yri-srap-ngŕ nrìn ghaam jhe.

Judge   Dím-gáai nréi jri-yruen yiu chró yri-srap-ngŕ nrìn ghaam gam nroi nhe?

Prisoner   Yhàn-wrai chró-yrùen yri-srap-ngŕ nrìn ghaam jhì-hrau, gó-jran-sì ngró wrúi srìng-wrài yhat go lruk-srap seui ge lróu-yràn, hó-yrí heui ló lróu-yràn gau-jai-gham, mŕ sái joi jrou-yré laak.

犯	**fraan**	to offend, commit a crime
偷嘢	**thàu-yré**	to steal things, theft
罪	**jreui**	a crime
罪名	**jreui-mrìng**	charge, accusation
成立	**srìng-lraap**	established, to establish
判	**pun**	to sentence
坐監	**chró-ghaam**	to be in prison
上訴	**sreung-sou**	to appeal to a higher court
法官	**faat-gwhùn**	a judge
大人	**Draai-yràn**	Your Honour, Your Excellency, Your Worship

辦法	**braan-faat**	*method, way, means*
生活	**shàng-wrut**	*to live, livelihood*
再次	**joi-chi**	*another time, a second time*
罰錢	**frat-chín**	*to fine, to be fined*
自願	**jri-yruen**	*voluntarily, willing*
成為	**srìng-wrài**	*to become*
老人	**lróu-yràn**	*the elderly, the aged*
救濟金	**gau-jai-gham**	*relief money*

 —————— **Grammar** ——————

4 More on 'lonely verbs'

You have met plenty of verbs which normally require objects (see Unit 4, grammar point 2, Unit 9, grammar point 12, Unit 15, grammar point 1), and you will recognise more as your Cantonese improves. **Thàu** (*to steal*) is another one, and you will notice that **yré** (*things*) is the supplied object. But you should not feel that because a verb has a fall-back object assigned to it you cannot embellish it – you could, for instance, say **kréui thàu-jó hóu dhò yré laak** (*he stole a lot of things*). The same applies to other verb–object pairings: **chró-ghaam** (*to sit in prison*) means *to be imprisoned*, but you can see from the dialogue that the verb and its object can be split (**kréui chró lréung nrìn ghaam** – *he's doing two years*).

5 Mrei *and* mróu

Both **mrei** (*not yet*) and **mróu** (*have not*) are used to form questions with the verb ending **-gwo**:

(a) **Nréi yráu mróu srik-gwo lrùng-hhaa qaa?**
(b) **Nréi srik-gwo lrùng-hhaa mrei qaa?**

These two examples can both be translated by *Have you ever had lobster?*, but note that the second one implies that at some time you probably will try it, so that you might prefer to translate (a) as *Have you ever had lobster?* and (b) as *Have you had lobster yet?*

Mrei (but not **mróu**) can also be used with the verb ending **-jó** when you want to know whether something has taken place yet. It is very common to greet someone with:

Nréi srik-jó fraan mrei qaa?   *Have you eaten yet?*

6 Can do/no can do?

In Unit 12 you met **tái-mȑ-dóu** (*could not see*) and Unit 15 introduced you to **wán-mȑ-dóu** (*cannot find*). In both cases you were left to guess what they meant, but you were owed an explanation and it is now time you had one. In the dialogue the prisoner says **yhat-dȓing wán-mȑ-dóu yré jrou** (*I'll certainly not be able to find work to do*). **Wán** of course means *to look for* and **dóu** you met in Unit 8, grammar point 10 meaning *to succeed in*, so **wán-mȑ-dóu** means *to look for but not succeed in it*, i.e. *to be unable to find*. Here are a few more examples:

tái-mȑ-dóu	*unable to see*
daap-mȑ-dóu bhaa-sí	*unable to catch the bus*
gwú-mȑ-dóu kréui hrai bhin-go	*can't guess who she is*

The positive form of this pattern uses **dhak** instead of **mȑ**, so **tái-dhak-dóu** means *able to see*, **daap-dhak-dóu** means *able to catch*, and **gwú-dhak-dóu** means *able to guess*. To ask a question you can of course, as always, put positive and negative together:

Nréi *daap-dhak-dóu daap-*   *Can you catch the bus?*
mȑ-dóu* bhaa-sí qaa?

But it would save breath to say:

Nréi *daap-mȑ-daap-dhak-dóu* bhaa-sí qaa?

7 As much as that

To stress the size of numbers it is quite common to add a **gam** (*so*) expression, just as in the dialogue the judge says **chró yri-srap-ngȑ nrìn ghaam gam nroi**. **Gam nroi** means *so long a time*, and the effect is to say *as long as twenty-five years in prison*. Here are some other examples:

Kréui yráu shàam-mraan mhan gam dhò.	*He's got as much as $30,000.*
Nréi yráu yri-baak brong gam chrúng.	*You weigh as much as 200 pounds.*
Ngró gáu-srap-yhat seui gam lróu.	*I'm all of 91 years old.*

8 Older *and* younger

You will need to be careful with *old*. **Lróu** means *really old, elderly, aged,* and is therefore the appropriate word in the term for *old age relief.* But when you are comparing ages (*Jack is older than Jill*) it would be absurd to use **lróu** if both people concerned are young. Cantonese prefers to use **draai** (*big*) for *old* in such a case:

Wròng Síu-jé draai-gwo Jhèung Síu-jé.	*Miss Wong is older than Miss Cheung.*
Ngró mróu nréi gam draai.	*I am not as old as you.*

It is not impossible to say **kréui lróu-gwo ngró**, but only if you are already very elderly and the person concerned is even more so.

 ——————————— **Exercises** ———————————

1 Mr Wong is insatiably curious. Unfortunately, although he writes down the answers, his memory is so bad that he can't remember what his questions were afterwards. Can you help him by supplying them (in Cantonese of course)? Here is his list of answers.

(*a*) **Ghàm-yrat hrai Shìng-krèi-yri.**
(*b*) **Lrèun-dheun Fhèi-ghèi-chrèung hái srìng-srí shài-brin.**
(*c*) **Ngró sing Jhèung.**
(*d*) **Dhi hhaa sei-srap-lruk mhan yhat ghàn.**
(*e*) **Yrau mr̀ hrai chhat-dím-jhung heui, yrau mr̀ hrai baat-dím-jhung heui, yhàn-wrai kréui srat-jroi mróu chéng ngró heui.**

2 Here's a quick and simple test. What are the opposites of the following?

(*a*) **Nràam-brin**	(*d*) **Chheut-brin**	(*g*) **Jhàn**
(*b*) **Nràam-yán**	(*e*) **Chheut-nín**	(*h*) **Jái**
(*c*) **Nhi-sue**	(*f*) **Chrìn-yrat**	(*i*) **Jhìu-jóu**

3

Chan

Cheung

Wong

Nhi shàam go yràn lréui-brin, bhin-go jeui draai qaa?

4 Tone practice time again. Put in the tone marks on the following where necessary.

(a) **Faai-dhi!** (*Hurry up!*)
(b) **fong-gaa** (*to be on holiday*)
(c) **sreung-brin** (*on top of*)
(d) **sruk shik** (*familiar with*)

(e) **yring-jhan** (*sincere*)
(f) **yhi-shang** (*doctor*)
(g) **ngroi-tou** (*jacket*)
(h) **nghaam-nghaam** (*a moment ago*)

5 Positive word-power. Dig into your vocabulary memory and find a word you know which is similar in meaning for each of the following.

(a) **brin-yhì**
(b) **gíng-chaat-chhe**
(c) **mr̀ hrai jhàn ge**
(d) **bhat-gwo**
(e) **mr̀ hó-yrí**

6 Complete the following unfinished words, remembering to get the tones right.

(a) ____-**wring** (*prosperous*)
(b) **fhòng-**____ (*aspect*)
(c) ____-**lréi** (*to repair*)
(d) **yram-**____ (*any*)
(e) ____-**seui** (*duty-free*)
(f) ____-**brin** (*convenient*)

19

第十九課　經濟
GHÌNG-JAI
Banking and finance

This unit provides you with some vocabulary for your own banking transactions and for discussing higher financial matters, and some useful grammar patterns for livening up your speech.

────── Dialogue 1 ──────

A customer has problems with his bank account.

小姐，呢張現金支票唔該你幫我兌咗佢，然後用嗰啲錢買五千蚊美金旅遊支票。

好呃。先生，重有乜嘢事呢？

嗱，呢張係我嘅銀行月結單，係今朝早收到嘅。張單上便寫明我個來往戶口上個月有赤字，而且重向銀行透支咗一萬三千蚊添。我實在冇向銀行透支過任何錢。我相信我嘅戶口一定唔會有赤字。唔該你幫我查一查，睇吓喺邊處錯咗。

好，請你交張月結單俾我喇，我會交俾有關嘅部門，有結果之後，銀行就會寫信俾你嘅嘞。

唔該晒。我希望你儘量快話我聽個結果係點樣。

好呃。我知道嘞。

唔該晒。我重想你幫我開一個外匯儲蓄戶口，好嗎？

好，冇問題。

呀，重有。今日馬克兌英鎊同埋港紙兌人民幣嘅兌換率係幾多呀？

我唔知嘛！請你去第三號櫃檯問嗰處嘅小姐喇！

Customer	Síu-jé, nhi jhèung yrin-gham jhì-piu m̀-ghòi nréi bhòng ngró deui-jó kréui, yrìn-hrau yrung gó dhi chín mráai ngf-chhìn mhan Mréi-gham lréui-yràu jhì-piu.
Teller	Hóu qaak. Shìn-shàang, jrung yráu mhat-yré sri nhe?
Customer	Nràa, nhi jhèung hrai ngró ge ngràn-hròng yruet-git-dhaan, hrai ghàm-jhìu-jóu shàu-dóu ge. Jhèung dhaan sreung-brin sé-mrìng ngró go lròi-wróng wru-háu sreung-go-yruet yráu chek-jri, yrì-ché jrung heung ngràn-hròng tau-jhì-jó yhat-mraan-shàam-chhìn mhan thìm. Ngró srat-jroi mróu heung ngràn-hròng tau-jhì-gwo yram-hrò chín. Ngró shèung-seun ngró ge wru-háu yhat-dring m̀ wrúi yráu chek-jri. M̀-ghòi nréi bhòng ngró chràa-yhat-chràa, tái-hráa hái bhin-sue cho-jó.
Teller	Hóu, chéng nréi ghàau jhèung yruet-git-dhaan béi ngró lhaa, ngró wrúi ghàau béi yráu-gwhàan ge brou-mrùn. Yráu git-gwó jhì-hrau, ngràn-hròng jrau wrúi sé-seun béi nréi ge laak.
Customer	M̀-ghòi-saai. Ngró hhèi-mrong nréi jreun-lreung faai wraa ngró thèng go git-gwó hrai dím-yéung.
Teller	Hóu qaak. Ngró jhì-dou laak.
Customer	M̀-ghòi-saai. Ngró jrung séung nréi bhòng ngró hhòi yhat go ngroi-wrui chrúe-chhuk wru-háu, hóu maa?
Teller	Hóu, mróu mran-trài.
Customer	Qaa, jrung yráu. Ghàm-yrat Mráa-hhaak deui Yhìng-bóng trùng-mràai Góng-jí deui Yràn-mràn-brai ge deui-wrun-léut hrai géi-dho qaa?
Teller	Ngró m̀ jhì bo! Chéng nréi heui drai-shàam-hrou gwrai-tói mran gó-sue ge síu-jé lhaa!

現金	**yrin-gham**	cash, ready money
支票	**jhì-piu**	cheque
兌	**deui**	to cash a cheque, to exchange currency
美金	**Mréi-gham**	American dollars
銀行	**ngràn-hròng**	bank
月結單	**yruet-git-dhaan**	monthly statement
收到	**shàu-dóu**	to receive
寫明	**sé-mrìng**	written clearly
寫	**sé**	to write
來往	**lròi-wróng**	coming and going; current (account)
戶口	**wru-háu**	bank account

赤字	**chek-jri**	(lit. *red characters*) in the red, deficit
透支	**tau-jhì**	overdraft, to overdraw
相信	**shèung-seun**	to believe, to trust
查	**chràa**	to check, investigate
錯	**cho**	error, wrong, incorrect
有關	**yráu-gwhàan**	relevant, concerned
部門	**brou-mrùn**	department
信	**seun**	a letter
儘量	**jreun-lreung**	to the best of one's ability, so far as possible
開	**hhòi**	to open
儲蓄	**chrúe-chhuk**	savings, to save
馬克	**Mráa-hhaak**	Deutschmark
英鎊	**Yhìng-bóng**	Pound Sterling
港紙	**Góng-jí**	Hong Kong Dollars
人民幣	**Yràn-mràn-brai**	Renminbi, RMB
兌換率	**deui-wrun-léut**	exchange rate

When *red* is *not* auspicious

It is hard to find red-coloured things which are not considered lucky by the Chinese, but to be *in the red* at the bank is no more desirable in a Chinese context than in a Western one. It is perhaps significant that the usual word for red (**hrùng**) is not used, but instead the word **chek** (which also means *red*) appears in the expression **chek-jri. Chek** has another meaning (*naked*) and appears in the term **chek-geuk-yhi-shang** (*barefoot doctors*), the practitioners who were trained to an elementary level in an effort to bring medical benefits to the most deprived areas of China as she strove to develop after the Communist Revolution of 1949. There is a link of poverty between the two uses of **chek**, it seems.

 —————————— **Grammar** ——————————

1 Positive commands with -jó

You first met the verb ending **-jó** in Unit 4, grammar point 4. It indicates that an action has been completed. The same verb ending also gives the idea *go ahead and do it!*, a polite and gentle exhortation. You will see an example in the dialogue where the customer says **mỳ-ghòi nréi bhòng ngró deui-jó kréui** (*please cash it for me*). Often the final particle **lhaa** gives additional force to the exhortation:

Srik-jó kréui lhaa!   *Eat it up!*

You should note that this use of **-jó** is always accompanied by an object, either **kréui** or a more specific noun:

Dáa-jó drin-wáa lhaa!   *Make the phone call!*

2 Lròi-wróng

Lròi-wróng means *coming and going*, so *a current account* is literally *a coming and going account*. You will sometimes hear people saying **lròi-lròi-wróng-wróng**, meaning *great to-ings and fro-ings*.

3 Verb me one verb!

As you will remember from Unit 15, **yhat-hráa** conveys the idea of doing something for a short while. You can also show this same idea by doubling a verb with **yhat** in the middle:

chràa-yhat-chràa   *run a little check*
tái-yhat-tái   *have a peep*

4 Cho (mistake)

Cho is a very useful little word. Its basic meaning is *incorrect, mistaken*, and that is the meaning which you will find in the dialogue (**tái-hráa hái bhin-sue cho-jó** – *and see where the error has occurred*). It can also be attached to other verbs as a verb ending:

Ngró thèng-cho laak.   *I misheard.*
Nhi go jri nréi sé-cho   *You've written this character*
laak.   *wrongly.*

In Unit 11 you met the same word **cho** in **mỳ-cho** (*not bad, pretty good*), and it appears yet again in another useful expression **mróu-cho** (*there's no mistake, quite right*).

Dialogue 2

Two puzzled friends discuss world finance.

上個禮拜五有幾間大銀行都公佈要增加利息。香港人做生意就會越嚟
越難嘞。我估下個禮拜香港股票市場又會有大災難嘞。

我估香港今年嘅通貨膨脹一定會超過百分之十。

我都估會嘞。如果係噉樣，今年會係香港連續第三年通脹超過百分之
十嘅嘞，不過通貨膨脹實在係乜嘢嚟嘅，我唔知。

老實講，我都唔知道係乜嘢嚟嘅。我只係知道我賺錢越嚟越唔夠。歐
洲嘅法國，德國，意大利同埋英國，佢哋嘅通脹重高過香港嘅喇！
但係我覺得美國嘅通脹比較歐洲國家嘅重嚴重啲添。

講起嚟，我唔明白點解最近幾年美國嘅經濟變得咁壞，美金貶值得咁
多？

係呀！我都唔明白。最近幾年美國都冇參加大規模戰爭喇，點解經濟
反而衰退呢？

對呢個問題，我哋兩個都係外行。我哋唔好再講啦！不如講啲比較容
易明白嘅嘢喇。喂，你幾時同我去睇跑馬呀？你成日都話想去，但
係好耐都冇去過。老實講，你想唔想去呀？

想係想，但係最近我冇乜錢，唔敢買馬嘞。

唔緊要㗎！你可以睇，唔駛買。嚟喇！嚟喇！星期六你一定要同我一齊
去玩。

Mr Wong	Sreung-go-Lrái-baai-ngŕ yráu géi ghàan draai ngràn-hròng dhou ghùng-bou yiu jhàng-ghàa lrei-shik. Hhèung-góng-yràn jrou shàang-yi jrau wrúi yruet-lrài-yruet-nràan laak. Ngró gwú hraa-go-lrái-baai Hhèung-góng gwú-piu srí-chrèung yrau wrúi yráu draai jhòi-nraan laak.
Mr Lee	Ngró gwú Hhèung-góng ghàm-nín ge thùng-fo-pràang-jeung yhat-dring wrúi chhiu-gwo baak-fran-jhì-srap.
Mr Wong	Ngró dhou gwú wrúi laak. Yrùe-gwó hrai gám-yéung, ghàm-nín wŕui hrai Hhèung-góng lrìn-jruk drai-shàam nrìn thùng-jeung chhiu-gwo baak-fran-jhì-srap ge laak. Bhat-gwo thùng-fo-pràang-jeung srat-jroi hrai mhat-yré lrài-gaa, ngró mŕ jhì.
Mr Lee	Lróu-srat góng, ngró dhou mŕ jhì-dou hrai mhat-yré lrài-ge. Ngró jí-hrai jhì-dou ngró ge chín yruet-lrài-yruet-mŕ-gau. Qhàu-jhàu ge Faat-gwok, Dhak-gwok, Yi-draai-lrei trùng-mràai Yhìng-gwok, kréui-drei ge thùng-jeung jrung ghòu-gwo Hhèung-góng ge lhaa! Draan-hrai ngró gok-dhak Mréi-gwok ge thùng-jeung

béi-gaau Qhàu-jhàu gwok-ghàa ge jrung yrìm-jrung-dhi thìm.

Mr Wong Góng-héi-lrài, ngró mř mrìng-braak dím-gáai jeui-gran-géi-nrìn Mréi-gwok ge ghìng-jai bin-dhak gam wraai, Mréi-gham bín-jrik-dhak gam dhò?

Mr Lee Hrai qaa! Ngró dhou mř mrìng-braak. Jeui-gran-géi-nrìn Mréi-gwok dhou mróu chhàam-ghàa draai-kwhài-mròu jin-jhàng lhaa. Dím-gáai ghìng-jai fáan-yrì shèui-teui nhe?

Mr Wong Deui nhi go mran-trài, ngró-drei lréung go dhou hrai ngroi-hóng. Ngró-drei mř-hóu joi góng laa! Bhat-yrùe góng dhi béi-gaau yrùng-yrì mrìng-braak ge yré lhaa. Wai, nréi géi-sí trùng ngró heui tái páau-mráa qaa? Nréi srèng-yrat dhou wraa séung heui, draan-hrai hóu nroi dhou mróu heui-gwo. Lróu-srat góng, nréi séung mř séung heui qaa?

Mr Lee Séung-hrai-séung, draan-hrai jeui-gran ngró mróu mhat chín, mř gám mráai-mráa laak.

Mr Wong Mř gán-yiu gaa! Nréi hó-yrí tái, mř-sái mráai. Lrài lhaa! Lrài lhaa! Shìng-krèi-lruk nréi yhat-dring yiu trùng ngró yhat-chrài heui wáan.

公佈	**ghùng-bou**	*to announce*
利息	**lrei-shik**	*interest*
越……越……。	**yruet . . . yruet . . .**	*the more . . . the more . . .*
市場	**srí-chrèung**	*market*
災難	**jhòi-nraan**	*disaster*
通(貨膨)脹	**thùng(-fo-pràang)-jeung**	*inflation*
超過	**chhiu-gwo**	*to exceed*
百分之十	**baak-fran-jhì-srap**	*ten per cent*
連續	**lrìn-jruk**	*in succession, consecutively*
嚟嘅/㗎?	**lrài-ge/gaa?**	*(final particle: for identification)*
歐洲	**Qhàu-jhàu**	*Europe*
法國	**Faat-gwok**	*France*
德國	**Dhak-gwok**	*Germany*
意大利	**Yi-draai-lrei**	*Italy*
比較	**béi-gaau**	*comparatively, to compare*
國家	**gwok-ghàa**	*country, state*
最近	**jeui-gran**	*recent, recently*
經濟	**ghìng-jai**	*economy, economic*
變	**bin**	*to change*
貶值	**bín-jrik**	*to devalue*
大規模	**draai-kwhài-mrou**	*large-scale*

戰爭	jin-jhàng	*war*
反而	fáan-yrì	*on the contrary, despite this*
衰退	shèui-teui	*to go into decline*
外行	ngroi-hóng	*layman, outsider*
不如	bhat-yrùe	*it would be better if*
跑馬	páau-mráa	*to race horses, horse-racing*

 —————— **Grammar** ——————

5 The more . . . the more . . .

There are two similar patterns using **yruet . . . yruet . . . .** There is an example of the first one in the dialogue: **yruet-lrài-yruet-nràan** (literally, *the more comes the more difficult*), *it gets more and more difficult.* You can add any adjective to the **yruet-lrài-yruet-** phrase:

Chró fó-chhe yruet-lrài-　　*It gets more and more expensive*
yruet-gwai.　　　　　　　*to travel by train.*
Kréui go jái yruet-lrài-　　*Her son gets taller and taller.*
yruet-ghòu.

The second pattern does not use **lrài** but instead uses two different adjectives or verbs to give the sense *The more it is this then the more it is that*:

Tái-bho, yràn yruet dhò　　*When watching football, the*
yruet hóu-wáan.　　　　　　*more people there are the*
　　　　　　　　　　　　　　more fun it is.

Wròng Táai yruet góng　　*The more Mrs Wong talks the*
yruet hhòi-sham.　　　　　*happier she is.*

6 Making fractions

Baak-fran-jhì-srap literally means *ten of one hundred parts* and therefore *ten parts in a hundred* or more usually *ten per cent.* All percentages are formed in the same way, so *12%* is **baak-fran-jhì-srap-yri**, and *75%* is **baak-fran-jhì-chhat-srap-ngŕ.** In fact, all fractions are made in this way too:

shàam-fran-jhì-yhat	*one-third*
sei-fran-jhì-shàam	*three-quarters*
srap-ngí-fran-jhì-srap-sei	*fourteen-fifteenths*

7 Final particle for identification

When something is defined or described for recognition by the listener, the speaker uses the final particle lrài-ge (*that's what it is*). The question form is lrài-gaa? (*what is it?*), and it is most often heard in hrai mhat-yré lrài-gaa? (*what is it?*).

8 Reluctant agreement

In the dialogue, Mr Lee is pressed to join Mr Wong at the races, and he has to admit that he would like to go but has a money problem. You should note the neat little pattern which allows reluctant agreement to be shown: it is verb-hrai-verb, draan-hrai . . . :

Ngró jhùng-yi-hrai-jhùng-yi kréui, draan-hrai ngró dhou mr`séung trùng kréui heui tái-hei.	*Yes, I like him alright, but I still don't want to go to the pictures with him.*
Wròng shìn-shàang leng-hrai-leng, draan-hrai mróu Jhéung shìn-shàang gam leng.	*Mr Wong is handsome alright, but he's not as handsome as Mr Cheung.*

9 Mróu mhat (not much)

Ngró mróu mhat(-yré) chín means *I haven't got much money*. Mhat-yré clearly is not acting as a question word here; it is used idiomatically to mean *any* or *much*. Quite often it can mean *whatsoever*, and in fact all the question words can act as *-ever* words, for example, bhin-go (*whoever*), bhin-sue (*wherever*), géi-dho (*however much*), géi-sí (*whenever*), dím-yéung (*however*):

Nréi heui bhin-drou qaa?	*Where are you going?*
Ngró bhin-drou dhou mr̀ heui.	*I'm not going anywhere.* (lit. *I'm not going to any wherevers.*)
Nréi géi-sí heui Yhìng-gwok qaa?	*When are you going to Britain?*
Ngró géi-sí dhou mr̀ heui.	*I'm not going at any time.*

☑ ———————— Exercises ————————

1 Mr Wong is on the phone to his stockbroker, and you can hear his end of the conversation. Can you supply what the stockbroker is saying (in Cantonese of course)?

Mr Wong   Chéng-mran, ghàm-yrat Yhìng-bóng deui Góng-jí hrai mŕ hrai ghòu-gwo jrok-yrat qaa?
Broker   *(No, it's not as high as yesterday.)*
Mr Wong   Dím-gáai Yhìng-bóng bín-jrik-jó gam dhò nhe?
Broker   *(The British government recently said they wouldn't raise interest rates.)*
Mr Wong   Nréi gwú hraa-go-lrái-baai Yhìng-bóng wrúi mŕ wrúi hoú-fhàan-dhi nhe?
Broker   *(I think the pound is sure to go a lot higher then.)*
Mr Wong   Nréi góng-dhak dhou-géi nghaam. Hóu, ngró jrau hraa-go-lrái-baai shìn-ji mráai Yhìng-bóng lhaa.
Broker   *(No problem. Phone me again at that time.)*
Mr Wong   Mŕ-ghòi-saai. Joi-gin.

2 Give simple answers to these simple alternative questions. You have a fifty-fifty chance of being right even if you do not understand the question!

(a) Draai-wrui-tròng hrai hái hhèung-háa dring-hrai hái srí-khèui nhe?

(b) Nréi yráu-breng ge srì-hrau gok-dhak shùe-fruk dring-hrai shàn-fú nhe?

(c) Geuk-jai yrung-lrài trìng-chhe dring-hrai hhòi-chhe nhe?

(d) Nréi gwú jóu-chhaan hrai mhat-yré qaa? Hrai yre-mráan srik ge dring-hrai yrat-táu srik ge nhe?

3 Which of (i) and (ii) is the correct translation of the following English sentences?

(a) *I can't go there with you.*
   (i) Ngró mŕ hó-yrí trùng nréi heui gó-sue.
   (ii) Ngró trùng nréi mŕ hó-yrí heui gó-sue.

(b) *I can't drive to the outlying islands.*
   (i) Ngró mŕ hó-yrí haí lrèi-dóu jhàa-chhe.
   (ii) Ngró mŕ hó-yrí jhàa-chhe heui lrèi-dóu.

(c)   *I won't be able to come until this afternoon.*
    (i)   Ngró hraa-jau jrau lrài-dhak laak.
    (ii) Ngró hraa-jau shìn-ji lrài-dhak.

(d)   *I like eating fruit salad.*
      (i)   Ngró jhùng-yi srik shàang-gwó trùng shàa-léut.
      (ii) Ngró jhùng-yi srik shàang-gwó shàa-léut.

(e)   *What do you intend to do when you go to Japan?*
    (i)   Nréi géi-sí heui Yrat-bún, séung jrou mhat-yré qaa?
    (ii) Nréi heui Yrat-bún ge srì-hrau, séung jrou mhat-yré qaa?

4 Write out the English translations of the five sentences which you decided were incorrect.

5

(a) Chràn Shàang qhuk-kéi, bhin-go jeui draai qaa?
(b) Nhi dhi yràn lréui-brin nréui-ge hrai baak-fran-jhì-géi qaa?
(c) Nràam-ge nhe?
(d) Hrai Chràn Shàang ghòu nhe dring-hrai Chràn Táai ghòu nhe?
(e) Chràn Shàang, Chràn Táai yráu géi-dho go jái qaa?

20

第二十課　郵政
YRÀU-JING

Using the postal system

In this unit you will learn some more about money words, how to give the date and how to cope with *the more . . . the more . . . .*

━━━━━ Dialogue 1 ━━━━━

A post office clerk patiently explains something to an anxious customer.

唔該俾十個郵柬，廿五個一蚊嘅郵票，同廿五個個八嘅郵票我。請問幾時有新紀念郵票賣呀？

十月十八號。

好呢！噉，下個月幾時有新首日信封買呀？

下個月十二號。

呢封信我想空郵去英國，請你幫我磅吓，要幾多郵費？

十二個六喇。

如果係平郵要幾多錢呀？要寄幾耐呀？

要三個二銀錢。差唔多要三個禮拜。

呢封信如果寄掛號要幾多錢呀？

掛號信嘅手續費係三蚊。

噉，呢封信我一共要俾幾多錢呀？

呀嘩吟要十四個六。

呢度係十五蚊。

找返四毫子俾你，多謝。

你哋有冇特快郵遞服務呀？

我哋呢間郵局太細嘞，暫時未有，請你去郵政總局喇。

Customer	Mr̀-ghòi béi srap go yràu-gáan, yraa-ngf́ go yhat mhan ge yràu-piu, trùng yraa-ngf́ go go-baat ge yràu-piu ngró. Chéng-mran géi-srì yráu shàn géi-nrim yràu-piu mraai qaa?
Clerk	Srap-yruet srap-baat-hrou.
Customer	Hóu qaak! Gám, hraa-go-yruet géi-srì yráu shàn sáu-yrat seun-fhung mraai qaa?
Clerk	Hraa-go-yruet srap-yri-hrou.
Customer	Nhi fhùng seun ngró séung hhùng-yràu heui Yhìng-gwok, chéng nréi bhòng ngró brong-hráa, yiu géi-dho yràu-fai?
Clerk	Srap-yri-lruk lhaa.
Customer	Yrùe-gwó hrai prìng-yràu yiu géi-dho chín qaa? Yiu gei géi-nroi qaa?
Clerk	Yiu shàam-go-yri ngràn-chín. Chhàa-mr̀-dho yiu shàam go lrái-baai.
Customer	Nhi fhùng seun yrùe-gwó gei gwaa-hrou yiu géi-dho chín qaa?
Clerk	Gwaa-hrou-seun ge sáu-jruk-fai hrai shàam mhan.
Customer	Gám, nhi fhùng seun ngró yhat-grung yiu béi géi-dho chín qaa?
Clerk	Hram-braang-lraang yiu srap-sei go lruk.
Customer	Nhi-drou hrai srap-ngf́ mhan.
Clerk	Jáau-fhàan sei hrou-jí béi nréi, dhò-jre.
Customer	Nréi-drei yráu mróu drak-faai yràu-drai fruk-mrou qaa?
Clerk	Ngró-drei nhi ghàan yràu-gúk taai sai laak, jraam-srì mrei yráu, chéng nréi heui yràu-jing-júng-gúk lhaa.

郵柬	**yràu-gáan**	*an air-letter form*
郵票	**yràu-piu**	*postage stamp*
個八	**go-baat**	*one dollar eighty cents*
紀念	**géi-nrim**	*memorial, to commemorate*
......號	**-hrou**	*day of the month* (in dates)
首日	**sáu-yrat**	*first day*
信封	**seun-fhung**	*envelope*
封	**fhùng**	(classifier for *letters*)
空郵	**hhùng-yràu**	*airmail*
郵費	**yràu-fai**	*postage*
平郵	**prìng-yràu**	*surface mail*
寄	**gei**	*to post*
幾耐?	**géi-nroi?** or **géi-nói?**	*how long?*

銀錢	**ngràn-chín**	*dollar*
手續費	**sáu-jruk-fai**	*procedure fee, handling charge*
一共	**yhat-grung**	*altogether*
呵嘩唥	**hram-braa(ng)-lraang**	*all told, altogether, all*
找(返)錢	**jáau(-fhàan)-chín**	*to give change*
特快郵遞	**drak-faai yràu-drai**	*express mail*
郵局	**yràu-gúk**	*a post office*
暫時	**jraam-srì**	*temporary, temporarily*
郵政總局	**yràu-jing-júng-gúk**	*general post office*

 ———— **Grammar** ————

1 Subtleties of classifiers

You are now happily at home with the idea of classifiers and the
way in which they help to describe or categorise the nouns which
follow them. Sometimes their ability to categorise makes them of
use in conveying shades of meaning. In the first line of the dialogue
the customer asks for **yraa-ngŕ go yhat mhan ge yàu-piu** (*25 one
dollar stamps*). Now if you think about it, the 'correct' classifier for
stamps should be **jhèung** because of their flat, sheet-like nature,
but in this case the customer is not thinking of them as physical
shapes but rather as items, so he uses **go** instead of **jhèung**. Don't
be alarmed if you occasionally hear people doing such things –
usually it is clear enough what is meant.

2 More on money

When whole dollars are involved, the word for *dollar* is **mhan**, as
you know. However, when there is a sum of dollars plus cents, the
word for *dollar* becomes the classifier **go** with or without the noun
ngràn-chín.
So:

> **lréung mhan** = *$2* and **srap-sei mhan** = *$14*

But:

> **lréung-go-sei (ngràn-chín)** = *$2.40c*
> **srap-sei-go-gáu (ngràn-chín)** = *$14.90c*

— 191 —

Fifty cents is more conveniently expressed as *a half* (**bun**) in such sums, so it is usual to say **shàam-go-bun (ngràn-chín)** for *$3.50c*, **srap-ngí-go-bun (ngràn-chín)** for *$15.50c*, and so on.

Ten cents as a sum is **yhat hrou-jí** or **yhat hrou**, so:

Kréui yráu lruk hrou-jí.	*He's got 60 cents.*
Ngró yráu ngí hrou-jí jhe.	*I've only got 50 cents.*

The smallest coin in circulation now in Hong Kong is the 10 cent piece, so there is no need to deal in single cents. The 10 cent piece is called **yhat go hrou-jí**, and the one dollar coin is **yhat go ngràn-chín**.

3 Dates

The months are simply expressed with numbers (see Unit 17, grammar point 5). Days of the month use the same number word (**-hrou**) that you met for addresses (**Fhàa-yrùen Drou yri-srap-baat hrou**) and bus numbers (**srap-ngí hrou bhaa-sí**), so *January 1st* is **Yhat-yruet yhat-hrou**, *May 23rd* is **Ngí-yruet yraa-shàam-hrou**, etc. The years are given in 'spelled out' number form followed by **nrìn**, as for example with **yhat-gáu-gáu-chhat-nrìn** (*1997*). Remember that the general always comes before the particular, so *17th April 1998* is:

Yhat-gáu-gáu-baat-nrìn Sei-yruet srap-chhat-hrou

And don't forget to add **nrìn** on the end when giving the year!

4 How long a time?

In Unit 8 you met **géi-sí?** (*when?*), the question word asking for a 'time when' answer. The question word asking for a 'time how long' answer is **géi-nroi?**:

Nréi géi-sí heui Yrat-bún qaa?	*When are you going to Japan?*
Ngró Srap-yruet sei-hrou heui.	*I'm going on 4th October.*
Nréi hái Yrat-bún séung jrue géi-nroi qaa?	*How long do you intend to stay in Japan?*
Ngró hái gó-drou séung jrue lréung go yruet.	*For two months.*

5 *A word you cannot forget*

Hram-braa(ng)-lraang just has to be the strangest word in the Cantonese language. It is peculiar because the three syllables are each completely meaningless on their own, and because it doesn't even sound much like a Cantonese word. Once heard it is very hard to forget, so we don't think you will have any difficulty with it. One of its meanings is *altogether*, as you will have seen from the dialogue:

> **Lrùng-hhaa, gáu-srap-sei mhan; hhaa, shàam-srap-yri-go-bun; hram-braa-lraang yhat-baak-yri-srap-lruk-go-bun ngràn-chín.**
>
> *Ninety-four dollars for the lobster; $32.50 for the prawns; $126.50 altogether.*

Its other meaning is *the whole lot* or *all*, and in this meaning it is usually accompanied by **dhou** (the adverb meaning *all* with which you are now very familiar):

Kréui-drei srèng-ghàa yràn hram-braang-lraang dhou jáu-saai laak.	*The whole family went away, every last one of them.*

6 Not for the time being

The last line of the dialogue contains the expression **jraam-srì mrei yráu** (lit. *temporarily not yet got*) – *for the time being it hasn't got it*. The expression is much used as a polite way of saying *not in stock* or *nothing yet* and it appears to offer hope that soon everything will be all right, but it would be best not to put too much faith in that hope, sometimes it seems to be merely a kindly way of saying *no*.

—————————— **Dialogue 2** ——————————

A tourist plagues his hotel clerk with questions.

我間房嘅信紙用晒嘞，你哋重有冇呀？咦！呢啲明信片設計得幾靚
嘛！我想買五張要幾多錢呀？

多謝十二個半啦，先生。

喺酒店附近有冇郵局呀？

寄明信片唔駛去郵局，喺呢處或者喺酒店大門口右便都有郵筒。

我唔係寄明信片，我想寄一個包裹返英國，點樣寄法呀？

哦，原來你想寄包裹。噉，好容易啫。你首先用白紙包好嗰個包裹，
　　然後寫上地址……

最近酒店嘅郵局喺邊處呀？

喺酒店門口向左便行大約十分鐘就到嘞。到咗郵局之後，你要填寫一
　　張寄包裹嘅表格，不過嗰張表格好簡單啫。包裹過磅之後，睇吓要
　　幾多錢，然後買郵票，貼上郵票，噉就得嘞！

我嘅包裹唔係好大，但係好容易爛嘅嘛！

噉就麻煩嘞，因為郵局唔保證包裹裡便嘅嘢冇爛嘅。

噉吖？等我諗一吓先。唔該晒。

Tourist	Ngró ghàan fóng ge seun-jí yrung-saai laak, nréi-drei jrung yráu mróu qaa? Yí! Nhi dhi mrìng-seun-pín chit-gai-dhak géi leng bo! Ngró séung mráai ngŕ jhèung yiu géi-dho chín qaa?
Clerk	Dhò-jre srap-yri-go-bun laa, shìn-shàang.
Tourist	Hái jáu-dim fru-gran yráu mróu yràu-gúk qaa?
Clerk	Gei mrìng-seun-pín mr̀-sái heui yràu-gúk, hái nhi-sue wraak-jé hái jáu-dim draai-mrùn-háu yrau-brin dhou yráu yràu-túng.
Tourist	Ngró mr̀ hrai gei mrìng-seun-pín, ngró séung gei yhat go bhàau-gwó fhàan Yhìng-gwok, dím-yéung gei-faat qaa?
Clerk	Qró, yrùen-lròi nréi séung gei bhàau-gwó. Gám, hóu yrùng-yri jhe. Nrei sáu-shìn yrung braak-jí bhàau-hóu gó go bhàau-gwó, yrìn-hrau sé-sréung drei-jí …
Tourist	Jeui krán jáu-dim ge yràu-gúk hái bhin-sue qaa?
Clerk	Hái jáu-dim mrùn-háu heung jó-brin hràang draai-yeuk srap fhàn-jhung jrau dou laak. Dou-jó yràu-gúk jhì-hrau, nréi yiu trìn-sé yhat jhèung gei bhàau-gwó ge bíu-gaak, bhat-gwo gó jhèung bíu-gaak hóu gáan-dhàan jhe. Bhàau-gwó gwo-bóng jhì-hrau, taí-hráa yiu géi-dho chín, yrìn-hrau mráai yràu-piu, tip-sréung yràu-piu, gám jrau dhak laak!
Tourist	Ngró ge bhàau-gwó mr̀-hrai-hóu-draai, draan-hrai hóu yrùng-yri lraan ge bo!
Clerk	Gám jrau mràa-fràan laak, yhàn-wrai yràu-gúk mr̀ bóu-jing bhàau-gwó lréui-brin ge yré mróu lraan ge.
Tourist	Gám qràa? Dáng ngró nám yhat-hráa shìn. Mr̀-ghòi-saai.

信紙	**seun-jí**	*letter paper*
明信片	**mrìng-seun-pín**	*postcard*
大門口	**draai-mrùn-háu**	*main doorway*
門口	**mrùn-háu**	*doorway*
門	**mrùn**	*door, gate*
郵筒	**yràu-túng**	*pillar-box*
包裹	**bhàau-gwó**	*parcel*
原來	**yrùen-lròi**	*originally, actually, in fact*
容易	**yrùng-yri**	*easy*
首先	**sáu-shìn**	*first of all*
白紙	**braak-jí**	*blank paper*
紙	**jí**	*paper*
包	**bhàau**	*to wrap up*
地址	**drei-jí**	*address*
近	**krán**	*near, close*
大約	**draai-yeuk**	*approximately*
填寫	**trìn-sé**	*to fill in a form*
表格	**bíu-gaak**	*a form*
簡單	**gáan-dhàan**	*simple*
貼上	**tip-sréung**	*to stick on*
保證	**bóu-jing**	*to guarantee*
諗	**nám**	*to think, to think about, to think over*

 ———————— **Grammar** ————————

7 Yrùen-lròi

The basic meaning of **yrùen-lròi** is *originally*, but you will probably most often meet it meaning *in fact, so now I understand how it is*. When people use the phrase they usually are acknowledging that they had been under a misapprehension about something, so it is a natural partner of the verb **yrí-wrài** (*to assume*) which you met in Unit 11:

> **Ngró yrí-wrài kréui hrai**
> **Yrat-bún-yràn, draan-hrai**
> **yrùen-lròi kréui hrai**
> **Jhùng-gwok-yràn.**

> *I thought she was Japanese but actually she is Chinese.*

8 The verb ending -hóu

Hóu of course means *good* and *very*, but as a verb ending it gives the idea that the action of the verb has been completed satisfactorily:

Nréi dhi mrìng-seun-pín   *Have you written your*
sé-hóu mrei qaa?   *postcards yet?*
Dhi seun ngró dáa-hóu laak.   *I've typed the letters.*

There is only a slight difference between **-hóu** and **-yrùen** as verb
endings: they both show that an action has come to an end, but
-hóu indicates that the result of the action is a satisfactory one.

9 Sréung *as a verb ending*

Sréung means *onto, to go up*. As a verb ending it also means *on* or
onto, and you will find that it often matches English usage quite
closely:

sé-sréung drei-jí   *to write the address on*
tip-sréung yràu-piu   *to stick on stamps*
Mr̀-ghòi nréi daai-sréung gó   *Please put on that hat.*
déng móu.

 ———————— **Exercises** ————————

1   You have not met some of the words in this exercise for quite
a while. Try writing out your translations of the sentences below, and if you have to look some of the words up make a list
of them for special study later.

   (*a*) **Wròng Shàang jeui mr̀ jhùng-yi yám yreuk-séui.**
   (*b*) **Mr̀-hóu dhaǹg-draai-deui-ngráan tái-jrue ngró.**
   (*c*) **Mr̀ hrap-kwhài-gaak ge bou-líu dhou dong hrai chi-
fo.**
   (*d*) **Hái draai-dong dóu-chín dhòng-yín hrai fhèi-faat lhaa.**
   (*e*) **Ngró-drei yiu dhò-dhi jue-yi ngró-drei dhi jái trùng
néui ge druk-shùe chrìng-fong.**

2   Give the Cantonese for the following dates and times.

   (*a*) *4th July*
   (*b*) *October 28th 1996*
   (*c*) *May 15th 2001*
   (*d*) *6.15 p.m., Sunday 11th December*
   (*e*) *31st August next year*

3 Choose which of the items in brackets best fits the sentence.

(a) **Jeui shìn yráu yràu-piu ge gwok-ghàa hrai (Jhùng-gwok/Yhìng-gwok/Yrat-bún).**

(b) **Sai-gaai drai-yhat ghàan yràu-gúk hrai hái (Lrèun-dheun/Náu-yeuk/Gwóng-jhàu).**

(c) **Yrì-ghaa sai-gaai sreung jeui gwai ge yhat go yràu-piu hrai (chhìu-gwo yhat-mraan Yhìng-bóng/yhat-mraan Yhìng-bóng/mr̀ gau yhat-mraan Yhìng-bóng).**

(d) **Yráu-dhi drei-fhòng, yràu-piu dong hrai (yrin-gham/shàn-fán-jing/fo-bún).**

4 Find suitable two-syllable Cantonese expressions using the clues supplied. The answer to the first one could be **chheut-ghaai** or perhaps **hràang-ghaai**.

(a) **Lrèi-hhòi qhuk-kéi. (____-____)**

(b) **Yhat go gwok-ghàa trùng drai-yri go gwok-ghàa dáa-ghaau. (____-____)**

(c) **Chhàa-mr̀-dho, jhik-hrai . . . . (____-____)**

(d) **Yrung fhèi-ghèi wran ge seun. (____-____)**

(e) **Hái sé-jri-lràu gwún-jrue nréi ge yràn. (____-____)**

(f) **Yhat go yràn mr̀ jeuk shaam. (____-____)**

5 As this is Unit 20 it is quite fitting that we should have a small crossword puzzle in the shape of the Chinese character for **yraa** (*twenty*). The clues are in English but the answers need to be in Cantonese.

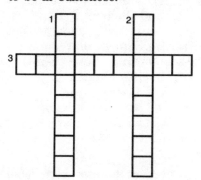

Clues

1 *Europe* (4–4)
2 *Do the washing* (3–5)
3 *To apply* (4–5)

6

Dóu-chrèung ge ghìng-lréi hóu mr̀ hhòi-sham laak! Nhi ngŕ go pràng-yráu dóu Lrèun-pún, hram-braang-lraang dhou yrèng-gán chín. Dou-yrì-ghaa-wrài-jí kréui-drei yhat-grung yrèng-jó ngŕ-mraan-sei-chhìn-lruk-baak mhan Mréi-gham. Yrèng jeui dhò ge hrai Jhèung Taai-táai, kréui yrèng-jó ngŕ-mraan-sei-chhìn-lruk-baak mhan ge shàam-fran-jhì-yhat. Drai-yri hrai Hrò Shìn-shàang, kréui yrèng-jó sei-fran-jhì-yhat. Drai-shàam hrai Wròng Shìn-shàang, yrèng-jó ngŕ-fran-jhì-yhat. Drai-sei hrai Lréi Taai-táai, yrèng-jó lruk-fran-jhì-yhat. Yrèng jeui síu ge hrai Chràn Shìn-shàang, kréui bhat-gwo* yrèng-jó yri-srap-fran-jhì-yhat jhe. (Chràn Shàang wraa mr̀-gán-yiu, yrèng ge chín mr̀ dhò draan-hrai dhou hrai hóu-gwo shùe!)

(a) Mr̀-ghòi nréi nám-yhat-nám, tái-hráa mrúi yhat go pràng-yráu yrèng-jó géi-dho chín nhe?

(b) Jrung yráu nhe . . . . Jhèung Táai yrèng-jó gam dhò chín séung chéng dhi pràng-yráu yám-jáu. Dhi jáu mr̀ prèng, mráai ngŕ go yràn ge jáu yhat-grung yiu béi sei-qraa-chhat-go-bun gam dhò. Jhèung Táai

ghàau-jó yhat jhèung yhat-baak mhan jí béi fó-gei,
yrì-ghaa dáng kréui jáau-fhàan géi-dho qaa?

* **bhat-gwo** means *but, however,* but it also can mean *only* and
is most often used in this way with numbers.

21

第二十一課　溫習(三)

– WHÀN-JRAAP (SHÀAM) –
Revision (3)

In this unit there are two short anecdotes about horses. The first is an old story about faith and unflappability. The second is a typical Chinese joke about someone who gets things wrong through being too literal-minded. The following exercises will help you revise what you have learned in Units 15–20.

─────────────── **Passage 1** ───────────────

Géi baak nrìn jhì-chrìn, hái Jhùng-gwok bhak-brou drei-fhòng, yráu yhat go sing Wròng ge yráu-chín-yràn. Kréui yráu hóu dhò yrau ghòu yrau draai yrau leng ge mráa, dhou hóu jhùng-yi nhi dhi mráa thìm. Yráu yhat yrat, yhat jek hóu leng draan-hrai géi lróu ge mráa mr̀-gin-jó.* Wròng Shìn-shàang dhi pràng-yráu go-go dhou gok-dhak hóu hó-shik, kréui-drei dhou gwú Wròng Shàang wrúi hóu nhàu, hóu mr̀ hhòi-sham, draan-hrai nghaam-nghaam shèung-fáan, kréui mr̀-jí mr̀ nhàu, yrì-ché jrung shèung-seun jek mráa hóu faai jrau wrúi fhàan-lrài thìm. Géi yrat jhì-hrau, jek lróu mráa jhàn-hrai fhàan-jó-lrài laak. Dhi pràng-yráu dhou wraa Wròng Shàang hóu-chói, kréui jí-hrai siu-hráa-gám wraa: 'Gó jek lróu mráa shik lrou, kréui wrúi wán lrou fhàan-lrài jhe.'

* mr̀-gin-jó (lit. *no longer could be seen*) lost, go missing.

─── **200** ───

─────── **Passage 2** ───────

Hóu nroi jhì-chrìn hái Gwóng-jhàu yráu yhat go yhi-shang.
Yráu yhat yrat kréui sé-jó yhat fhùng hóu gán-yiu* ge seun
béi jrue hái drai-yri go srìng-srí ge yhi-shang. Gó-jran-srì
Jhùng-gwok jrung-mrei yráu yràu-gúk, yrì-ché kréui hóu mròng
mr̀ dhak-hràan nhìng seun heui gó-drou, só-yrí kréui giu
kréui go jái bhòng kréui nhìng-heui. Kréui deui go jái wraa
'Nhi fhùng seun hóu gán-yiu, yiu jreun-lreung faai dou bo!
Nràa, geuk yruet dhò yruet faai: nréi lréung jek geuk mr̀ gau
sei jek geuk faai ge. Nréi bhat-yrùe yrung ngró jek mráa heui
lhaa! Faai-dhi qaa!'

Go hrau-shaang-jái jáu-jó, bràa-bhaa dáng kréui fhàan-lrài.
Kréui jhì-dou yhat jek mráa lròi-wróng gó go drei-fhòng dhou
yiu baat go jhung-tràu gam-sreung-háa. Gwú-mr̀-dóu kréui go
jái gwo-jó lréung yrat shìn-ji fhàan-lrài, deui bràa-bhaa hóu
hhòi-sham gám wraa: 'Bràa-bhaa, ngró fhàan-lrài laak. Nréi
wraa faai mr̀ faai nhe? Ngró séung-lrài-séung-heui git-gwó
séung-dóu yhat go hóu faai ge braan-faat. Nréi wraa geuk
yruet dhò yruet faai, lréung jek geuk mr̀ gau sei jek geuk faai
qhaa . . . gám, ngró lhàai-jrue jek mráa trùng kréui yhat-chrài
hràang . . . lréung jek geuk mr̀ gau sei jek geuk faai, lruk jek
geuk yhat-dring faai-gwo sei jek geuk, hrai mr̀ hrai qaa?'

* **gán-yiu** means *important*. You met it in Unit 2 in **mr̀ gán-yiu**
(*never mind, it doesn't matter*, or literally, *it is not important*).

 ─────── **Exercises** ───────

1   Did you manage to work out what **séung-lrài-séung-heui**
    means? If you skipped over it, go back and try again. And then
    make an intelligent guess at the English equivalents of the
    following.

    (*a*)   hràang-lrài-hràang-heui
    (*b*)   jáu-lrài-jáu-heui
    (*c*)   Ngró-drei góng-gaa góng-lrài-góng-heui dhou góng-
            mr̀-mràai laak.

2 Perhaps you know something about horses? Can you say which of the alternatives offered are correct?

(a) **Yhat jek póu-thùng ge mráa draai-yeuk yráu (ngʴ-baak brong/chhat-baak brong/yhat-chhìn brong) chrúng.**

(b) **Yhat jek mráa draai-yeuk dou (srap-ngʴ seui/yri-srap seui/yri-srap-ngʴ seui) jrau wrúi séi ge laak.**

(c) **Yhat jek mráa mrúi yrat jeui-síu yiu wran-drung (bun go jhung-tràu/yhat go jhung-tràu/sei go jhung-tràu) shìn-ji wrúi grin-hhòng ge.**

(d) **Yhat jek mráa mrúi yrat jeui-síu yiu srik (srap brong/ yri-srap brong/shàam-srap brong) yré.**

3

```
MAY 23                          MAY 24
Thursday                        Friday

10 am          _____
10.30 am       _____
12.15 pm       _____
3.30 pm        _____
6.45 pm        _____
7.30 pm        _____
```

Oh dear, it's my memory again! I have to keep a diary or I will forget what I have to do, but it seems that when I was filling it in for 23rd May I forgot to write down what it was I had to remember! I think this scrap of paper I found in my pocket has the information on it, but it's hard to understand. Can you fill in the diary entries for me in English, please?

Hái Draai-wrui-tròng trùng Jhèung Síu-jé srik qaan-jau. Trùng Hrò Síu-jé hái Hhèung-góng Jáu-dim yám baat go jri jáu, jrau yhat-chrài hràang ngʴ fhan jhung lrou heui tái-hei.

Dou lréui-yràu ghung-shi ló ghèi-piu.
Heui Wròng ghìng-lréi sé-jri-lràu bun go jhung-tràu jhì-chrìn jrau yiu dáa-drin-wáa giu dhik-sí lrài laak.

4   You have learned a lot of vocabulary by now – so much that you know more than one way of saying some things. Try finding another word with the same or almost the same meaning as the following.

   (*a*)   **draai-yeuk**   (*d*)   **tràu-shin**
   (*b*)   **yhat-grung**   (*e*)   **gaan-jhung**
   (*c*)   **bhat-gwo**   (*f*)   **dím-gáai**

 5   Here are a few more Chinese children's puzzles to make you groan. Try to work out the (fiendishly difficult) answers – in Cantonese please.

   (*a*)   **Jrok-yrat thìn-hei hóu yrit. Jhèung Shìn-shàang hái qhuk ngroi-brin jrou wran-drung, jrou-jó yhat go jhung-tràu gam nroi. Kréui dhou wraa mr̀-hrai-hóu-shàn-fú, mr̀ taai yrit. Dím-gáai nhe?**

   (*b*)   **Jhèung Shìn-shàang hrai yhat go lraap-saap-chhe shi-ghei, mrúi yrat kréui jhàa lraap-saap-chhe chheut-ghaai ge srì-hrau dhou yráu hóu dhò yràn nhìng dhi lraap-saap lrài kréui gaa chhe sue. Jí-hrai ghàm-yrat kréui jhàa-chhe chheut-ghaai, mróu yràn nhìng lraap-saap lrài. Dím-gáai nhe?**

   (*c*)   **Wròng Shìn-shàang mr̀ jrou-yré. Kréui yrat-yrat dhou yrung hóu dhò chín, nrìn-nrìn dhou heui lréui-yràu, srì-srì dhou mráai jeui gwai ge shàn chhe. Yri-srap nrìn jhì-hrau kréui srìng-wrai yhat go yráu yhat-baak-mraan mhan ge yráu-chín yràn laak. Dím-gáai nhe?**

6   No two people seem to agree exactly on anything. Here are some comments by different people about Mr Wong's new car. Can you translate their different views accurately into Cantonese?

   (*a*)   *It's a very handsome car.*
   (*b*)   *It's handsome, it's true, but not as handsome as Mr Cheung's new car.*
   (*c*)   *It's not very handsome.*
   (*d*)   *It's not big enough.*
   (*e*)   *It's too expensive.*
   (*f*)   *It's the most handsome car in the world.*
   (*g*)   *It's much more handsome than my car is.*

(h)   *It's just as large and just as expensive as Mr Cheung's new car.*

7   Supply the missing words in the following sentences. Go carefully – there may be more than one possibility and you should try to find the best alternative.

(a)   **Nhi ____ shìn-shàang hrai Wròng ghìng-lréi.**
(b)   **Kréui ____ yhat mhan dhou mr̀ háng béi gó go mróu chín ge yràn.**
(c)   **Ngró mràa-mhaa baat-srap-ngŕ seui gam ____.**
(d)   **Kréui lrài-jó ____-nroi qaa? Ngró mr̀ jhì, draai-yeuk lréung-shàam go shìng-krèi, wraak-jé yráu sei go shìng-krèi gam ____ laak.**
(e)   **Ngró ngŕ-srap-chhat seui, nréi bhat-gwo hrai sei-srap-gáu seui jhe. Ngró ____-gwo nréi baat seui.**

8   Usually one person picks up the bill when Cantonese people dine out, and 'going Dutch' is rare. Still, it is felt sometimes that for one person to pay for all would be too much, so different shares are agreed upon. Someone *draws a ghost's leg* (**wraak-gwái-geuk** – **gwái** is *a ghost*), a ladder diagram with one vertical line for each person, and a share of the bill written at the bottom of each. With the shares covered up, each person can add a horizontal line anywhere in the diagram or indeed can choose not to add a line at all. Then one by one they trace out their fate, going down their vertical until the first horizontal, which they must follow to the next vertical, down that to the next horizontal, follow that . . . and so on down to the bottom. Six friends have recently had two meals each costing $2000. On each occasion they agreed to make one share of $800, one of $500, one of $400, one of $300, and two zero-sum shares. Diagram A shows the *ghost's leg* as drawn at the first meal, and Diagram B shows four additional lines which four of the participants decided to put in at the second meal. You should have no difficulty in working out who had to pay how much each time and how the situation was changed by the extra lines.

(a)   **Wròng Shìn-shàang A-geuk yiu béi dhò-dhi dring-hrai B-geuk yiu béi dhò-dhi nhe?**
(b)   **B-geuk hrai bhin wái yiu béi baat-baak mhan qaa?**
(c)   **Jhèung Shìn-shàang A-geuk yiu béi, B-geuk dhou yiu béi. B-geuk kréui yiu béi dhò géi-dho chín qaa?**

Diagram A

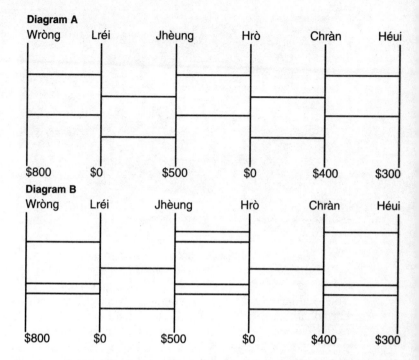

Diagram B

(d) **Kréui-drei yhat-chrài wáan A-geuk trùng B-geuk, gám, bhin wái yiu béi jeui síu nhe? bhin wái yiu béi jeui dhò nhe?**

9 Each of the sentences in this exercise uses one of the new grammar patterns from the last six units. If you can put them all into good Cantonese you can congratulate yourself on having really mastered some difficult material.

(a) *When my mother speaks on the telephone she speaks quite slowly.*

(b) *Waiter, this coffee is not hot enough.*

(c) *Would you like beer or water?*

(d) *That pen of yours which you bought last month is not as expensive as this one of mine.*

(e) *She told me to tell you what time you should come.*

(f) *Mr Wong doesn't even like eating lobster.*

(g) *Two-thirds of these books are in Chinese.*

(h) *He gets richer and richer.*

10

Hhèung-góng ge thìn-hei Chhat-yruet, Baat-yruet, Gáu-yruet hóu yrit. Thìn-hei yrit ge srì-hrau dhi yràn hóu jhùng-yi chró dhik-sí, dhik-sí yrau dhò yrau shùe-fruk. Dím-gáai shùe-fruk nhe? Yhàn-wai gaa-gaa dhou yráu lráang-hei. Yhat gaa dhik-sí hó-yrí chró-dhak sei wraak-jé ngɼ go yràn, mɼ-sái hóu dhò chín, hóu prèng jhe. Póu-thùng chhe yráu lràam-shik ge, yráu lruk-shik ge, braak-shik, hrùng-shik, hhak-shik, wròng-shik, mhat-yré shik dhou yráu, draan-hrai dhik-sí mɼ trùng, gaa-gaa dhik-sí dhou hrai hrùng-shik trùng-mràai ngràn-shik ge.

22

第二十二課　寫字樓
— SÉ-JRI-LRÀU —
The office

Some useful terms for the work environment and two or three really colloquial speech patterns to add liveliness to your conversation.

———— Dialogue 1 ————

Two friends discuss office working conditions.

呀陳，而家差唔多九點囉噃，點解你重喺呢處食早餐呢？唔駛返工咩？

唔係，我要返工，我返九點半呀。

你哋公司有彈性上班制度咩？

係呀。有九點同九點半兩班。

噉，幾點放工呀？

六點放工。喺下晝有九個字食晏晝。

工作時間都幾長噃！食晏晝嘅時間就太短嘞。過時工作有冇錢補㗎？

有。每個鐘頭補返三百五十蚊。

重有啲乜嘢福利呀？

每年有二十日係有薪水嘅假期。年尾有雙薪，有醫療津貼，有仔女教育津貼，女職員重有十個禮拜分娩假期。退休嘅時候重可以得到退休金添。王先生歡迎你加入我哋公司服務。

你講笑咩⁉ 我太老，冇用啦！

Mr Wong　Qaa-Chán, yrì-ghaa chhàa-mr̀-dho gáu-dím lo bo, dím-gáai nréi jrung hái nhi-sue srik jóu-chhaan nhe? Mr̀-sái fhàan-ghùng mhe?

Mr Chan Mr̀ hrai, ngró yiu fhàan-ghùng, ngró fhàan gáu-dím-bun qaa.

Mr Wong Nréi-drei ghung-shi yráu draan-sing sréung-bhaan jai-drou mhe?

Mr Chan Hrai qaa. Yráu gáu-dím trùng gáu-dím-bun lréung bhaan.

Mr Wong Gám, géi-dím fong-ghùng qaa?

Mr Chan Lruk-dím fong-ghùng. Hái hraa-jau yráu gáu go jri srik qaan-jau.

Mr Wong Ghùng-jok srì-gaan dhou-géi chrèung bo! Srik qaan-jau ge srì-gaan jrau taai dúen laak. Gwo-srì ghùng-jok yráu mróu chín bóu gaa?

Mr Chan Yráu. Mrúi go jhung-tràu bóu-fhàan shàam-baak-ngŕ-srap mhan.

Mr Wong Jrung yráu dhi mhat-yré fhuk-lrei qaa?

Mr Chan Mrúi nrìn yráu yri-srap yrat hrai yráu shàn-séui ge gaa-krèi. Nrìn-mréi yráu shèung-shàn, yráu yhì-lrìu jhèun-tip, yráu jái-néui gaau-yruk jhèun-tip, nréui-jhik-yrùen jrung yráu srap go lrái-baai fhàn-mrín gaa-krèi. Teui-yhàu ge srì-hrau jrung hó-yrí dhak-dóu teui-yhàu-gham thìm. Wròng Shìn-shàang fhùn-yrìng nréi ghàa-yrap ngró-drei ghung-shi fruk-mrou.

Mr Wong Nréi góng-siu mhe!? Ngró taai lróu, mróu yrung laa!

呀......	**Qaa-**	(familiar prefix for names and relationships)
早餐	**jóu-chhaan**	*breakfast*
返工	**fhàan-ghùng**	*to go to work*
彈性	**draan-sing**	*flexible*
上班	**sréung-bhaan**	*to go to work, go on shift*
制度	**jai-drou**	*system*
放工	**fong-ghùng**	*to finish work*
晏晝	**qaan-jau**	*midday, early afternoon, lunch-time; lunch*
工作	**ghùng-jok**	*work, job; to work*
長	**chrèung**	*long*
短	**dúen**	*short*
過時	**gwo-srì**	*overtime*
補	**bóu**	*to compensate*
福利	**fhuk-lrei**	*benefits, welfare*
薪水	**shàn-séui**	*salary*
假期	**gaa-krèi**	*holiday*
雙薪	**shèung-shàn**	*double salary*
醫療	**yhì-lrìu**	*medical*
津貼	**jhèun-tip**	*allowance, grant*

仔女	**jái-néui**	*sons and daughters, children*
職員	**jhik-yrùen**	*staff, employee, clerk*
分娩	**fhàn-mrín**	*to give birth*
退休	**teui-yhàu**	*to retire*
退休金	**teui-yhàu-gham**	*pension*
歡迎	**fhùn-yrìng**	*welcome, to welcome*

 ———————————— **Grammar** ————————————

1 Familiar terms of address

In Unit 6, grammar point 5 you learned that **Lróu** (*Old*) is used with surnames as a familiar way of addressing someone. You can refer to a younger person or a child by putting **Síu-** (*Little*) in front of their name. In both cases a surname which has a mid level, low level or low falling tone changes to a mid rising tone. Another way is to put **Qaa-** in front of the surname (again with the same tone changes). In fact, the sound **Qaa-** seems to be intimately connected with referring to or addressing people. It can be used with personal names as well (someone with the name **Chràn Jhi Bhak**, for instance, might be addressed as **Qaa-Bhak** by his family and friends) and it can be used with kinship terms (you could address your father as **Qaa-bhàa** instead of **Bràa-bhaa**). It is almost as though when you say **Qaa-** you are warning your listener that you are about to talk to them or to talk about a person.

2 Fhàan-ghùng *and* fong-ghùng

In Unit 3, grammar point 2 you met **fhàan** meaning *to return* or *to go where you usually go*: one of the examples was **fhàan sé-jri-lràu** (*to go to the office*). **Ghùng** means *work* and **jrou-ghùng** means *to do work, to work*. **Fhàan-ghùng** means *to go to work* in the same way that **fhàan sé-jri-lràu** means *to go to the office*, but *to finish work* and *to leave the office at the end of the day* both are expressed in the same way – **fong-ghùng**.

It is worth noting for your own use the colloquial way in which in the dialogue Mr Chan says that he goes in to work at 9.30: **ngró fhàan gáu-dím-bun**.

Fun with characters

The Chinese character used for **mhe?** is an interesting one. It shows a mouth and a sheep, and so indicates the bleating of a sheep, and that is rather what **mhe?** sounds like. The character for **maa?** shows a mouth and a horse, but you may find that a less convincing sound guide – every English-speaking person knows that horses go 'neigh' not 'maa', don't they?

3 The long *and the* short *of it*

Another pair of opposites: **chrèung** (*long*) and **dúen** (*short*). Both of them can be used for periods of time, as they are in the dialogue, but they are also used for lengths of things (*a long piece of string, a short pencil*) and even for more abstract things like *a long novel* and *a shortcoming*.

4 The tail again

In Unit 17 you met **yruet-mréi** (*the end of the month*), and in this unit there is **nrìn-mréi** (*the end of the year*). **Mréi** literally means *the tail*, but since tails are found at the end, it is logical enough that it should also mean *the end* and you will probably meet it quite often. One common expression is **drai-mhei** (*the last* – note the tone change), which of course contrasts with **drai-yhat** (*the first*).

5 Sons and daughters

Jái-néui means *sons and daughters*, and you need to bear that in mind when translating the word *children*. Only use **jái-néui** where *sons and daughters* would be appropriate. In English it would sound odd to say, *Oh look, there are several hundred sons and daughters over there in the school playground*; you would instead say *children*. Similarly in Cantonese, you would not use **jái-néui** in this case, you would use **sai-mhan-jái** (*children*).

Double salary

The Chinese have traditionally used two separate calendars, a lunar and a solar one. To keep them roughly in step, it has been necessary to add an extra month in seven lunar years out of every nineteen. So lunar years consist of either twelve or thirteen months. Chinese monthly salaries are nowadays usually paid according to the Western solar calendar, in which of course the years always have only twelve months, but it has become a custom among some employers to pay an additional month's salary every solar year as if it were a thirteen-month lunar year: its closest equivalent is perhaps the Western 'Christmas Bonus'. That is what is referred to in the dialogue as **shèung-shàn** (*double salary*).

—————— Dialogue 2 ——————

Interviewing a secretary for a job.

李小姐，你申請做我哋公司嘅秘書，我啱啱見過你打字嘞，表現都幾好。你識唔識用電腦呀？

經理先生，對唔住，我唔識。

唔識咩？今日嘅世界唔識用電腦唔得㗎！噉，你識唔識用傳真機呀？

呢啲先進嘅設備我見都未見過，當然唔識用喇。不過如果經理肯俾機會我，我會好俾心機學嘅。

你喺上海做過幾多年秘書呀？

差唔多有十七年嘞。

喺上海嘅寫字樓有幾多位秘書呀？

只有我一個係秘書，我要獨立處理一切公司嘅文件，而且要直接向經
理負責。

好喇！我就請你喇，不過第一個月係試用期，我想睇吓你嘅工作表現
先。其他詳細嘅福利同工作條件，等過咗試用期再講喇。你聽日可
以嚟開工嘞。

多謝經理。聽日見。

Manager	Lréi Síu-jé, nréi shàn-chíng jrou ngró-drei ghung-shi ge bei-shùe, ngró nghaam-nghaam gin-gwo nréi dáa-jri laak, bíu-yrin dhou-géi hóu. Nréi shik mr̀ shik yrung drin-nróu qaa?
Miss Lee	Ghìng-lréi shìn-shàang, deui-mr̀-jrue, ngró mr̀ shik.
Manager	Mr̀ shik mhe? Ghàm-yrat ge sai-gaai mr̀ shik yrung drin-nróu mr̀ dhak bo! Gám, nréi shik mr̀ shik yrung chrùen-jhàn-ghèi qaa?
Miss Lee	Nhi-dhi shìn-jeun ge chit-brei ngró gin dhou mrei gin-gwo, dhòng-yín mr̀ shik yrung lhaa. Bhat-gwo yrùe-gwó ghìng-lréi háng béi ghèi-wrui ngró, ngró wrúi hóu béi shàm-ghèi hrok ge.
Manager	Nréi hái Sreung-hói jrou-gwo géi-dho nrìn bei-shùe qaa?
Miss Lee	Chhàa-mr̀-dho yráu srap-chhat nrìn laak.
Manager	Hái Sreung-hói ge sé-jri-lràu yráu géi-dho wái bei-shùe qaa?
Miss Lee	Jí yráu ngró yhat go hrai bei-shùe, ngró yiu druk-lraap chúe-lréi yhat-chai ghung-shi ge mràn-gín, yrì-ché yiu jrik-jip heung ghìng-lréi fru-jaak.
Manager	Hóu lhaa! Ngró jrau chéng nréi lhaa! Bhat-gwo drai-yhat go yruet hrai si-yrung-krèi, ngró séung tái-hráa nréi ge ghùng-jok bíu-yrin shìn. Krèi-thàa chreùng-sai ge fhuk-lrei trùng ghùng-jok trìu-gín, dáng gwo-jó si-yrung-krèi joi góng lhaa. Nréi thìng-yrat hó-yrí lrài hhòi-ghùng laak.
Miss Lee	Dhò-jre ghìng-lréi. Thìng-yrat gin.

秘書	**bei-shùe**	*secretary*
打字	**dáa-jri**	*to type (lit. to hit characters)*
表現	**bíu-yrin**	*performance, to perform*
電腦	**drin-nróu**	*computer (lit. electric brain)*
傳真機	**chrùen-jhàn-ghèi**	*fax machine*
傳真	**chrùen-jhàn**	*fax, to fax*
先進	**shìn-jeun**	*advanced*

肯	háng	*to be willing to*
機會	ghèi-wrui	*chance, opportunity*
心機	shàm-ghèi	*mind, thoughts*
上海	Sreung-hói	*Shanghai*
獨立	druk-lraap	*independent, independently*
處理	chúe-lréi	*to handle, manage, deal with*
一切	yhat-chai	*every single one of, the whole run of, all*
文件	mràn-gín	*document*
直接	jrik-jip	*direct, directly*
負責	fru-jaak	*to be responsible*
試用期	si-yrung-krèi	*probationary period, trial period*
詳細	chrèung-sai	*detailed, minute, fine*
條件	trìu-gín	*a condition, terms*
開工	hhòi-ghùng	*to start work, to start a job*

 —————— **Grammar** ——————

6 Simply must

You probably found no difficulty with the sentence **Ghàm-yrat ge sai-gaai m̀r shik yrung drin-nróu m̀r dhak bho!** (*In today's world you simply must know how to use a computer!*). Note how the pattern works: it is **m̀r** + verb + **m̀r dhak**, that is, *if you don't* verb *it won't do!* or *you simply must* verb! Here are some other examples:

Gó dhi hhaa nréi m̀r srik m̀r dhak! *You really must eat those prawns.*

Wròng Táai wraa nréi m̀r heui taam kréui m̀r dhak. *Mrs Wong says you simply must go to visit her.*

7 Never even ...

In the dialogue Miss Lee says **gam shìn-jeun ge chit-brei ngró gin dhou mrei gin-gwo** (*I haven't even seen such newfangled equipment*). The pattern **gin dhou mrei gin-gwo** may have struck a chord with you – do you remember the **lrìn ... dhou ...** pattern which you met in Unit 17, grammar point 11? Here instead of **lrìn** + **dhou** the same verb appears twice + **dhou**, but the meaning is still *not even. ...*

8 Shàm-ghèi

Shàm-ghèi is quite a difficult word to grasp. Its closest equivalent in English is *the mind*, but perhaps the following examples of its most common usage will be the easiest way to come to terms with it:

Ngró wrúi hóu béi shàm-ghèi hrok.

I'll try my hardest to learn. (lit. I will very much give my mind to learning.)

Ngró mróu shàm-ghei heui.

I have no enthusiasm for going.

Kréui hóu mróu shàm-ghèi.

She's very out of sorts / listless / without enthusiasm / non-committal.

9 Direct *and* indirect

Jrik-jip literally means *directly in contact*, and so *directly*. Its opposite is gaan-jip (*touching at an interval*), that is, *indirectly*.

10 Fru-jaak (to be responsible to)

Note the way in which fru-jaak is used with heung. Miss Lee says in the dialogue that she jrik-jip heung ghìng-lréi fru-jaak (*was directly answerable to the manager*). You met heung first in Unit 6, where it meant *towards*, but here it may be better to think of it as meaning something like *vis-à-vis* or *as regards*. There was a similar example in the first dialogue of Unit 19: heung ngràn-hròng tau-jhì (*to be overdrawn at (vis-à-vis) the bank*).

 ———————— **Exercises** ————————

1 The following questions all use mhe? The short answer (either hrai or mr̀ hrai) has been supplied. In each case, supply the long full answer after the short one. For instance, the first answer would be Mr̀ hrai, ngró mr̀ hrai Mréi-gwok-yràn. Easy? Well, you may need to watch your step . . .

   (a) Nréi hrai Mréi-gwok-yràn mhe? Mr̀ hrai, . . .
   (b) Wròng Shìn-shàang dhi jái-néui yruet-lrài-yruet-wraai mhe? Hrai, . . .

(c)   Nréi mrei srik-gwo jóu-chhaan mhe? Hrai, . . .

(d)   Kréui mř-hrai-géi-jhùng-yi fhàan-ghùng mhe? Mř hrai, . . .

(e)   Yhìng-gwok-yràn trùng Jhùng-gwok-yràn yhat-yreung gam jhùng-yi tái-bho mhe? Hrai, . . .

2   Fill in the blanks in the following sentences.

(a)   Gáu go yràn yhat-go-yhat-go-gám hràang-lrou, drai-yhat go hó-yrí wraa hrai 'tràu-yhat go': drai-gáu go nhe? Hó-yrí wraa hrai 'drai-____ go'.

(b)   Wròng Síu-jé srèng-yrat dáa-drin-wáa ____ ngró, shàai ngró hóu dhò srì-gaan!

(c)   Chràn Táai baat-dím-gáu-go-jri shìn-ji fhàan sé-jri-lràu. Ngró ____ baat-dím.

(d)   'Kréui bràa-bhaa bhat-gwo jrou-gwo yri-srap nrìn yhi-shang jrau teui-yhàu laak.'
'Wràa, gam ____ srì-gaan! Kréui dhi breng-yràn tái yhi-shang yhat-dring yiu béi hóu dhò chín laa!'

3   Supply an appropriate verb ending for each of the blanks in the following sentences.

(a)   Whài-lrìm yrì-ghaa srik-____ fraan, chrì-dhi hó-yrí chheut-ghaai wáan.

(b)   Lráang qràa? Dhòng-yín mř gok-dhak lráang. Ngró jeuk-____ hóu nrúen ge shàam qaa.

(c)   Ngró mrei si-____ lrùng-hhaa. Hóu mř hóu srik qaa?

(d)   Dhi hhaa srik-____ laak; yrì-ghaa lrìn yhat jek dhou mróu laak.

(e)   Wai! Nréi wán bhin wái qaa? Hrò Síu-jé nhe? Qhòu, Hrò Síu-jé nghaam-nghaam hràang-____ jó laak. Kréui fhàan-lrài ngró wrúi wraa kréui jhì nréi dáa-gwo drin-wáa lrài laak.

4   The idea of this silly game is to climb the Peak in Hong Kong. But it is a game full of social significance: to live on the Peak (**shàan-déng**) is the height (so to speak) of ambition for many people in Hong Kong! You will need a dice and at least one opponent (if he/she/they cannot read the instructions, so much the better for you!). Start at the airport where you arrive penniless. Just as in real life, it's very hard to win! By the way, **héi-dím** (*lift-off point*) and **jhùng-dím** (*end point*) mean *Start* and *Finish* in board games like this.

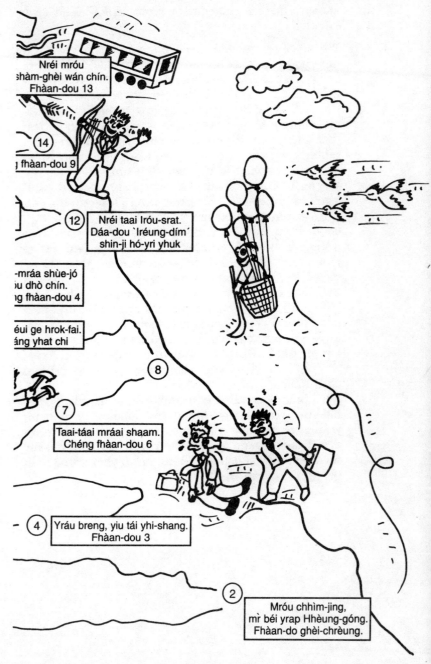

5 Here are some higher mathematical problems for you to solve (in Cantonese of course).

(a) Wròng Síu-jé ge shàn-séui mř ghòu, bhat-gwo hrai ngŕ-chhìn-sei-baak mhan yhat go yruet. Hóu-chói kréui nrìn-mréi yráu shèung-shàn. Gám, kréui yhat nrìn yhat-grung ló géi-dho chín qaa?

(b) Chràn Shàang Sei-yruet ge shàn-séui hrai yri-mraan-ngŕ-chhìn mhan. Hrò Shàang Sei-yruet fhàan-jó baat yrat ghùng, mrúi yrat ló ge chín yráu shàam-chhìn mhan gam dhò. Gó go yruet Chràn Shàang dring-hrai Hrò Shàang ló ge chín dhò nhe?

(c) Wròng Táai hóu hhàan. Yhàn-wrai chró drei-tit gwai-gwo chró bhaa-sí, kréui jrung-mrei chró-gwo drei-tit. Chró síu-bhaa dhou mróu chró bhaa-sí gam prèng, só-yrí kréui hóu síu daap síu-bhaa. Ghàm-yrat kréui hràang-lrou heui srí-chrèung, mráai-jó jeui prèng jeui prèng draan-hrai mř shàn-shìn ge hhaa trùng-mràai bun-ghàn ngràu-yruk, yrau mráai-jó yhat-dhi krèi-thàa sung. Ngràu-yruk mráai srap-ngŕ mhan yhat ghàn, dhi hhaa bhat-gwo yiu chhat-go-bun, krèi-thàa sung jí-hrai sei-go-baat ngràn-chín jhe. Kréui mráai-jó ge yré hóu chrúng, mř chró bhaa-sí fhàan qhuk-kéi mř dhak. Daap bhaa-sí yiu lréung-go-lruk. Nràa, Wròng Táai ghàm-yrat yhat-grung yrung-jó géi-dho chín qaa?

(d) Ngró bràa-bhaa séi-jó hóu nroi laak, mràa-mhaa jrung hái-sue; yráu sei go hhìng-drai, shàam go jí-mrui; yráu ngró taai-táai trùng-mràai ngŕ go jái-néui. Ngró-drei hram-braang-lraang dhou jrue hái yhat chràng mř draai mř sai ge láu. Chéng-mran yhat-grung yráu géi-dho go yràn qaa?

23

第二十三課　香港酒樓
HHEÙNG-GÓNG JÁU-LRÀU

Eating out in Hong Kong

No excuses need to be made for returning to the subject of food. You will find it the single most useful topic when talking to Chinese people.

 ——————— **Dialogue 1** ———————

A food-loving visitor talks to a Hong Kong gourmet.

我嚟咗香港差唔多有兩個禮拜嘞，對香港嘅酒家同餐廳都有好感。我
　覺得一個嚟香港玩嘅遊客如果唔去酒家試吓中國菜，噉，真係一個
　大損失嘞。
你好中意食中國菜咩？
喺香港中國菜唔只種類多，款式齊全，價錢平，而且色香味都係一流嘅。
請問你喺貴國做乜嘢生意㗎？
我係法國人，我開餐廳嘅。
唔怪得你對食物咁有認識喇。你最中意食乜嘢呀？
廣東點心同海鮮。
可惜最近幾年香港嘅海鮮越嚟越貴。喺酒家食咗海鮮之後我有時唔敢
　叫「埋單」，唔知帶嚟嘅錢夠唔夠。「污染」我估就係直接影響海
　鮮價錢嘅原因嘞。
重有一點，我估香港嘅酒樓同餐廳係世界上最多，最集中嘅嘞。你睇
　香港有一條街不過兩公里咁長之嘛，酒樓同餐廳就超過五百間嘞。
　我唔知邊處有咁多顧客日日都嚟幫趁呢？
你喺香港住耐啲，你就知點解嘅嘞。

— **219** —

Visitor Ngró lrài-jó Hhèung-góng chhàa-mr̀-dho yráu lréung go
lrái-baai laak, deui Hhèung-góng ge jáu-ghaa trùng
chhaan-theng dhou yráu hóu-gám. Ngró gok-dhak yhat
go lrài Hhèung-góng wáan ge yràu-haak yrùe-gwó mr̀
heui jáu-ghaa si-hráa Jhùng-gwok-choi, gám, jhàn-hrai
yhat go draai súen-shat laak.

Local Nréi hóu jhùng-yi srik Jhùng-gwok-choi mhe?

Visitor Hái Hhèung-góng Jhùng-gwok-choi mr̀-jí júng-lreui dhò,
fún-shik chrài-chrùen, gaa-chrìn prèng, yrì-ché shik-
hhèung-mrei dhou hrai yhat-lràu ge.

Local Chéng-mran nréi hái gwai-gwok jrou mhat-yré shàang-yi
gaa?

Visitor Ngró hrai Faat-gwok-yràn, ngró hhòi chhaan-theng ge.

Local Mr̀-gwaai-dhak nréi deui srik-mrat gam yráu yring-shik
lhaa. Nréi jeui jhùng-yi srik mhat-yré qaa?

Visitor Gwóng-dhùng dím-sham trùng hói-shin.

Local Hó-shik jeui-gran-géi-nrìn Hhèung-góng ge hói-shin yruet-
lrài-yruet-gwai. Hái jáu-ghaa srik-jó hói-shin jhì-hrau
ngró yráu-srì mr̀ gám giu 'Mràai-dhaan', mr̀ jhì daai-lrài
ge chín gau mr̀ gau. 'Whù-yrím' ngró gwú jrau hrai jrik-
jip yíng-héung hói-shin gaa-chrìn ge yrùen-yhàn laak.

Visitor Jrung yráu yhat dím, ngró gwú Hhèung-góng ge jáu-
lràu trùng chhaan-theng hrai sai-gaai sreung jeui dhò,
jeui jraap-jhùng ge laak. Nréi tái, Hhèung-góng yráu
yhat trìu ghaai bhat-gwo lréung ghung-lréi gam chrèung
jhi-mráa, jáu-lràu trùng chhaan-theng jrau chhìu-gwo
ngr̀-baak ghàan laak. Ngró mr̀ jhì bhin-sue yráu gam
dhò gwu-haak yrat-yrat dhou lrài bhòng-chan nhe?

Local Nréi hái Hhèung-góng jrue nroi-dhi, nréi jrau jhì dím-
gáai ge laak.

酒家	**jáu-ghaa**	*Chinese restaurant*
餐廳	**chhaan-theng**	*restaurant serving non-Chinese food*
好感	**hóu-gám**	*favourable impression, good opinion*
遊客	**yràu-haak**	*tourist*
菜	**choi**	*food, cuisine; vegetables*
損失	**súen-shat**	*a loss*
種類	**júng-lreui**	*type, kind, species, variety*
齊全	**chrài-chrùen**	*complete, all-embracing*
色香味	**shik-hhèung-mrei**	*appearance, aroma and flavour*
香	**hhèung**	*fragrant, nice-smelling*
一流	**yhat-lràu**	*first-rate*

貴國	**gwai-gwok**	*your country*
開	**hhòi**	*to run a business, start a business*
唔怪得	**mr̀-gwaai-dhak**	*no wonder*
食物	**srik-mrat**	*food*
認識	**yring-shik**	*to recognise, to be knowledgeable about, to understand*
廣東	**Gwóng-dhùng**	*Guangdong (province)*
點心	**dím-sham**	*'dim-sum', hot delicacies for breakfast or lunch*
海鮮	**hói-shin**	*seafood*
埋單	**Mràai-dhaan**	*May I have the bill? (in restaurants)*
污染	**whù-yrím**	*pollution, to pollute*
影響	**yíng-héung**	*to affect, influence*
原因	**yrùen-yhàn**	*reason*
點	**dím**	*a point, a spot, a dot*
集中	**jraap-jhùng**	*concentrated, centralised*
公里	**ghung-lréi**	*kilometre*
顧客	**gwu-haak**	*customer, client*
幫趁	**bhòng-chan**	*to patronise, give custom to*

 —————— **Grammar** ——————

1 Sung *and* choi

In Unit 4 you met the term **júe-choi** for *main course*, and it is the same word **choi** which appears in this unit meaning *food* or *cuisine*.

Jhùng-gwok-choi	*Chinese food*
Gwóng-dhùng-choi	*Cantonese food*
Bhak-ghìng-choi	*Peking food* (**Bhak-ghìng** = *Beijing/Peking*)
Sei-chùen-choi	*Sichuan food* (**Sei-chùen** = *Sichuan/Szechwan*)

The basic meaning of **choi** is *vegetables*:

Ngró-drei yráu yruk, dím-gáai mróu choi qaa?   *We have meat, why don't we have any vegetables?*

Both meat and vegetables are included in the word **sung** (see Unit 4), but **mráai-choi** and **mráai-sung** mean the same thing – *shopping for food*. Confusing isn't it?

Where does *Cantonese* come from?

The word Canton probably comes from a Portuguese romanisation of the Cantonese word **Gwóng-dhùng**. **Gwóng-dhùng** is the name of the province of which the capital city is **Gwóng-jhàu**. It is somewhat confusing that Canton became the name by which the city rather than the province became known to the West. It is even more confusing that in the province there are a number of Chinese languages spoken, of which the language we call Cantonese is only one. Casting the historical problems aside, the situation now is clear: the province is called **Gwóng-dhùng**, the capital city is called **Gwóng-jhàu**, and the language which you are learning, which is the language of **Gwóng-jhàu**, is known as **Gwóng-jhàu-wáa**. By the way, the official name of the city is actually Guangzhou, which is the Putonghua (Mandarin) version of **Gwóng-jhàu**.

---

2 Not only ... but also ...

The pattern which translates *not only ... but also ...* is quite straightforward: **mr̀-jí ... yr̀-ché ... (dhou) ....** **Dhou** is not essential to the pattern, but as so often happens when plural ideas are mentioned it is likely to be used:

> **Wròng Shìn-shàang mr̀-jí shik góng Yhìng-mràn yr̀-ché Yrat-mràn dhou góng-dhak hóu hóu.**
>
> *Mr Wong cannot only speak English, his Japanese is very good too.*

3 Shik-hhèung-mrei

You met **mrei** in Unit 4 in the term **hóu-mrei** (*delicious*). Its basic meaning is *flavour*. **Shik** means *colour* or *appearance*, and **hhèung** means *nice-smelling, fragrant* (as in **Hhèung-góng** – *Fragrant Harbour* = Hong Kong). The three together make up the three qualities which ideally all Chinese food is supposed to have – good appearance, good aroma, good flavour. As with other set phrases, do not be tempted to use the individual words outside this phrase. Of the three, only **hhèung** is a 'free' word which you can use in normal speech like any other adjective/verb:

Chràn Táai, nhi dhi sung hóu hhèung. Nréi jhàn- hrai hóu shik júe-sung bho!

Mrs Chan, this food smells wonderful. You really know how to cook!

4 Honorific words

Way back in Unit 1 you met **gwai-sing qaa?** (*what is your surname?*), and it was explained that this actually meant *what is your distinguished name?* (Later you met the same word **gwai** meaning *expensive*.) Chinese politeness traditionally demanded that other people's attributes and belongings were always spoken of as *precious, honourable, distinguished*, and so on, while one's own were always mentioned as *despicable, humble, miserable*, etc. In the dialogue the Hong Kong man is properly polite when he asks the visitor what his occupation is in his *honourable country* (**gwai-gwok**). Much of the very fancy honorific terminology is no longer used, you will be relieved to hear, but it is still polite to 'cry up' other people and to 'play down' yourself. You will find that when you try out your halting Cantonese on someone, he or she will inevitably respond by saying what wonderful Cantonese you speak – that is the polite thing for a Cantonese to say. Do not be fooled into believing him or her, and above all, even if you happen arrogantly to think he or she is correct, do not reply *I know I do* or *Thank you very much, I am a genius at languages.* You should always respond by saying, for instance, how poorly you speak it, or how ashamed you are at speaking so little, or how you can only say a very few words.

The extremes of politeness

Arthur Smith, in his famous book *Chinese Characteristics*, published in 1900, tells a Chinese story of a visitor who, while waiting in his best robes for his host to come in, is drenched in oil when a rat knocks a jar off the beam above his head. When his host enters, the guest explains what has happened: 'As I entered your honourable apartment and seated myself under your honourable beam, I inadvertently terrified your honourable rat, which fled and upset your honourable oil jar upon my mean and insignificant clothing, which is the reason of my contemptible appearance in your honourable presence.' Now, that's politeness!

Dialogue 2

William has his own way of beating inflation.

威廉，點解你咁客氣請我嚟呢間餐廳食飯呀？係唔係你今日生日呀？
　恭喜！恭喜！

我唔係今日生日。冇特別意義嘅，只係我聽到一個消息話呢間餐廳就
　快要拆啦，我又好中意喺呢間餐廳食嘢，所以我就邀請你嚟一齊食
　飯啫。

我唔知道你咁中意呢間舊餐廳嘅嗜。

係呀，我重好中意懷舊添，咦！……點解今日餐牌啲餸貴過昨日嘅咁多
　嘅？我昨日啱啱先至喺呢處食過飯啫！

對唔住啦，先生，你哋真係唔好彩嘞。我哋間餐廳啱啱由今日開始加
　價。如果你哋昨日嚟食飯，我哋嘅餐廳重未加價。

你哋昨日嘅食物全部都係賣舊價吖？

係呀。

好呃。我要一條昨日你哋賣剩嘅游水魚，一斤昨日賣剩嘅游水蝦，同
　埋一啲昨日賣剩嘅生果添。

哈！原來你對食物都懷舊嘅。

Mr Ho　Whài-lrìm, dím-gáai nréi gam haak-hei chéng ngró lrài
　　　　nhi ghàan chhaan-theng srik-fraan qaa? Hrai mr̀ hrai
　　　　nréi ghàm-yrat shàang-yrat qaa? Ghùng-héi! Ghùng-héi!

William　Ngró mr̀ hrai ghàm-yrat shàang-yrat. Mróu drak-brit yi-
　　　　yri ge, jí-hrai ngró thèng-dóu yhat go shìu-shik wraa nhi
　　　　ghàan chhaan-theng jrau-faai yiu chaak laa, ngró yrau
　　　　hóu jhùng-yi hái nhi ghàan chhaan-theng srik-yré, só-yrí
　　　　ngró jrau yhìu-chéng nréi lrài yhat-chrài srik-fraan jhe.

Mr Ho　Ngró mr̀ jhì-dou nréi gam jhùng-yi nhi ghàan grau
　　　　chhaan-theng ge bo.

William　Hrai qaa, ngró jrung hóu jhùng-yi wràai-grau thìm.
　　　　Yí! . . . dím-gáai ghàm-yrat chhaan-páai dhi sung gwai-
　　　　gwo jrok-yrat ge gam dhò gé? Ngró jrok-yrat nghaam-
　　　　nghaam shìn-ji hái nhi-sue srik-gwo fraan jhe!

Waiter　Deui-mr̀-jrue laa, shìn-shàang, nréi-drei jhàn-hrai mr̀
　　　　hóu-chói laak. Ngró-drei ghàan chhaan-theng nghaam-
　　　　nghaam yràu ghàm-yrat hhòi-chí ghàa-gaa. Yrùe-gwó
　　　　nréi-drei jrok-yrat lrài srik-fraan, ngró-drei ge chhaan-
　　　　theng jrung-mrei ghàa-gaa.

William　Nréi-drei jrok-yrat ge srik-mrat chrùen-brou dhou hrai
　　　　mraai grau gaa qràa?

Waiter　Hrai qaa.

William   Hóu qaak. Ngró yiu yhat trìu jok-yrat nréi-drei mraai-
jring ge yràu-séui yúe, yhat ghàn jrok-yrat mraai-jring
ge yràu-séui hhaa, trùng-mràai yhat dhi jrok-yrat
mraai-jring ge shàang-gwó thìm.

Mr Ho   Hhàa! Yrùen-lròi nréi deui srik-mrat dhou wràai-grau ge.

生日	**shàang-yrat**	*birthday*
恭喜	**ghùng-héi!**	*congratulations!*
特別	**drak-brit**	*special, especially*
意義	**yi-yri**	*meaning, significance*
消息	**shìu-shik**	*news, item of news, information*
就快	**jrau-faai**	*soon*
拆	**chaak**	*to demolish, tear down*
邀請	**yhìu-chéng**	*to invite*
懷舊	**wràai-grau**	*nostalgia, to be nostalgic*
餐牌	**chhaan-páai**	*menu*
開始	**hhòi-chí**	*to begin, to start*
加價	**ghàa-gaa**	*to increase price*
全部	**chrùen-brou**	*all, the whole lot*
......剩	**-jring**	*(verb ending: left over, surplus)*
魚	**yúe**	*fish*
哈！	**hhàa!**	*ha! ha!*

Different restaurants

You have now met three different words for *restaurant*: **jáu-
lràu**, **jáu-ghaa** and **chhaan-theng**. The first two are both
used in the titles of restaurants serving Chinese food, and
both include **jáu** in the name, probably reflecting the fact
that Chinese people generally only drink alcohol when they
are eating on special occasions. Restaurants which call
themselves **chhaan-theng** serve styles of cuisine other than
Chinese.

There is a similar distinction between different words for
eating. **Srik-fraan** would normally imply *eating a proper meal
of Chinese food*, whereas **srik-chhaan** means to have a meal
of Western food or some other non-Chinese variety. English-
style breakfast is quite popular with many Chinese, and the
word for breakfast used nowadays is usually **jóu-chhaan**,
but the evening meal is **mráan-fraan** or **mráan-chhaan** depending on the style of food eaten.

Oddly, there is no distinction between the word for 'food' in the pair of words usually used to contrast Western and Chinese cuisines. *Western food* is **shài-chhaan,** as you might expect, but *Chinese food* is called **Tròng-chhaan**.

 ———————— **Grammar** ————————

5 Birthdays

Shàang means either *to be born* or *to give birth to*. **Shàang-yrat** is *the day of birth, birthday.* **Shàang-yrat** is unusual in that although it doesn't appear to be a verb it doesn't seem to need any other verb either. Note the first speech of Mr Ho in the dialogue: **Hrai mr̀ hrai nréi ghàm-yrat shàang-yrat qaa?** (*Is it your birthday today?*) What he actually seems to be saying is *Is it the case that you are birthdaying today?* Don't worry too much about it; just accept that that is how **shàang-yrat** is usually used.

6 Inviting people

Yhìu-chíng means *to invite* and so does **chéng** (which is actually a colloquial version of the second element in **yhìu-chíng**). There is no real difference in meaning, but **yhìu-chíng** is slightly more formal than **chéng**.

7 Starting from . . .

Yràu means *from* (see Unit 6) and it pairs with **hhòi-chí** (*to begin*) to make a pattern for *starting from* . . . . In the dialogue the waiter says *yràu* **ghàm-yrat** *hhòi-chí* meaning *starting from today*. You can use the pattern quite freely:

Yràu **lruk-dím-jhung** *hhòi-chí* **yráu hóu dhò fó-chhe.**	*There are lots of trains from 6 o'clock onwards.*
Yràu **srap-baat seui** *hhòi-chí* **kréui jrau mrei srik-gwo yruk laa.**	*She hasn't had meat since she was eighteen.*

Swimming seafood

Cantonese cuisine excels in its preparation of seafood, but only if it is alive until the last possible moment before cooking is the food considered properly fresh. The best seafood restaurants (**hói-shin jáu-ghaa**) have large saltwater tanks in which the fish, prawns and shellfish are kept alive, and customers can select what they wish to eat from this *swimming seafood* (**yràu-séui hói-shin**).

 —————— **Exercises** ——————

1   Select the words from the phrases in brackets which will make sense of the following sentences.

(a)   Hhèung-góng yráu hóu dhò (yhat-grung/yhat-chai/ yhat-lràu/yhat-srì) ge jáu-dim.

(b)   Jeui-gran-géi-nrìn Hhèung-góng ge (ghìng-lréi/ghìng-gwo/ghìng-jai) yruet-lrài-yruet-hóu.

(c)   Hái Hhèung-góng, gíng-chaat (gwhàn-yràn/draai-yràn/lhàai-yràn/lróu-yràn) yhat-dring yiu yráu lréi-yràu.

(d)   Hhèung-góng ge bhaa-sí shi-ghei hhòi-ghùng ge srì-hrau yiu jeuk (gwhàn-fruk/brin-fruk/shùe-fruk/jai-fruk).

(e)   Ngró-drei géi-srì yráu (shàn-séui/yràu-séui/saan-séui/yreuk-séui) ló qaa?

2   When you have read the following passage carefully, answer the two questions in Cantonese.

Hái Hrò shìn-shàang qhuk-kéi bhak-brin lréung ghung-lréi gó-sue yráu yhat ghàan hrok-hraau. Hái hrok-hraau dhùng-brin ngf ghung-lréi hrai yhat ghàan yhì-yúen. Hái yhì-yúen nràam-brin lréung ghung-lréi jrau hrai gíng-chaat-gruk laak. Mréi-gwok ngràn-hròng hái gíng-chaat-gruk shài-brin shàam ghung-lréi gó-sue. Chéng-mran:

(a)   Yràu ngràn-hròng heui Hrò Shàang qhuk-kéi yráu géi-dho ghung-lréi qaa?

(b)   Ngràn-hròng hái Hrò Shàang qhuk-kéi bhin-brin qaa?

3   Here are some Chinese brain-teaser 'old chestnuts' for you to solve.

(a)   Síu-Jheung wraa: 'Ngró shàn-tái chrúng-lreung ge yhat bun joi ghàa yri-srap brong jrau hrai ngró shàn-tái ge chrùen-brou chrúng-lreung laak. Chéng-mran ngró hrai géi-dho brong qaa?'

(b)   Yráu yhat yreung yré, nréi jí hó-yrí yrung jó-sáu nhìng, mŕ hó-yrí yrung yrau-sáu nhìng. Nréi gwú hrai mhat-yré nhe?

(c)   Siú-Wóng wraa: 'Ngró yrì-ghaa géi-dho seui ngró mŕ wraa nréi jhì, draan-hrai shàam nrìn jhì-chrìn gó-jran-srì nghaam-nghaam jrau hrai ngró shàam nrìn jhì-hrau ge baak-fran-jhì-shàam-srap-shàam. Gám, nréi jhì mŕ jhì ngró yrì-ghaa géi-dho seui qaa?'

(d)   Wròng Shìn-shàang daai-jó yhat-baak mhan chheut-ghaai. Hái pou-táu mráai-jó shàam bún shùe, mrúi bún dhou hrai yri-srap-ngŕ mhan. Draan-hrai pou-táu ge fó-gei jí-hrai jáau-fhàan ngŕ mhan kréui. Dím-gáai nhe?

4   Can you remember your colours? Give the answers to the following questions in Cantonese:

(a)   Nréi jhàa-chhe gin-dóu hrùng-dhang yiu jrou mhat-yré nhe?

(b)   Lràam-shik ghàa mhat-yré shik hrai lruk-shik qaa?

(c)   Lràam-shik ghàa hrùng-shik hrai mhat-yré shik qaa?

(d)   Hóu dhò hóu dhò nrìn jhì-chrìn hóu grau ge drin-yíng hrai mhat-yré shik qaa?

5   Can you interpret for your friend who is about to foot the bill for a meal in a restaurant? Unlike you, he has not taken the trouble to learn Cantonese.

Friend	*Waiter, the seafood here is really delicious, very fresh and beautifully cooked. All three of the ideal qualities were superbly realised.*
You	____
Waiter	Ngró-drei nhi-drou dhi yúe dhou hrai yràu-séui ge, dhòng-yín shàn-shìn lhaa!
You	____
Friend	*May I have the bill, please.*
You	____

Waiter	**Dhò-jre. Yri-chhìn-baat-baak-gáu-srap mhan.**
You	___
Friend	*What?!! So much? That really isn't cheap!*
You	___
Waiter	**Shìn-shàang nréi yiu jhì-dou, yrì-ghaa yràu-séui yúe drak-brit nràan-mráai. Jrung yráu nhe, ngró-drei jáu-ghaa sung faai-jí, mrúi go gwu-haak sung yhat deui.**
You	___
Friend	*I have never bought such expensive chopsticks before. OK. It wasn't cheap but it was worth it. Here's $3000.*
You	___
Waiter	**Dhò-jre.**
You	___

6

Supply the caption for the speech bubble in Cantonese: '*This is a beautiful fish, sure to be very tasty. Who will give $1000?*'

24

第二十四課 嗜好

SRI-HOU

Leisure activities

This unit introduces you to hobbies. And there is a final word about **dhou**, the adverb which has cropped up again and again throughout this book.

 ——————— **Dialogue 1** ———————

Mr Cheung has changed his habits and Mr Wong wonders why.

老張，我知道你嘅嗜好係掉郵票同捉棋，有時都見你影相同畫畫，但係好少見你跳舞或者散步嘅嘛！

係呀！尤其是呢幾個月我畫咗好多幅畫。但係運動呢，連一次都冇做過。我最憎運動。

點解最近我見你晚晚食完飯之後就一個人離開屋企去花園散步呢？第一次見到你，我重以為你唔見咗嘢，出嚟搵，但係你唔會晚晚都唔見咗嘢㗎。

唉！我去散步係有個目的嘅。

嗰個目的係唔係秘密㗎？可唔可以講俾我聽呀？

唔係秘密，我只係想離開屋企一陣啫。

真奇怪勒！你一向都中意留喺屋企，好少出街嘅嘛！

老實講你聽喇，最近我個女參加咗初級鋼琴訓練班；我太太又參加咗歌劇訓練班。晚飯之後就係佢哋練習時間勒。你話我點可以留喺屋企呢？

——— **230** ———

Mr Wong	Lróu-Jheung, ngró jhì-dou nréi ge sri-hou hrai chróu-yràu-piu trùng jhuk-kéi, yráu-srì dhou gin nréi yíng-séung trùng wraak-wáa, draan-hrai hóu síu gin nréi tiu-mróu wraak-jé saan-brou ge bo!
Mr Cheung	Hrai qaa! Yràu-krèi-sri nhi-géi-go-yruet ngró wraak-jó hóu dhò fhuk wáa. Draan-hrai wran-drung nhe, lrìn yhat chi dhou mróu jrou-gwo. Ngró jeui jhàng wran-drung.
Mr Wong	Dím-gáai jeui-gran ngró gin nréi mráan-mráan srik-yrùen fraan jhì-hrau jrau yhat-go-yràn lrèi-hhòi qhuk-kéi heui fhàa-yúen saan-brou nhe? Drai-yhat chi gin-dóu nréi, ngró jrung yrí-wrài nréi mr̀-gin-jó yré, chheut-lrài wán, draan-hrai nréi mr̀ wrúi mráan mŕaan dhou mr̀-gin-jó yré gaa.
Mr Cheung	Qhàai! Ngró heui saan-brou hrai yráu go mruk-dhik ge.
Mr Wong	Gó go mruk-dhik hrai mr̀ hrai bei-mrat gaa? Hó mr̀ hó-yrí góng béi ngró thèng qaa?
Mr Cheung	Mr̀ hrai bei-mrat, ngró jí-hrai séung lrèi-hhòi qhuk-kéi yhat-jran jhe.
Mr Wong	Jhàn krèi-gwaai laak! Nréi yhat-heung dhou jhùng-yi lràu hái qhuk-kéi, hóu síu chheut-ghaai ge bo!
Mr Cheung	Lróu-srat góng nréi thèng lhaa, jeui-gran ngró go néui chhàam-ghàa-jó chhò-khap gong-kràm fan-lrin-bhaan; ngró taai-táai yrau chhàam-ghàa-jó ghò-krek fan-lrin-bhaan. Mráan-fraan jhì-hrau jrau hrai kréui-drei lrin-jraap srì-gaan laak. Nréi wraa ngró dím hó-yrí lràu hái qhuk-kéi nhe?

嗜好	**sri-hou**	*hobby*
揼郵票	**chróu-yràu-piu**	*to collect stamps*
捉棋	**jhuk-kéi**	*to play chess*
畫畫	**wraak-wáa**	*to paint, to draw*
跳舞	**tiu-mróu**	*to dance*
散步	**saan-brou**	*to stroll, to go for a walk*
幅	**fhuk**	*(classifier for paintings, drawings and photographs)*
憎	**jhàng**	*to hate, detest*
唔見咗	**mr̀-gin-jó**	*lost, to lose, to mislay*
唉!	**qhàai!**	*alas! (a sigh)*
目的	**mruk-dhik**	*purpose, aim, goal*
秘密	**bei-mrat**	*secret*
一陣(間)	**yhat-jran(-ghaan)**	*a moment, in a moment, for a moment*

奇怪	**krèi-gwaai**	*strange, weird, odd*
一向	**yhat-heung**	*all along, up to now*
留	**lràu**	*to stay, to remain; to leave behind*
初級	**chhò-khap**	*elementary, first-grade*
鋼琴	**gong-kràm**	*piano*
訓練班	**fan-lrin-bhaan**	*training class*
訓練	**fan-lrin**	*training, to train*
歌劇	**ghò-krek**	*opera*
練習	**lrin-jraap**	*to practise*

Grammar

1 These last few . . .

In Unit 19 you met **jeui-gran-géi-nrìn**, meaning *in the last few years*. Another way of saying the same thing is **nhi-géi-nrìn**, and you can extend either of the patterns to days, weeks and months too:

jeui-gran-géi-yrat =	*these last few days*
nhi-géi-yrat	
jeui-gran-géi-go-lrái-baai =	*these last few weeks*
nhi-géi-go-lrái-baai	
jeui-gran-géi-go-yruet =	*these last few months*
nhi-géi-go-yruet	

Géi is not essential to these patterns: you can be more specific if you wish, although normally only small numbers are involved:

jeui-gran lréung-shàam yrat =	*these last two or three*
nhi lréung-shàam yrat	*days*
jeui-gran sei-ngŕ nrìn =	*these last four or five*
nhi sei-ngŕ nrìn	*years*

2 Mr̀-gin-jó (lost)

Mr̀-gin-jó literally means *became unseen, not seen any more*, and it is a useful way of saying that you have lost or mislaid something:

| Ngró mr̀-gin-jó ngró dhi chín; mr̀-jhì hrai mr̀ hrai brei yràn thàu-jó nhe? | *I can't find my money; I wonder if it's been stolen?* |
| Kréui mr̀-gin-jó yràn laak. | *She went missing.* |

3 For a moment

Yhat-jran (or its longer form **yhat-jran-ghaan**) means *a moment of time*. It can be used as either a specific time or a duration of time, and its position can therefore be either in front of or after the verb in a sentence:

> **Ngró yhat-jran lrok-lrài lhaa!**
> *I'll be down in a moment!*

> **Hóu lhaa! Draan-hrai ngró bhat-gwo hó-yrí lrok-lrài yhat-jran jhe!**
> *OK, but I can only come down for a moment!*

4 In your opinion

Just in case you have not picked it up without being told, **nréi-wraa** or **nréi-tái** (*you say* or *you see*) both are used in the sense *in your opinion*. Similarly, **ngró-wraa** or **ngró-tái** can mean *in my opinion*.

It's the same the whole world over!

The hobbies which are mentioned in the dialogue are much the same as those you might find anywhere in the world: Cantonese people like sport and games and collecting things. Mind you, when Cantonese people talk about chess it may well be Chinese chess, which is played on a different board with different pieces and operates according to different rules from Western chess. Or it might be **wrài-kéi** (*surrounding chess*), which is played with black and white stones on the intersections of the lines on a multi-squared board: this tends to be known in the West under its Japanese name *go*. One hobby which is much more common among the Chinese than among Westerners is calligraphy (**shùe-faat**). Writing Chinese characters with a brush is a very high art form in China and Japan, and many people spend painstaking hours cultivating their skill.

Dialogue 2

Two mothers discuss the changing leisure pursuits of the young.

我覺得而家啲後生仔同我哋後生嘅時候好唔同.

你講邊方面唔同呢?

我講嘅係嗜好方面。我哋後生嘅時候好中意種花,養魚,養雀,養
狗,養貓等等。但係而家的後生仔就中意去的士高,卡拉OK,玩電
腦遊戲,呢的嗰樣嘅嘢。

係呀,我個仔可以一個人對住喫電腦遊戲機玩一晚都唔覺得癐。你
話,佢對呢方面幾有興趣呢。

李太,你要勸你個仔唔好玩咁多電腦遊戲嘞。專家話如果一個人習慣
自己同自己玩遊戲就會缺乏同別人溝通,漸漸就會養成孤獨嘅性
格,嗰樣係好危險嘅嘛!

我都覺得科學越進步,我哋就越依賴科技。而家連我哋嘅嗜好都受到
科技嘅影響慢慢改變,而且越變越快,越改越多。將來係點樣冇人
可以預知。係嘞,我一返到屋企就叫我個仔唔好再玩電腦遊戲嘞。

Mrs Wong	Ngró gok-dhak yrì-ghaa dhi hrau-shaang-jái trùng ngró-drei hrau-shaang ge srì-hrau hóu mr̀ trùng.
Mrs Lee	Nréi góng bhin fhòng-mrin mr̀ trùng nhe?
Mrs Wong	Ngró góng ge hrai sri-hou fhòng-mrin. Ngró-drei hrau-shaang ge srì-hrau hóu jhùng-yi jung-fhaa, yréung-yúe, yréung-jeuk, yréung-gáu, yréung-mhaau dáng-dáng. Draan-hrai yrì-ghaa dhi hrau-shaang-jái jrau jhùng-yi heui dhik-sri-ghou, khaa-lhaai-qhou-khei, wáan drin-nróu yràu-hei, nhi dhi gám-yéung ge yré.
Mrs Lee	Hrai qaa, ngró go jái hó-yrí yhat-go-yràn deui-jrue gaa drin-nróu yràu-hei-ghèi wáan yhat mráan dhou mr̀ gok-dhak gwrui. Nréi-wraa, kréui deui nhi fhòng-mrin géi yráu hing-cheui nhe.
Mrs Wong	Lréi Táai, nréi yiu huen nréi go jái mr̀-hóu wáan gam dhò drin-nróu yràu-hei laak. Jhuen-ghaa wraa yrùe-gwo yhat-go-yràn jraap-gwaan jri-géi trùng jri-géi wáan yràu-hei, jrau wrúi kuet-frat trùng brit-yràn khàu-thùng jrim-jím jrau wrúi yréung-srìng gwhù-druk ge sing-gaak, gám-yéung hrai hóu ngrài-hím ge bo!
Mrs Lee	Ngró dhou gok-dhak fho-hrok yruet jeun-brou, ngró-drei jrau yruet yí-lraai fho-grei. Yrì-ghaa lrìn ngró-drei ge sri-hou dhou srau-dou fho-grei ge yíng-

héung, mraan-máan gói-bin, yrì-ché yruet bin yruet
faai, yruet gói yruet dhò, jhèung-lròi hrai dím-yéung
mróu yràn hó-yrí yrue-jhì. Hrai laak, ngró yhat
fhàan-dou qhuk-kéi jrau giu ngró go jái mǐ-hóu joi
wáan drin-nróu yràu-hei laak.

同	**trùng**	*the same, alike*
種花	**jung-fhaa**	*to cultivate flowers*
養	**yréung**	*to rear, to keep (pets)*
雀	**jeuk**	*bird*
貓	**mhaau**	*cat*
的士高	**dhik-sri-ghou**	*discotheque*
卡拉OK	**khaa-lhaai-qhou-khei**	*karaoke*
遊戲	**yràu-hei**	*games*
瘡	**gwrui**	*tired, weary*
勸	**huen**	*to advise, to urge, to plead with*
專家	**jhuen-ghaa**	*expert, specialist*
習慣	**jraap-gwaan**	*to be accustomed to, to get used to; habit*
自己	**jri-géi**	*self, oneself*
缺乏	**kuet-frat**	*to lack, be short of*
別人	**brit-yràn**	*other people*
溝通	**khàu-thùng**	*to communicate*
養成	**yréung-srìng**	*to inculcate, to form, breed*
孤獨	**gwhù-druk**	*solitary, lone*
性格	**sing-gaak**	*temperament, disposition*
危險	**ngrài-hím**	*dangerous; danger*
進步	**jeun-brou**	*progress*
依賴	**yí-lraai**	*to rely on*
科技	**fho-grei**	*science and technology*
受	**srau**	*to suffer*
改變	**gói-bin**	*to change, alter*
將來	**jhèung-lròi**	*future, in future*
預知	**yrue-jhì**	*to predict*
一......就......	**yhat . . . jrau . . .**	*as soon as . . . then . . .*

The large Chinese characters for **ngrài-hím** (*danger*) read from left to right.

 ——————— **Grammar** ———————

5 Ghèi (machine)

The full word for *a machine* or *machinery* is **ghèi-hei,** but there are plenty of instances where **ghèi** on its own also means *machine,* usually when it is tacked onto other words:

yràu-hei	*games*	→	**yràu-hei-ghèi**	*games machine*
drin-sri	*television*	→	**drin-sri-ghèi**	*television set*
fhèi	*to fly*	→	**fhèi-ghèi**	*(lit. flying machine) aircraft*
dáa-jri	*to type*	→	**dáa-jri-ghèi**	*typewriter*
dáa-fó	*to strike fire*	→	**dáa-fó-ghèi**	*cigarette lighter*

6 Dhou *does it again!*

In Unit 22, grammar point 7 you saw how **dhou** could still convey the idea of *even* without the assistance of **lrìn.** In the dialogue there is another rather trickier example: **ngró go jái . . . wáan yhat mráan dhou mr̀ gok-dhak gwrui** (*my son can play the whole evening and still does not feel tired*). You may find it easier to see how **dhou** achieves its effect if you twist the English slightly: *my son even though he plays the whole evening does not feel tired.*

7 Self

Jri-géi means *self* and is a very useful word for emphasising individuality. It usually comes after a person's name or a personal pronoun:

Wròng Shìn-shàang jri-géi mř shik góng Yhìng-mràn.	*Mr Wong himself cannot speak English.*
Nréi jri-géi séung mř séung heui qaa?	*Do you yourself want to go?*

Jri-géi yhat-go-yràn means *all by oneself alone*:

Kréui jri-géi yhat-go-yràn chró hái-drou.	*He sat there all alone.*

Helping yourself

When you are eating a Chinese meal with chopsticks from communal bowls in the middle of the table, you will find that the host or other people will often select tasty morsels and put them in your personal bowl. Don't find this odd, it is meant as a great politeness. Of course it could be that they give you something which you do not want to eat, in which case you are at liberty just to leave it lying there. However, whether you want it or not, it can be embarrassing to be constantly waited on in this way, and it is polite to try to stop people doing it. Try saying **mř-sái gam haak-hei** (*no need to be so polite*), and following it with **ngró jri-géi lrài** (*I'll come at it myself*). If you have a really persistent host nothing you say will deter him, but at least you will have made the right disclaiming noises.

---

8 As soon as

One of the beauties of Cantonese grammar is that patterns of some complexity are often made up from very simple words. **Yhat** means *one* and **jrau** means *then*: you met them both long ago. However,

set them working together in a grammar pattern and they produce
As soon as . . . then . . . :

Kréui *yhat* chró chhe *jrau* tràu-wràn.	*He gets dizzy as soon as he gets in a car.*
Ngró *yhat* gin-dóu kréui, kréui *jrau* jáu-jó laak.	*As soon as I saw him he ran away.*
Wròng Taai-táai *yhat* chheut-jó ghaai, *jrau* m̀r gei-dhak-jó yiu mráai mhat-yré sung.	*No sooner had Mrs Wong got outside than she forgot what food she had to buy.*

Note that in this pattern both **yhat** and **jrau** act as adverbs and each comes before a different verb.

Exercises

1   Let's start with a couple of Chinese riddles.

   (*a*)   Can you guess (in English) what this represents?

   Yráu yhat yreung yré mróu chrúng-lreung ge, draan-hrai srap go yràn dhou m̀r hó-yrí tròi-héi kréui. Yrùe-gwó yre-mráan yhat lrài-dou, kréui jrau m̀r-gin-jó. Nréi gwú hrai mhat-yré nhe?

   (*b*)   And what is the answer to this one (in Cantonese)?

   Síu-Lréi deui Síu-Wóng wraa: 'Ngró ge shàang-yrat hái jrok-yrat ge jrok-yrat ge thìng-yrat.' Síu-Wóng wraa: 'Mróu cho, nréi ge shàang-yrat hrai thìng-yrat ge chrìn-yrat. Ghùng-héi! Ghùng-héi!' Síu-Lréi hrai géi-sí shàang-yrat qaa?

2   Join the following pairs of sentences into one by incorporating the idea in brackets. The answer to the first one is: **Wròng Síu-jé srik jóu-chhaan jhì-chrìn, jraap-gwaan heui saan-brou shìn.**

   (*a*)   **Wròng Síu-jé srik jóu-chhaan. Kréui jraap-gwaan saan-brou.** (*before*)
   (*b*)   **Ngró hái qhuk-kéi. Ngró m̀r daai móu.** (*when*)
   (*c*)   **Nràam-yán lruk-srap-ńg seui. Kréui-drei hó-yrí ló teui-yhàu-gham.** (*not until*)

(*d*) Ngró ghàm-jhìu-jóu tái bou-jí. Ngró jhì-dou ngró-drei
ghung-shi ge chrìng-fong hóu ngrài-hím. (*as soon as*)

(*e*) Chràn Shìn-shàang yám bhe-jáu. Kréui jhùng-yi yám.
(*the more . . . the more*)

3

**Chéng nréi yrung Gwóng-dhùng-wáa góng nhi sei fhuk
wáa lréui-brin faat-shàng dhi mhat-yré sri qaa.**

4 Here's a quick test of your place words. Supply the missing
words as rapidly as you can.

(*a*) Ngró hái nréi hrau-brin, gám nréi hái ngró ____.

(*b*) Sreung-hói hái Bhak-ghìng nràam-brin, gám Bhak-
ghìng hái Sreung-hói ____.

(*c*) Nréi hái gó-drou, gám ngró hái ____.

(*d*) Wròng Shàang hái Wròng Táai jó-sáu-brin, gám
Wròng Táai hái Wròng Shàang ____.

(*e*) Brou shùe hái braak-jí lréui-brin, gám braak-jí hái
shùe ____.

5 You are on Hong Kong Island and you want to get to the airport. You have managed to get through on the phone to the
airport enquiry office, but the person answering can only speak
Cantonese. You have a plane to catch, so you had better produce your best Cantonese and your keenest understanding. Ask:

(*a*) *Is there a bus which goes to the airport?*

(*b*) *How much is the fare from the Star Ferry Pier* (**Thìn-
shing Mráa-tràu**)?

(c)   How long will it take to get to the airport?
(d)   Is there a toilet on the bus?
(e)   What time does flight 251 take off?
(f)   When does flight 251 get in to London?

25

第二十五課　房屋
FRÒNG-QHUK
Household affairs

This unit teaches you some basic words for living accommodation and a little more about food.

 ━━━━━━━━━ **Dialogue 1** ━━━━━━━━━

Mr Wong's friend Mr Cheung lives alone in a large flat.

老王，歡迎你嚟探我。請入嚟坐喇！

咦！點解唔見張太同你哋啲仔女喋？

哦！佢哋半年之前已經移咗民去英國啦！而家只有我一個人住喺香港之嘛。

嘩，你間屋真係大嘞。我最中意你嘅露台。呢間屋有幾多間瞓房呀？

有三間瞓房，兩個廁所同洗身房，一間客廳一間飯廳，同埋一個廚房。

你哋嘅廚房設備都好齊全嘛……有洗衣機，洗碗機，煮食爐，碗櫃，重有微波爐添。

呢啲野我同太太都打算運去英國嘅，但係後來知道運費太貴嘞，而且，如果喺英國買新嘅，價錢都唔算太貴，所以我哋就決定唔運嘞，留喺香港自己用。

啲窗簾布同地氈都重係好新嘛！點解唔運去英國呢？

唉！唔好提地氈同窗簾布嘞。我嗰陣時都同你一樣，話要運去英國，但係我太太堅持要留返佢哋喺香港。佢嘅理由就係啲窗簾布嘅顏色太深嘞，唔好睇，啲地氈嘅花樣佢又唔中意。

我嚟咗咁耐，你都有斟茶俾我飲。我估喺呢半年你一個人住一定好孤獨嘞，老張，等我今日陪你一齊出街去飲茶逛公司喇。

Cheung Lróu-Wóng, fhùn-yrìng nréi lrài taam ngró. Chéng
yrap-lrài chró lhaa!

Wong Yí! Dím-gáai mr̀ gin Jhèung Táai trùng nréi-drei dhi
jái-néui gaa?

Cheung Qró, kréui-drei bun nrìn jhì-chrìn yrí-ghìng yrì-jó mràn
heui Yhìng-gwok laa! Yrì-ghaa jí yráu ngró yhat-go-yràn
jrue hái Hhèung-góng jhi-mráa.

Wong Whàa, nréi ghàan qhuk jhàn-hrai draai laak. Ngró jeui
jhùng-yi nréi ge lrou-tròi. Nhi ghàan qhuk yráu géi-dho
ghàan fan-fóng qaa?

Cheung Yráu shàam ghàan fan-fóng, lréung go chi-só trùng sái-
shàn-fóng, yhat ghàan haak-theng, yhat ghàan fraan-
theng, trùng-mràai yhat go chrùe-fóng.

Wong Nréi-drei ge chrùe-fóng chit-brei dhou hóu chrài-
chrùen bo . . . yráu sái-yhì-ghèi, sái-wún-ghèi, jué-srik-
lròu, wún-gwrai, jrung yráu mrèi-bho-lròu thìm.

Cheung Nhi dhi yré ngró trùng taai-táai dhou dáa-suen wran-
heui Yhìng-gwok ge, draan-hrai hrau-lròi jhì-dou wran-
fai taai gwai laak, yrì-ché, yrùe-gwó hái Yhìng-gwok
mráai shàn ge, gaa-chrìn dhou mr̀ suen taai gwai, só-
yrí ngró-drei jrau kuet-dring mr̀ wran laak, lràu hái
Hhèung-góng jri-géi yrung.

Wong Dhi chheung-lím-bou trùng drei-jhin dhou jrung hrai
hóu shàn bo! Dím-gáai mr̀ wran-heui Yhìng-gwok nhe?

Cheung Qhàai! Mr̀-hóu trài drei-jhin trùng chheung-lím-bou
laak. Ngró gó-jran-srì dhou trùng nréi yhat-yreung,
wraa yiu wran-heui Yhìng-gwok, draan-hrai ngró taai-
táai ghìn-chrì yiu lràu-fhàan kréui-drei hái Hhèung-
góng. Kréui ge lréi-yràu jrau hrai dhi chheung-lím-bou
ge ngràan-shik taai shàm laak, mr̀ hóu-tái, dhi drei-jhin
ge fhaa-yéung kréui yrau mr̀ jhùng-yi.

Wong Ngró lrài-jó gam nroi, nréi dhou mróu jhàm chràa béi
ngró yám. Ngró gwú hái nhi bun nrìn nréi yhat-go-
yràn jrue yhat-dring hóu gwhù-druk laak. Lróu-Jheung,
dáng ngró ghàm-yrat prùi nréi yhat-chrài chheut-ghaai
heui yám-chràa kwaang-ghung-shi lhaa.

露台	**lrou-tròi**	balcony
客廳	**haak-theng**	living room, lounge
飯廳	**fraan-theng**	dining room
洗衣機	**sái-yhì-ghèi**	washing machine
洗碗機	**sái-wún-ghèi**	dish-washer
碗	**wún**	a bowl
煮食爐	**júe-srik-lròu**	cooking stove
碗櫃	**wún-gwrai**	cupboard, dresser
微波爐	**mrèi-bho-lròu**	microwave oven
後來	**hrau-lròi**	later, afterwards
運費	**wran-fai**	transportation costs
決定	**kuet-dring**	to decide
窗簾布	**chheung-lím-bou**	curtains
地氈	**drei-jhin**	carpet
提	**trài**	to mention, bring up
堅持	**ghìn-chrì**	to insist, insist on
留返	**lràu-fhàan**	to leave behind
理由	**lréi-yràu**	reason
顏色	**ngràan-shik**	colour
深	**shàm**	deep
斟	**jhàm**	to pour into a cup, glass or bowl
陪	**prùi**	to accompany, keep company with
飲茶	**yám-chràa**	lit. to drink tea = to have a **dím-sham** snack meal
逛公司	**kwaang ghung-shi**	to go window-shopping
逛	**kwaang**	to cruise

Grammar

1 'Verb plus object verbs'

You may have found Mr Cheung's remark **yrí-ghìng yrì-jó mràn heui Yhìng-gwok laa** grammatically strange because **-jó** has split **yrì** and **mràn**. The reason is quite simple: the verb **yrì-mràn** (*to migrate*) is composed of **yrì** (*to move*) and **mràn** (*people*), so that it is actually a 'verb + object verb', and of course **-jó** is an ending which must be attached to a verb, not to an object.

2 Another classifier oddity

Mr Cheung uses the classifier **ghàan** for **fan-fóng** and for **haak-theng** and for **fraan-theng**, but he uses **go** for **chi-só** and **chrùe-**

fóng. Somehow toilets and tiny Chinese kitchens do not seem to qualify as proper rooms (rooms in which people socialise, perhaps), so they are often not given **ghàan** status.

3 Bowls *and other containers*

Wún (*bowl*) is a very handy word, because bowls are so much used at the Chinese table. There are **fraan-wún** (*rice bowls*), **thòng-wún** (*soup bowls*) and **chràa-wún** (*tea bowls*), not to mention **draai-wún** (*big bowls*) and **sai-wún** (*little bowls*). But **wún** is even more useful because it is also a classifier, as in **yhat wún thòng** (*a bowl of soup*) and **lréung wún braak-fraan** (*two bowls of boiled rice* – **braak-fraan** literally means *white rice*, hence *steamed* or *boiled rice* as opposed to **cháau-fraan**, *fried rice*). You can see how the two functions of **wún** operate in the following comparison:

shàam wún fraan	*three bowls of rice*
shàam jek fraan-wún	*three rice bowls* (the classifier for a bowl can be either **jek** or **go**)

Other container words or measure words work in the same way. Most common perhaps is **bhùi** (*a cup, a glass, a mug*):

lréung jek chràa-bhui	*two tea-cups* (note the tone change on **bhùi**)
lréung bhùi chràa	*two cups of tea*

4 Not any more

Way back in Unit 3, grammar point 6 you were given an example of the use of **laak** with **mr̀**. In the dialogue above, Mr Cheung says **ngró-drei kuet-dring mr̀ wran laak** (*we decided not to transport them after all*), that is, they had at first decided otherwise but not any more. **Mr̀** + **laak** is a very convenient way of conveying the notion *not any more*.

5 Deep *and* shallow: dark *and* light

Shàm literally means *deep* (**Nréi yiu síu-shàm bo! Gó-sue dhi séui hóu shàm!** – *You should be careful, the water is very deep there!*), and the opposite word *shallow* is **chín**. Both words are capable of being extended in use, so that you can describe someone's thought as **shàm**, for example. With colours, **shàm** means *dark* or *deep*, and **chín** means *light*, so **shàm-hrùng-shik** is *crimson* or *dark red*, and **chín-lràam-shik** is the colour sported by **Gim-krìu Draai-hrok** on boat race day.

Yám-chràa – more than a cup of tea

Cantonese people never say *let's go and have some* **dím-sham**; they always say *let's go and drink tea* (**yám-chràa**). **Yám-chràa** goes on in specialist tea houses and restaurants from early morning to about 2.30 p.m. What you order from the waiter is the type of tea you prefer to drink – Dragon Well Tea, Jasmine Tea, Iron Guan-Yin Tea, Chrysanthemum Pu-er, or whatever – and you then sit back and wait till someone comes by with a tray or trolley of **dím-sham** steaming hot from the kitchen. If you fancy what is there you ask for it, but otherwise you wait until another trolley comes round with something on it that you do want. There is great variety and you will find it hard to stop ordering. Until about thirty years ago the bill was calculated according to the number of little dishes left on your table when you had finished, but smart customers would slip dishes onto other people's tables and get up to other tricks to cut down the bill, so nowadays a running tally is kept on a menu slip in a holder on your table. And of course the tea will be charged for as well. **Yám-chràa** is a Cantonese must: one of the great gastronomic treats in a land where food is king.

Dialogue 2

Mr Wong looks at house purchasing.

先生，你睇呢座樓嘅管理唔錯嗮！廿四小時都有保安服務，每日保安人員會嚟兩次，有清潔工人打掃走廊同樓梯，每個月都有人檢查呢三架轆……好安全㗎！

係，都唔錯。有冇車位呀？

有一個車位包括喺屋價裡便。先生，到啦，請出轆喇。你睇呢度大門有法國電子鎖，壞人好難開㗎。

唔錯，唔錯。我哋入屋睇吓囉。

嗥，你睇，客廳同飯廳又大又光猛，個露台對住個海，真舒服嘞。

唔錯。可惜樓底太矮啫。

先生，唔算太矮啦，離地面都有九呎嘅啦。請過嚟呢處睇吓啲房間喇。

咦，點解冇套房廁所同沖涼房嘅咩？

有呃，主人房就有喇，嗥，請睇吓呢間喇。

嘩，重係用煤氣熱水爐咁落後嘅。

先生，如果你唔中意，我可以換一個電子熱水爐俾你。你睇，主人房
　　咁舒服，地方咁靜，一啲都唔嘈，喺呢處瞓覺一定會發好夢嘅。

我話唔係嘞。屋價咁貴，如果我買咗，會瞓唔著覺就真。

Salesman	Shìn-shàang, nréi tái nhi jro láu ge gwún-lŕei mŕ cho bo! Yraa-sei síu-srì dhou yráu bóu-qhon fruk-mrou, mrúi-yrat bóu-qhon yràn-yrùen wrúi lrài lréung chi, yráu chhìng-git ghùng-yràn dáa-sou jáu-lóng trùng lràu-thài, mrúi go yruet dhou yráu yràn gím-chràa nhi shàam gaa lhip . . . hóu qhòn-chrùen gaa!
Mr Wong	Hrai, dhou mŕ-cho. Yráu mróu chhe-wái qaa?
Salesman	Yráu yhat go chhe-wái bhàau-kwut hái qhuk-gaa lréui-brin. Shìn-shàang, dou laa, chéng chheut lhip lhaa. Nréi tái nhi drou draai-mrùn yráu Faat-gwok drin-jí-só, wraai-yràn hóu nràan hhòi gaa.
Mr Wong	Mŕ-cho, mŕ-cho. Ngró-drei yrap qhuk tái-hráa lo.
Salesman	Nràa, nréi tái, haak-theng trùng fraan-theng yrau draai yrau gwhòng-mráang, go lrou-tròi deui-jrue go hói, jàn shuè-fruk laak.
Mr Wong	Mŕ-cho. Hó-shik lràu-dái taai ngái jhek.
Salesman	Shìn-shàang, mŕ suen taai ngái laa, lrèi drei-mín dhou yráu gáu chek ge laa. Chéng gwo-lrài nhi-sue tái-hráa dhi fròng-ghaan lhaa.
Mr Wong	Yí, dím-gáai mróu tou-fóng chi-só trùng chhùng-lrèung-fóng ge mhe?
Salesman	Yráu qaak, júe-yràn-fóng jrau yráu lhaa. Nràa, chéng tái-hráa nhi ghàan lhaa.
Mr Wong	Wràa, jrung hrai yrung mrùi-hei yrit-séui-lròu gam lrok-hrau gé.
Salesman	Shìn-shàang, yrùe-gwó nréi mŕ jhùng-yi, ngró hó-yrí wrun yhat go drin-jí yrit-séui-lròu béi nréi. Nréi tái, júe-yràn-fóng gam shùe-fruk, drei-fhòng gam jring, yhat-dhi dhou mŕ chròu. Hái nhi-sue fan-gaau yhat-dring wrúi faat hóu mrung ge.
Mr Wong	Ngró wraa mŕ hrai laak. Qhuk-gaa gam gwai, yrùe-gwó ngró mráai-jó, wrúi fan-mŕ-jreuk-gaau jrau-jhàn.

座	jro	(classifier for massive things: *large buildings, mountains*, etc.)
管理	gwún-Iréi	*management, to manage*
小時	síu-srì	*an hour*
保安	bóu-qhon	*security, keep secure*
人員	yràn-yrùen	*personnel, staff*
清潔	chhìng-git	*cleanliness, to clean*
工人	ghùng-yràn	*worker, servant*
打掃	dáa-sou	*to sweep*
樓梯	Iràu-thài	*staircase*
檢查	gím-chràa	*check, inspect*
粒	Ihip	*lift, elevator*
安全	qhòn-chrùen	*safe, safety*
車位	chhe-wái	*parking space*
包括	bhàau-kwut	*to include*
屋價	qhuk-gaa	*house price*
度	drou	(classifier for *doors*)
電子	drin-jí	*electronic*
鎖	só	*a lock, to lock*
光猛	gwhòng-mráang	*bright*
海	hói	*the sea*
樓底	Iràu-dái	*the ceiling*
矮	ngái	*low, short in height*
離	Irèi	*distant from*
地面	drei-mín	*the floor*
呎	chek	*foot (length)*
套房	tou-fóng	*en suite*
沖涼房	chhùng-Irèung-fóng	*bathroom*
主人房	júe-yràn-fóng	*master bedroom*
煤氣	mrùi-hei	*town gas*
熱水爐	yrit-séui-Iròu	*boiler, water heater*
落後	Irok-hrau	*backward, old-fashioned*
換	wrun	*to change, exchange*
靜	jring	*quiet*
嘈	chròu	*noisy*
發夢	faat-mrung	*to dream*
瞓唔著(覺)	fan-mr̀-jreuk(-gaau)	*unable to get to sleep*

Grammar

6 Yraa-sei síu-srì

Síu-srì is an alternative word for **jhung-tràu** (*hour*) which you have met, and **yraa-sei síu-srì** is the regular way to say *24-hour* (as in *24-hour service*).

7 Workers

Ghùng-yràn means quite simply *work person*, but just like *worker* in English it implies that the person works for someone else, that he or she is not in charge. In Hong Kong it is the common word for *a house servant*, and there is a general assumption that house servants are female, so that if you have a male house servant you would refer to him as a **nràam-ghùng-yràn** (compare this with the example of policeman and policewoman described in Unit 17, grammar point 4).

The English invasion

Lhip is the Cantonese attempt at the English word *lift*, the proper Cantonese word being tediously long (**shìng-gong-ghèi** – *rising and falling machine*). You have met **bho** (*ball*), **bhaa-sí** (*bus*), **dhik-sí** (*taxi*), **shàa-léut** (*salad*) and **fhei** (*fare*). **Fhei-lám** is *film*, **sri-dho** is *a store*, **bho-sí** is *the boss*, **brat-lhaan-déi** is *brandy*, and there are many many more such words, but it seems that now the trend is away from using such words and towards a more pure Cantonese vocabulary. Incidentally, *to ride in a lift* is **chró-lhip**, although few lifts have seats in them.

---

8 Distant from

Lrèi means *to be distant from, to be separated from*, and it is very handy for showing distance relationships. In the dialogue the salesman says that the ceiling **lrèi drei-mín dhou yráu gáu chek ge laa** (*is nine feet from the floor*). Similarly, you might say:

Lrèun-dheun *lrèi* **Hhèung-góng** (**yráu**) *yhat-mraan-yhat-chhìn ghung-lréi.*
London is 11,000 kilometres from Hong Kong.

Yráu (*to have*) is the verb which appears with numbers most often. Its use in this pattern is optional, although you are more likely to put it in if you are trying to stress the notion *is **all** of 11,000 kilometres*.

The word most often associated with **lrèi** is **yrúen** (*far, distant*):

Gwóng-jhàu *lrèi* **Hhèung-**
góng mr̀-hrai-géi-*yrúen***.*

Canton is not very far from
Hong Kong.

Nréi qhuk-kéi *lrèi* **Draai-**
wrui-tròng *yrúen mr̀*
yrúen qaa?

Is your home far from the
City hall?

You will remember from Unit 20 that *to be close to* is a different pattern:

Thìn-shing Mráa-tràu *hóu*
krán **Draai-wrui-tròng.**

The Star Ferry Pier is very
close to the City Hall.

9 *A last look at* dhou

In the dialogue the salesman is put in a difficult situation – he has to contradict Mr Wong who claims that the ceilings are too low when in fact they are the usual height. What he does is to slip in an otherwise unnecessary **dhou**, and that somehow takes the confrontational edge off the contradiction. It is a standard politeness not to disagree too violently with someone else, but rather to show that while you cannot agree with them you do not wish to be offensive about it. In English you might say *that's not quite right* when what you mean is *that's wrong!* In Cantonese you would add in a **dhou**. So **mr̀ hrai!** sounds abrupt and rude (*it's not!*), but **dhou mr̀ hrai** gives the same answer in an acceptably soft way (*I'm afraid that's not the case*).

10 Bathrooms

In Unit 15 you learned that the word for *bathroom* is **sái-shàn-fóng**, and now you have met another and newer word, **chhùng-lrèung-fóng**. It seems that this newer term is slowly driving out the older one, but you are bound to come across both of them. There is a difference in their origins: **sái-shàn** (*to wash the body*) is *to have an all-over wash* or *to have a bath*, while **chhùng-lrèung** is really *to have a shower*, but the distinction is becoming blurred.

11 And that's for sure!

Jrau-jhàn means *then that would be true*, and it is used at the ends of statements to make them more emphatic. It coincides quite nicely with the English *and that's for sure!*, *and that's the truth!*

26

第二十六課　溫習（四）
— WHÀN-JRAAP (SEI) —
Revision (4)

The shortest unit in the book. Just a few exercises and a couple of passages of Cantonese for you to understand and to realise how far you have come in the space of twenty-five units. As usual, you will find translations of the passages at the back of the book, but you will probably not need them.

Of course you are not yet at native speaker standard, but you should find that you have reached the stage where you know enough to be able to hold a conversation and, more importantly, to find out more for yourself by asking and by working out what some of the things you hear must mean on the basis of what you already know.

Do persevere. Having come this far you have shown that you are capable of learning Cantonese. It would be a great pity to stop just when you have reached 'critical velocity' for take-off into the cheerful, exciting world of Cantonese conversation.

 ——————— **Exercises** ———————

1　Name the buildings or rooms which you associate with the following. The first answer is **gíng-chaat → gíng-chaat-gruk**.

（a）　**gíng-chaat**　　　　（e）　**bei-shùe**
（b）　**sái-yhì-ghèi**　　　（f）　**jhì-piu**
（c）　**yreuk-séui**　　　　（g）　**lrèun-pún**
（d）　**gong-kràm**　　　　（h）　**yràu-gáan**

2   Make the following sentences less aggressive by using **dhou**, other polite words such as **mr̀-ghòi**, **chéng** and **deui-mr̀-jrue**, or perhaps by rephrasing them in a softer way.

   (*a*)   **Mrái yhuk!**
   (*b*)   **Nréi góng-cho.**
   (*c*)   **Nréi mr̀ mrìng-braak.**
   (*d*)   **Ngró mr̀ trùng-yi.**
   (*e*)   **Ghim-krìu Draai-hrok mr̀ hrai sai-gaai sreung jeui yráu-méng ge.**

3   Here are the estate agent's details and plan of a flat which you want to buy. Explain to your wife in Cantonese what it is like, giving the size of the rooms, the address and other details.

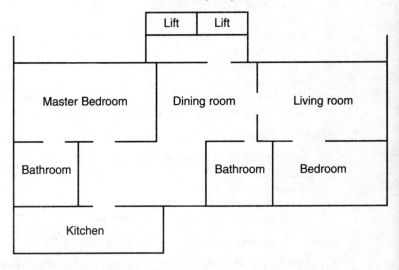

A TWO-BEDROOM FLAT
AT No.27 CANTON ROAD, 8TH FLOOR
PARKING SPACE INCLUDED IN THE PRICE
ONLY HK$5,500,000!

| Lift | Lift |

Master Bedroom   Dining room   Living room

Bathroom   Bathroom   Bedroom

Kitchen

4   Make meaningful sentences with these pairs of words. We have given simple models in the key to the exercises at the back of the book.

   (*a*)   **gwún-lréi**   **ghìng-lréi**
   (*b*)   **hhòi-chí**   **hhòi-chhe**

    (c) **hói-shin**   **shàn-shìn**
    (d) **yhat-lràu**   **jáu-lràu**

5 (a) **Bhin yreung yré trùng krèi-thàa ge yré m̀ trùng júng-lreui qaa? (yràu-gáan/yràu-séui/yràu-piu/yràu-gruk/yràu-fai)**

    (b) **Bhin yreung yré hái sé-jri-lràu lréui-brin mróu ge nhe? (drin-wáa/drin-nróu/drin-dhang/drin-yíng/drin-nrúen-lròu)**

    (c) **Bhin yreung deui ngró-drei ge shàn-tái hóu nhe? (dáa-bho/dáa-ghaau/dáa-gip/dáa-jri/dáa-drin-wáa)**

    (d) **Bhin yreung hrai jeui gwai nhe? (bou-jí/braak-jí/seun-jí/Góng-jí/m̀-jí)**

    (e) **Yrùe-gwó nréi séung heui ngroi-gwok, nréi yhat-dring yiu yráu bhin yreung 'jing' qaa? (bóu-jing/shàn-fán-jing/gíng-yrùen-jing/chhìm-jing)**

6 Put suitable final particles in the blanks in the following sentences.

    (a) **Ghàm-yrat ge thìn-hei m̀ hóu, ngró-drei m̀ heui yràu-séui ____.**

    (b) **Nhi gaa chhe gam prèng, nréi dhou m̀ jhùng-yi ____? Dím-gáai ____?**

    (c) **Kréui m̀ jhùng-yi ngró heui ____? Gám, ngró jrau m̀ heui ____.**

    (d) **Jhàa drin-dhaan-chhe hóu ngrài-hím ____. Dím-gáai nréi jrung béi nréi ge jái jhàa ____?**

7 Hái bhin-drou:

    (a) srik-dhak-dóu hói-shin qaa?
    (b) mráai-mráa qaa?
    (c) daap-dóu bhaa-sí qaa?
    (d) srik-dhak-dóu ngró taai-táai júe ge sung qaa?
    (e) gin-dhak-dóu Wròng Bei-shùe qaa?

8 Insert the missing classifiers in the following phrases.

(a)	yhat ____ drei-jhin		(d)	yhat ____ chhaan-tói trùng yí	
(b)	yhat ____ wáa		(e)	yhat ____ jai-fruk	
(c)	yhat ____ yrit-séui-lròu		(f)	yhat ____ draai-mrùn	

9 There are deliberate mistakes in each of the following sentences. Can you spot them?

(a) Lréi Shàang hóu yráu-chín, kréui lrìn yhat mhan dhou mróu.

(b) Ngró draai-gwo ngró mràa-mhaa.

(c) Gó chheut drin-yíng ngró mř tái-gwo.

(d) Kréui hràang srap-fhàn faai.

(e) Kréui shèui-yrìn hrai ghìng-lréi, yrì-ché shik dáa-jri.

—————— **Passage 1** ——————

Dragons (lrùng)

Hóu nroi hóu nroi jhì-chrìn hái Jhùng-gwok yráu yhat go hóu jhùng-yi wraak-wáa ge yràn. Kréui ge wáa wraak-dhak hóu hóu, yràu-krèi-si wraak lrùng, jhàn-hrai hóu-chrí wrúi yhuk ge yhat-yreung. Yráu yhat chi, yhat go draai-gwhùn jhì-dou kréui hóu shik wraak lrùng jrau hóu hhòi-sham gám deui kréui wraa: 'Ngró jri-géi dhou hóu jhùng-yi lrùng. Yrùe-gwó nréi háng bhòng ngró wraak yhat trìu lrùng, ngró wrúi béi hóu dhò chín nréi.'

Géi yrat jhì-hrau, git-gwó trìu lrùng jrau wraak-hóu laak, yrì-ché wraak-dhak hóu hóu, jrung khap-yrán-jó hóu dhò yràn lrài chhàam-gwhùn thìm. Draan-hrai jeui hó-shik jrau hrai trìu lrùng mróu ngráan ge. Draai-gwhùn mř mrìng-braak jrau mran kréui dím-gáai mř wraak ngráan nhe? Kréui wraa, yrùe-gwó wraak-jó ngráan jhì-hrau, trìu lrùng jrau wrúi fhèi-jáu ge laa!

Dhòng-yín kréui góng ge yré mróu yràn wrúi shèung-seun lhaa. Draai-gwhùn hóu nhàu, yhat-dring yiu kréui wraak-mràai deui ngráan. Jhàn krèi-gwaai, kréui yhat wraak-yrùen deui ngráan, trìu lrùng jrau yhuk-jó géi hráa, jhàn-hrai yràu jhèung jí sue tiu-jó chheut-lrài, fhèi-jáu-jó laak.

—————— **Passage 2** ——————

Sei-ngř-srap nrìn jhì-chrìn, gó-jran-srì Sreung-hói suen hrai yhat go hóu shìn-jeun ge draai srìng-srí, draan-hrai Jhùng-gwok krèi-thàa hóu dhò srìng-srí trùng-mràai hhèung-háa drei-fhòng dhou jrung hrai hóu lrok-hrau ge.

Yhat yrat, yráu yhat go hhèung-háa-yràn, Lréi Shìn-shàang, yráu-sri yiu heui Sreung-hói taam kréui ge pràng-yráu Wròng Draai Gwok. Wròng Shìn-shàang jrue hái yhat ghàan yrau draai yrau leng, chit-brei yrau chrài-chrùen ge jáu-dim lréui-brin.

Lréi Shàang lrài-dou jáu-dim, hái draai-tròng* dáng Wròng Shìn-shàang ge srì-hrau, gin-dóu yhat go lróu taai-táai mraan-máan gám hràang-yrap yhat ghàan fóng-jái lréui-brin. Lréi Shìn-shàang mrei gin-gwo lhip, só-yrí kréui mr̀ jhì gó gaa hrai lhip lrài-ge. Lréung fhàn jhung jhì-hrau, fóng-jái ge mrùn hhòi-jó laak, yhat go yrau leng yrau hrau-shaang ge síu-jé hràang-chheut-lrài.

Lréi Shàang hhòi-chí ge srì-hrau gok-dhak hóu krèi-gwaai, yrìn-hrau kréui jrau hóu hhòi-sham gám wraa: 'Srìng-srí yràn jhàn-hrai shìn-jeun laak: hraa chi ngró yhat-dring daai-mràai taai-táai lrài.'

*draai-tròng = *lobby, great hall*

——— APPENDICES ———

This section consists of two parts. The first is a summary of some of the basic principles of Cantonese grammar which you can use for quick reference. Where helpful it refers you back to earlier parts of the book where particular points are discussed in greater detail.

The second part is a brief introduction to Chinese characters; just a taste to give you a general feel for how they work.

——— Grammar summary ———

Contents

1 Adjectives

(*a*) Adjectives go before the nouns they limit:

yhat jek draai bhui   *a large cup* (Unit 1, grammar
point 3)

(*b*) All adjectives can also function as verbs. (Unit 1, grammar
point 3; Unit 13, grammar point 3)

(*c*) Adjectival clauses and phrases go before the nouns they
limit and are linked to them with **ge**:

ngró hóu séung mráai ge   *the car I very much want to*
chhe . . .   *buy . . .* (Unit 4, grammar
point 6; Unit 17, grammar
point 1)

2 Adverbs

(*a*) Fixed adverbs such as **dhou** (*all, both, also*), **jrau** (*then*),
joi (*again*) come immediately before verbs (although the
negative **mȑ** can be placed between a fixed adverb and a verb).
(Unit 1, grammar point 7; Unit 4, grammar point 9; Unit 6,
grammar point 3; Unit 8, grammar point 3; Unit 10, grammar
point 5; Unit 24, grammar point 8)

(*b*) Adverbs of degree such as **hóu** (*very*) and **taai** (*too*) go
immediately in front of adjectival verbs and auxiliary verbs such
as **séung** (*want to*) and **yiu** (*need to*) (but again the negative **mȑ**
can intervene).

(*c*) Adverbs of time when something occurs must come before
the verb, but not necessarily directly before the verb. (Unit 6,
grammar point 10; Unit 8, grammar point 2; Unit 24, grammar
point 3)

(*d*) Adverbs of duration of time come after the verb, but not
necessarily directly after the verb. (Unit 6, grammar point 12;
Unit 10, grammar point 9; Unit 20, grammar point 4; Unit 24,
grammar point 3)

(*e*)   Adverbs of location normally come before the verb, although not necessarily directly before the verb. However, if the location is the result of the action of the verb, the adverb comes after the verb:

Hái Yhìng-gwok Wròng   *Mr Wong has not got a house*
Shàang mróu qhuk.   *in Britain.*
Kréui chró hái sho-fáa-yí   *She seats herself on the sofa.*
sreung-brin.   (Unit 4, grammar point 3; Unit 12, grammar point 7)

(*f*)   Adverbs of manner can be made by joining adverbs to a verb with the verb ending **-dhak**:

Kréui jáu-dhak hóu faai.   *He runs very quickly.* (Unit 15, grammar point 2)

(*g*)   Adverbs can be made from adjectives by the formula **hóu** adjective **gám**:

hóu leng gám   *very prettily* (Unit 8, grammar point 9)

3   Alternatives

(*a*)   When *or* occurs in a question, it is translated by **dring-hrai**:

Nréi thìng-yrat heui dring-   *Are you going tomorrow or*
hrai hrau-yrat heui nhe?   *the day after?* (Unit 13, grammar point 6; Unit 16, grammar point 7)

(*b*)   When *or* occurs in a statement it is usually translated by **wraak-jé**:

Kréui wraak-jé lrài wraak-   *He'll come or he won't.* (Unit
jé mr̀ lrài.   16, grammar point 7)

(*c*)   When *or* occurs with numbers, indicating an approximate figure, two numbers are given together without any other device (although it is possible to separate them with **wraak-jé**):

lruk-chhat yrat   *six or seven days* (Unit 10, grammar point 4; Unit 13, grammar point 6)

4 Classifiers

(*a*) Whenever nouns are counted or specified with *this, that, which?, each, the whole*, the correct classifier must be placed between the number or specifier and the noun. (Unit 2, grammar points 4, 6; Unit 4, grammar point 8; Unit 12, grammar points 1, 5; Unit 13, grammar point 2; Unit 16, grammar point 3; Unit 17, grammar point 8; Unit 20, grammar point 1; Unit 25, grammar points 2, 3)

(*b*) The plural classifier and the classifier for uncountable things is **dhi**. (Unit 4, grammar point 8; Unit 12, grammar point 5; Unit 15, grammar point 3)

(*c*) The classifier can be used to form possessives in place of **ge**. (Unit 12, grammar points 3, 5)

(*d*) At the beginning of a sentence the classifer can be used with definite reference (like *The* in English). (Unit 12, grammar point 5)

(*e*) The classifier can be doubled in conjunction with the adverb **dhou** to give the meaning *each one of.* (Unit 5, grammar point 10; Unit 12, grammar point 5)

(*f*) A very small number of nouns do not need a classifier. (Unit 8, grammar point 6; Unit 9, grammar point 9; Unit 12, grammar point 5)

5 Commands

(*a*) Negative commands (*don't!*) are made with **m̀-hóu** or its more abrupt form **mrái**. (Unit 4, grammar point 11; Unit 16, grammar point 4)

(*b*) Positive commands (*do!*) use:

  (i)   abruptly spoken verbs (**jáu!** – *go!*) or
  (ii) (rather less forcefully) the final particle **lhaa!** or
  (iii) the verb ending **-jó** with a following object or
  (iv) some adjectival verbs and verb endings with the comparative **-dhi** ending. (Unit 3, grammar point 10; Unit 17, grammar point 7; Unit 19, grammar point 1)

6 Comparatives and superlatives

(*a*) Comparatives are formed with **-gwo** (*surpassing*). The pattern is **X** adjective-**gwo Y**. *A bit more* is expressed with **síu-síu**, and *a lot more* with **hóu-dhò**:

Ngró ghòu-gwo nréi.	*I am taller than you.*
Ngró ghòu-gwo nréi síu-síu.	*I am a bit taller than you.*
Ngró ghòu-gwo nréi hóu-dhò.	*I am a lot taller than you.* (Unit 12, grammar point 2; Unit 16, grammar point 9)

(*b*) Negative comparison uses the pattern **X mróu Y gam** adjective:

Nréi mróu ngró gam ghòu.	*You are not as tall as I am.* (Unit 16, grammar points 8, 9)

(*c*) If there is only an **X** and no **Y** the patterns are:

Ngró ghòu-dhi.	*I'm taller.*
Ngró ghòu hóu-dhò.	*I'm a lot taller.*
Nréi mróu gam ghòu.	*You're not so tall.* (Unit 16, grammar point 9)

(*d*) Superlatives make use of **jeui** (*most*), often adding **laak** after the adjective:

Kréui jeui ghòu laak.	*He is tallest.* (Unit 8, grammar point 4; Unit 16, grammar point 9)

(*e*) Equivalence is expressed by **X trùng/mróu Y yhat-yreung gam** adjective:

Ngró trùng nréi yhat-yreung gam ghòu.	*I'm just as tall as you are.*
Kréui mróu ngró yhat-yreung gam ghòu.	*He's not just as tall as I am.* (Unit 13, grammar point 4; Unit 16, grammar point 9)

7 Nouns

Nouns only have one form and do not change according to case, number or gender. The exception is the noun **yràn** (*person*) which has a plural form **yràn-drei**. However, this plural form is reserved for the meaning *other people* and as an oblique way of referring to oneself or to the person being addressed. It is *not* used in expressions such as *three people* which is **shàam go yràn**. (Unit 1, grammar point 9; Unit 2, grammar point 6)

8 Particles

Particles are words which for the most part have no meaning in themselves, but which add nuance or sentiment or some other gloss to a sentence or phrase. Some (such as **maa?, mhe?, qràa?, nhe?, shìn, thìm, bo, jhe**) are capable of clear definition, but usage of many others is not consistent among native speakers and so defies adequate definition. Unfortunately, all speakers of Cantonese use many particles, but they do not all use the same particles, nor do they all necessarily agree on which particle to use when. Often the ill-defined particles seem to add little or nothing to the meaning, and may be treated as 'voiced pauses' ('spoken commas' if you like) and ignored. (Unit 1, grammar point 11; Unit 3, grammar points 6, 8, 10; Unit 5, grammar points 2, 8; Unit 25, grammar point 4)

9 Passives

The passive construction is not common in Cantonese. It uses the pattern **X brei Y** verb, and the verb usually carries a verb ending of some kind:

Trìu yúe brei mhaau srik-gwo laak.
The fish was eaten by the cat.
(Unit 12, grammar point 4)

10 Possessives

(*a*) Possessives are formed with **ge**, which is positioned as if it were the English apostrophe *s* (*'s*):

Wròng Síu-jé ge nràam-pràng-yráu
Miss Wong's boyfriend (Unit 2, grammar point 2; Unit 17, grammar point 2)

(*b*) They can also be formed with the appropriate classifier (singular or plural) instead of **ge**:

ngró go jái   *my son*
ngró dhi néui   *my daughters* (Unit 12, grammar point 3)

11 Potentials

Potentials (*can, to be able*) are formed in three ways.

(*a*)   With the verbs **hó-yrí** and **shik**. **Hó-yrí** often implies *permission to* and so is rather like *may* in English, while **shik** indicates *acquired ability to* and so is like *to know how to*:

> **Ngró hó-yrí heui yràu-séui.**   *I may go swimming.*
> **Ngró shik yràu-séui.**   *I can swim.* (Unit 6, grammar point 11)

(*b*)   With the verb ending **-dhak**:

> **Ngró yràu-dhak séui.**   *I can swim* (= *may* or *know how to*) (Unit 6, grammar point 11)

(*c*)   With the positive ending **-dhak-dóu** and/or the negative ending **-mr̀-dóu**:

> **Nréi tái-mr̀-tái-dhak-dóu kréui qaa?**   *Can you see her?* (Unit 18, grammar point 6)

12 Questions

Questions do not change basic word order. There are four main ways of forming questions.

(*a*)   Using a question word such as **bhin?**, **mhat-yré?**, **géi-sí?** The final particle **qaa?** is often used in association with these question words:

> **Nréi séung mráai *mhat-yré* qaa?**   *What do you want to buy?*

Answers to these questions echo the form of the question, the answer appearing in the same place in the sentence as the question word:

> **Ngró séung mráai *dhi* choi.**   *I want to buy some vegetables.*

The question words **dím-gáai?** and **jrou-mhat-yré?** are exceptional in that they are usually answered by **yhàn-wrai ...** (*because ...*). (Unit 2, grammar point 1; Unit 3, grammar points 1, 3; Unit 8, grammar point 7; Unit 9, grammar point 8)

(*b*)   Using the 'choice-type' question form verb – negative – verb, again backed up often by **qaa?**:

> **Kréui** *shik mr̀ shik* **góng**   *Does he know how to speak*
> **Jhùng-mràn** *qaa?*   *Chinese?*

These questions can be simply answered *yes* or *no* by using the positive or negative form of the verb:

> **Mr̀ shik.**   *He doesn't (know how to speak Chinese).*
>   (Unit 1, grammar point 11)

(*c*)   Using a question particle such as **maa?, qràa?, mhe?, nhe?** at the end of the sentence:

> **Nréi hrai Jhùng-gwok-yràn**   *Do you mean to say you're*
> **mhe?**   *Chinese?*

Type (*c*) questions are often answered simply by **hrai** (*yes*) or **mr̀ hrai** (*no*):

> **Mr̀ hrai,** ngró mr̀ hrai   *No, I'm not Chinese.*
> **Jhùng-gwok-yràn.**
> **Hrai,** ngró hrai Jhùng-   *Yes, I am Chinese.* (Unit 1,
> **gwok-yràn.**   grammar points 4, 6; Unit 3,
>   grammar point 5)

(*d*)   Questions about past events can be asked using **mrei** or **mróu** and the verb endings **-jó** and **-gwo.** (Unit 18, grammar point 5)

13   Sentence order

(*a*)   The basic word order of Cantonese is subject – verb – object, just as in English:

> **Ngró jhùng-yi nréi.**   *I love you.*

(*b*)   Other word orders generally have in common that they put the stressed part of the sentence first regardless of whether it is the grammatical object, a time word, a location, or whatever:

Bhe-jáu **ngró jhùng-yi
yám.**
Thìng-yrat **kréui mr̀
lrài.**

*I like drinking beer (but not
those other drinks).
She's not coming **tomorrow**
(although she is coming today
and the day after tomorrow).*

14 Verb endings

(*a*) A number of suffixes can be attached directly to verbs to
convey aspects of meaning (**-gán** indicates that the action of the
verb is still going on, **-gwo** that it has been experienced at some
time, **-saai** that it is wholly committed, **-jó** that the action has
been completed, and so on). (Unit 4, grammar point 4; Unit 5,
grammar point 4; Unit 6, grammar points 9, 13; Unit 8, grammar
points 10, 11; Unit 11, grammar points 1, 3, 9; Unit 15, grammar
point 10; Unit 17, grammar point 9; Unit 19, grammar points 1, 4;
Unit 20, grammar points 8, 9)

(*b*) The suffix **-dhak** has two functions:

   (i) it enables adverbs of manner to be attached to verbs
and may be thought of as meaning *in such a way that*
(Unit 15, grammar point 2);

   (ii) it adds the notion *able to* to the verb (**góng-dhak** –
able to speak). (Unit 6, grammar point 11)

15 Verbs

(*a*) Verbs have only one form (they do not conjugate) and so
do not change according to tense or number or person. They
can be modified to some extent by verb endings tagged on to
show different aspects of meaning. (Unit 1, grammar point 8;
Unit 4, grammar point 4)

(*b*) Verbs are negated by **mr̀, mróu** or **mrei** placed before
them. There are two exceptions:

   (i) the verb **yráu** (*to have*) does not have a negative form
with **mr̀** or with **mróu**: normally the verb **mróu** (*not
to have*) is used as the negative of **yráu**; and

   (ii) the negative of the verb **yiu** (*to need*) is usually **mr̀-
sái** (*not need*). (Unit 3, grammar points 7, 9; Unit 4,
grammar point 5; Unit 18, grammar point 5)

(*c*)   Verbs normally have subjects, which may or may not be stated depending on whether they can be understood from the context. Exceptions are rare, although it is doubtful whether there is really any subject in expressions about the weather such as **lrok-suet** (*it is snowing*) or **lrok-yrúe** (*it is raining*).

(*d*)   Verbs do not all take objects, although some verbs such as **srik** (*to eat*) and **góng** (*to speak*) (called 'lonely verbs' in the units above) usually require a generalised object if a specific one is not mentioned. (Unit 4, grammar point 2; Unit 9, grammar points 2, 4, 12; Unit 15, grammar point 1; Unit 18, grammar point 4; Unit 25, grammar point 1)

(*e*)   Where there is a series of verbs together, it is normally the first of them which is the grammatically operative one, that is, the one which takes the negative or is acted upon by an adverb:

> **Nréi ghàm-yrat** *seúng mr̀* *seúng heui* **Bhak-ghìng qaa?**   *Do you want to go to Beijing today?*

(*f*)   Adjectival verbs. All adjectives can be used with a verbal function:

> **Kréui ge chhe** *hóu draai.*   *His car is very large.* (Unit 1, grammar point 3)

—— The Chinese writing system ——

Alphabetic systems attempt to show in writing the sounds people make when they speak. By converting the symbols on the page back into sounds, the reader can put him or herself in the position of a listener and so understand what the writer is 'saying'.

Ideographic systems, of which Chinese is the main example, do not make any serious attempt to show the sounds of speech. Instead, they try to show the ideas in a speaker's head when he or she speaks. The reader doesn't convert the written symbols back into sounds and then assign meanings to the sounds; he or she sees the symbols as meanings without having to go through the medium of sounds.

Each syllable of Cantonese is written with one character, and that symbol carries meaning, or in a small number of cases shows the function of the syllable. So the character 人 (**yràn**) carries the meaning *person*, while the character for the syllable 呢 **nhe?** is not actually meaningful in itself, but it does have the function of asking a follow-up question.

There are over 50,000 different Chinese characters in existence. This body of characters is large because, unlike the restricted number of sounds with which the language expresses itself, the number of different meanings is limitless and each meaningful or functional syllable needs its own unique symbol. A well-educated Chinese person will be able to write perhaps 3–4,000 characters and recognise maybe 5–6,000 without the aid of a dictionary. About 3,500 different characters are used in middle-brow newspapers.

The first characters (early second millennium B.C.) seem to have been pictures of the objects they represented, and some of those pictures remain standard today in a stylised form. 羊 (**yrèung**) is *a goat*, and it is not hard to see how the character derives from a picture of a goat's head with horns. 目 (**mruk**) is *an eye*, a squared-off vertical version of a picture of a wide open eye. William Tell fans with arrows through apples in mind will recognise the symbolism of 中 (**jhùng** – *middle*).

Gradually, other ways of creating characters were devised, some of them making use of similarities between spoken words; for example, it is no accident that the characters 由 (**yràu** – *from*) and 油 (**yràu** – *oil*) have the same element in common. But such common elements are at best an unreliable guide to pronunciation, and they can sometimes be downright misleading. It makes most sense to think of characters as being unique symbols for meanings rather than for pronounced sounds.

Chinese writing speaks more directly and more colourfully to the reader than does an alphabetic system. The two simple sounds **Jhùng-gwok** tell you that *China* is meant, but the characters for **Jhùng-gwok** 中國 mean *Middle Kingdom* and carry with them additional messages (*Middle* means *Central* and hence *Most important*, thus reducing other countries (**ngroi-gwok** – *outside kingdoms*) to a peripheral and unimportant status). You will find that once you have learned some characters they will take you over and romanisation will begin to feel very inadequate.

On the other hand, the sheer volume and clumsiness of the character base has made the computerisation of Chinese a very tough nut to crack. A computer can easily cope with storing the symbols and reproducing them – the problem is how to access them. The traditional Chinese methods used in printing and in dictionaries were slow and sometimes haphazard, and faster methods, such as accessing through romanisation, fall foul of homophones and of the many different dialects, each of which has its own way of pronouncing words. At present, Chinese computer software tends to offer the user a choice of several different access methods, but there are problems with all of them.

You may well have worked out for yourself by now that the use of unique symbols attached to meanings allows Chinese script to cope with the homophone problem very well. Two words may be pronounced the same and so be spelled the same in an alphabetic system, but their characters can be totally different and easily distinguishable one from the other. **Gáu**, as you know, can mean *nine*, but it can also mean *dog*. The two characters, however, are not at all confusing: 九 = *nine* and 狗 = *dog*. Similarly, 酒 (*alcoholic drink*) and 走 (*to run, to leave*) are both pronounced **jáu**, but there is no mistaking one character for the other.

Learning the thousands of characters necessary to be fully literate in Chinese is a time-consuming business (for Chinese people as well as for foreigners), and that is why you have learned through romanisation. A Chinese of course learns to speak at his or her mother's knee and so does not need romanisation using that particular language teaching method!

You may wish to learn to recognise some common characters. You will find that knowing them gives an extra dimension to learning Chinese, a very satisfying feel for the language which you have to experience to appreciate. Try to familiarise yourself with the few offered here which have come up in the units above. If you want more, you could look at the character versions of the dialogues.

See page 236 for the large Chinese characters for **ngrài-hím** (*danger*), which read from left to right.

See page 103 for the Chinese character for **trìng** (*to stop*).

See page 24 for the Chinese characters **dhik-sí** (*taxi*), which read from left to right on the door.

See page 52 for the Chinese characters for **sréung** (*board*), which can be seen on the front left door of the bus, in white. The other door reads **lrok** (*alight*).

See page 10 for the Chinese characters for **sé-jri-lràu** (*office*), reading from left to right.

See page 24 for the Chinese characters for **Yhì-yúen Drou** (*Hospital Road*), reading from left to right.

See page 42 for the Chinese characters above the shops, which read **Draai-gáam-gaa: Draai-chhàu-jéung** (*Great sale: Great lucky draw*) from left to right.

Writing a character is subject to certain rules of stroke order. You cannot write the different strokes in a random order or direction. If you do not observe the correct order it is difficult to get the character to balance properly, and it will probably become illegible if written in any kind of a hurry. Here are some useful characters written stroke by stroke for you to practise:

丨 卜 上 **sreung** (*above*); **sréung** (*to go up*)
丨 冂 口 中 **jhùng** (*middle*)
一 丁 下 **hraa** (*below*)
人 女 女 **nréui** (*female*)
丨 冂 冃 冊 田 甲 男 **nràam** (*male*)
丶 宀 广 广 庁 庁 盾 庿 庿 廁 廁　　　　所 **chi-só** (*toilet*)
丨 乚 屮 屮 出 出 丨 冂 口 **chheut-háu** (*exit*)
一 十 扌 扩 扩 扩 拉 拉 **lhàai** (*pull*)

The general rule is that you start at the top left-hand corner of the character and work downwards to finish at the bottom right, but the exceptions to this rule are numerous and you will need to find a teacher or a specialist book to guide you.

Incidentally, you may write your character text from left to right across the page as English does (that's the modern way), or from right to left down the page (that's the traditional way and of course means that you start at what would be the end of an English book), or indeed any way you like, because each character is a discrete entity – you can write round in a circle anti-clockwise if that's how the mood takes you. Chinese newspapers quite often print captions to photographs in a different direction from the rest of the text that they illustrate, and this produces no confusion, though if an English newspaper were to try it it would be *gnisufnoc yrev deedni*.

KEY TO THE EXERCISES

Unit 1

Exercises 1 (*a*) Kréui-drei hóu hóu. (*b*) Wròng Shìn-shàang hóu. (*c*) Jhèung Síu-jé dhou hóu. 2 (*a*) Jóu-sràn. (*b*) Ngró hóu hóu. Nréi nhe? (*c*) Joi-gin. 3 (*a*) mr̀. (*b*) mr̀. (*c*) hrai. (*d*) Mréi-gwok chhe. 4 (*a*) Yrat-bún chhe mr̀ gwai. (*b*) Kréui mr̀ hóu. (*c*) Nréi hóu leng. (*d*) Kréui-drei yiu mr̀ yiu chhe qaa? (*e*) Kréui dhou (hóu) leng. (*f*) Kréui-drei hrai Mréi-gwok-yràn. (*g*) Wròng Shìn-shàang mraai chhe. (*h*) Yhìng-gwok-yràn mr̀ mraai Mréi-gwok chhe.

Unit 2

True or false? (*a*) False. (*b*) False. (*c*) Perhaps: they are colleagues. (*d*) False.
Exercises 1 (*a*) Ngró sing . . . (add whatever your surname is). (*b*) Hrai, kréui hrai Jhùng-gwok-yràn. (*c*) Mr̀ mráai, ngró mr̀ mráai chhe. (*d*) Yráu, ngró yráu Yrat-bún pràng-yráu. 2 (*a*) *The watch and the pen are both Mr Ho's.* (*b*) *That watch is very handsome.* (*c*) *Mr Ho is going to ask Mrs Wong later.* (*d*) *Which pen is Miss Cheung's?* 3 (*a*) go. (*b*) -yràn. (*c*) bún. (*d*) mr̀. (*e*) mhat. (*f*) Bhin. (*g*) dhou. (*h*) mran. 4 You: Wròng Shìn-shàang, ngró séung heui Yhìng-gwok mráai Yhìng-gwok chhe./ Wong: Yhìng-gwok chhe hóu gwai./ You: Nréi yráu mhat-yré chhe qaa?/ Wong: Ngró dhou yráu Yhìng-gwok chhe. 5 Sei go Mréi-gwok-yràn. Shàam go Jhùng-gwok-yràn. Ngr̀ go Yrat-bún-yràn. Wròng Shìn-shàang mraai lréung go sáu-bhiu. Yhat go Mréi-gwok-yràn mráai bhat.

Unit 3

Here is the Wong family. C should address A as **Bràa-bhaa**. D should address B as **Mràa-mhaa**. D should address A as **Bràa-bhaa**. You should address D as **Wròng Síu-jé**. You should address B as **Wròng Taai-táai**. Probably C, since he is responsible enough to take his mother to the doctor's.
Questions.　1　(a) **Mr̀ hrai.** (b) **Mr̀ hrai.** (c) **Hrai.** (d) **Mr̀ hrai.**
(e) **Hrai.** 2　(a) **Hrò Shìn-shàang jrue hái Gaa-fhe Ghaai.** (b) **Jhèung Shìn-shàang jrue hái Fhàa-yrùen Drou.** (c) **Hrò Shìn-shàang ge láu mróu chhe-fròng.** (d) **Jhèung Shìn-shàang séung taam kréui.** (e) **Yráu, yráu hóu-dhò bhaa-sí heui Fhàa-yrùen Drou.**
Exercises　1　(a) **Hrò Shìn-shàang bràa-bhaa hrai yhi-shang.** (b) **Wròng Taai-táai hái qhuk-kéi jrou mhat-yré qaa?** (c) **Ngró mr̀ séung heui tái yhi-shang.** (d) **Ngró-drei yhat-chrài fhàan sé-jri-lràu.** 2　(a) **yhi-shang.** (b) **séung; qhuk-kéi.** (c) **yhi-shang.** (d) **Yhìng-gwok.** 3　**Wròng Shìn-shàang, hóu-nroi-mróu-gin. Nréi hóu maa? Taai-táai nhe? Nréi-drei yrì-ghaa hái bhin-sue jrue qaa? Deui-mr̀-jrue, Wròng Shìn-shàang, ngró yiu daap bhaa-sí heui Fhàa-yrùen Drou. Ngró yiu heui taam ngró bràa-bhaa, daai kréui heui tái yhi-shang.**

Unit 4

True or false?　(a) False. (b) False. (c) False. (d) False. (e) True.
Exercises　1　(a) **Wròng Shìn-shàang séung dáng Hrò Taai-táai yhat-chrài srik-fraan.** (b) **Hrò Taai-táai hái chrùe-fóng júe-gán fraan.** (c) **Hrò Taai-táai mran Wròng Shìn-shàang kréui júe ge sung hóu-mrei maa?** (d) **Hrò Shìn-shàang yráu mróu bhòng Hrò Taai-táai sáu qaa?** (e) **Hrò Taai-táai júe ge sung hóu-chrí jáu-lràu ge yhat-yreung.** 2　(a) **Shik, ngró shik júe ngràu-yruk thòng.** (b) **Mróu, ngró qhuk-kéi fru-gran mróu jáu-lràu.** (c) **Mróu, ngró mróu bhòng kréui sáu.** (d) **Ngró mr̀ nhàu.** (e) **Mr̀ hrai.** 3　(a) **Hái chrùe-fóng yráu lrùng-hhaa, dhou yráu shàang-gwó, yráu fraan, yráu thòng, yráu trìm-bán. Dhou yráu Jhèung Shìn-shàang.** (b) **Yráu, yráu Jhèung Shìn-shàang: kréui hrai lraap-saap-túng!**

Unit 5

Picture quiz.　(a) **Hóu prèng. Mr̀ leng.** (b) **Yráu lraan. Jhèung Síu-jé gó grin dhou yráu lraan.**

Just testing. (*a*) Kréui séung mráai hhaa. (*b*) Dhi hhaa baat-srap-ngŕ mhan yhat ghàn. (*c*) Krèi-thàa dong-háu ge hhaa chhat-srap-yri mhan yhat ghàn jhe. (*d*) Yhàn-wrai yráu séi hhaa!
Exercises 1 (*a*) Hrùng-shik ge Mréi-gwok chhe hóu gwai. (*b*) Ngró bràa-bhaa shik yràu-séui. (*c*) Wròng Taai-táai heui pou-táu mráai-yré. (*d*) Kréui ghàm-yrat mŕ séung srik-fraan. (*e*) Hrò Shàang mŕ srik Hrò Taai-táai jué ge sung. 2 (*a*) ghàan. (*b*) No classifier needed. (*c*) No classifier needed. (*d*) jhì. (*e*) jek. (*f*) Jek-jek. 3 (*a*) Wròng Táai yiu béi yri-srap-baat mhan. (*b*) Kréui yiu béi lruk-srap-sei mhan.

Unit 6

Testing again. (*a*) True. (*b*) False. (*c*) False. (*d*) False. (*e*) False.
Now test your skills. (*a*) Mŕ hrai Chràn Shìn-shàang drai-yhat chi, hrai Wròng Shìn-shàang drai-yhat chi. (*b*) Gim-krìu Draai-hrok mŕ hrai hái Lrèun-dheun fru-gran; yiu daap fó-chhè heui. (*c*) Hrai. (*d*) Hóu-chrí hrai.
Exercises 1 (*a*) (iii) Gim-krìu Draai-hrok hrai sai-gaai jeui yráu-méng ge draai-hrok jhì-yhat. (*b*) (i) Yràu Lrèun-dheun heui Gim-krìu Draai-hrok chhàam-gwhùn yiu daap chhe heung bhak hràng. (*c*) (ii) Yràu nhi-sue daap srap-ngŕ hrou bhaa-sí heui fhèi-ghèi-chrèung yiu géi-dho chín qaa? (*d*) (iv) Nhi-sue ge drei-hraa-tit-lrou mŕ heui fhèi-ghèi-chrèung jí heui srí-khèui. (*e*) (v) Nréi yiu gwo shàam go ghàai-háu dou draai mráa-lrou daap bhaa-sí heui fhèi-ghèi-chrèung. 2 Hái fhèi-ghèi-chrèung daap drei-hraa-tit-lrou heung dhùng hràng dou Draai-wrui-tròng lrok chhe. Hái Draai-wrui-tròng heung nràam hràng, gwo lréung go ghàai-háu, júen heung dhùng jrau dou laak.

Unit 7

Passage 1. *Yesterday mum asked us if we wanted to have salad. We all said we would like that. Mum said: 'Fine, so I'll make a lobster salad for you. Now, I'm going off to buy the lobster now, and you can go and buy some fresh fruit.' We bought lots of fresh fruit and prepared it all in the kitchen too. Mum came back half an hour later. She said: 'Today the lobsters are small and not fresh, so I didn't buy any, I only bought large prawns. You can pretend the prawn salad is lobster salad!'*

Exercises **1** (*a*) False. (*b*) Unknown. (*c*) True. (*d*) False. (*e*) False. **2** (*a*) Kréui mráai-jó draai hhaa fhàan qhuk-kéi. (*b*) Ngró-drei mráai-jó hóu dhò shàn-shìn shàa-léut fhàan qhuk-kéi. (*c*) M̀ shàn-shìn. (*d*) Shik, go-go yràn dhou shik jíng shàa-léut. (*e*) Yráu. **3** (*a*) Nréi srik-gwo ngràu-yruk shàa-léut maa? (*b*) Nhi jhì Mréi-gwok bhat hrai ngró jeui séung mráai ge bhat jhì-yhat. (*c*) Nhi chi hrai ngró drai-yhat chi lrài nréi sé-jri-lràu. **4** X: Deui-m̀-jrue, yrì-ghaa hóu jóu. X: Ngró hái qhuk-kéi. X: Ngró séung chéng nréi srik-fraan. X: Nréi hóu maa? X: Ngró dhou hóu. Nréi taai-táai nhe? X: Kréui dhou-géi hóu. Nréi trùng m̀ trùng ngró fhàan sé-jri-lràu qaa? X: Hóu. Nréi jhàa-chhe heui maa? X: Chró géi-dho hrou bhaa-sí qaa? X: Hóu, Lrài-baai-sei ngró trùng nréi yhat-chrài fhàan sé-jri-lràu. **5** (*a*) kréui mràa-mhaa. (*b*) yhat. (*c*) prèng. (*d*) m̀. (*e*) hó-yrí. **6** (*a*) Ngró-drei shàam go yràn nhi go Shìng-krèi-lruk daap fhèi-ghèi heui Yhìng-gwok wáan. (*b*) Wròng Taai-táai trùng Wròng Shìn-shàang yhat-chrài lrài ngró ge sé-jri-lràu. (*c*) Nréi ge júe-yi yhat-dring hrai jeui hóu ge. (*d*) Nhi ghàan draai-hrok hrai sai-gaai yráu-méng ge draai-hrok. (*e*) Lrèun-dheun hrai Yhìng-gwok jeui dhò yràn ge drei-fhòng jhì-yhat.

Passage 2. *Today I went to the office. Mr Ho told me he will be flying back to England on Thursday, and so would not be coming into the office after Wednesday. Mr Ho is one of my best friends, and I guess that he will not be returning here after he goes back this time. So, what can I give him as a present? I thought about it for a long while without having any ideas, and then went to ask Miss Wong and Mrs Cheung. Miss Wong said: 'How about if the three of us were to ask Mr Ho out for a meal?' Mrs Cheung said: 'It would be best if Mrs Ho could come with him too.'*

I think that women have the best ideas. Do you agree?

Unit 8

Have you understood? (*a*) drin-nrúen-lròu. (*b*) m̀ srat-yrung. (*c*) chrèung-gok. (*d*) mróu yrung-gwo.

Answer these questions if you can! (*a*) M̀ dhak. (*b*) Hrai lréung grin.

Exercises **1** Thìn-hei jrim-jím yrit, mráai lráang-hei-ghèi hrai srì-hrau laa. Lráang-hei-ghèi m̀ suen hóu gwai, draan-hrai hóu yrau-yrung. Yrùe-gwó mráai m̀ srat-yrung ge yré, jhik-hrai shàai chín. Ngró yrí-ghìng yrue-brei-jó ngró-drei

dhi lráang-thin shaam laa. 2 (*a*) Jhèung Síu-jé hrai hóu leng
ge Yrat-bún-yràn. (*b*) Ngró mr̀ séung mráai Chràn Shìn-shàang
pou-táu mraai ge Mréi-gwok bhat. (*c*) Ngró hóu séung srik
Hrò Táai jíng ge lrùng-hhaa. 3 (*a*) Sáu-tròi. (*b*) mrín-fai. (*c*)
Yhat tou leng ge. (*d*) shàn-shìn. 4 A creative test. 'Mr̀-hóu
nhàu lhaa! Ngró mr̀ hrai wraa nréi jhì nhi go mrit-fó-túng
hrai srat-yrung ge yré mhe?!'

Unit 9

Give the cartoon a caption. Nréi-drei gok-dhak nhi chheut
drin-yíng chi mr̀ chi-ghik qaa?
Exercises 1 (*a*) Hrò Shìn-shàang hóu-chrí ngŕ-srap seui
gam sreung-háa. (*b*) Srì-srì wran-drung deui grin-hhòng hóu
hóu. (*c*) Ngró jí-hrai jhùng-yi dáa-bho, pràa-shàan trùng yràu-
séui jhe. 2 sung/shàn-shìn. fó-gei/jáu-lràu. draai-gáam-
gaa/baak-fo-ghung-shi. lraan/lraap-saap-túng. hói-thaan/
yràu-séui. lrok-suet/drin-nrúen-lròu. 3 You: Wròng Shìn-
shàang, jóu-sràn. You: Nréi séung mr̀ séung yám bhe-jáu
qaa? You: Qhòu, gám gaa-fhe nhe? chràa nhe? You: Deui-mr̀-
jrue, ngró-drei mróu séui. Fó-gei wraa ngró jhì nhi-sue dhi
séui mr̀ hóu-yám. Dím-gáai mr̀ yám bhe-jáu qaa? You: Dhi
bhe-jáu hóu hóu-yám, hrai Yhìng-gwok bhe-jáu. Chéng yám
síu-síu lhaa. You: Qhòu, kréui jáu laak! 4 tái: yhi-shang/
drin-yíng/yré. júe: trìm-bán/yré. góng: yré. chhàam-
gwhùn: Gim-krìu Draai-hrok/chrùe-fóng. srik: yré/trìm-bán.
5 (*a*) Wròng Shàang srik-yré. (*b*) Wròng Táai júe-yré. (*c*)
Wròng Síu-jé mráai-yré. (*d*) Jhèung Shàang góng-yré. (*e*) Nhi
shàam go yràn yám-yré.

Unit 10

True or false? (*a*) Mr̀ hrai. Dhi yreuk-séui hrai mràa-mhaa
sreung-go-lrái-baai mráai-fhàan-lrài ge. (*b*) Hrai, mràa-mhaa
chi-chi dhou yiu kréui yrìu-wràn dhi yreuk-séui shìn. (*c*) Mr̀
hrai, kréui gok-dhak (hrai) go tróu mr̀ shùe-fruk. (*d*) Mr̀
hrai, kréui nghaam-nghaam yám-jó srap fhàn jhung jhe.
Exercises 1 (*a*) Yi-shang hái chán-só tái breng-yràn. (*b*)
Wròng Shìn-shàang hrai Jhùng-gwok-yràn. (*c*) Mràa-mhaa hái
pou-táu mráai-yré. (*d*) Hhèung-góng-yràn hái Hhèung-góng
jrue. (*e*) Wròng Whài-lrìm ge bràa-bhaa dhou hrai sing Wròng.
2 Nréi-drei lréung-go yràn yám-jó gam dhò mr̀ nghaam yám
ge yré deui shàn-tái mr̀ hóu ge! Nréi-drei dhou séung séi

qràa?! Wròng Shìn-shàang, nréi yám taai dhò bhe-jáu – mǐ-
hóu yám laa! Wròng Taai-táai nréi yám taai dhò gaa-fhe – mǐ-
hóu yám laa! 3   Nhi jek jhùe-jái heui-jó mráai-yré.   Nhi jek
jhùe-jái mróu lrèi-hhòi qhuk-kéi.   Nhi jek jhùe-jái srik-jó
ngràu-yruk.   Nhi jek jhùe-jái mróu srik-yré.   Nhi jek jhùe-
jái wraa: 'Qhòu! Qhòu! Qhòu!' jrau heui tái yhi-shang. 4   (a)
Chràn Shàang dáa-gán bho. (b) Kréui srik-gán lrùng-hhaa. (c)
Kréui yám-gán bhe-jáu. (d) Kréui tràu-wràn. (e) Kréui qáu-
gán. (f) Kréui tái-gán yhi-shang. (g) Kréui séi-jó laak.

Unit 11

Have you understood? 1   *'Yesterday I thought this chair was very
comfortable, but now . . . !'* **2**   You should have left: (a) srì-jhong.
(b) mǐ hhòi-sham. (c) grin ngroi-tou hóu leng. (d) sho-fáa-yí.
Exercises 1   srap-lruk go síu-jé.   yri-baak jhèung jí.   ngǐ-
chhìn-lruk-baak mhan.   yhat-baak-mraan go Jhùng-gwok-
yràn.   yhat-mraan-yri-chhìn-chhat-baak-ngǐ-srap.   baat-chhìn-
lrìng-shàam-srap-sei.   srap-yhat go jhung-tràu.   lréung jek
lrùng-hhaa. **3**   (a) grau-fún. (b) taai prèng. (c) mraai qhuk. (d)
jhì-chrìn. (e) yrit. (f) shài-nràam. **4**   Mrs Ho is going to eat
lobster on Monday; Miss Ho is going to see a film on Tuesday; and
Mr Ho is going climbing on Wednesday.

Unit 12

Whoops! Something is wrong!   (a) **Jek** is not the correct classifier for *students*: it should be **go-go**. (b) How can I say this sentence if it is true? (c) **Never ever** say **mǐ yráu** – it is always **mróu**.
(d) The classifier is missing. It should read **Gó lréung go Mréi-
gwok . . . .** (e) Must be wrong. How could the father be only eight
years old!
Exercises 1   (a) yrau chrúng yrau dhò. (b) sei go jhung-
tràu. (c) jhùng-hrok. (d) gaau-shùe shìn-shàang. **2**   (a) Ngró
go jái sái mǐ sái hrok Jhùng-mràn qaa? (b) Kréui mrúi mráan
dhou yiu jrou géi-dho go jhung-tràu ghùng-fo qaa? (c) Ngró
go jái hái Lrèun-dheun yrí-ghìng druk-gwo ngǐ nrìn Siú-hrok.
Yhìng-gwok hrok-shaang srap-yhat seui shìn-ji druk Jhùng-
hrok. Hhèung-góng hrai mǐ hrai yhat-yreung qaa? (d) Hái
nréi ge hrok-hraau druk-shùe, druk yhat nrìn yiu géi-dho
chín qaa? (e) Hrok-shaang sái mǐ sái mráai fo-bún trùng lrin-
jraap-bóu qaa? **3**   (i)(e). (ii)(a). (iii)(c). (iv)(b). (v)(d). **4**   (a)
Qhuk ngroi-brin yráu hei-chhè. (b) Wròng Shàang hái Wròng

Táai jó-sáu-brin. (c) Brou shùe hái sho-fáa-yí sreung-brin. (d) Ngró gwú kréui-drei mráai-yrùen yré fhàan-lrài. (e) Hái kréui chrìn-brin yráu hóu dhò séui. (f) Go mrit-fó-túng hrai Wròng Shìn-shàang mráai ge. (g) Kréui-drei go jái hái yí hraa-brin. (h) Wròng Táai yhat-dring hóu mr̀ hhòi-sham.

Unit 13

Exercises 1 (a) Chràn Táai ghàm-mráan hóu mr̀ dhak-hràan. (b) Ngró bràa-bhaa srèng-nrìn dhou mr̀ dhak-hràan. (c) Mr̀-ghòi nréi wraa béi ngró thèng nréi go jái thìng-yrat mròng mr̀ mròng qaa? (d) Kréui Lrái-baai-yri hóu mròng. (e) Ngró jeui mr̀ dhak-hràan ge srì-hrau hrai jhìu-jóu. 2 (a) Dhi. (b) ghaan . . . jek. (c) chrèung. (d) gaa. 3 mròng/dhak-hràan. shùe-fruk/shàn-fú. gaan-jhung/srì-srì. yrèng/shùe. hrok-shaang/shìn-shàang. jing-fú/srí-mràn. fhùng-fu/síu-síu. gáam-síu/jhàng-ghàa. 4 (a) Ngró gwú hrai Wròng Táai yrèng chín. (b) Mr̀ hrai, kréui hóu mr̀ hhòi-sham. (c) Drai-lruk jek mráa hrai sei hrou (mráa). (d) Gáu hrou mráa yrèng. (e) Hrai Wròng Taai-táai hóu shik dóu-mráa. (f) Mr̀ nghaam, gáu hrou mráa hóu-gwo sei hrou mráa. (g) Gáu hrou mráa dhou hóu-gwo shàam hrou mráa. (h) Mr̀ hrai, jeui hóu go jek mráa hrai gáu hrou mráa. (i) Nhi chrèung choi-mráa yráu lruk jek mráa. (j) Ngró gwú kréui-drei hrai shùe dhò-gwo yrèng laak.

Unit 14

Passage 1. *When Mr Wong's seven-year-old son came to school yesterday he cheerfully told me that his father had bought a new house last week. The house was large and looked nice, with three bedrooms, and there was a front garden and a garage as well. He said: 'Now I have a room to myself, it's really comfortable. But mummy has to share a room with daddy, so I think she must be unhappy. I don't know why daddy won't let mummy use the third bedroom. No one is using that room now, daddy has only put a lot of books in there, that's all.'*
Exercises 1 (a) Kréui hrai chhat seui. (b) Kréui mráai-jó yhat ghàan shàn qhuk. (c) Qhuk chrìn-brin yráu fhàa-yúen trùng-mràai yhat ghàan chhe-fròng thìm. (d) Hrai mràa-mhaa yiu trùng kréui yhat-chrài. (e) Drai-shàam ghàan fan-fóng lréui-brin yráu hóu dhò shùe. (f) Mróu. 2 (a) hhèi-mrong. (b) thìn-hei. (c) lráang-thin. (d) dáa-suen. (e) drin-yíng. (f) wran-

— 275 —

drung. (*g*) ghèi-yruk. (*h*) dhò-yrùe. (*i*) grin-hhòng. (*j*) nroi-yrùng. (*k*) síu-lrèun. (*l*) prìng-gwhàn. 3   (*a*) thìng-yrat. (*b*) Lrái-baai-yrat. (*c*) chrìn-yrat. (*d*) srèng-yrat. (*e*) jrok-yrat. (*f*) Yrat-bún. (*g*) ghàm-yrat. (*h*) yrat-yrat. (*i*) hrau-yrat. 4   (*a*)(i) *The first horse is No. 9.* (ii) *The first horse is not No. 9.* (*b*)(i) *Miss Jhung-shaan happens to be Japanese.* (ii) *Miss Jhung-shaan really is Japanese.* (*c*)(i) *He is going to Canton tomorrow.* (ii) *He is not going to Canton until tomorrow.* (*d*)(i) *Mrs Chan has been to the States more than ten times.* (ii) *Mrs Chan has been to the States dozens of times.* 5   (*a*) shùe-fruk. (*b*) trìng-chhe ge. (*c*) hóu dhò chín. 6   (*a*) Kréui sréung-tròng jhì-chrìn, srì-srì dhou heui taam kréui nràam-pràng-yráu. (*b*) Wròng Táai séung mráai gó gaa chhe, yhàn-wrai gaa chhe hóu leng. (*c*) Ngró mr̀ mrìng-braak gó go yràn lráang-thin séung mráai lráang-hei-ghèi jrou-mhat-yré qaa? (*d*) Gó dhi hhaa mr̀ shàn-shìn, só-yrí Chràn Táai mr̀ séung mráai. (*e*) Kréui srik-gán yré ge srì-hrau, mr̀ góng-wáa. 7   (*a*) Mráai gó gaa chhe yiu géi-dho chín qaa? (*b*) Wròng Shàang Shìng-krèi-géi (or géi-sí) lrèi-hhòi Yrat-bún qaa? (*c*) Hái Lréi Táai jó-sáu-brin gó jrek gáu-jái hrai bhin-go sung béi kréui gaa? (*d*) Gó dhi yràn yráu géi-dho go hrai gaau-shùe shìn-shàang qaa? 8   Across. 1 SRÍ-GAAN. 4 TIU. 5 BHO. 6 GIM-KRÌU. Down. 1 SÁU-TUNG. 2 GEI-DHAK. 3 NHI-DROU.

Passage 2.   Mr Ho bets on the horses.   *If a rich person wants to buy a horse then he goes and buys one, but that's a very expensive way to 'buy a horse'! In Hong Kong you will often hear poor people saying 'I think I'll buy a horse today.' What's the explanation? Have a guess, what could it mean if a poor person talks about 'buying a horse'? That's right, 'to buy a horse' means 'to bet on a horse', so when poor people say they want to buy a horse that means they want to bet on a horse.*

Mr Ho is not very rich. One day his good friend Mr Cheung phoned him up and asked him: 'There's horse-racing tonight. I'd like to invite you to go with me to the racecourse to enjoy ourselves. What do you say?' Mr Ho happily said 'Fine. Fine. Terrific idea!'

After finishing the phone call he told Mrs Ho. She said: 'You have never been horse-racing before, this will only be your first time. I wonder if you'll like it?' Mr Ho said: 'Oh, you're right. This will be my first time horse-racing. If I don't like it, I'll have to sit there with nothing to do! What can I do about it?' Mrs Ho said: 'You'd best buy a book before you go to the course. If you feel that it's fun watching the horses, then there's no need to read it. Otherwise, you can sit there and read. What do you think?' Mr Ho is a very docile man: he does whatever his wife says. So of course that evening before he went to the racecourse he bought a book.

Luckily Mr Ho found the racing quite good fun, and there was no need to read. But he didn't win a brass farthing, on the contrary he lost a great deal of money. When he went home he angrily said to his wife: 'Next time I go horse-racing I won't listen to you! When you bet on a horse you want to bet to win, you shouldn't bet to lose!'

Do you get it? The pun is in **mráai-shùe** which could be either *buy a book* or *bet and lose*, and superstitious gamblers believe that doing the one results in the other.

Exercise 9 *Mr Cheung came home from gambling at the dog track. His son asked him:*
'Daddy, how did the gambling go today? Did you win?'
'Won nine races out of ten.'
'Wow! Daddy, you really know how to gamble. You bet on ten races and only lost on one.'
'To tell you the truth, I didn't win a cent. I bet on ten races and the dog track was the winner on each race!'

Here the pun is on **gáu-chrèung** which sounds like either *dog track* or *nine races*. Mr Cheung's son naturally enough at first heard what he most wanted to hear, that his father had won handsomely.

Unit 15

Check on yourself. (*a*) Jáu-dim fròng-ghaan lréui-brin lráang-hei-ghèi mrit-fó-túng dhou mróu. (*b*) Ngŕ-shing-khap jáu-dim hrai jeui hóu jeui hóu ge jáu-dim. (*c*) Yráu-dhi ngŕ-shing-khap jáu-dim lréui-brin yráu chán-só trùng-mràai wran-drung fóng.

Exercises 1 (*a*) Nréi hrai Yhìng-gwok-yràn dring-hrai Mréi-gwok-yràn nhe? (*b*) Fó-chhe faai dring-hrai fhèi-ghèi faai nhe? (*c*) Kréui Lrái-baai-shàam dring-hrai Lrái-baai-sei lrài nhe? (*d*) Hrò Shìn-shàang séung heui Hhèung-góng dring-hrai Gwóng-jhàu nhe? (*e*) Hrai Lréi Táai mróu chín dring-hrai Chràn Táai mróu chín nhe? 2 (*a*) yrat-táu. (*b*) yhat-dring (yráu). (*c*) lráang-séui. (*d*) hhèng. (*e*) fó-gei. 3 (*a*) Kréui góng-dhak faai. (*b*) Wròng Shàang mráai hhaa mráai-dhak hóu prèng. (*c*) Nréi hràang-lrou hràang-dhak faai-gwo Jhèung Síu-jé. (*d*) Nréi

yám yrèung-jáu yám-dhak dhò-gwo ngró. (e) Lréi Shìn-shàang
jhàa-chhe jhàa-dhak mr̀-hrai-géi-hóu. 4 (a) jhèung. (b) jek.
(c) gaa. (d) ghàan. (e) trìu. (f) gaa. (g) ghàan. (h) jhèung. (i)
grin. 5 (a) Yhat ghàn chrúng-gwo yhat brong. (b) Hái Yhìng-
gwok mráai grin-hhòng bóu-hím hóu gwai. (c) Trùng-mràai
chró-gán fhèi-ghèi ge srì-hrau dhou yráu mrín-seui yrèung-
jáu mraai. (d) Mr̀-sái. (Remember the normal negative of yiu is
mr̀-sái.) (e) Hái Lrèun-dheun yráu sei go fhèi-ghèi-chrèung.
6 A shàam-dím-lréung-go-jri. B srap-dím-srap-yhat-go-jri. C
gáu-dím-bun. D chhat-dím-shaam-go-gwhat. E srap-yri-
dím-lrìng-gáu-fhàn(-jhung). F ngr̀-dím-srap-ngr̀-fhàn(-jhung).
ngr̀-dím-shàam (-go-jri). ngr̀-dím-yhat-go-gwhat. 7 Nréi Lrái-
baai-lruk lréung-dím-bun dou-jó mráa-chrèung.

Unit 16

Háau-srí. Ngró gwú yhàn-wrai gó go háau-srí-gwhùn paa-
dou tràu-wràn fan-jó hái-drou jhe.
Exercises 1 (a)(i). (b)(i). (c)(i). (d)(i) Generally Chinese people mention themselves first, in contrast to polite Western practice
which is to put the self last. (e)(i). 2 (a)(ii) *I also think he is a
Japanese.* (b)(ii) *I give away his ten dollars.* (c)(ii) *Mrs Lee is going
to Japan to get on a plane.* (d)(ii) Closest might be: *I and Mr Wong
are going to the City Hall to eat.* (e)(ii) *Whose wife is ill?* 3 A = Mr
Lee. B = Mrs Chan. C = Mr Chan. D = Mrs Lung. E = Mr Lung.
F = Mrs Lee. 4 (a) dáa-lràa-jeuk. (b) dóu-phe-páai. (c) chhàu
jéung-bán. (d) thèng gwóng-bo. (e) chhùng hrùng-dhang. (f)
tái drin-yíng. 5 Wròng Shàang ghòu-gwo Chràn Táai trùng
Wròng Táai, mróu Lréi Shàang Lréi Táai gam ghòu, draan-
hrai trùng Chràn Shàang yhat-yreung gam ghòu. Lréi Shàang
ghòu-gwo Wròng Táai hóu-dhò. Lréi Shàang jeui ghòu. 6 (a)
Wraai-yràn. (b) Ngr-wrui. (c) Shàu-lréi. (d) yhat-srì or yráu-srì.

Unit 17

You are a Hong Kong immigration official. Shìn-shàang,
mr̀-ghòi nréi ghàau bún wru-jiu trùng-mràai chhìm-jing béi
ngró lhaa. Nréi géi-sí séung lrèi-hhòi Hhèung-góng qaa? Nràa,
jing-fú kwhài-dring mr̀ jéun daai sáu-chheung yrap-lrài
Hhèung-góng: mr̀-ghòi nréi ghàau-béi drai-sei-srap-yhat-hrou
gwrai-tói ge gíng-chaat shàa-jín lhaa.

Exercises 1 (*a*) Wròng Shàang pràa-gán shàan. (*b*) Kréui hái sheung-yràn-chròng sreung-brin fan-gaau. (*c*) Kréui tiu-ghòu. (*d*) Kréui lhàai-jrue jek gáu. (*e*) Kréui chró hái sho-fáa-yí sreung-brin. (*f*) Kréui kréi hái yhat jhèung yí sreung-brin. **2** (*a*) gíng-chaat. (*b*) shìn-shàang. (*c*) shi-ghei. (*d*) fó-gei. (*e*) yhi-shang. **3** (*a*)(iv) shìn-ji. *She said she would come back on Monday, but she didn't return until Wednesday.* (*b*)(v) jhì-hrau. *After you had left I rang your wife.* (*c*)(ii) lrìn. *Last month Mrs Wong didn't even sell one car: her manager was very unhappy about it.* (*d*)(i) dhou. *He plays mah-jong every day, so he has no time to go shopping with me.* (*e*)(iii) jeuk shaam-kwràn. *It's not very convenient to wear a dress when swimming.* **4** (*a*) Yhat nrìn yráu shàam-baak-lruk-srap-ngí yrat. (*b*) Thìng-yrat hrai Lrái-baai-yrat. (*c*) Sei-yruet yráu shàam-srap yrat. (*d*) Shàam go shìng-krèi mróu yhat go yruet gam dhò yrat. (*e*) Shàam nrìn nroi-dhi. **5** (*a*) Kréi hái Chràn Táai jó-brin gó go síu-jé hrai Wròng Shàang srap-chhat seui ge néui. (*b*) Nréi hái Mréi-gwok lréui-yràu mráai ge Yrat-bún chhe hrai bhin yhat gaa chhe qaa? (*c*) Nréi nhi go grau ge mrit-fó-túng mř gau draai. Mráai yhat go draai-dhi ge, hóu mř hóu qaa?

Unit 18

Exercises 1 (*a*) Ghàm-yrat hrai Shìng-krèi-géi qaa? (*b*) Lrèun-dheun Fhèi-ghèi-chrèung hái srìng-srí bhin-brin qaa? (*c*) Gwai-sing-qaa? (*d*) Dhi hhaa géi-dho chín yhat ghàn qaa? (*e*) Nréi chhat-dím-jhung dring-hrai baat-dím-jhung heui nhe? **2** (*a*) Bhak-brin. (*b*) Nréui-yán. (*c*) Gó-sue. (*d*) Yrap-brin. (*e*) Grau-nín. (*f*) Hrau-yrat. (*g*) Gáa. (*h*) Néui. (*i*) Yre-mráan. **3** Wròng Shàang jeui draai. (Remember that **draai** is used for comparative age, not **lróu**.) **4** None of them need tone marks. (Aren't we rotten?!) **5** (*a*) brin-fruk. (*b*) chrèun-lrò-chhe. (*c*) gáa ge. (*d*) draan-hrai. (*e*) mř jéun. **6** (*a*) fràan-wrìng. (*b*) fhòng-mrin. (*c*) shàu-lréi. (*d*) yram-hrò. (*e*) mrín-seui. (*f*) fhòng-brin.

Unit 19

Exercises 1 Broker: Mř hrai, mróu jrok-yrat gam ghòu. Broker: Yhìng-gwok jing-fú jeui-gran ghùng-bou mř wrúi jhàng-gàa lrei-shik. Broker: Ngró gwú gó-jran-srì Yhìng-bóng yhat-dring wrúi ghòu hóu-dhò. Broker: Mróu mran-trài. Gó-jran-srì mř-ghòi nréi joi dáa-drin-wáa béi ngró lhaa. **2** (*a*) Hái srí-khèui. (b) Gok-dhak shàn-fú. (c) Geuk-jai yrung-lràai trìng-chhe qhaa-maa. (d) Jóu-chàan hrai yhat yrat drai-yhat chi srik yré. Hrai yrat-táu srik ge. 3 (a)(i). (b)(ii). (c)(ii). (d)(ii). (e)(ii). 4 (a) *You and I may not go there.* (b) *I cannot drive on the outlying islands.* (c) *I'll come in the afternoon.* (d) *I like eating fruit with salad.* 5 (a) Chràn Shàang jeui draai. (b) Nréui-ge hrai baak-fran-jhì-lruk-srap. (c) Nràam-ge dhòng-yín hrai baak-fran-jhì-sei-srap lhaa. (d) Hrai Chràn Táai ghòu. (e) Kréui-drei yráu shàam go jái.

Unit 20

Exercises 1 (a) *Mr Wong hates taking medicine.* (b) *Don't open your eyes wide and stare at me!* (c) *Materials which are not up to standard are treated as seconds.* (d) *It is of course illegal to gamble in a gambling den.* (e) *We should pay more attention to the study conditions of our children.* 2 (a) Chhat-yruet sei-hrou. (b) Yhat-gáu-gáu-lruk-nrìn Srap-yruet yraa-baat-hrou. (c) Yri-lrìng-lrìng-yhat-nrìn Ngí-yruet srap-ngí-hrou. (d) Srap-yri-yruet srap-yhat-hrou Lrái-baai-yrat hraa-jau lruk-dím-shàam-go-jri. (e) Chheut-nín Baat-yruet shàa-qraa-yhat-hrou. 3 (a) Yhìng-gwok. (b) Lrèun-dheun. (c) chhìu-gwo yhat-mraan Yhìng-bóng. (d) yrin-gham. 4 (a) chheut-ghaai/hràang-ghaai. (b) jin-jhàng. (c) draai-yeuk. (d) hhùng-yràu. (e) ghìng-lréi. (f) ló-tái. 5 1 QHÀU-JHÀU. 2 SÁI-SHAAM. 3 SHÀN-CHÍNG. 6 (a) Jhèung Táai yrèng-jó yhat-mraan-baat-chhìn-yri-baak mhan. Hrò Shàang yrèng-jó yhat-mraan-shàam-chhìn-lruk-baak-ngí-srap mhan. Wròng Shàang yrèng-jó yhat-mraan-lrìng-gáu-baak-yri-srap mhan. Lréi Táai yrèng-jó gáu-chhìn-yhat-baak mhan. Chràn Shàang yrèng-jó yri-chhìn-chhat-baak-shàam-srap mhan jhe. (b) Ngí-srap-yri-go-bun.

Unit 21

Passage 1. *Several hundred years ago in a place in the north of China there lived a rich man called Wong. He had lots of horses, all of them tall, mighty and handsome, and he loved them very much. One day a handsome but rather old horse went missing. Mr Wong's friends all felt it was a great pity and they thought that he would be angry and very unhappy, but quite on the contrary he was not only not angry but believed that the horse would come back very soon. After a few days the horse really did come back. His friends said Mr Wong was very fortunate, but he just smiled and said: 'That old horse knows what's what, (I knew) he could find the way home, that's all.'*

Passage 2. *Long ago there was a military officer in Canton. One day he wrote a letter of great importance to an officer in another city. At that time China did not have a Post Office, and he was very busy and had no time to take the letter there, so he told his son to take it for him. He said to his son: 'This letter is very important, it must get there quickly! Let's see, the more legs the quicker: your two legs won't be as quick as four legs. You had better use my horse to go. Hurry up!'*

The young man set off and his father awaited his return. He knew that a horse would need about eight hours to get to that place and back. Who could have guessed that it was two days before his son returned. He said cheerfully to his father: 'I'm back, Dad. Was I quick? I thought and thought and thought up a very fast method. You said the more legs the quicker and that two legs were not as fast as four... so I walked leading the horse along... if two legs aren't as fast as four, then six legs were bound to be faster than four legs, right?'

Exercises **1** Séung-lrài-séung-heui (lit. *think coming think going*) means *to rack your brains, to think and think.* (*a*) *walking up and down.* (*b*) *running to and fro.* (*c*) *We bargained and bargained but couldn't agree a price.* **2** (*a*) *An average horse weighs about 1,000 lbs* (**yhat-chhìn brong**). (*b*) *On average a horse dies at about 20 years of age* (**yri-srap seui**). (*c*) *A horse can only stay healthy if it exercises for at least half an hour a day* (**bun go jhung-tràu**). (*d*) *A horse must eat at least 20 lbs of food a day* (**yri-srap brong**). **3** *10 a.m.* *Call taxi. 10.30 a.m.* *To Manager Wong's office. 12.15* *Lunch in City Hall with Miss Cheung. 3.30 p.m.* *Get air ticket from travel company. 6.45 p.m.* *Drinks with Miss Ho at Hong Kong Hotel. 7.30 p.m.* *Cinema with Miss Ho.* **4** (*a*) **chhàa-mř-dho.** (*b*) **hram-braang-lraang.** (*c*) **draan-hrai.** (*d*) **nghaam-nghaam.** (*e*) **yráu-srì.** (*f*) **jrou-mhat-yré.** **5** (*a*) **Kréui yràu-séui, só-yrí mř yrit mř shàn-fú.** (*b*) **Kréui ghàm-yrat mř jhàa lraap-saap-chhe, kréui jhàa krèi-thàa chhe qaa.** (*c*) **Kréui yri-srap nrìn jhì-chhrìn hrai yhat go yráu yhat-***chhìn***-mraan mhan ge yráu-chhín yràn.** **6** **Wròng Shìn-shàang ge shàn chhe:** (*a*) **hóu leng.** (*b*) **leng-hrai-leng, draan-hrai mróu Jhèung Shàang ge shàn chhe gam leng.** (*c*) **mř-hrai-géi-leng.** (*d*) **mř gau draai.** (*e*) **taai gwai laa.** (*f*) **hrai sai-gaai sreung jeui leng ge chhe.** (*g*) **leng-gwo ngró gaa chhe hóu-dhò.** (*h*) **trùng Jhèung Shàang ge shàn chhe yhat-yreung gam draai yhat-yreung gam gwai.** **7** (*a*) **wái** (or **go,** but that is not really polite enough). (*b*) **lrìn.** (*c*)

lróu. (*d*) géi . . . nroi. (*e*) draai. 8   (*a*) Wròng Shàang A-geuk
yiu béi dhò-dhi (B-geuk kréui mř sái béi). (*b*) B-geuk hrai
Lréi Shàang yiu béi baat-baak mhan. (*c*) Jhèung Shàang A-
geuk yiu béi shàam-baak mhan, B-geuk yiu béi ngř-baak
mhan, jhik-hrai wraa kréui B-geuk yiu béi dhò yri-baak mhan.
(*d*) Béi jeui síu ge hrai Chràn Shàang: béi jeui dhò ge hrai
Lréi Shàang. 9   (*a*) Ngró mràa-mhaa dáa-drin-wáa (ge srì-
hrau) góng-dhak dhou-géi mraan. (*b*) Fó-gei, nhi dhi gaa-
fhe mř gau yrit. (*c*) Nréi séung yám bhe-jáu dring-hrai séui
nhe? (*d*) Nréi gó jhì sreung-go-yruet mráai ge bhat mróu ngró
nhi jhì gam gwai. or Nréi sreung-go-yruet mráai ge gó jhì
bhat . . . . (*e*) Kréui gìu ngró wraa béi nréi jhì nréi yiu géi-dho
dím jhung lrài. (*f*) Wròng Shìn-shàang lrìn lrùng-hhaa dhou
mř jhùng-yi srik. (*g*) Nhi dhi shùe yráu shàam-fran-jhì-yri
hrai Jhùng-mràn shùe. (*h*) Kréui yruet-lrài-yruet-yráu-chín.

Unit 22

Exercises 1   (*a*) Mř hrai, ngró mř hrai Mréi-gwok-yràn. (*b*)
Hrai, kréui-drei yruet-lrài-yruet-wraai. (*c*) Hrai, ngró mrei
srik-gwo jóu-chhaan. (*d*) Mř hrai, kréui hóu jhùng-yi fhàan-
ghùng. (*e*) Hrai, yhat-yreung gam jhùng-yi. 2   (*a*) mhei. (*b*)
béi. (*c*) fhàan. (*d*) dúen. 3   (*a*) -gán. (*b*) -jrue. (*c*) -gwo. (*d*) -saai.
(*e*) -hhòi. 5   (*a*) Chhat-mraan-lrìng-yri-baak mhan. (*b*) Hrai
Chràn Shàang ló ge chín dhò. (Hrò Shàang yhat-grung jí-hrai
ló yri-mraan-sei jhe.) (*c*) Wròng Táai ghàm-yrat bhat-gwo yrung-
jó yraa-yri-go-sei jhe. (*d*) Ngró qhuk-kéi yhat-grung yráu srap-
ngř go yràn. (Mř-hóu mř gei-dhak ngró lhaa!)

Unit 23

Exercises 1   (*a*) yhat-lràu. (*b*) ghìng-jai. (*c*) lhàai-yràn. (*d*)
jai-fruk. (*e*) shàn-séui. 2   (*a*) Yràu ngràn-hròng heui Hrò
Shàang qhuk-kéi jí yráu lréung ghung-lréi jhe. (*b*) Ngràn-
hròng hái Hrò Shàang qhuk-kéi dhùng-brin. 3   (*a*) Kréui
hrai sei-srap brong. (*b*) Hrai yrau-sáu. (*c*) Kréui yrì-ghaa lruk
seui. (*d*) Kréui jí-hrai ghàau-jó baat-srap mhan béi fó-gei jhe!
4   (*a*) Yiu trìng-chhe bo! (*b*) Lràam-shik ghàa wròng-shik
hrai lruk-shik. (*c*) Lràam-shik ghàa hrùng-shik hrai jí-shik.
(*d*) Hóu grau ge drin-yíng hrai hhak-braak-shik ge. 5   You:
Fó-gei, nhi-sue dhi hói-shin jhàn-hrai hóu-mrei, yrau shàn-
shìn yrau jíng-dhak leng. Shik-hhèung-mrei dhou hrai yhat-

lràu ge. You: *All our fish are live here, of course they're fresh.* You: Mr̀-ghòi mràai-dhaan lhaa. You: *Thank you. $2,890.* You: Mhat-yré wáa?! Gam dhò gé! Jhàn-hrai mr̀ prèng qaa! You: *You should know, sir, that it's very hard to buy live fish now. Added to that, our restaurant presents you with chopsticks, one pair for each customer.* You: Ngró mrei mráai-gwo gam gwai ge faai-jí qaa. Hóu lhaa. Mr̀ prèng, draan-hrai dhou dái. Nhi-drou hrai shàam-chhìn mhan. You: *Thank you.* 6 'Nhi trìu yúe jhàn-hrai leng, yhat-dring hóu hóu-mrei. Bhin-wái háng béi yhat-chhìn mhan qaa?'

Unit 24

Exercises 1 (*a*) A shadow. (*b*) Jrok-yrat. 2 (*a*) Wròng Síu-jé srik jóu-chhaan jhì-chrìn, jraap-gwaan heui saan-brou shìn. (*b*) Ngró hái qhuk-kéi ge srì-hrau, mr̀ daai móu. (*c*) Nràam-yán lruk-srap-ngr̀ seui shìn-ji hó-yrí ló teui-yhau-gham. (*d*) Ngró ghàm-jhìu-jóu yhat tái bou-jí jrau jhì-dou ngró-drei ghung-shi ge chrìng-fong hóu ngrài-hím. (*e*) Chràn Shìn-shàang yruet yám bhe-jáu yruet jhùng-yi yám. or Chràn Shìn-shàang yruet-lrài-yruet-jhùng-yi yám bhe-jáu. 3 (*a*) Yhat go sai-mhan-jái séung lhàai gáu, draan-hrai jek gáu mr̀ séung hràang. (*b*) Yhat go nràam-yán thèui-jrue yhat gaa wraai-jó ge chhe. Kréui taai-táai jhàa-jrue gó gaa wraai chhe. (*c*) Yráu yràn hhòi faai chhe chùng-gwo hrùng-dhang. (*d*) Gíng-chaat yrung sáu-chheung dáa-séi-jó yhat go yráu chheung ge wraai yràn. 4 (*a*) chrìn-brin. (*b*) bhak-brin. (*c*) nhi-drou. (*d*) yrau-sáu-brin. (*e*) chheut-brin. 5 (*a*) Chéng-mran, yráu mr̀ou bhaa-sí heui ghèi-chrèung qaa? (*b*) Yràu Thìn-shing Mráa-tràu heui ghèi-chrèung yiu géi-dho chín qaa? (*c*) Yiu chró géi-nroi (bhaa-sí) qaa? (*d*) Bhaa-sí yráu mróu chi-só qaa? (*e*) Yri-ngr̀-yhat-hrou bhàan-ghèi géi-dho-dím-jhung héi-fhèi qaa? (*f*) Yri-ngr̀-yhat-hrou bhàan-ghèi gèi-sí dou Lreùn-dheun qaa?

Unit 26

Exercises 1 (*a*) gíng-chaat → gíng-chaat-gruk. (*b*) sái-yhì-ghèi → chrùe-fóng. (*c*) yreuk-séui → chán-só or yhì-yúen. (*d*) gong-kràm → haak-theng. (*e*) bei-shùe → sé-jri-lràu. (*f*) jhì-piu → ngràn-hròng. (*g*) lrèun-pún → dóu-chrèung. (*h*) yràu-gáan → yràu-guk. 2 (*a*) Mr̀-ghòi nréi mr̀-hóu yhuk qaa. (*b*) Nréi góng-dhak dhou mr̀-hrai-géi-nghaam bo. (*c*) Nréi yráu-dhi mr̀-hrai-

géi-mrìng-braak qraa. (*d*) Ngró dhou mr̀ hó-yrí (or mr̀-wrúi)
trùng-yi. (*e*) Deui-mr̀-jrue, Ghim-krìu Draai-hrok dhou mr̀
hrai sai-gaai sreung jeui yráu-méng ge. 3   Taai-táai, gó chràng
láu yrau draai yrau leng. Júe-yràn-fóng hóu draai, yráu tou-
fóng chi-só trùng chhùng-lrèung-fóng; jrung yráu drai-yri ghàan
fan-fóng trùng-mràai drai-yri go chhùng-lrèung-fóng thìm.
Haak-theng trùng chrùe-fóng dhou-géi draai. Yráu lréung gaa
lhip, jrung yráu chhe-wái bhàau-kwut hái qhuk-gaa lréui-
brin. Drei-jí hóu hóu, jhik-hrai Gwóng-jhàu Drou yraa-chhat-
hrou baat láu. Gaa-chrìn hóu prèng: bhat-gwo yiu ngŕ-baak-
ngŕ-srap-mraan mhan Góng-jí jhe. Ngró hóu séung mráai!
4   (*a*) Ghìng-lréi ge ghùng-jok jrau hrai yiu gwún-lréi-hóu
kréui ge ghung-shi. (*b*) Hhòi-chí hhòi-chhe jhì-chrìn nréi yiu
jue-yi mhat-yré qaa? (*c*) Shàn-shìn ge hói-shin hóu hóu-srik.
(*d*) Hhèung-góng yráu hóu dhò yhat-lràu ge jáu-lràu. 5   (*a*)
yràu-séui. (*b*) drin-yíng. (*c*) dáa-bho. (*d*) Góng-jí. (*e*) chhìm-
jing. 6   (*a*) laa. (*b*) qràa . . . qaa. (*c*) mhe/qràa . . . lhaa. (*d*)
bo . . . nhe. 7   (*a*) hái hói-shin jáu-ghaa. (*b*) hái mráa-chrèung.
(*c*) hái bhaa-sí-jraam. (*d*) hái ngró qhuk-kéi. (*e*) hái sé-jri-
lràu. 8   (*a*) jhèung. (*b*) fhuk. (*c*) gaa. (*d*) tou. (*e*) tou. (*f*)
drou. 9   (*a*) It doesn't make sense: how can he be rich if he hasn't
got even $1? (*b*) How can you be older than your mother? (*c*) **Mr̀**
does not go with **-gwo**: it should be **mrei tái-gwo**. (*d*) It should be
hràang-*dhak* srap-fhàn faai. (*e*) **Yrì-ché** does not go with **shèui-
yrìn:** change **yrì-ché** to **draan-hrai.**

Passage 1.   *A very long time ago in China there was a man who
loved painting. His pictures were superb, especially when he was
painting dragons, they looked just as though they could move. Once a
high official, having got to know that he was good at painting dragons,
said to him with great delight: 'I myself love dragons too. If you were
willing to paint a dragon for me I would pay you very well.'*

*A few days later sure enough the dragon was done and very well
painted at that. It attracted a lot of people who came to look at it. But
alas the dragon had no eyes. The official was mystified and asked why
he had not painted the eyes. The painter replied that if he did so the
dragon would fly away.*

*Of course no one could believe what he said. The official was very
angry and insisted on him putting the eyes in. Strange as it may seem,
as soon as he had painted them the dragon gave a few shakes and
really did jump out from the paper and fly away.*

Passage 2. *Forty or fifty years ago Shanghai was considered a very advanced city, but many other cities and rural areas of China were still very backward.*

One day a certain Mr Lee came up from the country with matters about which he needed to see his friend Wong Tai Kwok in Shanghai. Mr Wong lived in a large and beautiful hotel with all possible facilities.

When Mr Lee got to the hotel and was waiting in the lobby for Mr Wong, he saw an elderly lady slowly walk into a tiny room. He had never seen a lift, so he didn't know that that was what it was. A couple of minutes later the doors of the little room opened and out walked a beautiful young lady.

Mr Lee at first thought it very strange, but afterwards he said gleefully: 'The city folks really are advanced: next time I'll be sure to bring my wife with me.'

CANTONESE–ENGLISH
—— GLOSSARY ——

The number in brackets shows the unit in which the entry is introduced.

baak *hundred* (11)
baak-fo-ghung-shi *department store* (8)
baak-fran-jhì-srap *ten per cent* (19)
baat *eight* (2)
baat-hrou *number 8* (3)
béi *to give, to give to, to* (4)
béi-gaau *comparatively, to compare* (19)
béi-ghìn-nréi *bikini* (8)
bei-mrat *secret* (24)
bei-shùe *secretary* (22)
bhaa-sí *bus* (3)
bhaa-sí-jraam *bus stop* (6)
bhàan classifier: *group of, gang of* (17)
bhaan-ghèi *scheduled flight* (15)
bhàau *to wrap up* (20)
bhàau-gwó *parcel* (20)
bhàau-kwut *to include* (25)
bhak *north* (6)
bhak-brin *the north side* (12)
Bhak-ghìng *Beijing (Peking)* (23)
Bhak-ghìng-choi *Peking food* (23)
bhat *pen, writing tool* (2)
bhat-gwo *but, however* (17)
bhat-gwo *only* (20)
bhat-yrùe *it would be better if* (19)
bhe-jáu *beer* (8)
bhin-drou? *where?* (3)

bhin-go? *who? which person? which one?* (2)
bhin-sue? *where?* (3)
bhin? *which?* (2)
bho *ball* (9)
bho-si *the boss* (25)
bhòng *on behalf of, for the benefit of* (10)
bhòng-báan *inspector* (17)
bhòng-chan *to patronise, give custom to* (23)
bhòng . . . sáu *to help . . . , give . . . a hand* (4)
bhui *a cup, glass, mug* (25)
bin *to change* (19)
bín-jrik *to devalue* (19)
bíu-gaak *a form* (20)
bíu-yrin *performance, to perform* (22)
bo! final particle: *'let me tell you!'* (5)
bóu *to compensate* (22)
bou-dou *check in, register, report for duty* (15)
bou-drou *report, to report* (18)
bóu-fhaan-sou *to make up for* (10)
bóu-hím *insurance* (15)
bou-jí *newspaper* (18)
bóu-jing *to guarantee* (20)
bou-líu *material, fabric* (11)
bóu-qhòn *security, keep secure* (25)
bràa-bhaa *father* (3)
braak-fraan *boiled/steamed rice* (25)
braak-jí *blank paper* (20)
braak-shik *white* (12)
braan-faat *method, way, means* (18)
brai! *oh dear! oh heck! alas!* (17)
brat-lhaan-déi *brandy* (25)
brei *by; to endure, to suffer* (12)
brei-bhik *to be forced to, compelled to* (11)
breng *illness* (10)
breng-yràn *a patient* (10)
brin-fraan *pot luck; a meal of whatever comes to hand* (4)
brin-fruk *plain clothes* (17)
brin-yhì *plain clothes, civilian clothes* (17)
brit-yràn *other people* (24)
brong *pound* (weight) (12)
brou *area, part, portion* (6)
brou classifier: for *books* (12)

brou-mrùn *department* (19)
bún classifier: for *books* (12)
bun *half* (4)
bún-chrìn *capital* (13)
bún-drei *local, indigenous* (18)
chaak *to demolish, tear down* (23)
cháau-fraan *fried rice* (25)
chán-só *clinic* (10)
cháng-shik *orange-coloured* (12)
che *steep* (16)
che-lóu *steep road* (16)
chek *foot* (length) (25)
chek *red, naked* (19)
chek-geuk-yhi-shang *barefoot doctor* (19)
chek-jri *in the red, deficit* (19)
chéng *please* (3)
chéng *to invite* (4)
chéng-mran *please, may I ask . . . ?* (6)
chéui-shìu *to cancel* (10)
chhàa-m̀r-dho *almost* (12)
chhaak-yrim *to test; evaluation* (12)
chhàam-ghàa *to take part in* (11)
chhàam-gwhùn *to visit* (6)
chhaan classifier: *a meal* (4)
chhaan-páai *menu* (23)
chhaan-theng *restaurant* (non-Chinese) (23)
chhàn-ngráan *with one's own eyes* (18)
chhat *seven* (2)
chhàu-jéung *lucky draw* (13)
chhe *car, cars* (1)
chhe-fròng *garage* (3)
chhe-wái *parking space* (25)
chheung-lím-bou *curtains* (25)
chheut classifier: for *films* and *stage plays* (9)
chheut *out* (17)
chheut-brin *outside, out, the outside* (12)
chheut-ghaai *to go out into the street* (18)
chheut-nín *next year* (8)
chhì-sin *crazy; mixed-up; off the rails* (16)
chhim-jing *visa* (15)
chhìn *thousand* (11)
chhìn-krèi *whatever you do don't; don't ever* (16)

chhìng-git *cleanliness, to clean* (25)
chhìu-gwo *to exceed* (19)
chhò-khap *elementary, first-grade* (24)
chhùng *to rush, dash against, 'jump'* (12)
chhùng-lrèung *to have a shower* (25)
chhùng-lrèung-fóng *bathroom* (25)
chi *time, occasion* (6)
chi-fo *seconds* (5)
chi-ghik *exciting* (9)
chi-só *toilet, lavatory* (10)
chín *money* (5)
chín *shallow, light (coloured)* (25)
chín-lràam-shik *light blue* (25)
chit-brei *facilities, appointments, equipment* (15)
chit-gai *design, to design* (11)
cho *error, wrong, incorrect* (19)
choi *food, cuisine; vegetables* (23)
choi-chhe *motor racing* (16)
choi-chhe-sáu *racing driver* (16)
choi-mráa *to race horses, horse-racing* (13)
chràa *tea* (4)
chràa *to investigate, check* (19)
chràa-wún *tea bowl* (25)
chrài-chrùen *complete, all-embracing* (23)
Chràn *a surname: Chan* (1)
chràng classifier: for *a flat, apartment: storey, deck* (3)
chràu-fún *to raise money, fund-raising* (13)
chrèui-bín *as you please, feel free* (4)
chrèun-lrò-chhe *patrol car* (17)
chrèung classifier: for *performances, bouts, games* (13)
chrèung *long* (22)
chrèung-gok *corner (of house, room, etc.)* (8)
chrèung-sai *detailed, minute, fine* (22)
chrì-dhi *later on* (2)
chrì-srin *charity* (13)
chrìn-brin *in front; the front side* (12)
chrìn-géi-nrìn *a few years ago* (18)
chrìn-mráan *the evening of the day before yesterday* (11)
chrìn-nín *the year before last* (10)
chrìn-yrat *the day before yesterday* (9)
chrìng-fong *situation, circumstances* (16)
chró *to sit* (3)

chró *to travel by* (6)
chró-ghaam *to be in prison* (18)
chró-hhòi-dhi *sit further away* (17)
chró-lhip *to ride in a lift* (25)
chró-mràai-dhi *sit closer* (17)
chròng *bed* (15)
chròu *noisy* (25)
chróu-yràu-piu *collect stamps* (24)
chrúe-chhuk *savings, to save* (19)
chrùe-fóng *kitchen* (4)
chrùen-brou *all, the whole lot* (23)
chrùen-jhan *fax, to fax* (22)
chrùen-jhan-ghèi *fax machine* (22)
chrúng *heavy* (12)
chrúng-lreung *weight* (15)
chúe-lréi *to handle, manage, deal with* (22)
dáa *to hit* (9)
dáa-bho *to play a ball game* (9)
dáa-drin-wáa *to make a phone call* (10)
dáa-fhùng *a typhoon, to have a typhoon* (8)
dáa-fó *to strike fire* (24)
dáa-fó-ghèi *cigarette lighter* (24)
dáa-ghaau *brawling, to fight* (18)
dáa-gip *robbery, to rob* (18)
dáa-hrò-bhaau *purse snatching, to pick pockets* (18)
dáa-jri *to type* (22)
dáa-jri-ghèi *typewriter* (24)
dáa-lréng-thàai *to tie a neck-tie* (10)
dáa-mràa-jeuk *to play mah-jong* (13)
dáa-sou *to sweep* (25)
dáa-suen *to intend; intention* (8)
daai *to lead, to bring, to go with* (2)
daai *to wear, put on (accessories)* (11)
daap *travel by/catch/take (public transport)* (3)
daap-dhak-dóu *able to catch* (18)
daap-mr̀-dóu *unable to catch* (18)
dái *to be worth it, a bargain, a good buy* (15)
dáng *let, allow* (5)
dáng *to wait, wait for* (4)
dáng-dáng *etc., and so on* (15)
dáng ngró beí *let me pay* (5)
déng classifier: for *hats* (11)

deui *cash a cheque, exchange money* (19)
deui classifier: *a pair of* (16)
deui *with regard to, towards* (9)
deui-mr̀-jrue *I'm sorry, excuse me, pardon me* (1)
deui-mrin *opposite, the opposite side* (12)
deui-wrun-léut *exchange rate* (19)
dhaan-chhe *bicycle* (16)
dhaan-yràn-chròng *single bed* (15)
dhak *OK, 'can do', acceptable* (5)
Dhak-gwok *Germany* (19)
dhak-hràan *to be free, at leisure* (13)
dhang *a light* (12)
dhàng *to stare, open the eyes* (17)
dhàng-draai-deui-ngráan *take a good look* (17)
dhi classifier: for plurals and uncountable things (4)
dhik-sí *taxi* (3)
dhik-sri-ghou *discotheque* (24)
dhò *many, much* (3)
dhò-dhi *a little more* (15)
dhò-jre (nréi) *thank you* (5)
dhò-jre-saai *thank you very much* (15)
dhò-yrùe *surplus* (9)
dhòng-yín *of course* (13)
dhou *all, both* (4)
dhou *also* (1)
dhou-géi *quite, rather, fairly* (3)
dhùng *east* (6)
dhùng-bhak *north-east* (6)
dhùng-brin *the east side* (12)
dhùng-nràam *south-east* (6)
dím *a point, spot, dot* (23)
dím qaa? = **dím-yéung qaa?** *how is it? how's things?* (10)
dím-gáai? *why?* (4)
dím-sham *'dim sum'* (23)
dím-yéung . . . -faat? *in what way?* (8)
dím-yéung? *how? in what way?* (5)
dong *to regard as* (4)
dong-háu *street stall* (5)
dou *to arrive, arrive at, reach* (6)
dóu *to gamble on, to bet on* (13)
dóu-bho *to bet on football* (13)
dóu-chín *to gamble with money* (13)

dóu-chrèung *casino* (13)
dóu-fhaan-thaan *to gamble at fantan* (13)
dóu-gáu *to bet on dogs* (13)
dóu-gwú-piu *to gamble on shares* (13)
dóu-mráa *to bet on horses* (13)
dóu-ngroi-wrui *to gamble on foreign exchange* (13)
dóu-phe-páai *to gamble at cards* (13)
dou-yrì-ghaa-wrài-jí *up to now* (18)
draai *big* (3)
draai-dong *gambling den* (13)
draai-fhong *tasteful, sophisticated* (11)
draai-gáam-gaa *a sale* (5)
draai-hrok *university* (6)
draai-kwhài-mròu *large-scale* (19)
draai-mrùn-háu *main doorway* (20)
draai-shèng *loud, in a loud voice* (11)
draai-tròng *lobby, great hall* (26)
Draai-wrui-tròng *City Hall* (6)
draai-yeuk *approximately* (20)
Draai-yràn *Your Honour, Your Excellency* (18)
draan-hrai *but* (6)
draan-sing *flexible* (22)
drai- (makes ordinal numbers) (6)
drai-mhei *the last* (22)
drai-yhat *the first* (6)
drai-yri *the second; the next* (6)
drak-brit *special, especially* (23)
drak-faai-yràu-drai *express mail* (20)
drei-fhòng *place* (6)
drei-háa *ground floor; the ground; the floor* (3)
drei-hraa-tit-lrou *underground railway* (6)
drei-jhin *carpet* (25)
drei-jí *address* (20)
Drei-lréi *Geography* (12)
drei-mín *the floor* (25)
drei-tit *underground railway* (6)
drei-tit-jraam *underground station* (6)
drin *electricity* (16)
drin-chhè *tram* (9)
drin-dhaan-chhe *motor bike* (16)
drin-jí *electronic* (25)
drin-nróu *computer* (22)

drin-nrúen-lròu *electric heater* (8)
drin-sri *television* (24)
drin-sri-ghèi *television set* (15)
drin-tròi *radio station* (13)
drin-wáa *telephone* (9)
drin-yíng *cinema film, movie* (9)
drin-yràu *petrol, gasoline* (16)
dring-hrai *or, or rather* (13)
drit-jreui *order* (12)
driu-tràu *to turn to face the other way* (16)
drou classifier: for *doors* (25)
drou *road, street* (3)
druk *to read* (12)
druk-lraap *independent, independently* (22)
druk-shùe *to study* (12)
dúen *short* (22)
faai *quick, quickly, fast* (15)
faai-dhi *get a move on!* (17)
faai-jí *chopsticks* (16)
fáan-ying *reaction, response; to respond, react* (16)
fáan-yrì *on the contrary, despite this* (19)
faat-gwhùn *a judge* (18)
Faat-gwok *France* (19)
faat-mrung *to dream* (25)
faat-shàng *to occur, happen, transpire* (18)
fai-yrung *cost, fee* (15)
fan(-gaau) *to sleep; to lie down; to go to bed* (16)
fan-lrin *training, to train* (24)
fan-lrin-bhaan *training class* (24)
fan-mr̀-jeuk(-gaau) *unable to get to sleep* (25)
fhaa-yéung *pattern* (11)
Fhàa-yrùen Drou *Garden Road* (3)
fhàa-yúen *garden* (3)
fhàan *to return, to return to* (3)
fhàan-ghùng *to go to work* (22)
fhaan-thaan *fantan* (13)
fhàn-mrìn *to give birth* (22)
fhei *a ticket; a fare* (15)
fhèi *to fly* (24)
fhèi-faat *illegal* (13)
fhèi-ghèi *aircraft* (6)
fhèi-ghèi-chrèung *airport* (6)

fhèi-ghèi-piu *air ticket* (15)
fhèi-lám *film* (25)
fho *a subject, a discipline* (12)
fho-grei *science and technology* (24)
Fho-hrok *Science* (12)
fhòng-brin *convenient* (17)
fhòng-mrin *aspect* (12)
fhui-shik *grey* (12)
fhuk classifier: for *paintings, drawings*, etc. (24)
fhuk-lrei *benefits, welfare* (22)
fhùn-yrìng *welcome, to welcome* (22)
fhùng classifier: for *letters* (20)
fhùng *wind* (8)
fhùng-fu *rich, abundant* (13)
fo-bún *textbook* (12)
fó-chhe *train* (6)
fó-gei *waiter* (4)
fong-gaa *to be on holiday, take days off* (9)
fong-ghùng *to finish work* (22)
fraan *rice, food* (4)
fraan *to offend, commit a crime* (18)
fráan-druk *to peddle drugs* (17)
fraan-theng *dining room* (25)
fràan-wrìng *prosperous* (13)
fraan-wún *rice bowl* (25)
fran-jí *element, member* (12)
frat-chín *to fine, be fined* (18)
fròng-ghaan *a room* (15)
fru-gran *nearby* (4)
fru-jaak *to be responsible* (22)
fruk-mrou *service, to give service* (15)
fún-shik *style* (5)
gaa classifier: for *vehicles, aircraft, machinery* (12)
gáa *false* (17)
gaa-chrìn *price* (11)
gaa-chrìn-páai *price tag* (11)
gaa-fhe *coffee* (3)
gaa-fhe-shik *brown* (12)
gaa-krèi *holiday* (22)
gaa-sái *driving, to drive* (16)
gaa? = ge + qaa? (2)
gaai-sriu *to recommend, introduce* (4)

gáam-síu *to reduce, cut down* (9)
gáan-dhàan *simple* (20)
gaan-jhung *occasionally, periodically* (10)
gaan-jip *indirectly* (22)
gaau-shùe *to teach* (12)
gaau-yruk *education; to educate* (12)
gám *in that case, so* (3)
gam *so* (4)
gám *to dare, to dare to* (18)
gam-nroi *so long a time* (18)
gam-sreung-háa *approximately, thereabouts* (9)
gám-yéung *in that case, so* (3)
gán-yiu *important* (21)
gau *enough* (16)
gáu *dog* (13)
gáu *nine* (2)
gau-jai-gham *relief money* (18)
gau-jhung *time's up, it's time to* (13)
ge final particle: *that's how it is and will stay!* (3)
ge links adjectives to nouns (4)
ge shows possession: *-'s* (2)
ge-laa final particle: gives strong emphasis (5)
géi *quite, rather, fairly* (3)
géi *several* (9)
gei *to post* (20)
géi? *how many?* (9)
gei-dhak *to remember* (9)
géi-dho? *how many? how much?* (5)
géi-gam . . . laak! *how very . . . !* (18)
géi-nrim *memorial, to commemorate* (20)
géi-nroi? *how long?* (20)
géi-sí? or **géi-srì?** *when?* (8)
géui-braan *to run, hold, conduct* (15)
geuk *foot, leg* (16)
geuk-jai *footbrake* (16)
ghàa-gaa *to increase price* (23)
ghàa-yrap *to join, recruit into* (17)
ghaai *street* (3)
ghaai-háu *road junction* (6)
ghàan classifier: for *houses* and *rooms* (3)
ghàau *to hand over* (15)
ghàau-thùng *traffic, communications* (12)

ghàau-thùng-dhang *traffic-light* (12)
ghàm-jhìu *this morning* (4)
ghàm-jhìu-jóu *this morning* (4)
ghàm-mráan *tonight, this evening* (11)
ghàm-nín *this year* (8)
gham-shik *gold-coloured* (12)
ghàm-yrat *today* (4)
ghàn *a catty* (= 20 ounces) (5)
ghèi-chrèung *airport* (6)
ghèi-frù *almost but not quite* (18)
ghèi-hei *machine* (24)
ghèi-piu *air ticket* (15)
ghèi-wrui *chance, opportunity* (22)
ghèi-yruk *muscle* (9)
ghìn-chrì *to insist, insist on* (25)
ghìng-gwo *to pass by* (11)
ghìng-jai *economy, economic* (19)
ghìng-lréi *manager* (15)
gho-krek *opera* (24)
ghòu *high, tall* (10)
ghùng-bou *to announce* (19)
ghùng-fo *homework* (12)
ghùng-grung *public* (12)
ghùng-gwhàan *public relations* (15)
ghùng-héi *congratulations, to congratulate* (23)
ghùng-jok *work, job; to work* (22)
ghùng-jrou *to work* (22)
ghung-lréi *kilometre* (23)
ghung-shi *a company* (8)
ghùng-yràn *worker, servant* (25)
gím-chràa *check, inspect* (25)
gím-hung *to accuse* (12)
Gim-krìu *Cambridge* (6)
gin *to see, to meet* (8)
gíng-chaat *policeman* (12)
gíng-yrùen-jing *warrant card* (17)
git-gwó *the end result* (16)
giu *to tell someone to, to order someone to* (17)
go classifier: for people and many objects (2)
gó *that, those* (2)
go-baat *one dollar eighty cents* (20)
gó-drou *there* (5)

gó-jran-srì *at that time* (10)
gó-sue *there* (5)
gói *to alter, to change* (usually for the better) (8)
gói-bin *to change, alter* (24)
gok-dhak *to feel* (9)
gón-jrue *hurrying to* (15)
góng *to speak, talk, say* (9)
Góng-jí *Hong Kong Dollars* (19)
gong-kràm *piano* (24)
góng-siu *to joke* (16)
grau *old, used* (8)
grau-nín *last year* (8)
grin classifier: for most items of *clothing* (5)
grin-hhòng *health* (9)
gruk *a bureau, department, office* (16)
gwaa-hrou *to register* (10)
gwái *a ghost* (21)
gwai *expensive; distinguished* (1)
gwai-gwok *your country* (23)
gwái-lóu *ghost fellow (Westerner)* (10)
gwai-sing-qaa? *what is your name?* (1)
gwhàai *well-behaved, obedient, a 'good boy'* (13)
gwhàan-hrai *relationship, connection, relevance* (13)
gwhàn-deui *army* (17)
gwhàn-fruk *military uniform* (17)
gwhàn-yràn *soldier, military personnel* (17)
gwhòng-mráang *bright* (25)
gwhù-druk *solitary, lone* (24)
gwhùn *an official, an officer* (16)
gwo *than* (12)
gwo *to go past, go across, go by* (6)
gwo-bóng *to weigh* (15)
gwo-chrúng *overweight* (15)
gwo-srì *overtime* (22)
gwok-ghàa *country, state* (19)
gwóng-bo *broadcast* (13)
Gwóng-dhùng *Guangdong (province)* (23)
Gwóng-dhùng-choi *Cantonese food* (23)
Gwóng-jhàu *Guangzhou (Canton)* (13)
Gwóng-jhàu-wáa *Cantonese language* (23)
gwrai-tói *counter* (15)
gwrui *tired, weary* (24)

gwú *to guess, reckon* (2)
gwú-dhak-dóu *able to guess* (18)
gwu-haak *customer, client* (23)
gwú-mr̀-dóu *unable to guess* (18)
gwú-piu *stocks and shares* (13)
gwún *to control, be in charge of* (12)
gwún-lréi *management, to manage* (25)
haak-hei *polite* (4)
haak-theng *living room, lounge* (25)
háau *to examine, to test* (16)
háau-srí *examination, test; to sit an exam* (16)
hái *at/in/on, to be at/in/on* (2)
hái-drou *at the indicated place* (11)
hái-sue *at the indicated place* (11)
háng *to be willing to* (22)
háu-brou *the mouth* (9)
hei-chhè *vehicle, car* (12)
Héi-dím *'Start'* (22)
héi-fhèi *to take off* (aircraft) (15)
héi-shàn *to get up in the morning* (10)
héi-yráu-chí-lréi *that's ridiculous! how could that be?* (16)
heui *to go to, to go* (2)
heung *towards* (6)
héung-srau *to enjoy; enjoyment, entertainment, treat* (15)
hhaa *prawn, shrimp* (5)
hhàa! *ha! ha!* (23)
hhaak-shik *black* (12)
hhàan *to save; be parsimonious, stingy* (8)
hhak-shik *black* (12)
hhèi-mrong *hope, to hope* (10)
hhèng *light (in weight)* (15)
hhèung *fragrant* (23)
hhèung-háa *countryside* (6)
hhìng-drai *brothers* (3)
hhòi *to open* (19)
hhòi *to run/start a business* (23)
hhòi-chhe *to start a car; drive a car* (16)
hhòi-chí *to begin, start* (23)
hhòi-ghùng *to start work, start a job* (22)
hhòi-sham *happy* (8)
hhùng *empty* (11)
hhùng-yràu *airmail* (20)

hing-cheui *interest* (13)
hó-nràng *it is possible that, possibly; possibility* (16)
hó-shik *It is a pity that, unfortunately* (11)
hó-yrí *can, may* (6)
hói *the sea* (25)
hói-shin *seafood* (23)
hói-thaan *beach* (8)
hóu *very; well, fine, OK, nice, good* (1)
hóu-chói *lucky, fortunately* (12)
hóu-chrí . . . mr̀-chrí . . . *to be more like . . . than like . . .* (6)
hóu-chrí . . . yhat yreung *just like* (4)
hóu-dhò *a lot more* (16)
hóu-gám *favourable impression* (23)
hóu-mrei *delicious* (4)
hóu-nroi-mróu-gin *long time no see* (3)
hóu-srik *delicious (to eat)* (4)
hóu-tái *good-looking, attractive* (13)
hóu-thèng *harmonious, melodic* (13)
hóu-wáan *good fun, amusing, enjoyable* (13)
hóu-yám *delicious (to drink)* (13)
hraa (yhat) chi *next time* (15)
hraa-brin *the underneath, under, beneath, the underside* (12)
hraa-go-lrái-baai *next week* (10)
hraa-go-yruet *next month* (17)
hraa-jau *afternoon, p.m.* (15)
hraa-pràa *chin* (9)
hràang *to walk* (15)
hràang-ghaai *to go out into the streets* (15)
hràang-hhòi-jó *not here* (17)
hràang-lrou *to walk* (9)
hràang-shàan *to walk in the country* (15)
hrai *to be* (1)
hram-braa(ng)-lraang *all told, altogether, all* (20)
hràng *to journey, to go towards* (6)
hràng-lréi *luggage* (15)
hrap-kwhài-gaak *to qualify, meet requirements* (17)
hrau-brin *the back, behind, rear* (12)
hrau-lròi *later, afterwards* (25)
hrau-mráan *the evening of the day after tomorrow* (11)
hrau-nín *the year after next* (10)
hrau-shaang *young* (12)
hrau-shaang-jái *youngsters* (12)

hrau-yrat *the day after tomorrow* (10)
Hrò a surname: *Ho* (1)
hrok-hraau *school* (12)
hrok-shaang *student, pupil* (12)
hròng-nroi-yràn *insider, expert* (15)
hrou *day of the month* (20)
hrùng-dhang *red light* (12)
hrùng-shik *red* (5)
huen *to advise, urge, plead with* (24)
huet *blood* (16)
jaak *narrow* (16)
jáan classifier: for *lamps* and *lights* (12)
jaan *to praise* (11)
jáau(-fhàan)-chín *to give change* (20)
jái *a son* (10)
jai-drou *system* (22)
jai-fruk *uniform* (17)
jái-néui *sons and daughters, children* (22)
jáu *alcoholic drink* (8)
jáu *to run, run away, leave* (3)
jáu-dim *hotel* (15)
jáu-ghaa *Chinese restaurant* (23)
jáu-lóng *passage, corridor* (8)
jáu-lràu *Chinese restaurant* (4)
jáu-nraan *to flee disaster, to be a refugee* (6)
jáu-wúi *reception, cocktail party* (11)
jek classifier: *'one of a pair'* (16)
jek classifier: for *animals* (5)
jeui *most* (6)
jeui-gran *recent, recently* (19)
jeui-síu *at least* (18)
jeuk *bird* (24)
jeuk *to wear (clothes)* (11)
jéun *to allow, permit* (17)
jeun-brou *progress* (24)
jéung-bán *prize* (13)
jhàa-chhe *to drive (a vehicle)* (6)
jhài *to put, to place* (8)
jhàm *to pour into a cup* (25)
jhàn(-hrai) *truly, really; true, real* (4)
jhàng *to hate, detest* (24)
jhàng-ghàa *increase, to increase* (13)

jhat-déi *quality* (5)
jhe final particle: *only, and that's all* (3)
jhek final particle: *only, and that's all* (3)
jhèun *bottle, bottle of* (10)
jhéun-tip *allowance, grant* (22)
Jhèung a surname: *Cheung* (1)
jhèung classifier: for sheet-like objects (11)
jhèung-lròi *future, in future* (24)
jhì classifier: for stick-like objects (2)
jhì *to know* (8)
jhì-chrìn *before* (10)
jhì-dou *to know* (8)
jhì-fhong *(body-)fat* (9)
jhì-hrau *after* (6)
jhi-mráa final particle: *'only'* (12)
jhì-nroi *within* (6)
jhì-piu *cheque* (19)
jhì-yhat *one of the . . .* (6)
jhik-hrai *that is, that is to say* (5)
jhik-yrùen *staff, employee, clerk* (22)
jhìu-jóu *morning, in the morning* (4)
jhoi-nraan *disaster* (19)
jhue *pig* (10)
jhue-jái *piglet* (10)
jhùe-yruk *pork* (10)
jhuen-ghaa *expert, specialist* (24)
jhuk-kéi *play chess* (24)
jhuk-kràu *soccer* (13)
jhung *clock* (15)
Jhùng-dím *'Finish'* (22)
jhùng-ghaan *in the middle of, in between* (12)
Jhùng-gwok *China* (2)
Jhùng-gwok-choi *Chinese food* (23)
Jhùng-gwok-wáa *Chinese language* (18)
Jhùng-gwok-yràn *a Chinese* (10)
jhùng-hrok *secondary school* (12)
Jhùng-mràn *Chinese language* (12)
jhung-tràu *an hour* (4)
Jhùng-yhì *Chinese medicine* (10)
jhùng-yi *to like, be fond of* (6)
ji *only then* (10)
jí *paper* (20)

jí(-hrai) *only* (4)
jí-mrui *sisters* (3)
jí-shik *purple* (12)
jí-yiu *so long as, provided that* (9)
jin-jhàng *war* (19)
jín-lráam *show, exhibition* (11)
jing *certificate, pass* (17)
jíng *to make, prepare* (4)
jing-fú *government* (12)
jing-hrai *just happens to be* (11)
jit-mruk *programme* (15)
jó(-sáu)-brin *on the left, the left(-hand) side* (12)
jó-yriu-yrau-báai *shaking from side to side* (10)
joi *in addition; again* (4)
joi-chi *another time, a second time* (18)
joi-gin *goodbye* (1)
jok-qáu *to retch, be about to vomit* (10)
jóu *early* (4)
jóu-chhaan *breakfast* (22)
jóu-sràn *good morning* (1)
jraam-srì *temporary, temporarily* (20)
jraap-gwaan *be accustomed to, used to; habit* (24)
jraap-háu *gate, gateway* (15)
jraap-jhùng *concentrated, centralised* (23)
jrau *then* (4)
jrau-faai *soon* (23)
jrau-jhàn *that's for sure!* (25)
jreui *a crime* (18)
jreui-mrìng *charge, accusation* (18)
jreui-qon *criminal case* (13)
jreun-lreung *so far as possible* (19)
jri *characters; five-minute periods* (15)
jri-géi *self* (24)
jri-qhòn *law and order, public order* (18)
jri-yruen *voluntarily, willing* (18)
jrik-jip *direct, directly* (22)
jrim-jím *gradually* (8)
jring *quiet* (25)
jro classifier: for massive things (25)
jrok-jhìu *yesterday morning* (4)
jrok-jhìu-jóu *yesterday morning* (4)
jrok-mráan *yesterday evening, last night* (11)

jrok-yrat *yesterday* (4)
jrong *run into, knock into* (16)
jrou *to do* (3)
jrou mhat-yré? *why? for what reason?* (3)
jrou shàang-yi *to do business, to run a business* (4)
jrou-ghùng *to work* (22)
jrue *to dwell, to live* (3)
jrung *even more* (8)
jrung *in addition, furthermore* (8)
jrung *still, yet* (3)
jrung-mrei *still not yet* (16)
júe *to cook* (4)
júe-choi *main course* (4)
júe-srik-lròu *cooking stove* (25)
júe-yi *idea* (6)
jue-yi *pay attention to* (15)
júe-yràn-fóng *master bedroom* (25)
júen *to turn, to change to* (6)
jung-fhaa *to cultivate flowers* (24)
jung-lréui *type, kind, variety, species* (23)
khaa-lhaai-qhou-khei *karaoke* (24)
khap-druk *to take drugs* (18)
khap-yràn *to attract* (13)
khàu-thùng *to communicate* (24)
khìng-gái *to chat* (11)
krán *near, close to* (20)
kréi *to stand* (17)
krèi-gwaai *strange, weird, odd* (24)
krèi-thàa *other* (5)
kréui *she, her, he, him, it* (1)
kréui-drei *they, them* (1)
krèung-ghàan *rape, to rape* (18)
krùen *right, authority, powers* (17)
kuet-dring *to decide* (25)
kuet-frat *to lack, be short of* (24)
kwaang *to cruise* (25)
kwaang-ghung-shi *to go window shopping* (25)
kwhài-dring *to regulate, lay down a rule* (17)
laa final particle: 'that's how the case stands now' (3)
laak final particle: 'that's how the case stands now' (3)
láu *a flat, a high building, a storey* (3)
leng *pretty, good-looking, handsome, of good quality* (1)

lhaa final particle: *urging co-operation or agreement* (3)
lhàai *to pull; to arrest* (17)
lhip *lift, elevator* (25)
lo final particle: *agreement with previous speaker* (15)
ló *to collect, to take* (15)
ló-tái *naked, nude* (17)
lràam-shik *blue* (12)
lraan *broken, damaged* (5)
lráang *cold* (8)
lráang-hei-ghèi *air conditioner* (8)
lráang-thìn *cold weather, winter* (8)
lraap-saap *rubbish* (4)
lraap-saap-túng *rubbish bin* (4)
lrài *to come, to come to* (3)
lrái-baai *week* (5)
Lrái-baai-yhat *Monday* (5)
Lrái-baai-yrat *Sunday* (5)
lrài-ge/gaa? final particle: *for identification* (19)
lràu *to flow* (16)
lràu *to stay, remain; leave behind* (24)
lràu-dái *ceiling* (25)
lràu-fhàan *to leave behind* (25)
lràu-thài *staircase* (25)
Lréi a surname: *Li* (1)
lrèi *distant from* (25)
lrèi-dóu *outlying island* (6)
lrèi-hhòi *to leave, depart from* (9)
lrei-shik *interest* (money) (19)
lréi-yràu *reason* (25)
lréng-thàai *neck-tie* (8)
lréui-brin *inside, in, the inside* (9)
lréui-yràu *to travel; tourism* (15)
Lrèun-dheun *London* (6)
lrèun-dou *the turn of, it has come to the turn of* (16)
lrèun-pún *roulette* (13)
lréung *two* (2)
Lrik-sí *History* (12)
lrin-jraap *to practise* (24)
lrin-jraap-bóu *exercise book* (12)
lrìn-jruk *in succession, consecutively* (19)
lrìn . . . dhou *even* (17)
lring *to cause, to make* (18)

lrìng *zero* (11)
lròi-wróng *coming and going; current (account)* (19)
lrok *to alight from* (6)
lrok-hrau *backward, old-fashioned* (25)
lrok-suet *to snow* (8)
lrok-yrúe *to rain* (8)
lróu *old, aged, elderly* (6)
lrou *road* (15)
lrou-bhin *the roadside* (17)
lrou-mrin *road surface* (16)
lrou-srat *honest, honestly* (13)
lrou-tròi *balcony* (25)
lróu-yràn *the elderly, the aged* (18)
lruk *six* (2)
lruk-dhang *green light* (12)
lruk-shik *green* (12)
lrùng *dragon* (26)
lrùng-hhaa *lobster* (4)
maa? final particle: makes questions (1)
mhaau *cat* (24)
mhan *dollar* (5)
mhat-yré? *what? what kind of?* (2)
mhàu-dhài *to squat down, to crouch down* (10)
mhe? final particle: *'Do you mean to say that ... ?'* (5)
mhi-yré? *what? what kind of?* (2)
móu *hat, cap* (11)
mr̀ *not* (1)
mr̀-cho *not bad, pretty good* (11)
mr̀ dhak *'no can do'* (5)
mr̀-gán-yiu *never mind, it doesn't matter* (2)
mr̀-ghòi (nréi) *thank you* (2)
mr̀-ghòi-saai *thank you very much* (15)
mr̀-gin-jó *lost, go missing* (21)
mr̀-gwaai-dhak *no wonder* (23)
mr̀-hóu *don't* (4)
mr̀-hrai-géi *not very* (3)
mr̀-hrai-hóu *not very* (3)
mr̀-jhì *I wonder* (11)
mr̀-jí *not only* (18)
mr̀-sái *no need to, not necessary to* (4)
mr̀-shùe-fruk *unwell, uncomfortable* (10)
mr̀-síu-dhak *not less than, must be at least* (15)

mráa *horse* (13)
mráa-chrèung *racetrack* (13)
mràa-fràan *trouble, troublesome* (12)
Mráa-hhaak *Deutschmark* (19)
mráa-lrou *road* (6)
mràa-mhaa *mother* (3)
mráai *to buy* (2)
mraai *to sell* (1)
mráai-choi *food shopping* (23)
mràai-dhaan *may I have the bill?* (23)
mráai-mráa *to bet on horses* (14)
mráai-sung *food shopping* (23)
mráan *evening, night* (6)
mraan *slow, slowly* (16)
mraan *ten thousand* (11)
mráan-chhaan *dinner, supper* (23)
mráan-fraan *dinner, supper* (23)
mrái *don't* (4)
mran *to ask a question* (2)
mràn-gín *document* (22)
mran-trài *problem, question* (15)
mràu-saat *murder, to murder* (18)
mrei *not yet* (10)
mréi *tail, end* (17)
mrèi-bho-lròu *microwave oven* (25)
Mréi-gham *American dollars* (19)
Mréi-gwok *America, USA* (1)
Mréi-gwok-yràn *American person* (1)
mrín-fai *free of charge* (5)
mrín-seui *tax-free, duty-free* (15)
mrìng-braak *to understand, be clear about* (12)
mrìng-seun-pín *postcard* (20)
mrit-fó-túng *fire extinguisher* (8)
mròng *busy* (10)
mróu *have not* (3)
mróu-mran-trài *no problem!* (15)
mrúi *each, every* (12)
mrùi-hei *town gas* (25)
mruk-dhik *purpose, aim, goal* (24)
mrùn *door, gate* (20)
mrùn-háu *doorway* (20)
nám *to think, think about, think over* (20)

Náu-yeuk *New York* (18)
néui *daughter* (17)
ngái *low, short in height* (25)
nghaam *correct* (13)
nghaam-nghaam *a moment ago, a moment before* (10)
nghaam-nghaam *exactly, precisely* (11)
ngí *five* (2)
ngí-shing-khap *five star grade, top class* (15)
ngr-wrui *misunderstand, get it wrong* (16)
ngráan *eye* (17)
ngràan-shik *colour* (5)
ngraang *hard, unyielding* (11)
ngrài-hím *dangerous, danger* (24)
ngràn-chín *dollar* (20)
ngràn-hròng *bank* (19)
ngràn-shik *silver* (12)
ngràu *cow, ox, cattle* (4)
ngràu-yruk *beef* (4)
ngró *I, me* (1)
ngró-drei *we, us* (1)
ngró-ge *my* (2)
ngroi-brin *outside, out, the outside* (12)
ngroi-gwok *foreign, foreign country* (18)
ngroi-gwok-wáa *foreign language* (18)
ngroi-gwok-yràn *foreigner* (18)
ngroi-hóng *layman, outsider* (19)
ngroi-tou *jacket* (11)
ngroi-wrui *foreign exchange* (13)
nhàu *angry* (4)
nhe? final particle: for rhetorical questions (5)
nhe? final particle: repeats same question (1)
nhi *this, these* (2)
nhi-drou *here* (5)
nhi-géi-go-lrái-baai *these last few weeks* (24)
nhi-géi-go-yruet *these last few months* (24)
nhi-géi-nrìn *these last few years* (24)
nhi-géi-yrat *these last few days* (24)
nhi-go-lrái-baai *this week* (10)
nhi-go-yruet *this month* (17)
nhi-sue *here* (5)
nhìng *to bring, to take* (16)
nràa! *there! here you are! here it is, look!* (5)

nràam *male* (9)
nràam *south* (6)
nràam-brin *the south side* (12)
nràam-chi(-só) *gentlemen's toilet* (17)
nràam-ghùng-yràn *male servant* (25)
nràam-hrok-shaang *boy pupils/students* (17)
nràam-pràng-yráu *boyfriend* (17)
nràam-yán *man, adult male person* (17)
nràan *difficult, hard* (17)
nréi *you* (1)
nréi-drei *you* (plural) (1)
nréi-tái *in your opinion* (24)
nréi-wraa *in your opinion* (24)
nréui *female* (17)
nréui-chi(-só) *ladies' toilet* (17)
nréui-gíng *policewoman* (17)
nréui-hrok-shaang *girl pupils/students* (17)
nréui-pràng-yráu *girlfriend* (17)
nréui-shìu-fròng-yrùen *firewoman* (17)
nréui-yán *woman, adult female person* (17)
nrìn *year* (8)
nrìn-mréi *end of the year* (22)
nroi *a long time* (3)
nroi-hóng-yràn *insider, expert* (15)
nroi-yrùng *contents* (9)
nrúen *warm* (15)
paa *to fear; to dislike* (8)
paak-wái *to park a car* (16)
páau-mráa *to race horses, horse-racing* (19)
pei-yrùe *for example, for instance* (16)
phe-páai *playing cards* (13)
póu-pin *common (widespread)* (18)
pou-táu *shop* (5)
póu-thùng *common (ordinary)* (18)
Póu-thùng-wáa *Putonghua (Mandarin)* (18)
póu-thùng-yràn *an ordinary chap* (18)
pràa-shàan *to climb mountains, walk the hills* (9)
pràng-yráu *friend* (2)
prèng *cheap* (5)
prìng-gwhàn *average, on average* (12)
prìng-yràu *surface mail* (20)
prùi *to keep company with* (25)

— **308** —

pun *to sentence* (18)
Qaa- prefix for names/relationships (22)
qaa? final particle: finishes a question (1)
qaan-jau *midday, early afternoon; lunch* (22)
qáu *to vomit* (10)
qhaa-maa! final particle: *'you should realise', 'don't you know'* (5)
qhaa? final particle: triumphantly scoring a point (8)
qhàai! *alas!* (24)
Qhàu-jhàu *Europe* (19)
qhòn-chrùen *safe, safety* (25)
qhòu *oh!* (surprise) (1)
qhuk *house* (3)
qhuk-gaa *house price* (25)
qhuk-kéi *family, home* (3)
Qou-mún *Macau* (13)
qràa? final particle: *'that's right, isn't it?'* (3)
qró! *oh, really! oh, now I understand!* (4)
saai-taai-yrèung *to sunbathe* (8)
saan-brou *to stroll, go walking* (24)
saan-séui *to scatter away* (17)
sai *small* (5)
sái *to drive* (16)
sái *to wash* (15)
sai-gaai *the world* (6)
sai-mhan-jái *children* (22)
sái-shàn *'to wash the body', to bathe* (15)
sái-shàn-fóng *bathroom* (15)
sái-wún-ghèi *dishwasher* (25)
sái-yhì-ghèi *washing machine* (25)
sáu-bhiu *wristwatch* (2)
sáu-chheung *handgun, pistol* (17)
sáu-jai *handbrake* (16)
sáu-jhuk *brothers (secret society)* (17)
sáu-jruk-fai *procedure fee, handling charge* (20)
sáu-shàn *to conduct a body search* (17)
sáu-shìn *first of all* (20)
sáu-trài *hand-held, portable* (8)
sáu-trài-drin-wáa *portable phone* (15)
sáu-yrat *first day* (20)
sé *to write* (19)
sé-jri-lràu *office* (2)
sé-mrìng *written clearly* (19)

sei *four* (2)
séi *to die* (5)
Sei-chùen *Sichuan (Szechwan)* (23)
Sei-chùen-choi *Sichuan food* (23)
sei-dím-bun-jhung *half past four o'clock* (15)
séi-jái *'dead-beats', 'bastards', 'rats'* (17)
sei-qraa-yhat *forty-one* (13)
séng *to wake up, recover consciousness* (16)
séui *water* (5)
seui *year of age* (9)
seun *letter* (19)
seun *to believe, to trust* (4)
seun-fhùng *envelope* (20)
seun-jí *letter paper* (20)
séung *to want to, intend to, would like to* (2)
séung-jreung *to imagine* (18)
seung-pín *photograph* (17)
shàa-jín *sergeant* (17)
shàa-léut *salad* (4)
shaa-qraa-yhat *thirty-one* (13)
shàai *to waste* (8)
shaam *clothing* (8)
shàam *three* (2)
shàam-go-gwhat *three-quarters past the hour* (15)
shaam-kwràn *a dress* (5)
shàan *mountain, hill* (9)
Shàan-déng *The Peak; mountain top* (22)
shàang-gwó *fruit* (4)
shàang-yrat *birthday* (23)
shài *west* (6)
shài-bhak *north-west* (6)
shài-brin *the west side* (12)
shài-chhaan *Western food* (23)
shài-nràam *south-west* (6)
Shài-yhì *Western medicine* (10)
Shài-yràn *Westerner* (9)
shàm *deep, dark (coloured)* (25)
shàm-ghèi *mind, thoughts* (22)
shàm-hrùng-shik *crimson, dark red* (25)
shàn *new; up-to-date* (5)
shàn-chíng *to apply* (17)
shàn-fán-jing *identity card* (17)

shàn-fú *hard, distressing* (12)
shàn-fún *new style* (11)
shàn-mràn *news* (13)
shàn-séui *salary* (22)
shàn-shìn *fresh* (4)
shàn-tái *the body* (9)
shàng-wrut *to live, livelihood* (18)
shat-braai *a loss, a failure* (12)
shàu-dou *to receive* (19)
shàu-lréi *to repair, to mend* (16)
shèui-teui *to go into decline* (19)
shèui-yrìn . . . draan-hrai . . . *although . . . yet . . .* (18)
sheung *classifier: a pair of* (16)
sheung *double* (9)
shèung *to wound; a wound* (16)
shèung-fáan *on the contrary* (11)
shèung-seun *to believe, trust* (19)
shèung-shàn *double salary* (22)
sheung-yràn-chròng *double bed* (15)
shi-ghei *driver* (12)
shik *to know how to, to be able to* (4)
shik-hhèung-mrei *appearance, aroma and flavour* (23)
shik-hrap *suitable to, fitting* (13)
shìn *first* (6)
shìn-jeun *advanced* (22)
shìn-ji *only then* (10)
shìn-shàang *Mr, Sir, gentleman, husband* (1)
shìn-shàang *teacher* (12)
shìng-gong-ghèi *lift* (25)
shìng-krèi *week* (5)
shìu-fròng-gruk *fire brigade* (17)
shìu-fròng-yrùen *fireman* (17)
shìu-shik *news, information* (23)
sho-fáa-yí *sofa, easy chair* (11)
shùe *a book* (12)
shùe *to lose* (13)
shùe-faat *calligraphy* (24)
shùe-fruk *comfortable* (10)
si *to try, to test* (11)
si-yrung-krèi *probationary period, trial period* (22)
sing *surname, to be surnamed* (1)
sing-gaak *temperament, disposition* (24)

síu *few; a little* (4)
siu *to smile, to laugh, to laugh at* (16)
Síu- *Little* (name prefix) (22)
síu-bhaa *minibus* (6)
síu-hrok *primary school* (12)
síu-jé *Miss, young lady* (1)
síu-lrèun *ferry* (6)
síu-shàm *careful* (16)
síu-síu *a little bit, somewhat* (5)
síu-srì *an hour* (25)
só *a lock, to lock* (25)
só-yrí *therefore, so* (4)
Sou-hrok *Mathematics* (12)
srap *ten* (2)
srap-fhàn *totally, 100 per cent* (18)
srap-go-baat-go *nine or ten* (10)
srat-jroi *in fact, really* (11)
srat-yrung *practical* (8)
srau *to suffer* (24)
sre-wúi *society* (12)
srèng- *the whole* (9)
srèng-yrat *the whole day* (9)
sréung *to go up, ascend* (17)
sreung-(yhat-)chi *last time* (15)
sreung-bhàan *to go to work, go on shift* (22)
sreung-brin *the top, on top of, above, the top side* (12)
sréung-chhe *to get onto a vehicle* (17)
sreung-go-lrái-baai *last week* (10)
sreung-go-yruet *last month* (17)
Sreung-hói *Shanghai* (22)
sreung-jau *morning, a.m.* (15)
sréung-shàan *to go up the hill* (17)
sreung-shi *superior officer, direct boss* (17)
sreung-sou *to appeal to a higher court* (18)
sréung-tròng *to attend class* (12)
sri *matter, business, affair* (2)
srí-chrèung *market* (19)
sri-dho *a store* (25)
srì-gaan *time* (3)
sri-hou *hobby* (24)
srì-hrau *time* (8)
srì-jhong *fashion* (11)

srí-khèui *urban area* (6)
srí-mràn *citizen* (12)
srì-srì (dhou) *always, frequently* (8)
srik *to eat* (4)
srik-chhaan *to have non-Chinese food* (23)
srik-fraan *eat, eat a meal* (4)
srik-mrat *food* (23)
srìng-jhik *result, score, report* (16)
srìng-lraap *established, to establish* (18)
srìng-srí *city, town* (18)
srìng-wrài *to become* (18)
sruk-shik *familiar with, well acquainted with* (15)
suen *to be regarded as, to be reckoned* (8)
súen-shat *a loss* (23)
suet-ghou *ice-cream* (8)
suet-gwrai *refrigerator* (15)
sung *food; a course other than rice or soup* (4)
sung *to deliver, escort, send* (6)
sung X béi Y *to give X as a present to Y* (4)
taai-táai *Mrs, wife, married woman* (1)
taai . . . (laa) *too . . . , exceedingly . . .* (4)
taam *to visit, to see* (3)
tái *to look at* (5)
tái-dhak-dóu *able to see* (18)
tái-hei *to see a play; to go to the cinema* (9)
tái-mr̀-dóu *unable to see* (18)
tái-shùe *to read* (14)
tái-yhi-shang *to see the doctor* (3)
tau-jhì *overdraft, to overdraw* (19)
teui-yhàu *to retire* (22)
teui-yhàu-gham *pension* (22)
thàu *to steal* (18)
thàu-yré *to steal things, theft* (18)
thèng *to listen* (6)
thèui *to push* (17)
thìm *final particle: as well, also, what's more* (8)
thìn-hei *weather* (8)
thìn-mràn-tròi *observatory* (8)
Thìn-shing Mráa-tràu *Star Ferry Pier* (24)
thìng-mráan *tomorrow evening, tomorrow night* (11)
thìng-yrat *tomorrow* (8)
thòng *soup* (4)

thòng-wún *soup bowl* (25)
thùng(-fo-pràang)-jeung *inflation* (19)
thùng-yrùng *stretch a point, get round the rules, accommodate* (15)
tip-sréung *to stick on* (20)
tiu-ghòu *to jump high; high jump* (10)
tiu-ghòu-mhàu-dhài *jumping up and down* (10)
tiu-mróu *to dance* (24)
tou classifier: *a set of, a suit of* (8)
tou-fóng *en suite* (25)
trài *to mention* (25)
tràu *the head* (10)
tràu-jéung *first prize* (13)
tràu-jue *to stake, to bet* (13)
tràu-shin *just now* (10)
tràu-tung *headache* (10)
tràu-wràn *dizzy* (10)
trìm-bán *dessert* (4)
trìn-sé *to fill in a form* (20)
trìng *to stop* (11)
trìu classifier: for long thin flexible things (8)
trìu-gín *a condition, terms* (22)
tròi *to carry, to lift* (16)
Tròng-chhaan *Chinese food* (23)
Tròng-yràn *a Chinese* (10)
tróu *stomach, abdomen* (10)
trùng *the same, alike* (24)
trùng *with, and* (3)
trùng-mràai *and, with* (2)
trùng-sri *colleague* (16)
trùng-yi *to agree* (8)
tung *pain, ache* (10)
verb + -dhak *in such a way that* (15)
verb + -dhak *can, able to* (6)
verb + -dóu *to succeed in* (8)
verb + -gán continuing action: *-ing* (4)
verb + -gwo *to have experienced* (6)
verb + -héi-lrài *when it comes to, once you start* (11)
verb + -hhòi *away from* (17)
verb + -hráa *have a little . . .* (5)
verb + -jó completed action: *-ed* (4)
verb + -jring *left over, surplus* (23)
verb + -jrue *ongoing state of* (11)

verb + -lrok-lrài *downwards* (11)
verb + -mràai *close up to* (17)
verb + -saai *completely* (15)
verb + -srèng *to become, . . . into* (8)
verb + -yrùen *finished* (6)
wáa *words, language, speech, saying* (4)
wáan *to play, to enjoy, to amuse oneself* (6)
wái classifier: polite for *people* (17)
wái! *hello!* (on the phone) (10)
wai! *hoy! hey!* (17)
wán *to look for* (2)
wán-dhak-dóu *able to find* (18)
wán-mr̀-dóu *unable to find* (18)
whàa! *wow!* (5)
Whài-lrìm Cantonese version of *William* (10)
whàn-jraap *to revise lessons* (12)
whù-yrím *pollution, to pollute* (23)
wraa *to say* (6)
wraa . . . thèng . . . *to tell someone something* (6)
wraa . . . jhì = wraa . . . thèng *to tell* (8)
wraai *bad* (12)
wraai *to go wrong, break down* (16)
wràai-grau *nostalgia, to be nostalgic* (23)
wràai-yrì *to suspect* (17)
wraak-gwái-geuk *'draw a ghost's leg'* (21)
wraak-jé *or; perhaps* (16)
wraak-wáa *to paint, to draw* (24)
Wrài-kréi *Surrounding Chess, 'Go'* (24)
wran *to transport* (11)
wran-dou *to arrive by transport* (11)
wran-drung *physical exercise; to exercise* (9)
wran-fai *transportation costs* (25)
wran-shùe *to transport* (11)
wran-shùe-dou *to arrive by transport* (11)
wring-chrì *swimming pool* (15)
Wròng a surname: *Wong* (1)
wròng-ngràu *brown cow* (12)
wròng-shik *yellow* (12)
wru-háu *bank account* (19)
wru-jiu *passport* (15)
wrúi *it is likely that* (future possibility) (8)
wrúi *to be able to, to know how to* (5)

wrun *to change, exchange* (25)
wúi *meeting; club, association* (13)
wún *a bowl* (25)
wún-gwrai *cupboard* (25)
yám *to drink* (8)
yám-chràa *'to drink tea'; have a dim sum meal* (25)
yhàn-wrai *because* (4)
yhat *one* (2)
yhat fhàn jhung *a minute* (10)
yhat-bhùn *general, common, the general run of* (12)
yhat-chai *every single one of, all* (22)
yhat-chrài *together* (3)
yhat-dhi *a little bit* (9)
yhat-dím-bun(-jhung) *half past one o'clock* (15)
yhat-dím-jhung *one o'clock* (15)
yhat-dring *certainly* (3)
yhat-go-gwhat *quarter past the hour* (15)
yhat-go-yràn *alone* (18)
yhat-grung *altogether* (20)
yhat-heung *all along, up to now* (24)
yhat-hráa *a little bit, one time* (15)
yhat-jran(-ghaan) *a moment, in/for a moment* (24)
yhat-jrik *straight, directly* (6)
yhat-lràu *first-rate* (23)
yhat-srì *momentarily, briefly* (16)
yhat-yreung *the same* (11)
Yhat-yruet *January* (17)
yhat . . . jrau . . . *as soon as . . . then . . .* (24)
yhì-lrìu *medical* (22)
yhi-shang *doctor* (3)
yhì-yúen *hospital* (10)
yhik *a hundred million, a billion* (13)
Yhìng-bóng *Pound Sterling* (19)
Yhìng-gwok *Britain, UK, England* (1)
Yhìng-gwok-wáa *English language* (18)
Yhìng-gwok-yràn *British person* (1)
Yhìng-mràn *English language* (12)
yhìu-chéng *to invite* (23)
yhuk *make a movement* (17)
yí *chair* (11)
yí! exclamation of surprise: *'hullo, what's this?'* (5)
Yi-draai-lrei *Italy* (19)

yí-lraai *to rely on* (24)
yi-shì *meaning, intention* (17)
yi-yri *meaning, significance* (23)
yíng-héung *to affect, influence* (23)
yíng-seung *to take a photograph, have a photo taken* (17)
yiu *must, need to* (3)
yiu *to want* (1)
yraa- . . . *twenty-*. . . (13)
yraa-yhat *twenty-one* (13)
yraa-yhat-dím *blackjack, pontoon* (13)
yram-hrò *any* (17)
yràn *person, people* (1)
yràn-drei *other people* (27)
Yràn-mràn-brai *Renminbi, RMB* (19)
yràn-sou *number of people* (13)
yràn-yrùen *personnel, staff* (25)
yrap *to enter* (5)
yrap-brin *inside, in, the inside* (12)
yrap-drin-yràu *to refuel, put petrol in* (16)
yrat *day* (6)
Yrat-bún *Japan* (1)
Yrat-bún-wáa *Japanese language* (18)
Yrat-bún-yràn *Japanese person* (1)
Yrat-mràn *Japanese language* (18)
yrat-táu *daytime, by day* (15)
yràu *a tour, to tour* (15)
yràu *from* (6)
yrau *furthermore* (5)
yráu *to have* (2)
yrau(-sáu)-brin *on the right, the right(-hand) side* (12)
yráu-breng *to be ill* (10)
yráu-chín *rich* (13)
yráu-dhi *some, a little bit* (10)
yràu-fai *postage* (20)
yràu-gáan *air letter form* (20)
yràu-gúk *post office* (20)
yráu-gwhàan *relevant, concerned* (19)
yràu-haak *tourist* (23)
yràu-hei *games* (24)
yràu-hei-ghèi *games machine* (24)
Yràu-jing-júng-gúk *General Post Office* (20)
yràu-krèi-sri *especially* (12)

yráu-méng *famous* (6)
yráu-mhat-yré-sri-qaa? *for what purpose? why?* (2)
yràu-piu *postage stamp* (20)
yràu-séui *to swim* (5)
yràu-séui-fu *swimming trunks* (8)
yráu-shàm *kind of you to ask* (1)
yráu-srì *sometimes* (13)
yráu-sri *to have something wrong with you* (16)
yràu-túng *pillar-box* (20)
yráu-yhat-dhi *some, a little bit* (10)
yráu-yràn *somebody* (11)
yráu-yrung *useful* (8)
yrau . . . yrau . . . *both . . . and . . .* (5)
yré *thing, object* (8)
yre- . . . *twenty- . . .* (13)
yre-máan *night-time, at night* (15)
yrèng *to win* (13)
yreuk *medicine* (10)
yreuk-séui *(liquid) medicine* (10)
yreung *kind, sort, type* (13)
yréung *to rear, keep (pets)* (24)
yrèung-jáu *liquor, (non-Chinese) alcoholic drinks* (15)
yréung-srìng *to inculcate, form, breed* (24)
yreung-yreung *all kinds of, all sorts of* (13)
yri *two* (2)
yrì-ché *moreover* (9)
yrì-ghaa *now* (2)
yrí-ghìng *already* (8)
yrì-mràn *to migrate, immigration, emigration* (17)
yrí-wrài *to think, to assume, to regard as* (11)
yrìm-jrung *serious, desperate* (10)
yrin-gham *cash, ready money* (19)
yrìn-hrau *afterwards, after that* (10)
yring-jhan *serious, sincere* (16)
yring-shik *to recognise; to understand* (23)
yrit *hot* (8)
yrit-séui-lròu *boiler, water-heater* (25)
yrìu-wràn *to shake up* (10)
yrue-brei *to prepare, get ready* (4)
yrùe-góng *fishing port* (6)
yrùe-gwó *if* (4)
yrùe-gwó-mr̀-hrai(-nhe) *otherwise* (12)

yrue-jhì *to predict* (24)
yrúen *distant, far* (25)
yrùen *dollar* (13)
yrùen-lròi *originally, actually, in fact* (20)
yrùen-yhan *reason* (23)
yruet *moon, month* (17)
yruet-git-dhaan *monthly statement* (19)
yruet-mréi *end of the month* (17)
yruet . . . yruet . . . *the more . . . the more . . .* (19)
yruk *meat, flesh* (4)
yrung *to use, to spend* (4)
yrùng-yri *easy* (20)
yúe *fish* (23)